PRAISE FOR *STARVING UKRAINE*

"This is an important work for several reasons: it speaks to our current dangerous climate of fake news, attacks on journalists, and the loss of independent news sources, while demonstrating the vital importance of a robust press, an informed citizenry, and local activism. More so, in describing the fierce battle over Canadians' understanding of the Holodomor, it offers a powerful lesson on the complexity of coming to terms with the atrocities of our own past. Indeed, in many ways, Serge Cipko carefully documents a story that is playing out in Canada once again, but this time, the struggle is over the current reporting of—along with the acceptance or rejection of Canadians over—our own legacy of colonial violent policies, including that of the residential school system. For this reason, this book matters greatly to Canadians—it is the story of us now." —JAMES DASCHUK, author of *Clearing the Plains: Disease, Politics of Starvation, and the Loss of Aboriginal Life*

"This is a carefully researched, comprehensive and ground-breaking study. It explores hitherto unknown Canadian connections, uncovers many surprises, and is a must-read for students of the Holodomor." —MYROSLAV SHKANDRIJ, author of *Ukrainian Nationalism* and *Russia and Ukraine*

"There is no comprehensive study of the Canadian reaction to the famine in the English or Ukrainian language [...] and so this is a major contribution. It is an interesting story and an important one for Canadian and Ukrainian history. Cipko has assembled a rich collection of documents about the dissemination in Canada of news about the Great Ukrainian Famine and how Canadians... reacted to this information. He has compiled a bibliography of historical literature on that tragedy presented as famine, genocide and Holodomor.... The work [is] also an important contribution to the study of Canadian mainstream and ethnic newspapers, how they handled information on foreign catastrophes." —ROMAN SERBYN, editor of *Famine in Ukraine, 1932–1933*

"Well-researched... and readable.... I believe this work to be an important contribution.... [It] examines the contemporary state of knowledge in Canada about Soviet Ukraine during 1932–33, the time of the Great Famine, and puts this knowledge into a wider context." —THOMAS M. PRYMAK, author of *Gathering a Heritage: Ukrainian, Slavonic, and Ethnic Canada and the USA*

STARVING UKRAINE

The Holodomor and Canada's Response

SERGE CIPKO

© 2017 University of Regina Press

All rights reserved. No part of this work covered by the copyrights hereon may be reproduced or used in any form or by any means—graphic, electronic, or mechanical—without the prior written permission of the publisher. Any request for photocopying, recording, taping or placement in information storage and retrieval systems of any sort shall be directed in writing to Access Copyright.

Cover design: Duncan Campbell, University of Regina Press
Text design: John van der Woude, JVDW Designs
Copy editor: Alison Jacques
Proofreader: Anne James
Indexer: Sergey Lobachev, Brookfield Indexing Services
Cover art: The "Bitter Memories of Childhood" monument memorializing the Holodomor was erected in the spring of 2015 in Regina, Saskatchewan, Canada. It is an exact copy of the life-size bronze statue by sculptor Petro Drozdowsky, whose original statue is located near the entrance to the National Holodomor Museum in Kyiv, Ukraine. Photo by Duncan Noel Campbell.

Library and Archives Canada Cataloguing in Publication

Cipko, Serge, 1961-, author
    Starving Ukraine : the Holodomor and Canada's response / Serge Cipko.

Originally published: Regina, Saskatchewan : University of Regina Press, 2017.

Includes bibliographical references and index.
ISBN 978-0-88977-560-2 (softcover)

1. Ukraine—History—Famine, 1932-1933—Public opinion. 2. Ukraine—History—Famine, 1932-1933—Press coverage. 3. Famines—Ukraine—Press coverage. 4. Public opinion—Canada—History—20th century. 5. Ukraine—Foreign public opinion, Canadian. 6. Ukraine--Relations--Canada. 7. Canada—Relations—Ukraine. I. Title.

DK508.8378.P83C57 2018   947.708'4   C2018-903895-0

University of Regina Press, University of Regina
Regina, Saskatchewan, Canada, s4s 0a2
tel: (306) 585-4758 fax: (306) 585-4699
web: www.uofrpress.ca

We acknowledge the support of the Canada Council for the Arts for our publishing program. We acknowledge the financial support of the Government of Canada. / Nous reconnaissons l'appui financier du gouvernement du Canada. This publication was made possible with support from Creative Saskatchewan's Creative Industries Production Grant Program.

This publication also received generous financial support from the following: Shevchenko Scientific Society of Canada Scholarly Publications Support Programme; Canadian Foundation for Ukrainian Studies, Scholarly Publications Support Program; Holodomor Research and Education Consortium of the Canadian Institute of Ukrainian Studies; Alberta Ukrainian Commemorative Society.

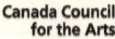 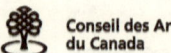 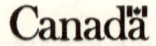 

CONTENTS

Chronology of Major Events   vii
Acknowledgements   xi

Introduction   xiii
Chapter One   "We Are Starving Terribly": 1932   1
Chapter Two   "Open Your Eyes, Unite in a Common Protest":
     Winter 1933   19
Chapter Three   "Starvation, Real Cause of Soviet Trial": Spring 1933   51
Chapter Four   "What to Believe about Russia": Summer 1933   65
Chapter Five   "What Are 1,000,000 in a Population of 162,000,000?":
     Autumn 1933   93
Chapter Six   "Hunger Bennett":
     The Pro-Soviet Community in Canada   129
Chapter Seven   "A Blessing from Heaven":
     Aid and Appeals, January–June 1934   159
Chapter Eight   "A Great Responsibility": Canada, the USSR, and
     the League of Nations, July–December 1934   185
Conclusion   213

Appendix   225
Notes   229
Bibliography   321
Permissions Acknowledgements   335
Index   337

CHRONOLOGY OF MAJOR EVENTS

January 22, 1918: The government of the Ukrainian National Republic—the Rada—declares independence.

1918–21: A war ensues in the former Russian Empire, which leads to the loss of Ukrainian independence and Bolshevik victory.

1921–23: A famine begins in 1921. The Volga, Urals, Ukraine, and North Caucasus are the hardest-hit areas. The famine claims at least three to four million lives in 1921–22. The government in Moscow under Vladimir Lenin accepts help from abroad.[1] The Union of Soviet Socialist Republics is founded in December 1922. Soviet Ukraine is one of its constituent republics. Lenin adopts the New Economic Policy (NEP) in March 1921, which introduces a mixed economy and allows for private landholdings.

1928: The NEP is abolished by Lenin's successor, Joseph Stalin, who launches the First Five-Year Plan. Industrialization and agricultural collectivization are emphasized. Large-scale collective farms are created at the expense of independent farms. There is widespread peasant resistance to the collectivization campaign, and wholesale deportations take place. The so-called *kulaks*, the wealthier peasants, are a main target of the campaign.

1929–31: The Great Depression begins. In Canada, the Conservative Party led by Richard Bedford Bennett wins the 1930 general election. In 1931, the Conservative government imposes a partial embargo on trade with the Soviet Union; in response, the Soviet Union imposes a complete embargo on imports from Canada.

1931–32: Policies of collectivization and grain requisition quotas continue in the Soviet Union.

February 1932: The *Toronto Star* reports that forty Ukrainian peasants, fleeing "an impending famine," were shot by Soviet frontier guardsmen as they attempted to swim across the river into Romania.

August 7, 1932: The Five Ears of Corn Law is promulgated. Also known by other names, this law decreed that collective farm property was considered to belong to the state, and severe penalties, including death, would be meted to those stealing state property.

October 1932: Stalin sends Viacheslav Molotov, chair of the Council of People's Commissars of the Soviet Union, and Lazar Kaganovich, secretary of the Central Committee of the Communist Party, to Soviet Ukraine and the North Caucasus to supervise officials in their grain-procurement drive. To assist in the drive, "thousands of communist cadres from Ukraine and Russia were mobilized to find grain that the peasants had stored in order to survive the winter and spring. Procurement teams often took all foodstuffs, not only grain, from peasant homes. While famine also broke out in other parts of the Soviet Union in 1932–33, it was...especially intense in Ukraine and the Kuban [North Caucasus]."[2]

October 10, 1932: Opening of the Dnipro Hydroelectric Station (*Dneprostroi*), the largest power plant in the USSR and among the biggest in the world.

December 14–15, 1932: Resolutions attack the existing Ukrainianization policy in Soviet Ukraine and other parts of the USSR and call for its discontinuance in the Ukrainianized raions of the Northern Caucasus and in other parts of Russia, recommending a switch from Ukrainian to Russian in such districts.

December 27, 1932: A decree introduces a compulsory passport system and entrusts a new workers' and peasants' militia—under the supervision of the secret police—with its enforcement. Urban centres, beginning with Moscow, Leningrad, and Kharkiv, were to be purged of non-Communist and suspect elements and "secured as communist strongholds, from which the discontented, starving peasantry will be banned."[3]

January 7, 1933: Stalin proclaims the success of the First Five-Year Plan.

January 22, 1933: Stalin signs an order to prevent peasants leaving Ukraine and the North Caucasus in search of food in other parts of the Soviet Union.

May 13, 1933: Prominent Soviet Ukrainian writer Mykola Khvylovy commits suicide.

July 7, 1933: Soviet Ukrainian statesman Mykola Skrypnyk commits suicide. The London *Times* links his death to Soviet agricultural practices in Ukraine.

September 29, 1933: Representatives of fourteen members of the Council of the League of Nations discuss the famine behind closed doors and decide to defer the matter to the International Committee of the Red Cross.

November 16, 1933: The United States recognizes the Soviet Union.

June 24, 1934: Kyiv replaces Kharkiv as the capital of the Ukrainian Soviet Socialist Republic.

September 17, 1934: Delegates of four dozen nations gather in Geneva to debate and then vote on whether to admit the USSR to the League of Nations. Although most, including Canada, vote for acceptance, the Canadian delegate mentions the famine during the debate.

ACKNOWLEDGEMENTS

I have been the fortunate beneficiary of all sorts of assistance. I begin by conveying my gratitude to the people who read the manuscript and provided helpful comments: Myroslav Shkandrij and John-Paul Himka. And Yurij Kotovych, who not only read and provided feedback on the manuscript but also played a vital role in obtaining support for the project. I express my appreciation, too, to the peer reviewers of the manuscript and for all the assistance rendered by the University of Regina Press.

In the course of work for the book, I also consulted with and/or received help from Jars Balan, J. Laurence Black, Liudmyla Hrynevych, Bohdan Klid, John Lehr, Andrij Makuch, Orest Martynowych, Peter Melnycky, Myron Momryk, Marshall Nay, Kirk Niergarth, Roman Serbyn, Roman Shiyan, and Mykola Soroka. I would also like to acknowledge Kateryna Kod and Ihor Rudyk.

A special word of thanks goes to Roman Procyk, who, together with Zenon Kohut, arranged for archival material to be brought to me from Philadelphia (the Ielysaveta Skoropadska Papers). On the subject of archives and libraries, I thank the staff of the Bohdan Medwidsky Ukrainian Folklore Archives, Edmonton; Library and Archives Canada, Ottawa; the Library of St. Vladimir's Ukrainian Orthodox Church, Calgary (Father Taras Krochak and Mykola Woron); the Provincial Archives of Alberta, Edmonton; the Saskatchewan Archives Board, Regina; the University of Alberta Library (Rutherford Library and Inter-Library Loan Department); the Ukrainian Canadian Archives and Museum of Alberta, Edmonton; the Ukrainian Catholic Archeparchy of Winnipeg Archives, and the Ukrainian Cultural and Educational Centre (Oseredok), Winnipeg.

The research and writing could not have been done without the financial support of the Alberta Ukrainian Commemorative Society, the Alberta Society for the Advancement of Ukrainian Studies, John Boyko, the Bishop Budka Charitable Society, the Canada-Ukraine Foundation, the Knights of Columbus–Bishop Greschuk Assembly, the Knights of Columbus–Fr. Dydyk Council, the Knights of Columbus–Fr. Hannas Council, the John and Marie Koziak Foundation, Peter and Doris Kule, Nicholas and Pat Melnik, Alann, Anne, and Jule Nazarewich, the Ukrainian Canadian Benevolent Society, and the Ukrainian Catholic Brotherhood of Canada–Edmonton Eparchy.

In past years I was commissioned to carry out research through the Ukrainian Canadian Archives and Museum of Alberta, the Ukrainian Pioneers' Association of Alberta, and the Holodomor Research and Educational Consortium (HREC) at the Canadian Institute of Ukrainian Studies. I thank Jars Balan for facilitating those research assignments and for sharing his own material with me. Some of the material that was gathered has been used in this book. Thanks to HREC, which was founded through a generous gift by the Temerty Family Foundation, and also to the Kule Ukrainian Canadian Studies Centre at the Canadian Institute of Ukrainian Studies (CIUS), I was able to present research findings at sponsored panels of the Canadian Association of Slavists and at other forums.

It was a pleasure working with the University of Regina Press, including acquisitions editor Karen May Clark and the meticulous copyeditor Alison Jacques, and I express my gratitude to all concerned.

Last, but not least, I wish to acknowledge the support of my family—my wife, Jacqueline Tait, and daughters, Anastasia and Saoirse Cipko—who have had to bear with me during the time I spent devoted to this project.

It remains to be said that I alone am responsible for any shortcomings that the reader may detect in this study.

INTRODUCTION

When he broke the third seal, I heard the third living creature saying, "Come!" And I saw, and behold, a black horse, and its rider had a balance in his hand; and I heard what seemed to be a voice in the midst of the four living creatures saying, "A quart of wheat for a denarius, and three quarts of barley for a denarius; but do not harm oil and wine!"

— Revelation 6: 5–6 *(Catholic Comparative New Testament)*

On New Year's Day of 1932, an Alberta newspaper announced that the Soviet government had issued a special stamp. "Four riders are shown in a mad race across the face of the stamp," the *Irma Times* reported, "on which is roughly outlined a map of the European section of the Soviet Union." The stamp, the newspaper remarked, bore a design that was "strikingly similar to the traditional picturizations of the four horsemen of the Apocalypse."[1]

The stamp was intended to mark the tenth anniversary of the organization of the Red Army's first regular detachment. But a reader or two of that account may well have thought later, as events unfolded in the Union of Soviet Socialist Republics (USSR), that the image may have served as a harbinger of what was to come in parts of the very territory delineated. For anyone inside or outside the Soviet Union who was familiar with the Book of Revelation, of the Four Horsemen of the Apocalypse the one atop the black horse symbolized famine.[2] Indeed, the Book of Revelation was invoked during the course of contemporaneous reporting in 1932, if not in reference to famine in the Soviet

Union then in regard to analogous conditions in China: "Disease and famine, two others of the horsemen of the Apocalypse," reported Associated Press (AP) staff correspondent Morris J. Harris, were riding "'rough-shod' over China."³

Harris's description of conditions in China does not appear to have been disputed, but the same cannot be said about reports of famine in the areas of the Soviet Union where it struck during 1932 and 1933. In 1934, British journalist Lancelot Lawton decried the Soviet government's attempt to conceal the famine from the outside world. "At the end of 1932 and the beginning of 1933 came famine, chiefly in Ukrainia and the North Caucasus," he wrote in the periodical *Fortnightly Review*. Lawton went on to declare that "no more remarkable instance of suppression has been recorded in history than the Bolshevik concealment of this great calamity." The Soviet government, he said, "to the present day" would not acknowledge that a famine had occurred, which Lawton described as a "pose of ignorance" that was "absurd" because "the fact has been proved by a host of eye-witnesses, including foreigners of repute."⁴

Figure 1. Soviet commemorative stamp from 1930, issued for the tenth anniversary of the First Cavalry Army. Personal collection of the author.

The two areas mentioned by Lawton—Soviet Ukraine and the North Caucasus—were disproportionately affected by the famine, or rather, the famines, of the era. For by the beginning of the 2000s, historians had become aware that they "were dealing with a series of famines," rather than a single Soviet famine, which were "clearly connected to a general phenomenon and thus sharing profound similarities, but also profoundly different from each other; among them the 1932–33 Ukrainian-Kuban Holodomor and the 1931–33 Kazakh tragedy stood out."[5] The term "Holodomor" comes from the Ukrainian words *moryty holodom* and means "extermination by hunger." According to historian Olga Andriewsky, the popularization of the term is usually attributed to Ivan Drach, a prominent writer and the first leader (elected in 1989) of the reformist People's Movement of Ukraine for Reconstruction.[6]

Historian Stanislav Kul'chyts'kyi distinguishes between the famines that took place in the Soviet Union during 1932 and 1933. The famines that occurred in three regions of the Soviet Union in 1932 and 1933—specifically, in the Ukrainian Soviet Socialist Republic (Ukrainian SSR), the North Caucasus (where many of the inhabitants were of Ukrainian ancestry), and the Lower Volga Krai—were, he argues, the consequence of large-scale actions aimed at the deliberate destruction of the peasants through starvation. Collectors under the supervision of the Soviet state security service came to villages and requisitioned grain and other foodstuffs. At the beginning of 1933, measures were introduced to stop peasants from leaving their districts of residence.[7] Both the coerced removal of food from the villagers and the controls placed on their movement condemned many, mostly in the countryside, to a slow and agonizing death. Distinctions are also made by French historian Nicholas Werth, who argues that "there was a strong, qualitative specificity to the Ukrainian case, at least from the second half of 1932 onwards." In his view, "the answer to the question 'Was the Holodomor a genocide?' can only be 'yes.'" Werth goes on to say that "Kazakh herdsmen, Russian peasants of the Volga region, deportees from all over the Soviet Union ... were not victims of a genocide," but they died "massively, in silence and total oblivion" and "they too should not be forgotten."[8] In Ukraine, starvation occurred simultaneously with an assault on the Ukrainian language and culture[9] and, in Kuban—in the Russian North Caucasus (Severo-Kavkazskii krai, or the North Caucasian Territory of Russia)—with the reversal of a Ukrainianization policy.[10]

Even if the famine had been proved by a host of eyewitnesses, as Lawton notes, there were journalists who downplayed its gravity both at the time of the famine and during its aftermath. In a book about Ukraine and its diaspora during the famine, Mykhailo Marunchak writes of Western correspondents who, through their writing about the USSR, helped the cause of Soviet propaganda. Two particular examples are the infamous Walter Duranty of the *New York Times* and the lesser-known Pierre van Paassen of the *Toronto Star*.[11] In 1936, van Paassen, who had earlier written about the famine, wrote a piece about Spain, which that year was enveloped in a civil war. He ridiculed the "reactionary press" that, he said, was "so frightened," or at least pretended to be, that it saw "the Four Horsemen of the Apocalypse dragging a chariot" bearing down on Madrid; according to van Paassen, the chariot's passengers were "Bela Kuhn, the Cheka, a Ukrainian famine, Herod slaughtering the innocents and Jack the Ripper in the uniform of the Red army."[12]

In 1934, the same year that Lawton's piece was published in the *Fortnightly Review*, the *Christian Science Monitor* correspondent William Henry Chamberlin—very likely one of the eyewitnesses and "foreigners of repute" whom Lawton had in mind—posed a question about the famine: "Is it conceivable that the famine of 1932–33 could have taken place if civil liberties had prevailed in the Soviet Union, if newspapers had been free to report the facts, if speakers could have appealed for relief, if the government in power had been obliged to submit its policy of letting vast numbers of the peasants starve to death to the verdict of a free election?"[13] Although newspapers in the Soviet Union were "not free to report the facts," and in spite of Soviet attempts to suppress news about the famine, stories about mass starvation traversed its borders and reached countries such as Canada. In her memoirs, the British noblewoman and Scotland's first female member of Parliament Katharine Marjory Stewart-Murray, the Duchess of Atholl, wrote about "a young man named Malcolm Muggeridge" who "had brought ghastly descriptions of the famine in the Ukraine, which he had seen." The Scottish Unionist Party member of Parliament for Kinross and West Perthshire also mentioned another British journalist, the Welshman Gareth Jones. By March 1933, the Duchess of Atholl recalled, "some of us in the House of Commons" were hearing from Jones "of the appalling famine in the Ukraine, news of which was officially concealed from the outside world."[14]

Canadians were also reading the stories provided by these two journalists, and later on by Chamberlin and others, and these received comment in newspaper editorials. Indeed, a survey of the Canadian press in the years 1932 to 1934 shows that developments in the Soviet Union were covered extensively in newspapers from the Atlantic to the Pacific. This fact deserves to be better known and understood. In the discussion that follows, several topics are explored, including the questions of when the news about the famine broke in Canada and how the stories about developments in the USSR were presented to readers of Canadian newspapers.

Kul'chyts'kyi postulates the notion of "three Ukraines" during the time of the famine to which Moscow policymakers paid attention: Soviet Ukraine, Kuban in the North Caucasus (in Russia), and western Ukraine (in Poland).[15] Some twenty-nine million people inhabited the Ukrainian SSR in 1926; six to seven million Ukrainians dwelled in western Ukraine (primarily the regions of Galicia and Volhynia) in Poland, where they formed that state's largest national minority; and an additional 455,000 Ukrainians lived under Czechoslovakian rule in Transcarpathia (Subcarpathian Rus') and 760,000 under Romanian jurisdiction (310,000 in Bukovyna and 450,000 in Bessarabia).[16] In Kuban—which today is in the Krasnodar krai of Russia—there were 1.7 million Ukrainians.[17]

To these "three Ukraines" one conceivably could add a fourth: the Ukrainian diaspora. In the 1920s and early 1930s, the Ukrainian diaspora was emerging as a political force. Thousands of Ukrainians lived as political exiles in such major European centres as Paris, Berlin, and Prague. Leaders of short-lived governments during the 1917–21 war for independence were among them, including the head of the Ukrainian National Republic (UNR), Symon Petliura (assassinated in

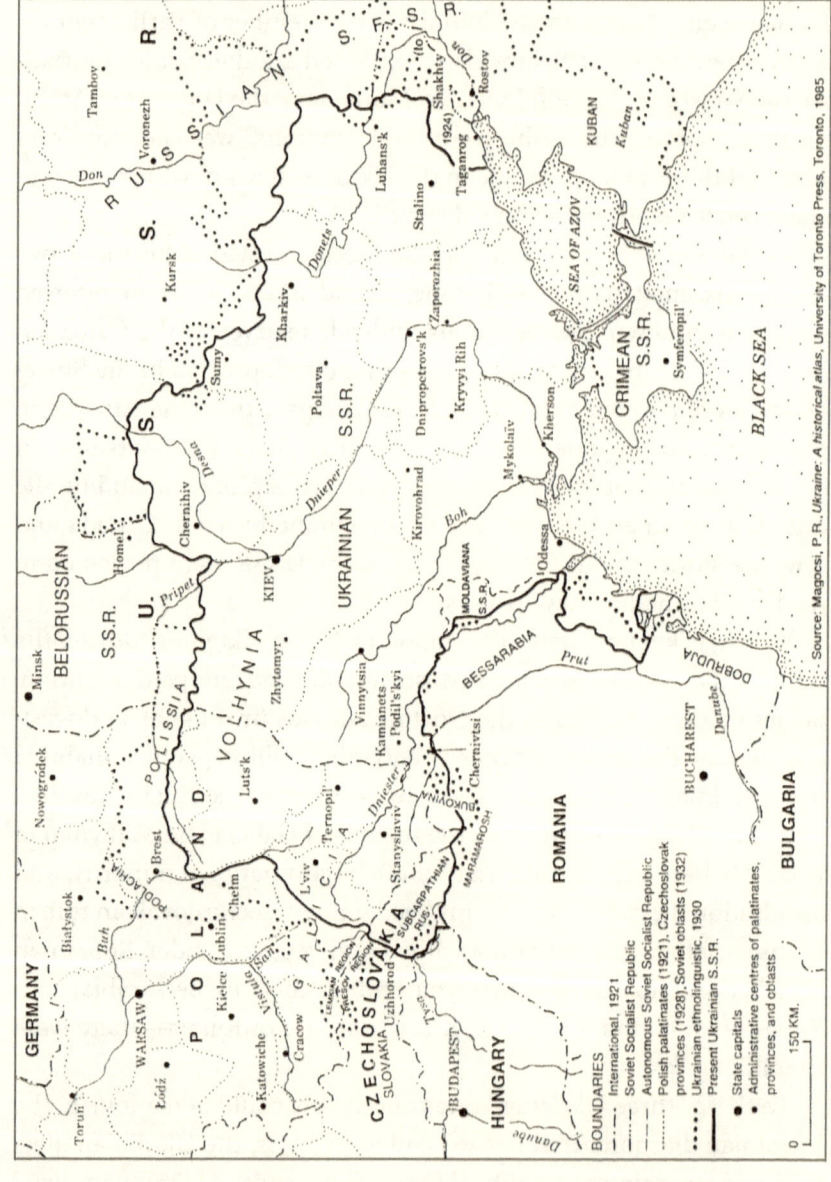

Figure 2. Map of Ukraine, 1933.

Paris in May 1926), and Pavlo Skoropadsky, who briefly established a monarchy in Ukraine (a state governed by a hereditary "hetman") and later lived in Berlin.[18] Apart from the political refugees, many thousands more Ukrainians had emigrated to western Europe or across the Atlantic Ocean to countries in North and South America. By 1933, the number of people outside western Ukraine and the Soviet Union with some ethnic Ukrainian ancestry may have approached (or even surpassed) a million.[19] The largest Ukrainian communities were in Canada and the United States. In Canada, Ukrainians were an especially significant numerical factor in the Prairie provinces of Alberta, Saskatchewan, and Manitoba, where they established organizations and periodicals.[20] Apart from the people enumerated in the Canadian census as Ukrainians, there were others in Canada who had emigrated or whose parents had emigrated from Ukraine—among them, Germans and Jews.

To the initial questions, others can be added: What was the nature of the coverage in the Ukrainian-language press in Canada? How did the pro-Soviet segment of the Ukrainian community respond to the stories about famine in the Soviet Union? What relief efforts existed among Ukrainians, Mennonites, and others in Canada? How did the Canadian government respond to petitions about the famine? These questions are probed in this book. With one exception, the chapters are arranged chronologically. The delineation does not follow any particular organizational principle, other than, in 1933, to group the months into seasons. In 1933, the greatest number of deaths from famine occurred in the six-month period between March and August.[21] The narrative that follows begins with the early months of 1932, before the start of the famine, and ends with the close of 1934, focusing especially on September of that year, when a debate took place at a general meeting of the League of Nations over the admission of the Soviet Union into its fold.

As these various questions are probed in the following chapters, this study will, it is hoped, help elucidate how mainstream and ethnic newspapers handled information on a foreign catastrophe and the extent to which these two domains of journalism interacted. It will also provide examples of the ties that existed between Canada's immigrant communities and their former homeland. The objective of the book is to illustrate as much as possible how the famine was presented to Canadians in real time. In order to stay within the 1932–34 timeframe to a feasible extent, the discussion is necessarily more descriptive than analytical. Knowledge about the famine has grown considerably since 1991 and thus readers may draw their own conclusions from the picture that the newspapers presented to their readers from 1932 to 1934 compared with what we know today of the events.

The number of newspapers in Canada at the time was large even though it was not a large country in terms of population. In 1932, the country's huge land mass surrounded by three oceans—the Arctic, Atlantic, and Pacific—was home to only about ten million people. Canada's population was informed about domestic events and about the world beyond the national frontiers: both citizens and unnaturalized immigrants supported many newspapers, some of which appeared in languages other than English and French. In 1932, according to the *Winnipeg Free Press*, forty-three newspapers were published in Canada in a foreign language. These included nine dailies (three Chinese, three "Jewish," two Japanese, and one Finnish), seven Ukrainian periodicals (six in Winnipeg and one in Edmonton), six in German, three Icelandic, three Hungarian, three Italian, two Swedish, two Danish, two Norwegian, two Polish, and one Spanish.[22]

Regardless of the language in which the newspapers were published, their editors received, printed, and occasionally commented on news about the Soviet Union, including the reports of widespread famine. A good many Canadians had origins in territories that in 1932 were part of the USSR. According to the census of 1931, Canada was home to 88,736 Mennonites, a significant portion of whom traced their roots to Soviet Ukraine (including as recently as the 1920s). Some among the 156,726 Jews in Canada also had origins in Soviet territories. The census also counted 225,113 Ukrainians and 88,148 Russians (ethnic Russians, Ukrainians, or others from the former Russian Empire) in Canada.[23]

The majority of the 225,113 Ukrainians in Canada had come from regions that before 1914 were part of Austria-Hungary but after the Great War were under the jurisdictions of Poland or Romania and, to a much lesser extent, Czechoslovakia. A minority had also come from regions in the Russian Empire that later were part of Soviet Ukraine in the multi-ethnic successor state, the USSR. The USSR was founded in 1922 and Soviet Ukraine was one of its republics (the others that were constituted that year or later on as the decade progressed were Armenia, Azerbaijan, Belarus, Georgia, Russia, Tajikistan, Turkestan, and Uzbekistan). According to the Soviet census of 1926, of the 29,018,187 inhabitants of the Ukrainian SSR, about 80 per cent identified their ethnicity as Ukrainian. The largest minorities were Russians (2,677,166), Jews (1,574,428), and Germans (393,924). In 1926, one out of nine ethnic Ukrainians lived in urban centres, where they formed a little under half (47.2%) of the inhabitants of those cities. Ethnic Ukrainians constituted 87.5 per cent of the Ukrainian SSR's rural population.[24]

The Ukrainian community, the largest of the eastern European groups in Canada, keenly followed developments in the homeland after the close of the war. On January 22, 1919, the Ukrainian National Republic (central and eastern Ukraine) united with the Western Ukrainian National Republic. Many Ukrainians in Canada supported the short-lived independent state that resulted, but, after the victory of the Bolsheviks, a minority was sympathetic to the new Communist order in Soviet Ukraine. Between 1932 and 1934 the mainstream press in Canada mentioned activities of various Ukrainian groups across the country. From these reports, it could be inferred that there were two main camps in the Ukrainian community: one in favour of an independent Ukraine and another that supported Soviet Ukraine within the USSR. Two large churches were in the former camp: the Ukrainian Catholic Church and the Ukrainian Orthodox Church, both of which had parishes across the country. Secular nationwide organizations that were close to both churches included the Ukrainian Sporting Sitch Association of Canada (to the Ukrainian Catholic Church) and the Ukrainian Self-Reliance League of Canada (to the Ukrainian Orthodox Church). In 1932, in response to the emergence of the militant Organization of Ukrainian Nationalists in western Ukraine under Poland, the Ukrainian National Federation was founded in Canada as a group sympathetic to that movement. In the other camp belonged the pro-Soviet Ukrainian Labour-Farmer Temple Association.

The Ukrainian community supported a vibrant press. By 1930, Ukrainian-language weeklies and monthlies in Canada had a combined circulation of more than sixty thousand. The voice of the Ukrainian Sporting Sitch Association (a movement that favoured a monarch or "hetman" in Ukraine) was heard in the Ukrainian Catholic weekly *Ukraïns'ki visty* (Ukrainian News), published in Edmonton, and in the pro-Conservative weekly *Kanadyis'kyi farmer* (Canadian Farmer), in Winnipeg. Owned by a publisher of Czech orgin, Frank Dojacek, *Kanadyis'kyi farmer* had over fourteen thousand subscribers in 1930. The organ of the Ukrainian Self-Reliance League was *Ukraïns'kyi holos* (Ukrainian Voice), in Winnipeg, while that of the Ukrainian National Federation was *Novyi shliakh* (New Pathway), published originally in Edmonton and later in Saskatoon. *Ukraïns'kyi holos* had about fifteen thousand subscribers. The Ukrainian Labour-Farmer Temple Association published the periodical *Ukraïns'ki robitnychi visty* (Ukrainian Labour News) in Winnipeg. *Ukraïns'ki robitnychi visty* had more than eight thousand subscribers in 1930.[25] All of these periodicals featured news about developments in the western Ukrainian territories under Poland, Romania, and Czechoslovakia and in central and eastern regions (often referred to as "Greater Ukraine") in the USSR.

The existence of separate groups within the Ukrainian community was reflected in their responses to the famine. The Ukrainian Self-Reliance League was notable for its mounting of protest rallies. The Ukrainian National Federation often included the plight of Ukrainians in western Ukraine in its protests about the famine. Monetary collections for famine victims (sent to a relief committee in Berlin) were more intrinsic to the Ukrainian Sporting Sitch Association. As for the pro-Soviet segment of the community, its leaders denied that a famine existed.

During the 1920s, one of the developments in Soviet Ukraine that Canada's Ukrainian community observed was the introduction of a policy of Ukrainianization, under which the use of Ukrainian language and culture increased in public life. Eventually, Ukrainian schools were opened outside Ukraine, in other places in the USSR inhabited by Ukrainians, including the Russian Far East and much closer to the republic, in Kuban. From 1928, the Ukrainian newspapers, and the press in Canada in general, were also covering such other developments as the Soviet Five-Year Plan—which entailed an ambitious industrialization program—and the collectivization of agriculture—the replacement of individual farms by state-run collective ones, a process that included coercion.

Chapter One

"WE ARE STARVING TERRIBLY"
1932

Collectivization, Grain Requisitions, and Bread Shortage

Before the summer of 1932, stories printed in the Canadian press indicated problems in the Soviet countryside. In early April, the *Edmonton Journal* quoted the Riga correspondent of the London *Times* about the temporary suspension of collectivization of peasants into state farms while shock brigades were being organized to hasten spring seeding.¹ A couple of months later, the *Journal* made reference to a letter, dated April 12, from a man in the district of Minsk, in Soviet Belarus, to his daughter in northern Alberta. The letter said that wheat was scarce, as "all the grain was taken away from us and sold last fall."²

Other stories about the Soviet Union published during May 1932 were more enthusiastic. At the end of that month, the *Toronto Star* reported on Stanley Hood, who had visited the USSR as a guest of Soviet trade unions. "In the Ukraine at Gorlovka [Horlivka, Donetsk Oblast], contrary to reports I have seen in Canadian newspapers, living conditions are very satisfactory," Hood declared. He had seen the "largest mining machine plant in the world at Gorlovka and found workers working under ideal conditions," and at "Dnieprostroy [Dniprostroi] we saw a city of 220,200 where formerly there were only wheat fields." Hood then offered a prediction: "I believe that at the end of the next five-year plan Russian workers will be better off than Canadian workers.

Working conditions are better now than Canadian conditions, but of course they are rationed on food."³ The First Five-Year Plan, introduced by Soviet leader Joseph Stalin in 1928, emphasized the development of heavy industry. One of its manifestations was the construction of the Dniprostroi Dam (now Dniprohes), a hydroelectric power station on the Dnipro River near the southeastern Ukrainian city of Zaporizhzhia. Opening in 1932, it came to be the biggest Soviet power plant of the era and one of the largest in the world.⁴

Yet another article in the Canadian press in May referred to a scarcity of food in the Soviet countryside, including Ukraine—a place where the "harvest was above the average last year."⁵ Indeed, by the end of that month there were also reports of actual deaths from starvation.⁶ In June, Dr. George Ezekial Leiken, formerly a rabbi in the Volga region of Russia, visited Edmonton and there declared that the Soviet Union "had been selling grain while her people starved."⁷

Andrew Cairns

By that time, the agricultural specialist Andrew Cairns of Islay, Alberta, who had gone to the USSR as an official of the Empire Marketing Board, had penned his first report, dated May 3, 1932, about the situation in the Soviet countryside.⁸ While in Moscow, Cairns had learned of food shortages in the rural districts. Later, he had travelled to Saratov and agricultural districts along the Volga River, and then to rural areas in western Siberia, Kazakhstan, Ukraine, the Crimea, and the North Caucasus. Cairns had witnessed "people dying of hunger on the streets of Kiev."⁹ His disclosures were not published in the Canadian (or any) press but did circulate privately in official circles in the United Kingdom and Canada.¹⁰

Although Cairns's report officially was not made public, the *Globe* noted on May 26 that the Department of Trade and Commerce had received information from a "reliable observer who has just made a comprehensive survey of conditions in the agricultural districts." While the observer is not named, one wonders if it was Cairns. The unnamed observer told "a vivid story of his travels, of hungry people, gross mismanagement," and other problems. Peasants were said to be consuming the "seed wheat on account of the almost unbelievable shortage of food." Reports of conditions in Ukraine and the Volga region were described as "simply appalling." People in the towns and cities, the observer reported, were sending bread to relatives in the countryside. He went on to say that the peasants "were too poor in physical and mental vigor to offer really effective direct resistance," but that there was "plenty of passive resistance."[11]

Cairns had visited the USSR on a diplomatic visa. His accounts were made available to the British embassy in Moscow and, through it, the British Foreign Office. The British ambassador to Moscow, Sir Esmond Ovey, remarked that it was a pity that Cairns's revelations about starvation and other Soviet problems could not "be broadcast to the world at large as an antidote to Soviet propaganda in general." The reason for not publicizing the findings stemmed from hopes within the Foreign Office that Cairns could be sent again to the USSR—and fears that he would be denied a visa.[12] Cairns made known to Alberta's premier his intention to return to the USSR: he hoped to go in the autumn of 1933, he told John E. Brownlee in a letter from London dated December 8, 1932. By then, Cairns intimated, he would have attained a better knowledge of Russian, and when in the USSR would do some driving in his own car, thereby avoiding "as much as possible the use of Government guides." He thus expected to improve on the information he had collected in his first tour. Brownlee had requested, in a letter the previous month, more details about that trip. His was one of many such requests that Cairns had received, and Cairns had been resisting sharing further thoughts about the investigative visit. His preference, he explained to Brownlee, was for "people to draw their own conclusions from the evidence contained in my reports," and because he was planning a second tour, he would be in a position to better assess the agricultural situation in the USSR. Moreover, considering that the forecasts he had cabled were indeed coming to bear over the previous three months, "we did not think it advisable to endanger the chances of my securing a visa for a return visit by giving any publicity to my recent tour."[13]

Despite this reluctance, Cairns made an exception for the Alberta premier. He shared with Brownlee his disappointment with some of the reactions to his reports. Some people, Cairns said, had concluded from them that he was an anti-socialist who was in "favour of having no truck or trade with the Russians." Cairns expressed regret at such opinions, feeling that he had "really tried hard to refrain from expressing personal judgements" and had given a "simple chronological account of what I saw and the evidence I gathered." He also thought that his "several years [of] active participation and unshakeable faith in the farmers' co-operative movement in Canada" should have put to rest any charge of bias against socialism. Moreover, continued Cairns in his letter to the leader of the United Farmers of Alberta government, he was not against but in favour of trade with the Soviet Union, because, in his opinion, countries with a surplus of foodstuffs could through barter or another arrangement render the Soviet people a "great service."[14]

Brownlee had asked his correspondent at the Empire Marketing Board in London some specific questions, which Cairns proceeded to answer. One centred on whether the Soviet standard of living was better now or during the period before the war. In Cairns's estimation, if the population as a whole was taken into consideration, then the standard of living was "certainly lower than it was in the pre-war days." He would never say so publicly, he confided, because discussions of that subject "always arouse emotional as well as intellectual responses," because of contradictions in the evidence regarding prewar conditions, and because he would prefer an opportunity to elaborate any public statement before making it. Cairns then remarked that he could not bring himself "to believe, taking the country as a whole, conditions could possibly have been as bad as in pre-war days as they are at present." Cairns mentioned an unnamed English agriculturalist, who lived in the USSR for many years, and a Mr. Bennett, who occupied a minor position at the British embassy in Moscow and was "anything but a Tory," as well as a Mr. Bernhardt, the general manager of the Superintendents Company in the USSR, as being of the same opinion. He pointed to the sharp loss of livestock over the past years with no sign of improvement and referred to an enclosed confidential report by Dr. Otto Schiller, the agricultural attaché of the German embassy in Moscow, to illustrate the lack of recovery in the Volga region. Leningrad was experiencing a serious outbreak of spotted typhus, or "famine fever," Cairns said, which was being kept secret from the outside world; he added that, following a bad harvest, he would not be surprised if famine claimed many victims in the Volga region over the winter. His conclusion, therefore, he told Brownlee, was that conditions were worse now than at any other time "with the exception of the disastrous famine in 1920–21 when, as you will remember, possibly 2,000,000 or more people died of starvation."[15]

Among the insights that Cairns shared with the Alberta premier was his perception of discrimination against the peasantry in favour of the urban population. The latter, in his view, was being given a standard of living "above its productivity" through the "harsh and cruel measures of confiscation and persecution of large classes of the peasantry." The government had "been 'paying'" agricultural producers only an "infinitesimal fraction of the open market price for their produce." Cairns described a countryside that was "polluted with weeds," "stripped of livestock," and "teeming with people constantly on the move looking for food." He noted that the Ukrainian Communist Party was rumoured to have protested to Moscow about the need to make drastic changes to its policies. Yet he doubted that there would be any effective organized opposition to the Soviet regime as it "would be put down by the army." Cairns predicted "widespread starvation this winter" and suggested that if a world wheat conference were held, the main exporting counties could offer a "substantial amount of grain" to the USSR. He doubted "very much if the Government will be so foolish as to push their grain collecting punitive expeditions as hard as they did last year, as they must be aware of the inevitable consequences which such pressure would have on next year's harvest."[16] In spite of his own and officials' hopes, Cairns never did return to the USSR.

The Assassination of French President Paul Doumer

In the same month Cairns penned his report, May 1932, news of the assassination of France's president, Paul Doumer, made headlines in national newspapers and shocked the world. The assassin was identified as Paul Gorguloff [Pavel Gorgulov], a physician.[17] He had lived in

France for four years and described his motive as a reaction to French policy toward the USSR: "France always helped Bolshevism," Gorguloff maintained.[18] A later report claimed he was born in "Raviscala in the Caucasus, and was trained as a Cossack." His mother, according to the *Vancouver Sun*, lived in Labinsk ("where the family originated").[19] Sometime in the past she had been classified as a "kulak" and had her property seized by the state. The Russian term *kulak* ("tightfisted"; Ukr. *kurkul*) originally denoted wealthy farmers, but over time as the collectivization drive was in effect it came to signify any peasants resisting the Soviet agricultural policy. Gorguloff linked his assassination of the French president with the condition of the Soviet peasantry. "I fought to save France in the war and I fight now to save the Russian peasants," he said when his death sentence was pronounced.[20] After Gorguloff was guillotined in Paris, his eighty-two-year-old mother and his aunt, both of the same place in Kuban, were arrested. The crime of which they were accused was the theft of state grain, a violation that could fetch the death penalty. It was expected that clemency might be granted them on account of their ages.[21]

Flight across the Dnister River

The signs of a troubled Soviet countryside were reinforced by several stories in the Canadian press about desperate attempts made by peasants to cross the Dnister River from Soviet Ukraine to Romania. Direct communications had ceased after World War I. Roads had been destroyed and diplomatic relations between Bucharest and Moscow terminated. The last bridge across the river—connecting Tighina (now Bender) and Tiraspol (both cities today are in the breakaway Moldovan Transnistria region)—had been bombed in 1919 by UNR troops as they retreated into Romania. In 1924, on the Soviet side of the river, the Moldavian Autonomous Soviet Socialist Republic (Moldavian ASSR) was formed as an autonomous republic within the Ukrainian SSR. Ukrainians formed nearly half of the population of the territory (which today comprises the Moldovan Transnistria region and areas in Ukraine) and Moldovans almost a third.[22] In separating the Soviet Union from Romania, the Dnister River divided, in the opinion of Romanian historian Alexandru-Murad Mironov, not two countries but "two distinct worlds."[23]

In February 1932 the *Toronto Star* reported that forty Ukrainian peasants had been shot by Soviet frontier guardsmen while attempting to swim across the river into Romania. They were fleeing "an impending famine," as the Soviet government was engaged in grain seizures for the army stationed on the Soviet-Manchurian border.[24] In March 1932, the *Charlottetown Guardian* reported how villagers had tried to flee to Romania by hiding their wives and children in barrels placed on wagons. They would "drive down to the river bank as though to get water," according to the newspaper from Prince Edward Island, and then "whip up their horses and race across the ice toward the Rumanian shore."[25]

The Ukrainian-language press in Canada also commented on the attempted crossings of the Dnister River. Edmonton's *Ukraïns'ki visty* cited the weekly *Tryzub* of Paris (the unofficial organ of the UNR government-in-exile), which said that in spite of stricter border controls, refugees continued to come to Romania. The majority of them (Moldovans) were given refuge in Romania, but Ukrainians, it said, were sent back to the Communist authorities. The main reason given was the cost of maintaining the refugees. The Romanian government was apparently spending no less than 50,000 lei a day on the refugees who came in 1931 and 1932 and those who were still coming (according to the *New York Times* on 15 May 1932, the value of 20,000 lei was about 120 U.S. dollars).[26] Jewish refugees were receiving support from Jewish charities, *Ukraïns'ki visty* continued, and German refugees were directed to Germany, as a result of an agreement between Romania and that country. For the Moldovans, Romanians had collected around a million lei. A special committee in Chişinău (Kishinev) looked after them. "Only Ukrainians," the newspaper demurred, "remained without help."[27] The subject of Soviet border guard killings of peasants attempting to cross the border to Romania was one that the American Ukrainian daily *Svoboda* suggested might be raised at the Imperial Conference that would convene in Ottawa in July 1932. Another was the grain shortage in Ukraine caused by the dumping of Soviet wheat in Europe in competition with Canadian wheat. "This constitutes a double reason for the interest shown by the Canadian and the Ukrainian farmers of Canada," the Jersey City–based newspaper said. The treatment of the Ukrainian minority in Poland was also mentioned.[28]

A report about post–World War I refugees in Romania noted that a "certain infiltration across the Dniester" had taken place for some years "until the vigilance of the guards on both sides of the river, who were apt to shoot at sight, put an end to the movement." The movement "resumed in 1932, at the time of the collectivization campaign in Ukraine; most of those who came in this way remained in Bessarabia." No statistics were presented except for the spring of 1932, during which, according to the report, two thousand Ukrainians were said to have arrived.[29] Soviet control of the border tightened in 1933, making crossings even more difficult. The Italian scholar Alberto Basciani wrote that in 1933, "attempts to escape across the Dnister into Romania continued, even though the high numbers of the previous year were no longer being recorded, with the partial exception of the month of June, when the Romanian authorities noted the arrival from the USSR of 61 refugees."[30] To prevent families from fleeing across the Dnister, the Soviet authorities decided to erect on the left bank of the river a two-metre-tall fence with barbed wire.[31]

The issue of the attempted crossings of the Dnister River was discussed by Romania's members of Parliament and senators. Denys Maier-Mykhalsky's speech in the senate on April 19, 1932, was mentioned in *Ukraïns'kyi holos*. According to this report, the senator from Bukovyna appealed to the interior ministry not to return the refugees from Ukraine, for to do so was tantamount to delivering a death sentence. The Bukovynian lawyer argued that not only would deportation under such circumstances constitute an antihumanitarian act but it would also be counter to the Romanian constitution, which, he pointed out, did not recognize the death penalty. The Ukrainian National Party member urged that countries bordering the USSR that did not have sufficient funds to address the problem of refugees approach the League of Nations and apply for support. *Ukraïns'kyi holos* said that Senator Maier-Mykhalsky received broad applause for his speech, but there does not seem to have been much action on the part of the League of Nations.[32]

Emigration from Canada to the USSR

Meanwhile, as stories about difficulties in the Soviet rural sector persisted—a Canadian Press (CP) dispatch in March 1932 noted that no fewer than forty million peasants would require food relief, for example, and reports about fear of a famine continued throughout the year[33]—a migration movement trickled from Canada to the USSR. In March 1932 the *Edmonton Journal* mentioned a party of twenty people of Ukrainian and Russian background who had just left Drumheller (southern Alberta) for the USSR. These mine workers were apparently guaranteed work in the Don Basin region.[34] Members of that party may have read the pessimistic reports about the Soviet Union. But they also may have read the articles then circulating, especially in pro-Communist publications, that presented the USSR in a positive light—and which emphasized the Five-Year Plan, education, and the promise of full employment. Five months later, the *Edmonton Journal* reported that two hundred "Russian" emigrants, from different parts of Canada (some of whom were born in the country), had set sail to the USSR from Halifax on the liner *Gripsholm*. All had been promised jobs.[35]

"Starving for the Five-Year Plan"

Indeed, as the Canadian press tracked the progress of the Soviet Five-Year Plan during the course of 1932,[36] journalist Pierre van Paassen, writing in August in Toronto's *Globe*, alluded to pressures on food supplies in the Soviet Union. He gave readers the impression that there was no reason for alarm. People were hungry, van Paassen said in his piece titled "Ukraine Starves for Five-Year Plan," but there was no actual famine. Foodstuffs were "obtainable only at exorbitant prices, prices which are actually prohibitive to the poorer peasants." He then offered this interpretation of the situation: "What has happened is this: 'Comrade' Stalin has gone too fast." Van Paassen went on to say that the Soviet dailies *Pravda* and *Izvestia* reported facts and criticized them "to the extent of demanding the death penalty of hundreds of men who blundered with those grain collections, thereby setting whole peasant districts against the Government, which it must be obvious, cannot afford internal opposition much longer without endangering its own life."[37] A month later, Toronto's *Telegram* announced that van Paassen and the *Globe* had parted ways. It was difficult, the *Telegram* scoffed, for the journalist to serve two masters (the *Globe* and the *Star*). "To the Globe he wrote of the woes of Ukraine," the *Telegram* noted in an editorial; "To the Star he tells of the wondrous accomplishments of Soviet Russia and of the 'greatest human experiment of history.'"[38]

"We Have Now Reached the Point That We Are Dying of Hunger"

Van Paassen may have indicated that there was no cause for alarm, but letters received in Canada from relatives in the USSR sounded desperate. One such letter, written in June 1932, was sent by a woman in Soviet Ukraine to her husband in Saskatchewan. He in turn forwarded it to the newspaper *Ukraïns'ki visty*, which then published it. "We have now reached the point that we are dying of hunger," the mother of five told her husband. "Your children are pleading that you not forget us because we are living on only sorrel soup, there is nothing else." There had been bread before but "now we are starving terribly, ten times worse than during the famine of ten years ago. You remember well how it was." Her heart ached when she looked at the children "swelling from starvation." The letter went on to say that people from her area travelled "for bread to far-off places" and "after two or more weeks when they return they bring very little bread." People were "already feeding on dead horses" and no longer recognized one another as they turned gaunt. The woman feared for what might happen to her and the children. They had not been able to plant the fields "since there were no seeds." She had traded some clothing for bread and brought back some flour, but now was "left with nothing else to barter. It is sad to look at the starving people, as they trade their last pieces of clothing." God, she thought, and her husband in Canada were the family's best hope for survival.[39]

"Proposal Not Necessary in the Absence of Real Need"

Disquieting reports continued. In August 1932, an *Edmonton Journal* account indicated that there were delays in harvesting in Ukraine and the North Caucasus—areas that, it said, had experienced a devastating drought the previous year. According to the *Journal*, Soviet newspapers were blaming poor organization and "increased activities of the Kulaks against collective farmers in the form of grain thefts and general persecution" for the fact that only 65 per cent of grain had been harvested in Ukraine.[40] The *Globe* reported food shortages, saying that vegetables were lacking for the winter months, and grain reserves, with the exception of army supplies, had been consumed.[41]

In fact, much hunger was already occurring in the Soviet Union, particularly in the two areas mentioned by the *Edmonton Journal*: Ukraine and the North Caucasus. Although major famine had yet to be confirmed by the mainstream Canadian press, sometime in the summer of 1932 the Ukrainian Self-Reliance League of Canada had already approached the Canadian Red Cross about the matter of dispensing relief. The exact date is unknown, but the approach stemmed from a district meeting of the league in Hafford, Saskatchewan. Prices for prairie grain had fallen, the local harvest was a good one, and there was plenty of wheat to share with starving brethren in Soviet Ukraine. All that was needed was confirmation on the Soviet side that the aid would be permitted. In October 1932 the national office of the Canadian Red Cross replied. On October 20, Elsie F. Moir, secretary to the national commissioner in Toronto, wrote to Mrs. Mary E. Waagen, honorary acting commissioner of the Red Cross Society in Calgary, informing Waagen that "In this morning's mail I received a letter from the League of Red Cross Societies" with which a copy of a communication it had received from the Alliance of Red Cross and Red Crescent Societies of the USSR was enclosed. It read: "I have just received your letter of September 9th regarding the desire expressed by a group of Ukrainians to send part of their harvest to their compatriots. While expressing my most sincere thanks for the interest you have been good enough to take in this matter, I have the honour to inform you that in view of the satisfactory harvest this year, the Executive Committee of the Alliance of Red Cross and Red Crescent Societies of the USSR believes that the carrying out of the Canadian citizens' proposal is not necessary in the absence of real need." Moir then added that Waagen "may wish to go into this matter a little further" and, if so, could "discuss it with Dr. Biggar when he sees you on his return trip."[42]

Meanwhile, in September 1932, reports that appeared in newspapers such as the *Toronto Star* suggested a protracted struggle between Soviet authorities and a recalcitrant peasantry. In one account, peasants were said to be showing resistance to Soviet agricultural policy by staging an exodus to the cities.[43] Another noted that a decree signed by Stalin fixed the amount of meat and grain that the various regions were required to deliver to the government at low prices, hoping to "extract more food from a reluctant peasantry."[44] Later that month, the *Toronto Star* quoted a British newspaper, the *Morning Post*, about food riots in the Russian city of Yekaterinburg.[45]

"Excoriation of the USSR"

At the same time, other Soviet-related content in the *Toronto Star* was more upbeat. Thorton Purkis, an "advertising counsel," shared impressions of the Soviet Union that were described as "tremendously enthusiastic."[46] Descriptions of the mighty Dnipro hydroelectric station seemed to evince advancement while those making reference to "kulaks" implied an element that formed an obstacle to progress. Pierre van Paassen described the largely U.S.-designed Dniprostroi as the "world's most powerful hydro-electric station" and called the "region here in the Ukraine Republic" the "heart and nerve centre of the whole five year plan."[47]

In October 1932 the *Toronto Star* reprinted an editorial from the *Cobourg World* (Ontario) about the USSR, which criticized the "excoriation of Soviet Russia" by Toronto newspapers. The piece acknowledged that "Russians face short rations," but countered "so do thousands of Canadians this coming winter." It added that when Walter Duranty, "winner this year of the coveted Pulitzer Prize for journalism," said that Communism was the best system of government for the USSR, "it means that this whole interesting and terrifying business can not be dismissed with our damnation."⁴⁸ Days later, the same Toronto newspaper ran a piece by van Paassen titled "Reconstruction or Revolution." Van Paassen declared, among other things, that in Ukraine, where "the agrarian policy failed utterly last year, the most pitiless publicity was given to the causes by the [Soviet] newspapers." Nobody was spared, he added; "Nobody was shielded. Much to the delight, by the way, of the purveyors of anti-Soviet news, who are stationed in Warsaw, Riga and Bucharest."⁴⁹

Rhea Clyman

In September 1932 the *Toronto Telegram*, a rival to the *Toronto Star*, presented its readers with a series of articles about the USSR penned by Rhea Clyman (a special correspondent for the *Telegram*, London's *Daily Express*, and other newspapers), who had spent four years in the Soviet Union. That month, Clyman was expelled from the Soviet Union because of articles she had written about that Eurasian state.⁵⁰ Some of them appeared in the *Telegram* in September 1932, others later, in May and June 1933. In a story titled "Girl from New Toronto Begs Bread in Russia; Father Lured by 'Job,'" the twenty-eight-year-old writer asserted that she had visited Kharkiv, the capital of Soviet Ukraine, and had been "anxious to get away." The "great Ukrainian capital," Clyman wrote, "was in the grip of hunger." She noted that beggars "swarmed around the streets," the stores "were empty," and the workers' bread rations had "just been cut from two pounds a day per person to one pound and a quarter." She also related the story of Alice Mertzka, a girl who had "come begging to our hotel room for food." Mertzka had lived in "New Toronto for nine years" and her father worked for the Massey Harris Company. "Three years ago," Clyman related, "she and her father came back to Russia to get work at the tractor plant in Kharkov. 'Now we are without bread,' she told me."⁵¹ The *Redcliff Review* in Alberta remarked that Clyman's expulsion was the first of a foreign correspondent in ten years, although representatives of CP and the *Berliner Tageblatt* had been refused permission to enter the Soviet Union in recent years.⁵²

It was probably an account by Clyman published in the *Daily Express* that the *Charlottetown Guardian* had in mind when, in January

1933, it referred to sensational stories in the London newspaper about the situation of the USSR's agricultural population.⁵³ Those stories, according to the Charlottetown newspaper, mentioned "dire famine" in Ukraine and the "same condition" in the North Caucasus. There were "even tales of cannibalism, unauthenticated ... but possible." The story went on to discuss another report about Soviet agriculture that had appeared in the January 1933 issue of the magazine *Current History* (published by the New York Times Company). That account mentioned neither "dire famine" nor cannibalism. The closest it came to either was to say that the peasantry was reduced to conditions "not much above the famine level."⁵⁴

Death of Nadezhda Alliluyeva

Two months earlier, news had broken of the death of Stalin's wife, Nadezhda Alliluyeva. A short announcement of her death, appearing in the *Toronto Star* on November 9, 1932, remarked that no other details were available.⁵⁵ The next day, the *Star* said that according to rumour, Alliluyeva had died after consuming poisoned food intended for her husband.⁵⁶ The *Globe* commented on her death by referring to journalist Frederick Griffin's talk before the Toronto Women's Press Club, during which he had extolled the liberties enjoyed by Soviet women. Anne Anderson Perry had responded by bringing up Alliluyeva: "Apparently one of the liberties enjoyed by Stalin's wife was that of tasting her husband's food before he ate it, so that he might avoid poisoning. And apparently it was through the exercise of this liberty that she met her death."⁵⁷ However, it later emerged that it was not the poisoning of food but rather the treatment of those who produced it that possibly led to the demise of the Soviet leader's wife—by her own hand.⁵⁸

Resistance

By the time of Nadezhda Alliluyeva's suicide, and ahead of the *Charlottetown Guardian*'s editorial, in November 1932, *Ukraïns'ki visty* was reporting not only widespread famine but also resistance to Soviet government policies. The newspaper said that according to news from Berlin (the source was not specified), actions against Soviet representatives in rural localities had, in a single month, led to eighty-seven deaths and another forty-four later on in hospital. It added that the Soviet security forces claimed to have uncovered an organization in Ukraine, headquartered in Dnipropetrovsk, that aimed to incite a general strike as a protest against the export of grain abroad while the population was starving.[59]

Reports of Cannibalism in the Ukrainian-Language Press

That same month, *Ukraïns'ki visty* also contained stories about cannibalism. According to "the press," these stories said, there had been instances of cannibalism in right-bank Ukraine (west of the Dnipro River). Specific cases involving names, villages, and actions were given. One of the cases had occurred in the village of Molodechni, Buky raion (district), where Viktor Ivasenko had cut up two children, partially consuming them and selling some of their flesh in the market. *Ukraïns'ki visty* also related the case of Marta Zakharchenko, of the village of Kharkivka in the same raion, who had dismembered her son Borys and fed the parts to his siblings. In the village of Kyshyntsi, *Ukraïns'ki visty* said, the flesh of a deceased four-year-old was found fried in a pan; a mother had consumed her two-month-old child in the village of Polianka, while in the village of Balanivka children were constantly disappearing. In the meantime, the newspaper continued, the number of deaths by starvation was increasing. Every night several dozen corpses were brought to the cemeteries of Kyiv, Kharkiv, and Zhytomyr. These were victims of death by starvation, said the paper, their corpses gathered daily on the roads leading to those cities. But all of this, *Ukraïns'ki visty* declared to its readers scattered across Canada, was being kept secret by "the Bolsheviks" so that the world would not know the true state of affairs in the USSR.[60] Indeed, that very same month, on November 29, the Soviet Union signed a nonaggression pact with France.[61]

New Soviet Punitive Measures Introduced

During December, news of stiffer penalties for workers was among the reports about Soviet developments. *Ukraïns'ki visty* mentioned a decree punishing absences of workers without a doctor's certificate. They could be penalized by withdrawal of workers' food stamp books and in other ways that would affect the entire family. Living quarters could be taken away for not reporting to work. That month *Ukraïns'ki visty* also cited Duranty on peasants fleeing the countryside.[62] Toronto's *Globe* cited the Soviet newspapers *Izvestia* and *Pravda* about the issuance of sharp warnings to peasants against hoarding grain. A "kulak" had been sentenced to death and his wife to ten years' imprisonment after a government grain collector had been slain. Editorials in the Soviet newspapers singled out Ukraine and the Volga region as places that were lagging behind in grain collections, in contrast to Moscow province and the Tatar republic, which had fulfilled their quotas.[63]

Silver for Food

The year 1932 closed with Canadian newspapers reporting on the practice of the sale of silver articles in exchange for food and clothing and on the food situation in the USSR. Food stores were accepting any kind of silver, the *Toronto Telegram* reported, just as gold had been accepted.[64] The same newspaper also carried a report about the round-up in cities of "unproductive elements" who had then been put to work, presumably in convict labour camps. The aim, apparently, was to uproot the "kulaks."[65]

An editorial in the *Winnipeg Free Press* at the start of December discussed the "food scarcity" in the Soviet Union. The Five-Year Plan was in some ways successful, it noted, with up to 75 per cent of the industrial program having been accomplished. But what had fallen "woefully behind," the editorial said, was the food supply. The plan had envisaged that one-third of peasant holdings would be socialized by 1933, but in fact, the editorial pointed out, twice that number and four-fifths of cultivable land had been collectivized. The editorial attributed one of the failures of the new system to the peasants' lack of socialization. It also stated that as the collectivization drive ensued with full determination, "the peasant resistance took the form of killing off the livestock and abandoning the production of surplus food stuffs." The producers and private traders were "thrown on the scrap heap," but the managers of the collective farms could not immediately "take over the complicated business and maintain its balance." The editorial remarked that peasants, forced by food shortages, had migrated to urban centres and construction camps by the millions. But while *Ukraïns'ki visty* had already begun publishing accounts of cannibalism in Soviet Ukraine, the *Free Press* perceived only food shortages but no famine in the USSR. "Reliable correspondents do not claim that the Soviet is faced with famine," it said, "but rather by a woeful scarcity of food."[66]

Chapter Two

"OPEN YOUR EYES, UNITE IN A COMMON PROTEST"
Winter 1933

In 1933 the famine was discussed in the Canadian mainstream press alongside such other Soviet-related stories as the matter of lifting restrictions (introduced in 1931) on Canadian trade with the USSR, the possibility of U.S. recognition of the Soviet Union, and the threat of deportation to the USSR of a Doukhobor leader in Canada, Peter Verigin. In the United States, the presidential election of November 8, 1932, had resulted in the defeat of the Republican Party's incumbent, Herbert Hoover, and the victory of the Democratic Party's Franklin Delano Roosevelt. The United States had never recognized the Soviet Union, a policy that Hoover had maintained during his presidency. But after his defeat there were signs that the new government under Roosevelt might gradually move in a different direction.

Col. Herbert John Mackie

At the start of the year, the press mentioned problems in grain requisitioning and food shortages in the Soviet Union. An *Edmonton Journal* story published on January 3, 1933, concerned the sentencing to death of "three of the highest Communist party and Soviet officials in the

Orekhovsky district" of Ukraine and imprisonment of eight others "upon their conviction of treason in sabotaging the government's grain collection plan." The three to be executed were charged with "arbitrarily lowering the government's grain collection quotas, and falsely reporting on the extent of the crop to the central authorities, and branded as counter-revolutionaries, traitors and betrayers of the working class."[1] Later in the month, A. C. Cummings of the *Journal*'s London bureau noted that some news reports "say that before the next harvest comes round [the Soviet Union] may face a worse food shortage than she has known for years."[2] Yet that seemed to contradict what Col. H. J. Mackie—described as "prominent in recent years as an intermediary between Canadian and Russian industrialists"—had suggested earlier in the month. Mackie had been shown dispatches from Calgary that proposed bartering Canadian wheat for Soviet oil.[3] "I discussed Russia's wheat supply with Mr. Bogdanov [chair of the Amtorg Trading Corporation]," Mackie had said, adding that Bogdanov's "latest information was that wheat collections in Russia during the past month were above expectations and...his opinion was Russia would not be forced to import wheat."[4] The matter of Canadian trade with the USSR was discussed extensively in the press, with considerable pressure applied on the Canadian government to lift its partial embargo.[5]

Memorandum of the Birmingham Bureau of Research on Russian Economic Conditions

In the midst of the debate about Canadian trade with the USSR, including the much-discussed proposal of an exchange of Soviet oil for Canadian cattle, in mid-January 1933 the *Montreal Gazette* featured an editorial about the Soviet Union that referred to the prevalence of famine. Considering the interest in the topic of trade with the USSR, the editorial began, it was important to obtain reliable information about the situation there. It observed that the Birmingham Bureau of Research on Russian Economic Conditions had issued a memorandum "whose conclusions are based upon a very careful study under the auspices of the Russian Department of the University of Birmingham." The report, the editorial said, declared that the Soviet population was experiencing a famine "without a crop failure." Socioeconomic factors rather than physical ones such as climate were blamed for an "unfavorable grain situation," including the "system of compulsory deliveries of grain at prices fixed by the Soviet Government."[6]

Canadians in the USSR

Indeed, by January 1933, Canada's prime minister knew, if not about the extent of the famine, at least that conditions in the USSR were such that ex-residents of Canada wanted to leave the former and return to the latter. During the Great Depression, so-called hunger marches were organized in the United Kingdom, Canada, and other countries. During one such march in Canada in January, a set of demands was presented to Prime Minister R. B. Bennett by hunger marchers who had travelled to Ottawa. In reply, Bennett brought up the subject of the Soviet Union. He revealed that he had just been informed by his minister of labour of requests from six former residents of Canada for aid to resettle in Canada from the USSR. "They had found," the prime minister was quoted as having said, "that conditions in the Soviet were much different from those represented by the deputation."[7]

It is not known who these six individuals were, but this may not have been the first time that the Canadian government had been informed of such requests from former residents and it probably was not the last.[8] On March 27, 1933, the British embassy in Moscow forwarded extracts of letters it received to London, and these may have been shared with Canadian counterparts. One of the letters was said to have come "from a Russian now in Ukraine who lived for many years in Canada." He returned in 1922, lived on the land "neither rich nor poor," then in 1932 was "'dekulakised,' my house taken and I and my family put under the open sky." William Strang, counsellor at the British embassy in Moscow, noted, "There is no doubt that both the embassy and the Consulate receive considerably more of these letters than at any time since the present Mission was established."[9]

In February 1933, during a debate in the House of Commons, Canada's prime minister used the word "starvation" in reference to the USSR. The prompt was a statement by William Richard Motherwell, the Liberal member of Parliament (MP) for Melville, Saskatchewan, about the sale of wheat and the USSR. Motherwell, a former federal minister of agriculture, said, "The whole trouble with our calculations ... is that just when we think Russia will cease to export wheat because of her home requirements, she starts to export; she becomes an exporter of wheat when it is well known that later in the same year she will have to import wheat." To which R. B. Bennett interjected, "While the population dies of starvation."[10]

Stalin Declares Success of the Five-Year Plan

That same month, *Toronto Star* journalist Frederick Griffin announced that Stalin had broken "a silence of eighteen months" to broadcast the "success, almost triumph" of the Five-Year Plan. Speaking before the Communist Party of the Soviet Union on January 7, the Soviet leader had justified the velocity of the program and the sacrifices incurred. "The conditions of the moment, the growth of armament in capitalist countries, the collapse of the idea of disarmament, the hatred of the international bourgeoisie for the U.S.S.R.—all this forced the Party to intensify the strengthening of the defensive power of the country, the foundation of its independence," he asserted. When Stalin turned to the agricultural sector, he remarked that collective farms now embraced over seventy per cent of all peasant farms and more grain could be collected annually. He defended the pace of collectivization: "it was undoubtedly right ... even though things have not been accomplished here without some people being carried away with the enthusiasm." The question, Stalin told his listeners, was no longer whether or not the collective farm would or would not be, but rather one of strengthening the system. "Wrecking elements" had to be driven out and reliable Communist cadres needed to be selected for the collectives to ensure they became good, Soviet farms. He considered the struggle against the "kulaks" an unfinished one: as a class they "had been crushed, but not beaten completely."[11]

Insurrection in Kuban

That same month, too, in its 11 February 1933 issue, under the title "Soviet Russia Fascinates Young Lethbridge Couple," the *Edmonton Journal* published the impressions of Charles Richert, an "irrigation expert from Alberta...[serving as a] consultant engineer in the building of a 100,000-acre irrigation project...in the sub-Caucasian lands at the eastern end of the Black Sea." Writing in the summer of 1932, Richert spoke of the Soviet people as "great lovers of music and the theatre, [who] drink lots of wine and vodka and above all enjoy elaborate meals. I am told, however, that the latter now bear only a faint resemblance to former times." He added that "with copious rains...the crops are wonderful and soon will be ready for the combine. We have fruits such as mulberries and strawberries in abundance and last fall ate the greatest amount of grapes in our lives."[12] There was no indication that acute food shortages were being experienced. In part, this was because, although the report was published in early 1933, it actually described the period before the major famine.

Yet elsewhere in the Caucasus region, villagers were being expelled en masse. The *Toronto Telegram* and *Star* wrote of the wholesale deportation of the population of three villages in Kuban, around 45,000 people in total, to the far north of the USSR for obstructing the grain collection.[13] That news elicited a plea from Countess Alexandra L. Tolstoy, the daughter of the celebrated Russian writer Leo Tolstoy, in the United States. An article in the *Border Cities Star* of Windsor, Ontario, datelined Philadelphia, announced that she had appealed to the world to help the Soviet people. In a statement she sent to the League of Nations and to leaders in Europe, China, and Japan, Tolstoy urged them to "Open your eyes. Unite in a common protest against the tortures of 160 million of defenseless Russian people." The countess asserted that conditions in the USSR were now worse than in the days of Ivan the Terrible. The current Soviet regime was answering "pitiful pleas for bread with 'bullets and gas.'" In Kuban whole families were executed and 45,000 people—women and children—were driven out of their homes to be sent to Siberia, where they would meet a certain death. She went on: "Now, in the year 1933, when in the Northern

Caucasus a bloody slaughter is going on, when thousands of people are shot and exiled daily, and my father is not here to protest, I feel that it is my duty to raise my weak voice against this wholesale murder." The "Bolsheviki," she said, began by "prosecuting class enemies, religious people, old priests, scientists, professors. Now the turn has come for the working classes, the peasants."[14]

Ukraïns'ki visty spoke of a revolt that was driven by the threat of death from starvation. The periodical said that the revolt began in the Tikhoretsky district of Kuban—a region with a large ethnic Ukrainian population that dated back to the late eighteenth century, when Zaporozhian Cossacks from Ukraine had resettled there. The rebellion came to encompass five counties. Under the leaderships of Gen. Hovoryn and "Otomans" Selykhov, Babanyn, and Borsukov, six thousand Cossacks had gathered and cleared the district of "Bolsheviks," taking over an area of 250 square miles. "Even descendants of the Zaporozhian Cossacks in their sixties and seventies took part in the insurrection," the periodical told its readers. The insurgents set up a temporary Cossack government. An army dispatched from the city of Rostov against them was defeated and the insurgents obtained additional materials. On the sixth day of the insurrection, tanks and airplanes were deployed against the insurgents. Twelve leaders were executed and 45,000 Kuban inhabitants were banished to the Solovetsky Islands. Thousands of villagers were killed.[15]

Countess Tolstoy's appeal was mentioned in Canada's House of Commons by Franklin W. Turnbull, the Conservative MP for Regina, during an attack on the Co-operative Commonwealth Federation. The CCF, a coalition of labour and left-wing groups, had recently been founded in Calgary, in August 1932. James Shaver Woodsworth was elected as its leader. In 1931, Woodsworth travelled to the Soviet Union.[16] Turnbull and others used this visit as a way to discredit the CCF. Thus, the reference to Countess Tolstoy was made in the context of the Regina MP's statements about the CCF and Canada's trade relations with the Soviet Union. On February 23, 1933, Turnbull declared in the Green Chamber: "We hear the continual cry whether we should trade with Russia....They sound the praises of what is going on over there, telling what wonderful things Stalin is doing for Russia.

But Tolstoy's daughter is praying for her murdered fellow citizens in Russia, and asking the nations of the world if they cannot come to their rescue and stop the slaughter."[17]

The Ukrainian Bureau in London

Among the archival papers of R. B. Bennett are several publications of the former Ukrainian press bureau at 40 Grosvenor Place, London. Founded by an affluent Ukrainian in the United States, Jacob Makohin, as an information and lobbying centre in the aftermath of the 1930 pacification of Ukrainians in Poland, the Ukrainian Bureau was directed by Vladimir Kaye (Kysilewsky) from Canada.[18] The bureau published an irregular bulletin, which it mailed to politicians and others in the United Kingdom and abroad. Information it collected and disseminated about Ukraine was printed in the Ukrainian-language press in Canada.[19] The February 15, 1933, issue of the bulletin included five articles about the situation in Soviet Ukraine: "Ukraine and the Five Year Plan," "Dissention in the Ukrainian Communist Party," "Failure of the Anti-God Campaign," "Terrible Depression in Soviet Ukraine," and "New Passport System to Harry Starving Refugees." Much discussion was about the famine. Ukraine had already "suffered from the horrors of famine," the bulletin noted in its article about the Five-Year Plan, but the incidence of famine had been "generally local and not widespread." It attributed the present food shortage not to "unfavourable weather conditions, but to doctrinaire rulers, who, totally disregarding the human factor, have relentlessly forced their policy on a hostile countryside, depriving those who grow the food." It added, in uppercase letters, that the suffering was "felt more intensely in the Ukraine which is the largest and most important agricultural area (as well as one of the great industrial areas) and is moreover, with its overwhelmingly non-Russian population, the special target of the central government which realises that the separatist movement is gaining in intensity as a result of the desperate conditions to which Ukraine is now reduced."[20]

In its article about dissension in the Communist Party of Ukraine, the bulletin reported that the Soviet secret police had discovered a "strong organization" among the party's peasant members that was "taking steps to protect the peasants against the Agrarian Policy of the State." The group, the bulletin said, called itself the "Rural Communist Blo[c]" and was "carrying on a most serious opposition to the requisition of wheat."[21] The bulletin's article about repression in Ukraine noted that the Soviet regime had followed its mass deportation of Kuban Cossacks with a similar campaign in rural areas of Ukraine where the grain plan had not been fulfilled or where the population was "hostile to the central administration." About twenty thousand people were deported from Poltava and other areas, including members of the Communist Party, according to the bulletin. For some, the deportation amounted to a death sentence. When one of the trains transporting deportees pulled into the station in Kursk, Russia, "six peasants were found frozen to death in one of the trucks." The bulletin also called attention to punitive expeditions sent to punish peasants who hid grain.[22]

The article "New Passport System to Harry Starving Refugees" referred to the Soviet measures to counter the migration of the Ukrainian population to the cities and northern parts of the USSR. According to the bulletin, a decree of December 27, 1932, introduced a compulsory passport system, and a new workers' and peasants' militia under the supervision of the secret police was entrusted with its enforcement. Urban centres, beginning with Moscow, Leningrad, and Kharkiv, were to be purged of non-Communist and suspect elements, the bulletin noted; those cities were to be "secured as communist strongholds, from which the discontented, starving peasantry will be banned."[23]

The Alberta Wheat Pool's Barter Proposal

While Ukrainian-language periodicals in Canada had earlier drawn their readers' attention to cases of cannibalism in Soviet Ukraine, the mainstream Canadian press was saying little at this time about actual famine in the USSR. The Rev. E. E. Shields of Chicago was quoted by the Canadian press in February 1933 as saying in Toronto that "there are well-authenticated reports of cannibalism in certain areas of the U.S.S.R.," and he referred to "instances where the authorities gave people permission to go to the morgues and obtain bodies for human food." But there was little elaboration.[24]

There was, however, broader acknowledgment of major difficulties being experienced in the Soviet countryside. In 1932 and 1933, Canada had wheat—and lots of it. Ukrainian farmers in Canada had already suggested that surplus wheat could be transferred to people who were in need of it in Soviet Ukraine. That sentiment was echoed at the turn of 1933 by the Alberta Wheat Pool (AWP) when, in a year-end statement, it proposed the bartering or credit sale of Canada's surplus wheat to the USSR. The statement said that the elimination of the surplus would improve world wheat prices, "aid Russia in its need of the grain," and bring about benefits to all the participating countries. Through barter, Canada could take what it needed in exchange for the wheat. "Reliable information suggests a more serious situation in the way of disruption of food in that vast country than is generally realized," said the AWP, which advocated allotting a considerable portion of the entire "world's surplus wheat" to the USSR on generous credit terms or in exchange for commodities. "This would undoubtedly save millions from near starvation while disposing of the surplus," the statement stressed, and would "combine humanitarianism with hardheaded business."[25] Canadian trade with the Soviet Union had been a topic of considerable discussion ever since the imposition of a partial embargo by the Conservative government in 1931. A year after the United Kingdom had diplomatically recognized the USSR, Canada did the same. But the Dominion government did not send a trade commissioner to Moscow, although a Soviet trade agent came to Canada. That agent's welcome "was extinguished when it was found that he was carrying on Bolshevistic propaganda." This had happened during the Mackenzie King–led Liberal government. Not long after R. B Bennett took office, trade between the two states was restricted almost to a minimum by an embargo imposed on the main Soviet exports to Canada. Oil was not affected, but coal, lumber, asbestos, and certain furs were.[26] In retaliation, Moscow imposed a complete embargo of Canadian imports.

Meanwhile, a strong business lobby urged the Canadian government to lift its embargo and consider the sale of cattle to the Soviet

Union. Among other forums, such discussions took place in the Manitoba legislature, in Winnipeg. Ralph H. Webb, mayor of Winnipeg and the Conservative member for Assiniboia, was among the debaters on trade relations. Not long after he was elected a member of the Legislative Assembly (MLA), the Winnipeg mayor made a startling statement in the legislature. In February 1933, he told fellow members that he read between thirty and fifty letters daily from the USSR that "asked for food, clothing, shoes, and not for money." Webb added that people "would be astonished if they learned how much was going out of Winnipeg every week for the needy of Russia."[27]

David Toews and Col. Herbert John Mackie

In March 1933, the *Toronto Telegram* said that the Soviet government was feeding people in the North Caucasus where there was crop failure "due to reluctance of the farmers to produce," but was doing so selectively, with food being allowed "only [to] those showing diligent work."[28] In fact, March was an important turning point in Canada with respect to the famine because in the middle of that month the Legislative Assembly of Saskatchewan took an unusual step: It suspended its regular business in order to devote attention exclusively to the topic of the famine.

The catalyst appears to have been the local Mennonite community. Over the course of previous months, the Mennonite board in the town of Rosthern had been receiving letter after letter from the USSR describing famine conditions. In January, David Toews, the head of the board, had been reading the statements made by Col. Herbert Mackie—a former MP and president of the Canadian Committee of the Save the Children Fund during the 1921–23 Soviet famine—about the Soviet Union and decided to appeal to him. "My dear Colonel, you at one time were at the head of the Save the Children organization in Russia," Toews wrote to Mackie, whom he knew. "The need is as great as it was in 1921 and 1922," he continued. "I believe you are the man who should again put himself at the head of such an organization and I am sure that with your influence in Russia, you could again become the savior of millions of children who are now dying."[29]

The following month, Toews took issue with Mackie's claim that there was no forced labour in the USSR and decided to write a letter to the *Star-Phoenix* of Saskatoon. Those who knew Mackie "know that he is a friend of Russia on account of his business interests in that country," wrote Toews. He then addressed the issue of business with the USSR: "Whether business transactions with Russia will finally result in benefit or detriment to Canada, I will not try to answer. I believe that our prime minister has good reason to be skeptical on this point. Dealing with brutal, treacherous rogues is always hazardous, because you never know when they might stab you in the back." Toews then referred to the appeal by Countess Tolstoy that had recently been reported in the Canadian press. "Countess Tolstoy is reported to have said that not since the time of Ivan the Terrible ... has there been as much suffering in Russia as there is at the present time," he wrote. "And we believe that not even during the regime of that notorious lunatic has there been such general suffering as there is in Russia at present." The Mennonite community, Toews said, had been receiving on average one hundred letters a day from the Soviet Union—and "some days there are as many as five hundred." The letters were coming from all parts of the USSR, "from the erstwhile prosperous settlements in the Ukraine, from the settlements along the Volga River, from northern regions south of Archangelsk, northern Siberia, the desolate regions of the Ural Mountains, and central Asia, where many of the formerly prosperous people have been exiled and where they are kept in such a state that they are perishing." Toews wrote that even though most of the letters were written carefully for fear of being censored, "enough leaks out for us to know that thousands, yea millions, are at present perishing for want of food or clothing. . . . We know from many letters that they [the farming population] are in rags and without food—people in Russia are perishing in the millions." The Mennonite leader said that in all the letters they received "there is a cry for bread—people are dying of starvation." Further, people who had committed no crime "except gleaning some ears of wheat after harvest" were sent to exile or shot. "But the world will take no notice," Toews said. He was prepared to share the contents of the letters with anyone interested in learning about the conditions in the USSR.[30]

Impressed with the USSR

While Toews wrote of the desperate letters sent to the Mennonite board from the USSR, others wrote in Saskatchewan newspapers in praise of that state. In January the *Leader-Post* of Regina published an article titled "Soviet State Impresses Two Western Men." The two men were J. (John) Brown, a logger from British Columbia, and "Jack" (Sam[?]) Patterson, a miner from the Coleman district of Alberta. Having recently travelled to the USSR to "investigate working conditions" there, Brown and Patterson had been in Leningrad (now St. Petersburg) on November 7, 1932, for the October Revolution parade and had visited a tractor plant somewhere in Ukraine. Upon their return, in a talk at the Regina Labor Temple, the men emphasized that they had seen improvements in machinery, betterment of housing for workers, increased committees for self-government and control of industries, and equal pay for equal work. The tractor plant they had visited in Ukraine was "turning out 100 tractors a day, with spare parts," Patterson said. He added, "The farming methods in the Soviet state were a threat to all Canadian farmers, for it would be possible under the Soviet plan to lay wheat down in Winnipeg at as low as 25 cents a bushel. Collective farms, plowed by tractors, sowed by aeroplanes and reaped by combines, were the reason for the low cost." Brown, for his part, declared that "99.5 percent of all the reports you read in the capitalist press are lies."[31] In the same issue of the newspaper, an editorial quoted the positive impressions of the USSR expressed by Lord Passfield, "better recalled as Sydney Webb, and long a pillar in the British Socialist movement." After sharing what Webb had to say—including statements that more was being spent on education per head in the USSR than in the UK and that Soviet industrial production rates were high—the editorial commented that his observations helped "to throw light on perhaps the most striking experiment social and economic history has yet yielded." Reports varied as to how the Soviet Union was coming along, the editorial said: "Some observers are enthusiastic, some are skeptical, while others are far from being impressed." The *Leader-Post*, this editorial affirmed, believed "in providing its readers with information and the viewpoint of reputable observers so that its readers may know what is going on."[32]

Positive portrayals of the USSR could also be found in other newspapers. In February 1933, the *Border Cities Star* reported on an address about Soviet life by Herbert Spencer Clark, an electrical engineer and the secretary of the Robert Owen Foundation. Clark had visited the USSR in 1931 as a member of a group led by U.S. Protestant missionary and educator Sherwood Eddy. At his talk, which was sponsored by the Windsor branch of the League of Nations Society, he showed his audience of 1,500 packed into the auditorium of Windsor's Walkerville Technical School lantern slides that depicted examples of progress in the USSR. Clark likened developments in the USSR with those made during the Renaissance, Reformation, and French Revolution and suggested that with the passage of time the importance of the Bolshevik Revolution would become apparent to the rest of the world. People were still sent to Siberia, but they were building roads and toiling in the lumber camps under humane conditions, he claimed. One of the pictures Clark showed was of a "comely woman and her babe." Clark, according to the *Border Cities Star*, asked his listeners to bear the woman's "buxom figure" in mind when they "read accounts telling how the Russians were starving." She was "typical of the well-fed appearance the people presented at the time of his visit," he said.[33]

Clark's portrayals did not go unchallenged. George Herman Derry, a sociologist and president of Marygrove College in Detroit, and Walter E. Ellis, a graduate of Queen's University who had worked as a construction engineer in Magnitogorsk, Russia, also spoke at a meeting of the Windsor branch of the League of Nations Society, presenting instead a negative picture of conditions in the USSR.[34] Then John A. Willis, of Windsor, Ontario, but writing from London, England, wrote a letter to the *Border Cities Star* in response to Clark's address. Willis had worked as a chief architect in Kyiv and Dnipropetrovsk, Ukraine, and Sverdlovsk, Russia. Among the points of Clark's lecture he touched on was the reference to the "comely woman," who, Willis suggested, may well have been a member of an OGPU (All-Union State Political Administration, the Soviet secret police)[35] or an army official's family. The rest of the population, he said, subsisted on "thin soup, soggy black bread, and substitute tea." Willis also wrote of the breakdown of the collective farms, where "in spite of the good weather, the crops were a failure, due only to the passive resistance of the peasant."[36]

In Vernon, British Columbia, when J. F. Fox of Vancouver addressed a group on behalf of the National Unemployed Workers' Association and spoke glowingly of the USSR, a woman from the audience cried out that Canada was a paradise compared with the Soviet Union. The woman, about whom details were not given, mentioned letters received from relatives that told of thousands dying from starvation. Fox was also challenged by a man in the audience who said his own brother had died from starvation under the Soviet regime. Fox's response was not to deny that starvation existed, but to put the blame for it on the famished. The people who were starving in the USSR, according to Fox, were persons who were "too proud to soil their hands in the Soviet's campaign of productive toil." They deserved "nothing better than starvation."[37]

W. L. Mackenzie King: Leader of His Majesty's Loyal Opposition

In February 1933, David Toews also wrote to W. L. Mackenzie King, the former prime minister and now leader of the opposition in the House of Commons. On February 14, he gave King a copy of a letter he was sending to the press. "Our people in Russia are perishing for want of food and I must say that our people are not the ones who are suffering most," he told the Liberal Party leader. Millions were dying of starvation, Toews continued, and it seemed to him that "these conditions should be kept in mind when questions relating to Russia are being discussed in Parliament."[38] Still later in February, Cyril March of Prince Albert, Saskatchewan, also wrote to King. He intimated that he had received a letter from Gerard Ens of Rosthern, who was closely associated with the Canadian Mennonite Colonization Board and for whom March had served as a solicitor during the immigration of Mennonites to Canada from the USSR in the 1920s. Ens told March that his relatives in the USSR were suffering from lack of food and suitable woolen clothing. He added that Bishop Toews was for some time getting an average of over a hundred letters a day at the Mennonite board office in Rosthern.

"These reports show that in the settlements where the Mennonites in the Ukraine, in the Odessa district are suffering severely from lack of food [sic]," March said in his letter to King. He went on to say that Canada's vast quantities of wheat could be used not only to help but also to provide an opportunity to change Soviet attitudes toward Canada, ultimately leading to expanded trade between the two countries.[39]

King wrote his reply on March 13, 1933. He said that in putting arguments in support of trade with the USSR the Liberals were, as far as the present administration was concerned, battering their heads against a stone wall. The embargo that Bennett had in effect, King surmised correctly, would remain in place until the government was out of office. That did not mean, however, that the Liberal opposition would not continue to press the government on the issue of trade, King continued. He also told March that he had "brought the contents of your communication to the attention of some of our Saskatchewan Members, and others from the West with a view to having them more fully informed and better prepared when the subject comes up anew for discussion."[40] The subject may have come up again in the federal Parliament, but it was not in any specific way linked with the famine.

On March 11, David Toews wrote once more to King. "Conditions in Russia are getting so terrible," he declared, "that thousands of our people as well as very many other people in Russia are at present dying of starvation, the last little supplies of food having been taken away from them by the authorities." He then reasoned that "while millions of people in Russia are dying from want of food or clothing," there seemed to be no market for western Canadian grain and "no way to get grain for relief purposes into Russia." Toews conjectured that perhaps by allowing grain to come into the USSR such action would demonstrate the failure of the Five-Year Plan. He intimated that "we have been trying every possible way" to send help to the USSR but that these efforts had not been sufficient, considering the conditions. People were perishing and the Mennonite board was receiving thousands of letters. "Sometimes we have had as many as 550 letters from Russia with one mail," Toews stated. He wondered if King knew of a more effective relief action, similar to that of 1921–22 with the Save the Children Fund or Herbert Hoover's American Relief Commission. "The grainaries

[sic] of our people here in Canada are filled with wheat, money is so very scarce and we must see our people in Russia perishing under our very eyes without being able to move," a frustrated Toews affirmed to the former prime minister.⁴¹

By that time, the *Winnipeg Tribune* had published a letter about conditions in the USSR obtained from a person identified only as "citizen." The "authentic letter," dated December 20, 1932, was received in Canada in February and published on March 2, 1933. The letter writer, a person identified as J. L., possibly a Mennonite, expressed profuse gratitude for a parcel that had been received—without which "we would have starved to death long time ago [sic]." The letter writer noted that their mother was eighty-two years old and worked the "whole spring and summer" for which she was not given anything to eat. Then she "went gleaning and managed to pick about 1½ poods (60 pounds)." Neighbours had dug up and taken potatoes that had been planted; in the fall, pumpkins, beets, and poppies had also been stolen. The family might be able to manage until Christmas, "citizen" in Canada was told, "but we don't know what will happen to us after that." The letter from the USSR stated that the addressee's uncle had been sent to the Solovetsky Islands and that "Peters Ladim and Philips Ivan and many others" had been banished. The deportations had ceased and people were "simply chase[d] out of the house," everything of value taken. In the letter writer's village the fields and gardens were "overgrown with weeds and the people suffer untold miseries. Many people have died of starvation." The letter writer begged for bread.⁴²

The Legislative Assembly of Saskatchewan and the Famine

On March 16, 1933, the *Regina Leader-Post* quoted from a letter that was read out the previous day in the provincial legislature: "I suppose you are aware of the fact that a terrible famine exists in Russia, particularly so in the Ukraine." The recipient of the letter was Dr. John M. Uhrich, Liberal member for Rosthern, an area whose population included many Mennonites. The letter came from an unnamed resident of the riding. By now, the local Mennonite board was apparently receiving, on average, seven to eight hundred letters a week that were coming "over from there," and the concerned resident proposed that Canada send surplus wheat—the amount suggested was ten to twenty million bushels—to the USSR by way of either a barter arrangement or "whatever way that could be effectively arranged." It was reasoned that such an intervention by Canada would have several effects: it would save many lives, Canada could dispose of surplus wheat, and it would draw the attention of local Soviet sympathizers and others to the so-called "Communist paradise" where "thousands, millions are starving with no hope for relief as long as the present regime [in the Soviet Union] is carried on."[43]

Uhrich told the legislature that this was only one of many letters that had been received concerning conditions in the Soviet Union. He alone, Uhrich said, had received eight or nine such letters over the previous few days. He suggested that the legislature adjourn its regular affairs to discuss the situation in the USSR. In response to a question on how the letters were obtained, Uhrich explained that he had gotten them "through having made a contribution for some people over there recently." He added that the house ought to discuss the matter in order to "open the eyes of the people" to conditions in the Soviet Union over the previous few months. He wanted to know what could be done. Murdoch A. MacPherson, attorney general of the province, recommended that the matter be discussed under the resolution on trade with the USSR.

According to the newspaper from Saskatchewan's capital, "Cabinet ministers, back benchers, Liberals, Conservatives, and Independents all united" to take part in the ensuing discussion and "in urging help." Among the speakers that afternoon was the premier of the province, James T. M. Anderson (Conservative). He read out excerpts of a letter that had come from a Canadian who had recently visited the Soviet Union: "No bread here because the government exported too much grain. Some were dying of starvation. The purchasing power of the average monthly income in Kiev is $5." After reading other extracts, the Saskatchewan premier remarked that anything the legislature could do in terms of arousing public interest in the situation should be done.

The *Leader-Post* then turned to the letters mentioned by James F. Bryant, the province's minister of public works. These letters spoke about the theft of foodstuffs from trains, which, Bryant pointed out, was a capital offence. Another MLA told of a letter he had that mentioned a case of starving parents who had been shot to prevent their further suffering. When it came time for James G. Gardiner to speak, the leader of the Liberal opposition declared: "We go to church Sunday after Sunday and never hear a word that people in one of the great countries of the world are starving. Something is wrong that is of greater importance than reforming banks and currency." He continued that there was "no better way for the Anglo-Saxon countries to act than to provide 20,000,000 bushels of wheat."[44] Gardiner said he could see that there was a chance the Soviets might use the wheat "for planting to compete with Canadian wheat," but, he stressed, "we should bury our economics. Bury ideals like that and act in the interests of humanity." He added, "We must say these people must not die. We must try to do the right thing and the right thing in connection with the Russian situation is to feed these boys and girls."[45]

The next day, MLAs returned to the legislature to vote on a resolution relating to trade with the USSR and the matter of the famine. That resolution read as follows:

> That this assembly requests the Dominion government to accord the fullest measure of assistance to the promotion of trade between Canada and other countries on a barter and exchange basis, and that this principle of trading be especially considered in regard to the possibility of Canada supplying Russia with wheat and cattle to the end that the present suffering from lack of food by residents of that country may, to some extent, be alleviated and that this action may also have some beneficial effect on the price levels of these commodities.[46]

The resolution was passed unanimously.

The Legislative Assembly of Saskatchewan and the Famine: Aftermath

The story remained in the news for a number of days, so that the federal government was certainly aware of the plight of people in the

USSR. And certainly so, too, was the leader of His Majesty's Loyal Opposition in Ottawa. On the day that the legislature in Regina passed its resolution on barter, King penned a reply to Toews. "I have received this morning the letter signed by Mr. Enns [sic] and yourself," he wrote on March 16. "I can appreciate your feelings with respect to the plight of your friends in Russia and wish very much that I could make a suggestion which would be of some service in helping to meet the situation." King went on to note that when the Save the Children Fund had been established, he had just come into office and was able to obtain the support of his party for the contribution that Canada was making at the time. The current government, he said, had an attitude toward the USSR that was "wholly different from that of the Liberal party." King, as he had once before, compared trying to influence the government on its Soviet policy to "simply battering our heads against a stone wall." Perhaps, he suggested, the government might pay more heed to representations made independently of the house.[47]

In Saskatchewan, Gardiner's reference to the church touched a raw nerve. In a sermon delivered on Sunday, March 19, and reported in the *Leader-Post* the next day, Rev. Samuel Farley of the First Presbyterian Church in Regina expressed the hope that such statements about the church would be withdrawn. It was not the duty of the church to tell the government what it should do "in such a crisis," Farley said, or to dictate how it conducted foreign policy. Its duty was to "proclaim the gospel of Jesus Christ." He then asked, "Has the government of Russia made an application to the outside world for relief for its starving millions?" Had the Soviet government even admitted that millions were starving, he continued, and should "a country offer relief, where such has not been sought, and to a country that last year exported approximately 25,000,000 bushels of wheat from her own shores"? The Presbyterian minister acknowledged that he "may be reminded" that the starving were making their own appeal for succour but wondered whether the relief would even reach those in need of it. The relief might be used by the Soviet government for other ends, perhaps as "seed wheat to the detriment of the other wheat growing countries of the world, or exported to meet their own commitments abroad."[48] Farley then asked to whom the churches would send the relief, since the Soviet leadership had repudiated religion and converted places of worship into "places of amusement." It meant, in his view, that only the Soviet government was to be dealt with—a government in which he had little faith. Farley concluded his sermon by expressing the opinion that the famine matter was best addressed by international governments, not by the church. The church had done its duty and now it was for "our people and the governments to carry out her teachings." While he was "far from being opposed to our legislature making overtures to the federal parliament to send 20 or 50 million bushels of wheat to help Russia," he stated, "I respectfully submit this is an international problem in which the main exporting countries, Canada, United States, Australia, and the Argentine, should all have a share."[49]

It does not seem that Gardiner's statement was ever withdrawn. On the contrary, a day later, the *Leader-Post* published the full text of Gardiner's speech.[50] At least one reader of the *Leader-Post* agreed with the Presbyterian minister. "What possible control could we have over the wheat, after it crossed the Russian border, that would assure its ultimate destination and use as intended?" J. E. Sanderson asked in a letter published in the paper. And then, in a reference to the ongoing debate over trade with the USSR, Sanderson posed another question: "If it is true that the powers now ruling in Russia have so betrayed and robbed their own people, could Canada ever hope to establish trade relations of any kind that would benefit either itself or the common people[?]"[51]

The *Star-Phoenix* of Saskatoon commented on the resolution in the context of Canadian trade with the Soviet Union. Because the resolution asked the federal government "to take an attitude directly opposite to that which it displayed in recent negotiations," the *Star-Phoenix* opined that the resolution was "for all intents and purposes a censure of the Bennett government." The newspaper did not consider the discussion that had preceded the passing of the resolution as particularly purposeful. "Human suffering is suffering whether in Russia or Canada," it said, "and if trade will relieve it in either or both countries, then obviously trade should be encouraged whether by barter or in any other way, instead of being discouraged and made difficult or impossible."[52]

An editorial in the *Leader-Post* published on March 21 commented on the breakdown in the "machinery of agricultural production" in the USSR. The shortage of food there, the editorial said, was "due, apparently, to the fact that the former tillers of the soil having no direct interest in the results of tillage, have not concerned themselves with crop production." Production was now the job of the state. The editorial included an excerpt from a letter that portrayed famine conditions, but no link was made with the pleas heard in the Saskatchewan house for succour. Rather, the paper emphasized the Communist system: "Communism appears to have just as many flaws as capitalism, with the added peril that it operates through a dictatorship." Still, the letter was there to allow readers to form their own conclusions. The excerpt of the letter printed in the newspaper, "from a Russian who is working on a state farm," spoke of "a terrible famine." Because the government demanded an excessive amount of grain, a quantity that could not be procured, "the sharpest measures are taken against us." Officials ordered the return of grain that had been given to the members of the collective farm in the autumn as payment for work done, but half of it had already been consumed. The imprisonment of many and "the sale of those few, miserable things that we called our own" followed. The people were left without bread. "There are no words to describe the things that are going on here," the letter writer went on to say, noting that people "eat the carcasses of dead horses, pigs and dogs. Men and women go from place to place begging for food. But there is none. Beets and pumpkins are the only eatable things which the more fortunate still do possess." In spite of the hunger, people continued to go to work as before: "In the morning at six o'clock at the sound of the trumpet we start to work and quit at 6 p.m. We still are threshing. We have to thresh the straw and chaff for the second time, in the hope to find some kernels." Yet for all the work, "we are not paid, and still different payments are demanded of us." No one dared to protest: "All this we bear quietly. Nobody ventures to say a word. The prisons are overcrowded." It was not simple to leave. Many people left their homes to wander, the letter writer said, but it was "not permissible to ride on the trains. It is said that in the near future everyone must have a passport, and that such will only be given at the place of birth." The letter writer, reporting that people who had changed their homes since 1930 would be compelled to return to their former residences, dreaded what could come from such a policy.[53]

The same letter was published on the letters' page of the *Winnipeg Free Press*, also in March. The person who submitted it, identified as "formerly of Russia," spoke of two letters received from the Soviet Union during February and stated that both had come from members of a collective farm in Ukraine.[54] It is not clear whether "formerly of Russia" was a member of the Mennonite community or of another, but at this time Mennonites in Canada—on the basis of the receipt of such letters—were still countering pro-Soviet portrayals. A day after the *Leader-Post* editorial appeared, the *Star-Phoenix* reported on a meeting that took place in Hague, Saskatchewan (a community with a significant Mennonite population). It was attended largely by "farmers who came from Russia, the majority still having relatives there." Those present heard about George H. Williams's positive portrayal of the USSR and criticized that depiction.[55] Williams, of Semans, Saskatchewan, was a former president of the United Farmers' of Canada (Saskatchewan section), which had sponsored a five-week inspection trip of the Soviet Union in the summer of 1931.[56]

On March 24, 1933, the *Leader-Post* again penned an editorial about conditions in the USSR. It referred to statements made by G. R. Holland while addressing the Canadian Legion in Victoria, BC. Holland had been in the USSR (it is not clear exactly where) for the past two years instructing Soviet citizens in the assembly and operation of agricultural machinery. The editorial said he would "prefer to eke out a bare existence in Canada than attempt to survive the hardships of the [Soviet] working class." Holland spoke of the constant fear of arrest and incarceration, which drove inmates to suicide, and asserted that foreign Communists in the USSR were now hoping to return to their former countries. The editorial remarked that the *Leader-Post* was inclined to accept only about half of "what comes out" of the USSR "one way or the other." But it did not believe that the letters that came from the Soviet Union "telling of conditions there have been inspired by a 'propaganda mill' for the purpose of discrediting anyone." The editorial referred to "several observers of international note," who had said that while "other phases of the Five-Year Plan had worked out fairly close to schedule," the "breakdown of agricultural production was the most serious problem faced by the Soviet authorities." The editorial repeated the belief that the food shortage owed to "the fact that the state farms, up to the present, had not produced food as plentiful as was the case when the people tilled the land under the profit system." It said that given the lack of production "it is not difficult to imagine that in a thickly populated country the starvation stage could quickly be reached. And it is starvation the people are writing about from Russia."[57]

The Saskatchewan legislature story was covered by newspapers all across the country. The *Border Cities Star* included it and also reprinted an editorial from the *Brandon Sun*, which it titled "People Who Like Soviet Rule Should Read This." The editorial said that the "scene was unprecedented in the history of the Saskatchewan House" and done as a way to suggest to the federal government that something might be done to help the people who are starving. It noted that the Liberal leader asserted that Canadian wheat should be shipped to the USSR not in barter and exchange, but as charity. The *Brandon Sun* said this was all very well, but no one knew what would become of the wheat, goods, or cash shipped as relief. It maintained that the USSR had no interest in the "hungry mouths," that the Soviets "would rather be rid of the non-militaristic muscles and unmechanical minds, or casual weakly laborers." The editorial then asked who could find a way to save the victims "with red jailers in all strategic positions and to whose interest it is to grind the starving to death." It called the last major Canadian campaign to "save the children" of the USSR "a suspicious fiasco" conducted by Communists in North America. No one seemed to know where the funds went on that occasion, it alleged. At the same time, the editorial agreed that "something should be done in the name of humanity and Christianity" for the starving.[58]

Toronto's *Globe* commented that if food were sent from Canada to the USSR there was no guarantee that it would ever reach those in need. It pointed out that the Soviet passport system had been introduced in order to "drive the jobless from the cities to fend for themselves in a country denuded of food by the Soviet authorities." The *Globe* then tied the Saskatchewan legislature story with that of the arrest in the USSR of British engineers from the Metropolitan-Vickers company: "In the face of the letters read at Regina, what are the deported ones to do but starve? And, considering the studied indifference to the requests of the British Government, what faith can one have in Moscow?"[59]

As for Gardiner himself, he held to his view that the federal government should try to address the matter of starvation in the USSR. On March 18, 1933, J. M. Speechly of Parkside, Saskatchewan, wrote to the provincial leader of the opposition to tell him that he had read about the conditions in the USSR and that he for one "would be pleased to see our Government at Ottawa, send help to the starving Russians." Such a move, Speechly said, would "be a Christian act."[60] Gardiner replied that he was glad to learn that Speechly felt "something should be done for those who are suffering in Russia at the present time." He agreed with Speechly that it was a "matter which should be dealt with primarily by the Ottawa Government in so far as we in Canada are concerned." The MLA for North Qu'Appelle also expressed his regret that "we should have a great country like Russia, in this enlightened age, so far apart from all the other great nations of the world, more particularly in a religious way, as to render the bringing of assistance to their people so difficult as it is at present."[61]

The Legislative Assembly of Saskatchewan and the Famine: Response in the Ukrainian Community

The Saskatchewan house's discourse on the famine did not generate much discussion in the Ukrainian-language press in Canada, but it did evoke a response within the community. W. S. Plawiuk, in a letter to the editor of the *Edmonton Journal*, wrote that thousands of letters had been received by Ukrainian Canadians in the fall of 1932, asking not for money, but for grain and flour. "We tried to make arrangements to collect 400,000 to 500,000 bushels of wheat to be shipped to Ukraine," he said, "but the Soviet government through their charitable institutions refused to accept our offer, stating: 'In view of satisfactory harvest this year, proposal is not necessary in the absence of real need.'"[62] Plawiuk was referring to the approach made from the Hafford, Saskatchewan, branch of the Ukrainian Self-Reliance League of Canada to the Canadian Red Cross. In fact, not long after the province's elected representatives met in Regina that day in March—specifically, on March 25—their deliberations were referenced at a gathering of around three hundred persons in a community hall in Hafford, which was organized under the auspices of the Ukrainian Self-Reliance League.[63] The assembled composed a letter to Premier Anderson, dated March 31, containing resolutions. The first resolution was an expression of gratitude: the three hundred Canadian citizens of Ukrainian origin assembled in the community hall in Hafford "WISH TO EXPRESS OUR HEARTY APPRECIATION of the efforts taken by the Government in trying to help the starving people in Ukraine." Two other resolutions concerned a protest against the spreading of Communist propaganda among Ukrainians in Canada and the famine in Ukraine. As far as the latter was concerned, the group expressed "the opinion that this third famine in Ukraine is purposely perpetrated by the Red Chieftains in [the] Kremlin in order to extirpate the Ukrainian peasants, who so obstinately oppose their terrible Procrustean experiment."[64]

The first speaker at the Hafford rally was a Mr. Sarchuk, who was described as the principal of the school in Krydor, Saskatchewan, nearly twenty-five kilometres away. He was likely the same Sarchuk who wrote a letter to Premier Anderson about a public meeting in Krydor that took place the same day as the one in Hafford. In that letter, W. J. Sarchuk, acting secretary of the Resolution Committee, informed the premier that 250 people had gathered in Krydor on March 25, 1933, and adopted several resolutions. One was to protest the "reign of terror" in Ukraine—"the aim of which is the extermination of the Ukrainian people." Another was directed against Communist propaganda and asked the provincial government to use its power to check it. A third resolution concerned the discussions within the Saskatchewan legislature ten days earlier: "We, furthermore, petition the Government to use their influence to bring into realization the project of helping the starving millions in Ukraine, as it was discussed in the Legislative assembly on March 15th last."[65] The Saskatchewan premier forwarded copies of both letters containing the resolutions to the prime minister of Canada.[66]

Mennonite Relief Efforts

No concrete action seems to have stemmed from the Saskatchewan resolution. As Jamie Glazov notes, Canada "avoided any formal diplomatic contact or large-scale business relations with Moscow throughout the 1930s."[67] Support for barter had been building up steam.[68] The prime minister received a report about proceedings in the Saskatchewan legislature. In a letter to Mr. Ernest Edward Perley (Liberal MP for Qu'Appelle, Saskatchewan) dated March 21, 1933, Saskatchewan public works minister Bryant wrote: "The question of trade with Russia came up for discussion, and when it came up an effort was made led by Dr. Uhrich to discredit George Williams and the Farmer-Labor party who have been holding Russia up as the ideal socialistic state, by reading letters received from people in Russia telling how the ordinary small farmer was practically starving, and absolutely at its wits ends." He pointed out that hundreds of letters written by people in the USSR— "revealing an appalling state of starvation existing in many of the rural areas of the country"—had been received. The discussion had taken place "with a view to discrediting the propaganda in favour of Russia that has been spread among the Farmer-Labor party during the last two or three years and a resolution was passed to the effect that all efforts to exchange commodities by means of barter should be encouraged. But the reference to the Federal Government guarantee was cut out."[69]

No mention was made of the Mennonites' reasons for having these letters read, which was to remove obstacles for relief and come to the rescue of the famished population. It soon became apparent that there would be no repeat of the massive relief undertakings of the previous decade. As Frank H. Epp put it, while the plight of the Soviet people was a tragic one, "tragic also was the fact that the world at large turned a deaf ear and indifferent heart to the cries for help coming from the Soviet hell."[70] When Toews raised the matter of Mennonites in the USSR from 1930, Epp noted, he was told by British officials that the United Kingdom did not interfere in the internal affairs of another state, especially when British citizens were not involved, while American officials considered diplomatic representations to be useless when the United States had not recognized the USSR. In the case of Canada, "there was little encouragement from Prime Minister R.B. Bennett."[71] Toews was frustrated that nothing was being done to alleviate suffering in the USSR. Epp wrote that at a time when there was some interest in the Communist experiment—in the Depression era, the USSR was presented by the Soviets as a land freed of unemployment—there was some skepticism about stories of human misery in the USSR. This was "in part a reaction to the excesses of World War I propaganda, when it had first been used on a mass scale to manipulate the psychology of whole nations." But it was convenient and profitable also, Epp remarked, to believe the best about the USSR.[72]

Letters flowed from the Soviet Union to Mennonites in Canada both before and after March 15. In just four months, from January to April 1933, the Rosthern board office had received about seven thousand letters from the USSR pleading for help.[73] When it seemed that the Canadian government was not interested in either facilitating immigration or organizing aid, it became apparent that, if anything was to be done, then the Mennonite community itself would have to take the initiative. At the start of February 1933, Toews had already applied himself to mobilizing the community for relief action. On February 3, at a brotherhood meeting of the Rosenorter Mennonite Church, Toews posed the question: "How can we rescue our brothers in Russia from the famine that besets them at this time?" He informed those present that over a thousand letters begging for help had been received in the previous three weeks. "Brethren," he challenged the group at the meeting, "will we be asked some day: 'In the year 1933 I was hungry in Russia and you did not give me food?'" He then exhorted, "We must gather donations and we must help," and he quoted a stanza of the hymn "Throw out the Lifeline":

Soon will the season of rescue be o'er,
Soon will they drift to eternity's shore;
Haste then, my brother, no time for delay,
But throw out the lifeline and save them today.[74]

These letters were crucial at a time when, as historian Colin Neufeldt notes, Soviet government laws and restrictions "prevented

Soviet Mennonites from taking any collective action to alleviate their suffering and hunger."[75] The Soviet government's own efforts to mitigate the famine were few and far between. The local Red Cross had established some relief centres in a number of Mennonite-populated areas, but, as Neufeldt points out, officials were "hamstrung by government red tape in their attempts to provide succour to those in need." Meanwhile, Soviet government officials ignored petitions for relief that came from collective farm executives.[76] The hunger drove some Mennonites to try to migrate within the USSR—in some cases as far as Siberia, where food was "reportedly more readily accessible"—and circumvent the strictly controlled passport system.[77] For Mennonites who remained in Ukraine, the visits of foreign delegations, receipt of aid from the West, and establishment of Torgsin stores[78] across Ukraine could result in temporary improvement. Indeed, it is very plausible that the Soviet regime, in its desire for foreign currency with which to buy certain goods from the West, encouraged the receipt of aid from relatives abroad. The letters sent abroad before 1933 often were not censored, as Neufeldt observes: "In many respects, the Soviet government actually appears to have encouraged the delivery of foreign parcels and letters to its citizens until 1933, as is evidenced by the fact that the Soviet government did not routinely censor or destroy all foreign letters and packages, even though it often censored and destroyed letters written by Soviet Mennonites to their relatives or friends living in other regions of the USSR."[79] The letters that were read (in English translation) in the Saskatchewan legislature and printed in newspapers during 1933—with identifying information such as names and places of residence withheld—seem to have eluded strict censorship.

The Mennonites in Ukraine, where many ethnic Germans of other denominations also dwelled, drew the interest of Berlin. Germany had an embassy in Moscow and consulates in Kharkiv, Kyiv, and Odesa. The Germans had set up a relief organization, Brüder in Not (Brethren in Need), which was allowed to conduct some work in the USSR. After the Nazis assumed power, the Soviet authorities curbed the number of parcels coming into the USSR in the early months of 1933 and the number of letters going out to the West.[80] During this time, comments made by German chancellor Adolf Hitler about the famine were quoted in the *Winnipeg Free Press*. Addressing a large crowd on March 3, Hitler had pointed to conditions in the USSR as evidence of the failure of Communism to surmount capitalism. "Millions are starving," he had declared, "in one of the world's greatest granaries."[81] Neufeldt points out that some of the restrictions imposed after the Nazis had gained office were only temporary, "as the Soviet government did not want to jeopardize the progress it had made with Germany." Brüder in Not and other groups could resume relief efforts in mid-1933, within certain limitations.[82]

The coordination of relief from Canada was not straightforward. The effort was concentrated on sending care packages to individual addresses supplied by donors in Canada and was determined in part by the letters received from the USSR.[83] After a period of negotiation, the Soviet government agreed to a specific method of forwarding relief from abroad to individuals there. A monopoly agreement was made with a single firm in each of the countries in question. The German firms with which Canadian and American Mennonites worked were, successively, Herman Tietz, Fast and Brilliant, and Fast and Company. Donated monies and addresses were forwarded to Benjamin H. Unruh of Karlsruhe, Germany, who in turn forwarded them to the appropriate company; the company then forwarded the money to the Torgsin supply house of Moscow, which had distribution centres across the USSR; and the Torgsin would then supply a package of requested materials, consisting of food and/or clothing, to the addressee. According to Epp, "This was a satisfactory method of dispatching relief supplies and hundreds of Mennonites otherwise doomed to die in the Ukraine and Caucasus were saved from starvation." However, its effectiveness was reduced through some degree of duplication, as Mennonite families in the USSR wrote letters to all the foreign addresses they knew. Moreover, in some localities "receivers of relief were coerced to give up what they received and to seek more from abroad."[84] In 1932, the contributions for Soviet relief that passed through the Rosthern board office amounted to $39,573.71. The amount shot up the following year, with $62,073.77 traversing the board treasury in 1933.[85]

The difficulties that could be experienced in the attempts to provide help to relatives were detailed in a letter from Franklin W. Turnbull,

Conservative MP for Regina, to Prime Minister Bennett, dated March 24, 1933. Turnbull related a case that concerned a person in Regina who had sent registered letters containing money to relatives in the USSR. The "letters arrived without the money," he told Bennett. "Consignees were raided at night; all their property, even to their furniture, was taken"; further, their rations were eliminated and they were told that "they must purchase their food henceforth only from the 'Torgsin,' which sells for foreign exchange only."[86]

The assistance rendered by the Mennonite community in Canada and from other places seems to have ensured a lower mortality rate among their coreligionists in Ukraine, who—when compared with the ethnic Ukrainian population—had suffered disproportionately during the preceding dekulakization campaign.[87] Neufeldt states that "it seems likely that no more than 3% to 8% of the Mennonite population in Ukraine and the Crimea lost their lives during the 1932–33 famine. This estimate is in keeping with the observations of some Mennonites who noted that the percentage of deaths in a number of Mennonite villages was generally lower than the percentage of deaths in neighbouring non-Mennonite communities, and particularly Ukrainian villages, which often saw between 6% and 18.8% of their inhabitants die in 1932 and 1933."[88] The plight of the Mennonite community during the famine was also reported in Canada's Ukrainian-language press. In one example, *Ukraïns'kyi holos* mentioned I. Iu. Simons of Saskatchewan, who had received a letter from his brother in the village of Mykolaivske where, in a single week in May 1933, forty people had died from starvation.[89]

Gareth Jones

It was not long before the stories that were related in the Saskatchewan legislative chamber were confirmed by British journalists. In March 1933 the *Manchester Guardian* published a three-part article about the famine by Malcolm Muggeridge, although he did not append his name to it.[90] In Canada, also in March, the Welsh journalist (and former private secretary to Prime Minister David Lloyd George) Gareth Jones was mentioned by American journalist and Pulitzer Prize winner

H. R. Knickerbocker in the *Toronto Star*. Jones had arrived in Berlin after a long walking tour of Ukraine and other parts of the USSR, Knickerbocker wrote, and was the "first foreigner to visit the Russian countryside since the Moscow authorities forbade foreign correspondents to leave the city." The reason for the prohibition, according to Jones, was the famine. A summary of first-hand observations by Jones was then provided. Jones said that he had walked through villages and thirteen collective farms. Everywhere "was the cry, 'There is no bread. We are dying.'" That cry, he asserted, came from every part of the Soviet Union, "from the Volga, Siberia, White Russia, the North Caucasus, Central Asia." He "trampled the black earth region, because that was once the richest farm land in Russia, and because the correspondents have been forbidden to go there to see for themselves what is happening."[91] Yet such claims by Jones were being denied by Walter Duranty, the Moscow correspondent for the *New York Times* and, like Knickerbocker, a Pulitzer Prize winner. Duranty's rebuttal to Jones's revelations appeared in the *Border Cities Star* under the heading "Hungry but Not Starving."[92] Both Jones's revelations and Duranty's rebuttal were mentioned in the *Vancouver Sun*. That newspaper began by noting Jones's statements about the pleas for bread and also his remark that writer George Bernard Shaw was the most despised person in the USSR after Stalin. Shaw, who had earlier travelled to the Soviet Union, had given "accounts of...plentiful food." Then, in the same story, the *Sun* indicated that Jones's statements were contested by Duranty.[93]

Indeed, at that time, the Soviet regime officially denied the famine. Notwithstanding the excerpts of letters that were read out by Saskatchewan MLAs in the middle of March 1933, by the close of that month Canadian newspapers were publishing Soviet denials of the famine. The *Lethbridge Herald*, for instance, reported that in spite of the serious food shortages in many parts of the USSR, "official quarters vigorously denied reports published abroad that the nation is suffering from famine. A statement that thousands were dying of starvation was branded as 'non-sensical.'"[94]

Chapter Three

"STARVATION, REAL CAUSE OF SOVIET TRIAL"
Spring 1933

On the Eve of Protest Rallies

During April, May, and June 1933, Canadian daily newspapers included accounts of rallies organized by the Ukrainian community to draw attention to conditions in the Soviet Union. In the preceding two months the Ukrainian-language press, with the exception of the pro-Soviet periodicals, had contained further material about the famine in "Greater Ukraine" and elsewhere and related topics. *Ukraïns'ki visty* wrote about the Volga region, where grain reportedly lay under the snow because villagers were fleeing to the cities to escape collectivization.[1] It also mentioned the case of a Ukrainian worker who had returned to Philadelphia after a visit to Moscow, Kharkiv, and Kyiv and had seen hunger in Soviet Ukraine.[2] The newspaper commented on the deportation of up to twenty thousand people from the Poltava and other areas—a story that had been also published in the bulletin of the Ukrainian Bureau in London—and the punitive actions against villagers who were trying to hold back some grain for themselves. *Ukraïns'ki visty* perceived the deportations as a means of Russification; taking the place of the deportees, it said, were Russian settlers.[3] Another article noted the lack of bread in Soviet Ukraine and remarked that hunger-related disturbances were an everyday occurrence in such cities as Kharkiv, Kyiv, and Odesa.[4]

Rose Kritzevosky

Thus, members of the Ukrainian community were reading stories such as these before the rallies were staged in protest against Communist rule in Ukraine. By now, as well, one or two former citizens of the USSR had come to Canada and shared rare first-hand accounts. Readers of the *Winnipeg Tribune* learned in February 1933 of the case of Rose Kritzevosky, a thirty-year-old woman who had "got out of Soviet Russia more by luck than good management" and was bound for Saskatchewan. By the previous November, Kritzevosky's relatives in Tisdale had sent a hundred dollars to the Soviet authorities for a passport. When asked by a reporter what the USSR was like, Kritzevosky replied that "there was terrible starvation and many people were dying in the rural districts." It is not clear where in the Soviet Union she was from, it only being revealed that her aged parents were "still in Russia."[5] But at a time when Soviet citizens were risking their lives to cross the Dnister River into Romania or to scramble into Poland, her case was rare. The *Tribune* noted that it was an offence for Soviet citizens to possess foreign currency and that the fees required to leave the USSR had risen in December 1932. A decree issued at the start of that month stipulated that Soviet labourers could leave the country only upon payment of US$283, "with a double fee for non-laborers."[6] A couple of months earlier, the *Toronto Telegram* had commented on the prohibitive cost of departing the USSR. Whereas before it had been almost impossible to obtain permission to leave for residence abroad, now, the newspaper announced at the close of November 1932, it would be "granted to all those who can raise the funds." An exit visa was to cost five hundred rubles, in gold or foreign currency, for workers, but a thousand rubles for other classes. The *Telegram* predicted that the "exodus is not likely to be extensive."[7]

A Rally in Saskatoon

More rallies in April followed the ones staged in Krydor and Hafford, Saskatchewan, the previous month. In Saskatoon, people packed the city's Legion Hall on Sunday, April 2, to hear "reports of famine horrors in the Ukraine." The hall was filled to overflowing, the *Star-Phoenix* said. According to the report, the meeting—presided over by John Hnatyshyn, a University of Saskatchewan graduate (in arts and law), and Joseph Melnyk—comprised people from all Ukrainian denominations and sections in the province, except the pro-Communists, and "several hundred people were unable to gain admission." Letters from Ukraine that were read aloud made reference to "many instances of cannibalism." One of the speakers, J. W. Stechishin, emphasized Soviet mismanagement but also Russian colonial policy as reasons for the famine. This policy, stemming from fear of Ukrainian separatism, included wholesale deportations, imprisonment, and the seizure of food. While famine was raging, Stechishin observed, the Soviet Union was exporting foodstuffs. Resolutions passed at the meeting called on the British, Canadian, and Saskatchewan governments to assist the starving population of Ukraine and to use their influence to help stop exports of foodstuffs from areas experiencing famine. Among other things, the meeting's attendees also "decided to ask the Soviet government to set up machinery to remedy the famine conditions."[8]

A Rally in Edmonton

That same weekend, about four hundred people attended a meeting of the Ukrainian National Federation and the Ukrainian War Veterans' Association in Edmonton. The *Edmonton Journal* reported that speakers at the rally referred to "Communistic internationalism" as a "new cover for extreme fascism" and stated that "thousands of Ukrainians" were "starving to death, thousands have been exiled to Siberia, and thousands have been jailed for asking for justice."[9] On April 13, the *Journal* ran a more comprehensive report on the meeting, which mentioned that letters were read that referred to famine in Soviet Ukraine and instances of cannibalism. One of the resolutions at the meeting charged that "famine conditions in the Ukrainian territory, probably the richest section of eastern Europe, were due to the Soviet system and acts of the Russian authorities." The *Journal* story continued: "Action by the provincial, dominion and British governments to initiate a movement with other nations and humanitarian organizations to help the starving people and also urge upon the Soviet government the need of stopping exports from Ukraine was urged in a resolution passed by the meeting." Dr. I. Verchomin, one of the speakers at the meeting (at which Communist propaganda and actions in Canada were also condemned), described the attempt made in 1932 by the Ukrainian community through the Red Cross to have grain shipped from Canada to Ukraine.[10] Around the same time, the *Toronto Telegram* reported on anti-Communist rallies organized in Toronto and St. Catharines under the auspices of the Ukrainian Self-Reliance League of Canada, though these events were not specifically associated with the famine.[11]

"A Syndicate with All Kinds of Food"

Meanwhile, the Ukrainian Catholic newspaper *Ukraïns'ki visty* steadily provided more and more commentary on the famine as the year progressed, publishing items during April and May 1933 that included a letter alluding to the problem of sending food packages to the USSR (and the fact that the Torgsin stores accepted only foreign currency); a story about peasants executed for not fulfilling the spring sowing plan; a report of women gathering at the Ispolkoma (executive committee) building in Dnipropetrovsk to voice their protest at starving for the Five-Year Plan; and an account of the famine by journalist Gareth Jones.[12]

The mainstream press also occasionally discussed issues related to the famine in the spring of 1933. In April, the *Calgary Herald* perceptively observed that not all news from the Soviet Union came by cable; the Soviet authorities allowed letters to go out, which told a different story. While this seemed strange at first, the newspaper noted that it became less so when one dug beneath the surface. It then shared a letter received by a "Calgary Russian from relatives in the Soviet Republic" in which the letter writer said that his father, appointed a commissar of the village collective farm, had been sentenced to six years' imprisonment at the Solovetsky Islands after someone had stolen a sack of barley at threshing time. The family had not heard from him since. The letter writer then spoke of "a syndicate [in the city] where there are all kinds of merchandise and food to be bought cheap, but only for dollars. You send the money to the syndicate and they will send us as much goods as they feel like." Their "winter allowance" had kept the family "only till Christmas." Now they were weak and sick with starvation but had to work. People were dying "like in the flu" and buried in mass graves, the letter said. The *Herald* commented that when one understood where the dollars would go and "guesse[d] how little the 'syndicate' will give for them to the sufferers," then it was not so difficult to comprehend why such letters were permitted to pass the censors.[13]

An Appeal to the League of Nations

In May 1933, the Ukrainian-language press in Canada discussed an appeal to the League of Nations by an "association of nations oppressed by Moscow," the details of which had been published in Swiss newspapers on April 28. The appeal asserted that economic measures taken by the Soviet authorities had provoked famine in Ukraine and in the provinces of the south of the USSR; it also referred to the introduction of the passport system and the expulsion of people from the cities.[14] Later in May, an article in *Ukraïns'ki visty* discussed the "terrible famine" in Ukraine, the Caucasus region, Russia, and Siberia. This article stated that there was no bread because there was no grain—and there was no grain seed for sowing. Kyiv had seen an outbreak of typhus, and hundreds of people there were dying daily. In Kuban, people were wandering from place to place searching for food. *Ukraïns'ki visty* reported increases in unemployment, in crime (especially in Odesa), and in the number of orphans. Revolts were quickly suppressed.[15]

Nicholas Ignatieff on the Metropolitan-Vickers Trial and the Famine

Over the first four months of 1933, it was not the famine that made front-page news in the mainstream press but rather the arrests and trial in

Moscow of six British engineers who were employees of the electrical engineering firm Metropolitan-Vickers. As reporter Walter Duranty put it, "there occurred the sensational trial of the Metro-Vickers engineers, which caused more ink to flow abroad than anything which had happened in Russia since the case of the Roman Catholic priests ten years before."[16] Arrested in January 1933, the engineers along with a number of Soviet citizens were accused of carrying out espionage and sabotage on behalf of Great Britain. Whitehall demanded the release of the detained British citizens. The Kremlin refused. The British government then imposed an embargo on trade with the USSR. The engineers were tried in April 1933 and subsequently released; British trade with the USSR resumed.

The whole affair took place as multitudes were dying of starvation. An observer or two may have wondered what the point of the trial really was, for there were doubts about the Soviet charges. On the front cover of its issue of late April 1933, the Canadian magazine *Saturday Night* announced with the heading "Starvation, Real Cause of Soviet Trial" an article, written by Nicholas Ignatieff, that began on page 2. Ignatieff began by stating that the trial had taken place under the conditions of a Communist dictatorship, which not only had complete control over the domestic media but had "muzzled effectively the reports of foreign correspondents." The article outlined some of the challenges that the Soviet regime faced, including a decline in 1932 of its export trade and a shortage of foreign currency. The engineers, then, were convenient scapegoats who could be used to divert the attention of Soviet workers from local problems. The trial was also used, according to the article, to show off Soviet might to the United States, which had not yet recognized the USSR. Ignatieff mentioned the introduction of the passport system, which was designed to remove the unemployed from the cities to the countryside—"there to shift for themselves as best they can." Among the conditions Ignatieff described was the rule of terror in the Soviet countryside. An attempt had been made to rectify Soviet agriculture by the use of force, he wrote. OGPU troops had come to the countryside, executed leaders of resistance, deported communities, and brought in shock brigades to take part in the seeding campaign. Ignatieff characterized the food situation in parts of the USSR as "catastrophic." The foreign correspondents confined to Moscow, he said, could "not begin to picture the gravity of the situation"; yet in Canada "thousands of Russians" had been "deluged for months by urgent appeals for help by their starving relatives and friends in Russia." He then referred to the letters that had been read aloud at—and had "shocked"—the Saskatchewan legislature, as well as several more received by people in Toronto, which he had personally read. One had come from the Kyiv region (where the Toronto-based Ignatieff himself was born and of which his father had been governor).[17] A translated extract from the letter, included in the *Saturday Night* article, related cases of mothers who had killed their children, the high incidence of death by starvation, burials of the dead in trenches without coffins, and cannibalism; Ignatieff mentioned also having received a second independent testimony regarding cannibalism. He attributed the food shortage to peasant resistance to ruthless Soviet policies.[18]

The April 1933 piece reflected Ignatieff's understanding of the Soviet situation at the time. In another article he wrote for *Saturday Night* later in the year, Ignatieff repeated similar notions in a more detailed discussion about the famine. This time, he referred to Soviet denials of the famine and Duranty's contradictory reports that ultimately acknowledged that millions had died. Ignatieff maintained that the famine was not the result of unfavourable weather conditions or the lack of seeding and harvesting campaigns; rather, he repeated his interpretation that it was due to peasant resistance that resulted in poor cultivation, weeds in the fields, and the destruction of buildings, livestock, machinery, and grain stocks. The disorganization of transport was also a factor. And grain production was down while the population had risen since 1913. Ignatieff asserted that it was easier to control undernourished peasants. Many years ago, he said, Leon Trotsky[19] had advised that peasants should be "treated as enemies and driven into submission." Apparently, Stalin also believed this was correct—that the peasants could not be made into proletarian Communists—and thus was "driving them relentlessly."[20]

Ignatieff was not the only person at the time to mention the famine in relation to the Metropolitan-Vickers trial. Across the Atlantic

Ocean, the Right Honourable Winston S. Churchill wrote a commentary in which he attributed the trial to the Kremlin's need to find scapegoats for Soviet domestic failures. "The Five-Year Plan is breaking down," the Conservative member for Epping wrote in London's *Daily Mail* on April 20, 1933. Its failure, Churchill continued, was becoming "daily inconcealable" and even "the brutalized, down-trodden Russian masses can feel disaster in the air. ... Everywhere there is a shortage of food. One of the greatest granaries of the world is ceasing to function. In whole districts there is famine."[21]

As for the accused British engineers themselves, one turned out to have a Canadian tie. Allan Monkhouse, who had served in the Canadian Expeditionary Force and whose aunt and sister-in-law lived in British Columbia, visited Canada in 1934, addressing the Empire Club about the USSR in November. He alluded to Soviet agriculture in his address, though he made no specific mention of the famine.[22]

Malcolm Muggeridge

In May 1933 some Canadians learned of the revelations about the famine by a British journalist, who was unnamed but was undoubtedly Malcolm Muggeridge.[23] The *Winnipeg Free Press* informed readers that over the previous several weeks, a correspondent for the *Manchester Guardian* had travelled through the Volga region, the North Caucasus, and Ukraine. This correspondent asserted that the USSR was tending toward a slave state and that there was not only a famine in "the most fertile parts" of the USSR, but also a military occupation. In Ukraine and the North Caucasus, grain collection was conducted with such thoroughness and brutality that the peasants no longer had bread. The correspondent described deportations, the neglect of fields now overwhelmed by weeds, the absence of cattle, and a starving and terrorized population; only the OGPU and military were sufficiently fed. He noted that "hunger" was the word he heard most in Ukraine, a country with a language and art of its own. Its towns and little villages "seemed just numb and the people in too desperate a condition even actively to resent what happened." The correspondent—who wondered why "so many obvious and fundamental facts" about the USSR were not "noticed even by serious and intelligent visitors"—was told by Communists that the development of agriculture was following that of heavy industry. The plan for the year was to plant "so many hectares which will produce so many poods of grain."[24]

A month later, the *Winnipeg Free Press* again ran a piece that referred to an article written by Muggeridge for the *Fortnightly Review*. Titled "Soviets' War on the Peasants," the article described a battle between the government and the peasants witnessed by the writer during a recent visit to Ukraine and Kuban. On the one side, he said, were "millions of peasants, starving, often their bodies swollen with lack of food," and on the other were "soldiers, members of the [O.]G.P.U.," who were carrying out the "instructions of the dictatorship of the proletariat." Muggeridge likened the latter to a swarm of locusts that had gone through the country "and had taken away everything edible." Thousands of peasants had been shot or exiled—"sometimes whole villages." Some of the most fertile land in the world, he lamented, had been reduced to a "melancholy desert."[25] Muggeridge's revelations were also covered by the francophone press in Canada.[26]

"Liquidation of a Nation": Editorials in *Ukraïns'ki visty*

In June, *Ukraïns'ki visty* turned its attention to other issues related to the USSR: the pausing of the Ukrainianization program in schools in Ukraine; resistance to the "Bolsheviks" by starving villagers with axes, scythes, and other implements; the militarization of the Soviet border with Poland; a Ukrainian protest rally in Philadelphia (during which opposition to any U.S. recognition of the USSR was voiced); and the incidence of cannibalism in Kuban.[27] One item in the paper cited the American correspondent Donald Day, who said that as many people had already perished in the current famine as had died in the one of 1921–22. It went on to say that any relief that existed was of a concealed nature and limited to twenty-eight cities, which would be using grain that came from the Black Sea ports. A second stock of grain was on its way to Leningrad to feed the industrial population. Meanwhile, declassed elements were sent from the cities to work on fields. As for the villages, the periodical said, famine had reached such proportions that thousands were dying weekly, and the cities offered no guaranteed refuge; according to *Ukraïns'ki visty*, nonproletariat persons were required to leave the twenty-eight cities within ten days (a decree on March 28, 1933, had forbidden people from leaving their villages without special permission). Meanwhile, the article continued, news of cannibalism had become more and more frequent. It also said the post office did not accept packages of bread addressed to villages.[28] *Ukraïns'ki visty* did not say where Day's article had appeared, but on June 4, a story about the famine by the American journalist, datelined Warsaw, was published on the front page of the *Vancouver Province*. There, in addition to his estimate that as many deaths from starvation would occur in Ukraine alone as had occurred in all affected areas during the 1921–22 famine, Day referred to travellers' accounts and diplomatic reports. Soviet Ukraine comprised 2 per cent of the territory of the USSR and 19 per cent of its population, but, as Day pointed out, it had formerly accounted for 22 per cent of the grain harvested. Yet in spite of that statistic, Ukraine had "been abandoned to starvation by Moscow." Day wrote of the passport system that was introduced to expel declassed elements from Ukrainian cities. Reports about the "condemned people" asserted that "they are practically hired on collectivized farms, as beasts of burden"; their reward for plowing and harrowing during the spring was a daily "bowl of porridge." The article went on to say that among the village population, the famine had "reached a point where thousands are dying of hunger a week," and the food situation in the cities "quarantined by the [O.]G.P.U. from the countryside" was not significantly better. By way of example, Day related the story of a cook employed at a "foreign consulate" in Kharkiv who had written that he expected to "retire shortly with a small fortune realized from selling potato peelings and other garbage to a crowd which gathers at the back door of the consulate each day."[29]

During June 1933, *Ukraïns'ki visty* published several major editorials relating to the famine. The first, which appeared on June 14, stated that Ukrainians were feeling the pain from both a moral and physical torture—moral in the sense of the liquidation of a nation and physical in the sense of the liquidation of people. From the time Moscow had taken control of Ukraine, the editorial said, it had eliminated its associations, press, publishing houses, and political parties. Nothing like that was happening to Ukrainians in Czechoslovakia, Poland, or even Romania. There was also an assault on religion and the churches.[30] And more recently, the aim had been to destroy Ukrainians not only in a national sense but also physically as a people, the editorial continued. The Soviet state was taking grain for the cities and export, it said, while Ukrainians were perishing from hunger. Some, trying to flee by crossing into Poland and Romania, would face a barrage of bullets from the guns of soldiers stationed along borders: "They shoot at them and send dogs at them much like America did with black slaves." Uncle Tom's Cabin, the newspaper asserted, had resurfaced. The editorial expressed regret that Ukrainians abroad had not taken action at the level of Jewish protests against the persecution of Jews in Germany. Nothing was being said, it observed, about the destruction of Greater Ukraine in the parliaments of states where Ukrainians lived—such as Poland, Czechoslovakia, Romania, and Canada, where they had political representatives—or in other public forums. The editorial expressed the conviction that protesting was far from all that had to be done; the Ukrainian community as a whole needed to systematically be made "conscious" of Bolshevism in Ukraine, and for that to happen, anti-Bolshevik actions were necessary. The editorial argued that Ukrainian immigrants in Europe and the Americas had a national obligation to do this, to inform all peoples, verbally and in print.[31]

The editorial writer may or may not have known that the famine had been raised the month before in the Legislative Assembly of Manitoba. Dr. Cornelius W. Wiebe, a Mennonite who represented the riding of Morden and Rhineland as a member of the Liberal Party, spoke about the famine on May 3, drawing the legislature's attention to constituents who had learned of the plight of relatives in the USSR. "These people, most of them living in the Ukraine, have been dying in large numbers both from actual starvation and from undernourishment as a result of excessive levies made on farm products by the Soviet authorities," Wiebe had said, adding that the "people had protested and pleaded with the authorities without avail." In contrast to the much more publicized Saskatchewan case, Wiebe had no motion in connection with the famine but rather wanted to share the information with his fellow members of the assembly.[32] Wiebe's statements in the Manitoba legislature were quoted in the *Winnipeg Free Press* and summarized in *Ukraïns'kyi holos*; the latter noted the 1932 Ukrainian Self-Reliance League's approach to the Canadian Red Cross with the offer of grain for the starving people of Ukraine.[33]

"The Anti-Christ from Moscow is destroying Ukraine," began an editorial in *Ukraïns'ki visty* a week after the first. Religious life had been eliminated, Ukrainian education eradicated, people deported and replaced by Russians, and everywhere there was famine and cannibalism, lamented the editorial. The world could see it all happening, but did not protest in the way it had with the anti-Jewish actions in Germany. The editorial declared that Ukrainians living outside "the Soviet hell" had a duty to unmask the international hypocrisy and, at the same time, not to miss any opportunity to inform the world of Moscow's "demonic policy" of liquidating an entire people. Portraying the "Bolsheviks" as thick-skinned but nonetheless sensitive to intelligent anti-Soviet actions, the editorial drew the readers' attention to the English-language monthly *Investigator* published in London, England, by members of the Hetmanite movement. Each had to do his or her anti-Soviet action, *Ukraïns'ki visty* concluded, and organizations had to engage in joint actions.[34]

The Edmonton weekly had begun to report on such joint actions, albeit seemingly among Ukrainian Catholics, in Alberta, including a public meeting of the Ukrainian Sporting Sitch Association, the Ukrainian Catholic Parish, and a fraternal association, held in Calgary on June 3, 1933. The assembled petitioned the federal and provincial governments to implement measures against Communism in Canada and to not allow the Kremlin to fulfill its plans of a mass deportation of Ukrainians and their replacement by Russians.[35] A gathering in Halych, Alberta, on June 18, also passed a resolution that was sent to the federal government, asking that efforts be made to stop the "mass murder, famine, and deportations in Ukraine."[36]

Sophie Slusarenko

Earlier in 1933, Canadians had read the account of Rose Kritzevosky. In May and June, some were also reading about Sophie Slusarenko, a woman from Perehonivka (in the Kyiv region), Ukraine. Slusarenko was passing through Winnipeg on her way to Edmonton to join her husband, who had immigrated to Canada some five years earlier. She confirmed the existence of widespread hunger in her country: "There is not enough bread or potatoes in Ukraine, let alone other bare necessities," she said, adding that six hundred people in her village had died of starvation. Slusarenko traced the problem back to 1931, when "nationalization of agriculture was started on a large scale." But conditions since then had become much worse: "There were not enough cows to provide milk for the children and most of the horses had been eaten by the starving people." Slusarenko painted a picture of a police state. Riots in Perehonivka, for instance, had been suppressed by armed force and any criticism of the Soviet order was "invariably followed by a swift removal to the Solovetsky Island, or to Archangel." Workers in the local sugar factory were "slightly better off than the agrarians" but there, too, "an armed force [is] continued to maintain discipline."[37]

Meanwhile, in June the USSR had reportedly agreed to a reduction in wheat output. "With a famine reported in the Ukraine!" exclaimed the *Winnipeg Free Press*. "When man became intelligent he discovered the amazing possibilities of absurdity," the newspaper remarked.

Chapter Four

"WHAT TO BELIEVE ABOUT RUSSIA"
Summer 1933

Suicide of Mykola Skrypnyk

In July 1933, news broke that a prominent Soviet Ukrainian leader, Mykola Skrypnyk, had taken his own life. From 1927, Skrypnyk had served as the people's commissar of education in Ukraine, but was removed from that post after Stalin sent Pavel Postyshev from Moscow to that republic to take control of the local Communist Party. Skrypnyk had overseen Ukrainianization in Ukraine and in Soviet places outside the Ukrainian SSR inhabited by Ukrainians. After Postyshev arrived in January 1933, Skrypnyk's policies were denounced and he was removed as education commissar; he served as head of the State Planning Committee of the Ukrainian SSR from February until his death on July 7.[1]

An AP wire story in the *Globe* said that the Communist Party's central committee, in announcing the suicide, had charged that it was a "cowardly act" and due to Skrypnyk's falling into the hands of Ukrainian nationalistic counterrevolutionaries. The fifty-one-year-old had only recently been dismissed from his post for displaying "rotten liberalism" toward anti-Soviet elements.[2] The suicide generated much discussion in the Ukrainian community abroad. In London, the Ukrainian Bureau's bulletin printed extracts from its coverage in the British press. An extract from the London *Times* was presented in Ukrainian-language periodicals in Canada.³ The *Times* correspondent in Riga reported that Skrypnyk had come "into conflict with the central authorities in connexion with the disastrous agricultural policy, which has produced widespread famine and distress, particularly in the Ukraine."⁴ The earlier suicide of a prominent Ukrainian writer, Mykola Khvylovy, in May 1933, was also reported in the Ukrainian-community press.⁵

A Canadian MP Returns from a Visit to the USSR: Humphrey Mitchell

Another talking point in July was the reaction of Humphrey Mitchell, the Labour MP for East Hamilton, Ontario, to his recent visit to the USSR. Mitchell, who had also visited Germany, had travelled to the USSR with a trade union delegation of cooperative workers from the United Kingdom, the country of his birth.⁶ In a message to Mayor John Peebles of Hamilton, Mitchell said that he had not seen "such suffering in my life" as he had witnessed in the Soviet Union.⁷ Editorials in several Canadian newspapers commented upon Mitchell's description of conditions in the USSR. Toronto's *Globe*, for example, remarked that "Mr. Humphrey Mitchell, Hamilton member of Parliament, has been visiting in Russia. He writes that he never saw such suffering as he witnessed in the land of the Soviets. And Mr. Mitchell is a calm, level-headed representative of Labor. Evidently he got away from the beaten paths that Moscow has prepared for notable visitors, such as Mr. George Bernard Shaw."⁸

An editorial in Windsor's *Border Cities Star* asked if the MP for East Hamilton was taking his political life in his hands with his letter to Mayor Peebles. After all, the newspaper pointed out, Mitchell was a supporter of J. S. Woodsworth, the head of the CCF—a party that "seems to look with so much favor on the Russian experiment." The editorial remarked that while there were people who stood on soapboxes to extol the virtues of the USSR, the fact was that they had no personal knowledge of the Soviet Union. Instead, much news was coming out of the USSR, the editorial said, and a good portion of it was along the lines of Mitchell's account. The pro-Soviet sympathizers were writing off "such reports" as lies of the capitalist press, but they would not be able to dismiss so easily the statement provided by a "well-known Canadian like Mr. Mitchell, M.P., a Labor parliamentarian and, as we have said, a supporter of Mr. Woodsworth." Canada had its problems, stated the editorial, "but our people are not starving."[9]

Mitchell was also mentioned in an editorial in the *Edmonton Journal*. In response to contradictory reports about the situation in the USSR, the *Journal* published its editorial under the title "What to Believe about Russia." It began by pointing out that when "much is being written about Russia by those who have had the opportunity of acquiring a thorough knowledge of conditions there, little attention deserves to be paid to conclusions reached by visitors who cannot have had the time to make anything more than surface observations." Many of those observers came away with the idea that the country was in much better shape than the outside world thought, the editorial went on to say, but that was not the impression received by such people as Mitchell. The newspaper specified that Mitchell's letter mentioned suffering "among those who appeared to be peasants and unskilled workers."[10]

A Canadian Newspaper Publisher Returns from the USSR: Robert J. Cromie

The title of the *Edmonton Journal* editorial was apt when set against the background of other stories circulating at that time, which raised doubts or skepticism about the famine, including a statement by a Canadian newspaper publisher following a visit to the Soviet Union. In July 1933, at a time when the Canadian government was being lobbied to expand trade with the Soviet Union, Robert J. Cromie, publisher of the *Vancouver Sun*, said in reference to the famine that "some critics say that conditions were not too bad in Moscow, but down in the Ukraine people were starving. Someone from the Ukraine told me that the people in Moscow are starving, too." Everything that one heard about the USSR, he continued, was in fact both "true and untrue."[11]

By the time Cromie uttered those words, the famine had made it to the front pages of two Canadian dailies. In addition to the article by Donald Day that ran in the *Vancouver Province* in early June 1933, a United Press story on the famine, by Richard Sallet, appeared at the bottom of the front page of the *Montreal Star* on July 8.[12] Sallet, described as a professor at Northwestern University, announced that ten million people had starved to death in the previous six months in southern and eastern USSR. The suffering was particularly acute, he noted, in the Volga, Ukraine, and North Caucasus regions. Sallet pleaded for aid to be furnished. It was not a question of friendship or animosity to the USSR, he said, but one of "starving humanity." He urged the American Red Cross and churches in the United States to cooperate in assisting the starving people and suggested that Washington, DC, could try to influence Moscow on the matter of relief provision.[13]

But for some reason—possibly because the story was datelined Berlin—Sallet's plea did not seem to elicit much subsequent attention in the Canadian press. Rather, Canadian newspapers appeared to be more interested in what Cromie had to say about the USSR. In August 1933, Cromie elaborated on certain points that he had made earlier, and his observations were accorded extensive coverage. For instance, he thought the USSR should not be measured by the standards of the United States or Canada, and he maintained that major strides were being made. "It took Japan only 30 years to modernize industrially," he said, while the USSR was "doing it in 10." In terms of the famine, Cromie said that he had heard from an official that conditions in Leningrad were not too bad, but that they were terrible in Moscow, while in Ukraine, where there was a harvest shortage, there was cannibalism. The story of cannibalism frightened him, Cromie noted, because it had been told to him by a "high British official." He then presented the facts as he "saw them." There had been a food shortage in Ukraine, he said, which he described as "the Kansas of Russia." Cromie noted that of the USSR's population of 185 million, 30 million people lived in Ukraine—the figure of 185 million was considerably higher than what was reported in the Soviet census of 1926 (148 million), though the figure for Soviet Ukraine was closer to the mark. He left it to readers to judge "how far from the truth was the statement that the Ukraine was starving and that they were practicing cannibalism," based on a conversation he related: "Going through a Moscow art museum," Cromie said, "I noticed a couple of groups of 20 or 30 boys and girls, 13 to 15 years old." He stopped one of the girls and asked her "if things were bad down in the Ukraine." Yes, she replied: "the crops had not been very good and there was a little bit of trouble." In fact, Cromie continued, her parents had "discussed allowing her to come on this trip, but after 'long talks' they finally dug down and put up the money. Her father was a farmer who had joined the new co-operative group." Cromie said he then talked with a couple of other children, and "their story was pretty much the same." Cromie then concluded: "The point is that the farmers of the Ukraine were represented to me as starving to death and practicing cannibalism, and yet here were 20 children from the Ukraine district whose parents had put up 75 rubles each for them to come down and have a five-day visit to Moscow—18-hour train ride away."[14]

Cromie's comments about the Soviet Union were subsequently publicized across Canada, in both the English- and the French-language press.[15] His statements also seem to have commanded some interest in Ottawa; H. H. Stevens sent a copy of a memorandum to Arthur Merriam, R. B. Bennett's private secretary, for the attention of the prime minister. Dated August 31, 1933, the memorandum, whose author is not identified, began by noting that Cromie was delivering lectures about the USSR a month or so after his return. On August 15, he had lunched with Mr. Woodsworth of the CCF at the Vancouver Club. The author of the memorandum wondered if Cromie (the name misspelled as "R.J. Crombie") was "wholly philanthropic in his expenditure of time and money in going to Russia and now advocating their cause."[16]

Cromie's statements about the famine did not go unchallenged in Alberta. In August, the *Edmonton Bulletin* printed a letter to the editor, signed "Canadian"; its writer remarked that Cromie, had he gone to the provinces, would have seen hundreds of thousands of famished orphans and millions of "declassed" people starving and without shelter. People with relatives in the USSR, this letter writer went on to say, could provide more reliable information about the real state of affairs there.[17] In a letter published in September in the *Calgary Herald*, Henry S. Gold of Delia, Alberta, described Cromie's claim that there was no starvation in Ukraine as "incredible." To counter Cromie's statement, Gold quoted from a letter that former Russian premier Alexander Kerensky had written in June to the *Times* of London.[18]

Cromie's position also prompted comments within his home province of British Columbia. On August 16, he addressed the Victoria Chamber of Commerce. It was quite clear from his remarks, reported the city's *Daily Colonist*, that Cromie considered the USSR not the "Chamber of Horrors" he apparently had been led to believe but rather a well-managed state run by a government whose incentive was to "work for the people as a whole, free from corrupting influences."[19] However, on the same page, the *Daily Colonist* ran an editorial on the Soviet Union. It was axiomatic that anyone who had lived and worked there, the editorial began, knew more about prevailing conditions than "any chance visitor who has spent a few weeks there and been shown what he or she is wanted to see under Soviet tutelage." The editorial then referred to "evidence," coming in a "steady stream," about a regime that maintained itself in Moscow through "terrorism" and focused on Countess Tolstoy's publicized statements about the USSR, which included remarks about the famine: "The Bolshevik government has been robbing the people, taking away their bread, their food, and sending it abroad," the countess had said. The Soviet government needed the currency, in her view, for machinery and also for financing propaganda. If the cultivators hid bread for their families, they were punished, she continued; she then referred to the "crowds of famished peasants" who, when "confronted with death," were fleeing Ukraine—"formerly...the granary of the world."[20] The *Vancouver Province* also covered Cromie's Soviet impressions, comparing them with Mitchell's disclosures: "Humphrey Mitchell, Labor M.P. for Hamilton East, saw people starving in Russia. Mr. R. J. Cromie of the Vancouver Sun saw 50,000 Russians betting on a football match at Moscow. The Toronto Star would like to know if the two things had any connection."[21]

Canadians who were sympathetic to the USSR, or at least turned a blind eye to the conditions there in the hope that full trade relations would resume, were more inclined to make reference to Cromie. Sovietophiles in Canada preferred the accounts of former French prime minister Édouard Herriot to those about the existence of widespread famine in Soviet Ukraine. Herriot, who visited the USSR in August and September 1933, said that he had not seen "anything resembling a famine" in Ukraine.²² Cromie's statement (along with comments made by Herriot and others) was also recalled in a letter to the *Manchester Guardian*, part of an exchange in the British newspaper about conditions in the USSR and the famine.²³ Yet if Cromie referred to people from Ukraine he had met in Moscow to make a point about the famine, at least one other Canadian who was visiting the USSR's

Food Shortage During Wheat Glut

WORLD CONFERENCE on WHEAT CONTROL   BURNING WHEAT in IDAHO

REGULATION of wheat growing and distribution is a problem which representatives of 31 countries battled to solve in a world conference in London under chairmanship of Prime Minister R. B. Bennett of Canada. While the delegates met, reports from Russia told of 100,000 Soviet children being organized to guard against grain thefts and to retrieve stray kernels dropped by harvesters in the North Caucasus field. Despite reports, Soviet officials deny there is a food shortage. Although drouths seriously cut the wheat crops of the United States, Canada and Argentina, this year, holdover crops continue to mount, due to lack of consumption. Total unsued wheat in Canada also amounts to some 315,000,000 bushels. And Europe, exclusive of Russia, has produced 100,000,000 bushels this year. At a period when there are millions of hungry people in every country in the world, the grain crops carried over are the largest in the world's history. The United States is beginning to subsidize exports to the Orient as one outlet. In the meantime the grain farmer fears the depressing effect on prices of larger surpluses.

Figure 3. No pictures associated with the famine were published in any of the mainstream newspapers or Ukrainian-language weeklies consulted. In the absence of any photographs, the *Saskatoon Star-Phoenix* used images from the 1921–23 famine to accompany its story about food shortages at a time of a wheat glut. This photograph was published on August 28, 1933, p. 7.

capital around the same time relied on a visitor from that southern Soviet republic to illustrate a different one.

P. H. Boivin of Granby, Quebec, speaking before the Old Boys' Association of Collège Mont-Saint-Louis, Montreal, informed his audience that, during a summer visit to the USSR, "he had met a farmer who had come to Moscow from the Ukraine who told of the death from starvation of his wife and son and daughter. In the Ukraine there have been over a hundred persons accused of cannibalism."[24]

Édouard Herriot

Édouard Herriot's visit to the USSR in the late summer of 1933 was well covered in the Canadian press. In May 1932, Gorguloff had assassinated French president Paul Doumer, apparently because Gorguloff perceived France as being too friendly to the USSR. Subsequently, France moved not further from but ever closer to the Soviet Union.[25] Herriot returned to the fore as prime minister after the assassination, serving for a third time between June 3 and December 18, 1932. Afterward, although no longer prime minister, he remained "the leader of the most powerful political party in France (Radical-Socialist)" and worked toward better relations between France and the USSR.[26] Ukraine was among the places in the USSR that the former French prime minister visited. After his stay there, Herriot dismissed the famine "scarecrow" as a "product of the Hitlerite propaganda department."[27] A Franco-Soviet accord was signed and, following it, the French government applied pressure on Russian émigrés. Gregory Semenov, editor of the Paris-based Russian-language newspaper *Vozrozhdenie*, was summoned to the French foreign ministry over an article attacking Maxim Litvinov during the Soviet foreign minister's visit to France in August 1933. Then, on September 29, Semenov was summoned to the Prefecture of Police and "warned about statements in his paper to the effect that Herriot made a mistake when he said that there was no famine in Russia." Afterward, three detectives were stationed in the street near the *Vozrozhdenie* office, because, one of the detectives said, according to a staff member, the "paper was following a policy interfering with good relations existing between the two countries since France had adopted a policy of rapprochement with the Soviets." For his part, Semenov asserted that the summonings to the foreign office and police prefecture would have no effect on the newspaper's policy. *Vozrozhdenie* would continue to "tell the truth," he said, adding that "he had accurate information that there was a bad famine in Russia."[28]

On the day that *Le Matin* announced Herriot had left Rostov-on-the-Don and was now in Moscow, that Paris newspaper published an appeal by Jan Tokarzewski-Karaszewicz—a former Ukrainian National Republic diplomat living in exile in the French capital—for an official humanitarian mission to visit Soviet Ukraine. Describing the situation there as "terrifying," Tokarzewski-Karaszewicz said that the country was gripped by famine and a typhus epidemic. People were dying, he said, and Ukraine was being depopulated. It was necessary to send an official mission to Soviet Ukraine to investigate conditions there—and, Tokarzewski-Karaszewicz stressed, a Franco-Ukrainian committee had been struck for that very purpose.[29] French-language newspapers in Canada were aware of the coverage in France of Herriot's visit to the USSR. *La Presse* reacted by referring to a commentary in *Le Matin* and publishing an extract of a letter from the North Caucasus (received in Paris) that described famine conditions.[30]

An Article in *Maclean's* Magazine: J. K. Calder

By the time of Herriot's visit to the Soviet Union, Canadians had already been hearing the stories related by engineers who had returned from there following expiry of their employment contracts. In 1932, Soviet officials stated that six thousand foreign specialists and skilled mechanics of various nationalities were then in the USSR. Soviet trade representatives abroad reportedly received "tens of thousands" of applications for jobs.[31] Perhaps the best-known Canadian engineer in the Soviet Union was J. K. Calder. Born in Ingersoll, Ontario, Calder served as the chief construction engineer for Bryan and Detwiler Company. Commissioned to work on projects in the USSR, he had departed for the Soviet Union in 1929. Before his return to Canada, in May 1933, he had supervised the construction of the Stalingrad and

Chelyabinsk tractor plants, the Magnitogorsk steel mills and blast furnaces, and various other projects. In July 1933, the Canadian magazine *Maclean's* shared with its readers the engineer's impressions after his several years in the Soviet Union. "He has had as many as 18,000 men, from all parts of Russia," *Maclean's* told its readers, adding that the Canadian engineer had "seen more of conditions under Soviet rule than probably any other foreigner."[32]

In a description of his years in the USSR, Calder assessed the food situation. It had been bad for the last year, for which he blamed not the policymakers but the producers of the food. The impression in Europe, Canada, and the United States, he said, seemed to be that food shortages were more or less due to crop failure. But in Calder's opinion, in Ukraine "the farmers absolutely refused to work." Their rationale was that the government had taken all the grain for export the previous year, "leaving them without enough for their own requirements." Believing that the regime would do the same in 1932, the farmers did not "put the crops in" and consequently there was a shortage of grain. Calder said he had been told "by prominent Russians that the leaders of this movement have been shot or banished to Siberia and Kazakstan [sic]." Further, the government also sent party leaders and the state police to Ukraine to supervise the seeding on collective farms, to ensure that the practice was not repeated. Calder then denied that any mass mortality had resulted from famine in Ukraine. "Except in one area [Kazakhstan] which I shall describe in my next article," he declared, "I have never heard of many actual deaths from starvation." He asserted that the "people have little or nothing to eat," but claimed that the Soviet populace could "get along on less real food and do more hard work on it than any other people that I have ever seen."[33]

The Border Cities Workers' Educational Circle (Windsor, Ontario)

Meanwhile, Mitchell's statements were being referenced during exchanges about the Soviet Union at a meeting in Windsor, Ontario. The Border Cities Workers' Educational Circle (BCWEC) was at this time sponsoring meetings to draw attention to conditions in the Soviet

Union. Eugene Volodin of that organization had already written a letter to the *Border Cities Star*, prior to its editorial on Mitchell, complaining that efforts to provide relief to starving people in the Soviet Union were undermined by the lack of cooperation by Soviet authorities. Volodin's letter, published in the paper in June 1933, had begun with a declaration that "we Russians, as Canadian citizens, residents of the Border Cities and members of the Border Cities Workers Educational Circle," had assembled in Windsor's Polish Canadian Citizens' Club in order to "raise our voice against the recognition of the government of the country of our birth by the government of Canada." Volodin noted that "From many regions we are daily in receipt of letters reporting numerous cases of cannibalism," and that the Soviet government was "restricting to receive any kind of help outside of the land of the so-called Communism."[34] The following month, a *Border Cities Star* article mentioned a letter, received by J. Domino of East Windsor from a brother in the USSR, that told of "terrible suffering and starvation." The letter claimed that eight or nine persons a week were dying from starvation in an unnamed village, including the letter writer's daughter. A story of cannibalism was related, along with a report of people "dying on the street who are too weak to work for the government and have been evicted from their home."[35]

Such information was to be the basis of a BCWEC meeting at Windsor's Prince Edward School on the evening of July 21, 1933. The meeting took place as planned but was disrupted by pro-Communists, leading to the summoning of city police reserves. "The meeting called by Eugene Volodin under auspices of the Workers Educational Circle was kept in a constant uproar," reported the *Border Cities Star*. "Parked in the rear of the hall, the Reds maintained a steady barrage of howls." Members of the organizational committee remonstrated with the disturbers, but "combat was averted on several occasions and the two police officers on duty in the meeting showed excellent judgment." The contingent of Communist sympathizers "had concluded the Internationale and was filing out of the building as the scout cars loaded with officers reached the trouble scene." Volodin had granted a pro-Soviet sympathizer five minutes to state his case. Jack Miller of the Workers' Ex-Servicemen's League declared, before he was "howled down" after three minutes, "I find it my duty to stand here tonight in defence of the Soviet Union, the only country which has solved the greatest issue confronting any capitalistic country. And to think that any capitalistic country would utilize the White Russians to spread false propaganda and to sabotage the progress of the Soviet Union when we find on our own doorstep people starving to death. Would you sacrifice the people of one-sixth of the world for one man, Humphrey Mitchell[?]" The speakers that evening included K. Talan, secretary-organizer of the circle. Commissioner Bennett and Oscar Kitching, recently resigned as president of the Windsor branch of the Labor Party, attended as guests. The guests and Miller spoke in English, while Volodin spoke in both English and Russian, and others gave their messages exclusively in Russian. In his speech, I. Michailoff of Detroit, "organizer of the Cultural Workers Association of North America," recounted that his parents had died of starvation on a farm in the USSR. Another speaker, L. Krotkoff, a member of the Great Russian War Veterans' Association, told of letters from relatives who mentioned "the confiscation of their property." A. S. Odoevteff [Odoevzev?], a civil engineer, described conditions in the USSR. When it came Kitching's turn to speak, he remarked that all he could go by was "what has been translated from letters." He added that "it seems to be now that there must have been plenty of false reports sent out about Russia before this. I heard Mr. [James S.] Woodsworth and A.E. Smith paint wonderful pictures of Russia. But I heard a different story from two men who recently came back. And then Humphrey Mitchell sends word that conditions are terrible. So, therefore, there must be something in those letters that is true. The Soviet must have placed a ring of steel around the workers. And that's why I stand here tonight opposed to any dictatorship, whether imposed by the Communists in Russia or the Nazis of Germany."[36]

The resolution adopted by "Canadian citizens of Russian birth" at the meeting held that July evening was published by the *Border Cities Star*. According to the BCWEC, 740 people had taken part in the meeting. In consideration of information about conditions in the USSR that had been derived from "thousands of letters from relatives and friends" and "men and women who have recently returned from that unfortunate country," the resolution supported the Bennett administration's practice of "refusing to trade with the Soviets" and asked that the Canadian government urge the United Kingdom that it was also not in London's interest to trade with the USSR. Another resolution asked the Canadian government to put an end to the "teaching of the doctrine of Communism to the youth of Canada," and one other requested that the "Border Cities Branch of the League of Nations immediately petition the League of Nations in Geneva to appoint a special commission to investigate and report on living conditions in the U.S.S.R."[37] A clipping containing the resolution was sent to the prime minister's office by S. Odoevzev, vice-president of the Society of Russian World War Veterans in Detroit. In his covering letter, Odoevzev wrote that, by the initiative of the Society, a meeting organized by the BCWEC was held in Windsor to protest the brutal ways in which the Soviet regime was "trying to fulfill their absurd program in experimenting on human beings." The information provided in the clipping, he continued, could help the prime minister "in serving this country and saving it from growing influence of Communists."[38]

In September 1933 the BCWEC hosted Jacob Margolis, who came to speak on the Soviet Union. The speaker was identified in the *Border Cities Star* only as "Jacob Margolis of Pittsburgh," but he was surely the anarchist lawyer whom Emma Goldman called a "very able friend."[39] The speaker from Pittsburgh reviewed the past fifteen years of Communism in the Soviet Union and declared that famine existed in 1933 because of the Soviet "policy of exporting foodstuffs and natural resources for the erection of a capital structure." If millions of people were starving, he said, it was "not due to natural causes but through social usages that have been foisted upon them." Margolis quoted Lenin on the necessity for the revolution to march forward even if it "costs half the population of Russia" to illustrate the fanaticism behind the Soviet scheme.[40]

In July 1933, another group identified as Russian staged a protest, elsewhere in Ontario. The Russian-Canadian Workers' Federation held a meeting on July 6 at the Masonic Temple in Chatham. The assembly, chaired by F. Konosevych of Brantford, drafted a resolution that protested such practices as the Soviet denial of aid from abroad to assist starving people.[41]

Editorial in the *Winnipeg Free Press*

That same month, the *Winnipeg Free Press* published an editorial about the famine. Titled "Famine over Russia," it noted that stories from the USSR over the previous six months had not made for pleasant reading. Even the *New York Times* correspondent, "who has been particularly kind in his efforts to find advantages in the collectivization of farms" (undoubtedly Duranty), had remarked that food shortages had caused "heavy loss of life." The death rate was much higher for peasants and others who had not received bread rations, the editorial continued, and it was believed that in Ukraine, the North Caucasus, and the Lower Volga region alone the number of dead was around three million. The editorial referred to German newspapers that, based on interviews with travellers, reported that the farther an observer went into the interior beyond Odesa "the greater was the 'misery.'" These travellers spoke of "starved children with emaciated limbs and swollen abdomens who were seen along the railroad track, not occasionally but as a common spectacle," of field mice being in demand as food, and of reports of cannibalism. The editorial went on to say that it was significant that travel in the USSR had been substantially restricted and that foreign correspondents were forbidden to leave Moscow without special permission. The only gleam in the picture, according to the *Free Press*, was that the recent harvest was good, meaning there would be sufficient food for all, "so that the countryside which produces the harvest may not have a repetition of a condition which has strewn its roadsides with dead and famishing men, women and children."[42]

Indeed, foreign journalists had just recently been summoned by Soviet authorities and told that they could not travel outside the Moscow area without a special permit. Yet the restriction, as a *Manchester Guardian* correspondent noted, had already existed. The "present system of rigorous restriction of the correspondents' freedom of movement," the correspondent said, seemed "primarily designed to prevent foreign observers from visiting the southern and south-eastern regions of the Soviet Union, Ukraina, and the North Caucasus" where "hunger prevailed in some parts, at least, of those regions." The correspondent thought it odd that the restriction should be imposed at a time of reports of a good harvest.⁴³ The link with the famine was also made in the *Toronto Telegram*.⁴⁴ Winnipeg's *Kanadyis'kyi farmer* mentioned the ban in an article about the famine that also referred to the appeals by the Ukrainian Catholic hierarchy and Cardinal Innitzer.⁴⁵

The Catholic Church and the Famine

In July 1933, a month after *Ukraïns'ki visty* had lamented in an editorial the lack of effective action on the famine question in places where Ukrainians lived and had political representation outside the Ukrainian SSR, the Ukrainian Civic Committee for the Salvation of Ukraine was initiated in Lviv. Branches were opened across western Ukraine and some were also established abroad. One of the aims of the Lviv-based committee was to "mobilize the opinion of the world"; it hoped to do this through churches and the League of Nations, among other vehicles.⁴⁶ The committee was formed at a time when efforts had been made to improve relations between Poland and the Soviet Union. A *New York Times* report suggested that the creation of the committee was awkward for Warsaw in view of its recent relations with Moscow. The "[Ukrainian] National Democrats oppose any action that appears treacherous to the Poles but greatly embarrassed the Polish Government by creating a special relief committee for 'starving brethren' in Soviet Ukrainia in spite of Soviet denials of famine," the report in the *Times* said.⁴⁷

On July 24, Metropolitan Andrei Sheptytsky and the Ukrainian Catholic bishops of western Ukraine issued a statement of protest against the famine. That joint statement was printed in the *Western Catholic*. The Ukrainian Catholic bishops in Galicia declared "Ukraine to be in the clutches of death, its people dying of starvation and the situation, resulting from Bolshevik action, growing worse from day to day." The bishops appealed for a worldwide protest.⁴⁸ The newspaper *Le Devoir* also reported on the letter, as did the French-language Manitoba weekly *La Liberté*, but otherwise it does not seem to have received coverage elsewhere in Canada.⁴⁹ The bishops' statement did, however, come to the attention of the Archbishop of Vienna, Cardinal Theodor Innitzer, who organized the Interconfessional and International Relief

Committee for the Starving Districts of the Soviet Union.[50] The cardinal's efforts commanded international press attention. In Canada, the press reported his statement that even at a time of a new harvest in the USSR, catastrophe loomed just four months in the future and, once again, millions of lives would be lost. At a time when the world was almost choked with a surplus of wheat and food, the archbishop of Vienna said, people were starving in the USSR. He warned that famine, accompanied by infanticide and cannibalism, threatened people of different religious and ethnic background equally.[51]

Indeed, in terms of reactions to the famine, the cardinal seems to have received far more press coverage than the pope. The *Western Catholic* was an exception among Canadian newspapers in reporting on the response of the leader of the Catholic world to the news that millions were dying of starvation in the USSR. "As stoic as he is pious," the account in that weekly began, "seldom does Pope Pius XI give way to his emotions before friends or strangers in his great audience hall at the Vatican." However, the pontiff "shed bitter tears not long ago when one of his Jesuits stood before him and recounted the plight of the starving millions in Soviet Russia." That Jesuit, the report said, "was one of the few if not the only living person ever to see His Holiness weep." The unnamed Jesuit had returned to the Vatican from a "secret visit" to the Soviet Union, where he had conveyed words of support from the Holy See to Catholics and other Christians. He informed the pope of the food shortages and "described how thousands of poor people wander aimlessly across the land in search of enough black bread and dried fish to keep body and soul together." An estimate of "between 10 and 12 million deaths from starvation" was provided. The report went on to say that, as those words were spoken, "the Jesuit was shocked to see tears streaming down the face of the pontiff." After recovering, Pope Pius XI discussed plans "for sending several hundreds of Catholics" into the Soviet Union "by the fall of this year to organize relief." The cost of such an expedition—which ultimately was never put into operation—was estimated to run in "the millions," but the "pontiff is said to be determined to carry it out, despite the fact general economic conditions have not spared the Holy See."[52] Soon after, in a story about religious freedom in the USSR and Soviet-Italian relations, *Le Devoir* of

Montreal mentioned a speech by the pope to the faithful in September 1933, in which "the Holy Father said that he feels a profound interest in Russia because of the suffering of the Russian people."⁵³

An Editorial in the *Edmonton Journal*

An *Edmonton Journal* editorial about the famine, at the start of September 1933, mentioned Cardinal Innitzer. Two days earlier, the paper had published an interview with Peter J. Lazarowich, an Edmonton barrister who had recently returned to the city after almost a year in Europe. A part of Lazarowich's time abroad had been spent in Prague, a major centre of Ukrainian émigré scholarly life. He had also stopped in London, where he helped with the Ukrainian Bureau and presented a paper on Ukrainians in Canada at the Royal Institute of International Affairs.⁵⁴ In the interview published in the *Journal*, Lazarowich said that Ukraine was "today...the centre of the most appalling famine in its history due to the internal strife and bad government in the various states."⁵⁵

And so it was Lazarowich's reference to a famine in Ukraine that prompted the *Journal*'s editorial of September 1. Under the title "Russia's Famine," the editorial began by drawing attention to Lazarowich's statement about an appalling famine in the granary of Europe—a statement that "must have proved startling to many readers." How could this be so, the editorial noted that its readers might ask, when the previous two or three weeks had seen reports of large crops in Europe and a reduction of the supplies needed to be purchased? But the barrister's statement was supported by other sources of information, the newspaper continued, including the appeal made by Cardinal Innitzer. The editorial also pointed to fundraising efforts in Germany to "relieve distress among the Russo-German inhabitants of the Ukraine." An American correspondent, the editorial said, on the basis of hearing what a fellow American and two Germans returning from the USSR had to say, "cabled that the indications were that the estimate of 4,000,000 deaths due to malnutrition in rural Russia during recent months was too low." The *Journal* further observed that even Duranty, who represented the *New York Times* and dismissed the famine reports as an exaggeration or malignant propaganda, acknowledged there had been some deaths: specifically, that deaths in the winter and spring had occurred at four times the normal rate. The editorial expressed the belief that the food shortage in the USSR was due not to climatic conditions, which had been responsible for the 1921–22 famine, but "solely to the government's farm collectivization policies."[56]

Editorials about the famine appeared in the French-language press in Canada as well. In one, titled "Rumours of Famine" and published in September 1933, *La Presse* referred to "a major Belgian journal" that specialized in Soviet affairs; this journal stated that the famine in the USSR had commenced in 1932 and "in 1933 it continued to expand and encompass the most fertile regions of the country, taking thousands of lives."[57] The journal to which *La Presse* referred was *CILACC*; *La Presse* had earlier published extracts from this periodical.[58] As well, CILACC material devoted to the famine was republished in the November 1933 issue of the Roman Catholic series *L'Oeuvre des tracts* of Montreal.[59]

The League of Nations and the Famine

The efforts of organizations such as the Ukrainian Civic Committee for the Salvation of Ukraine had the effect of increasing pressure on the League of Nations to consider acting on the matter of the famine. In September 1933, Johan Ludwig Mowinckel, president of the Council of the League of Nations, received a delegation from Lviv; that same month, he also received a letter from the Liaison Committee of Women's International Organizations. The letter, dated September 26, was published in the Ukrainian-language press in Canada. On behalf of the organization, Miss Corbett Ashby asked Mowinckel to "bring to the notice of the Council of the League the desperate condition of the famine stricken population of Soviet Ukraine." The league had repeatedly rendered "invaluable services to the cause of humanity," Ashby wrote, and she entreated its president to "submit to the Council the present need for League action in any form which you may think wise." The committee, she added, was "unanimous in their decision to appeal" to him. Ashby enclosed some notes about the situation in Ukraine. There appeared to be a serious famine, the notes said, but details were hard to come by because it was virtually impossible for a visitor in Soviet Russia to obtain permission to visit Soviet Ukraine. In spite of the efforts of recently reinforced frontier guards, Ashby's notes claimed that a large number of inhabitants were escaping. The notes continued that there had been a famine in 1932 and that seed grain for 1933 had been eaten, and, in spite of this, the population had been enfeebled and unable to prepare the ground sufficiently. Quotas were set regardless of circumstances, and "troops were sent to guard the crops and prevent the peasants from stealing the half ripe corn for food." The peasants were considered too weak for rebellion. Losses in two villages (Zalyvanshchyna and Kumanivka, today in Vinnytsia Oblast) were specified in order to illustrate the extent of the calamity. Cannibalism was said to be rife. In spite of the potential consequences to letter writers, the notes went on to say, letters were "openly being sent abroad describing the state of the country and appealing for help." Attention was then drawn to the appeals of the Ukrainian Catholic Church in western Ukraine, the Comité de secours aux affamés de l'Ukraine et de Kouben, in Brussels, and Brüder in Not of Germany.[60] In another letter, written to Mowinckel on September 25 by Milena Rudnycka and Zenon Pelensky of the Ukrainian Civic Committee for the Salvation of Ukraine in Lviv, reference was made to the willingness of Ukrainians in Canada to provide famine aid. "The Ukrainians of the West, who are outside the Soviet Union, as well as the Ukrainians who are citizens of Canada and the United States," the letter said (in French), were "ready to make available to their starving brethren grain and other foodstuffs if the League of Nations makes possible their transport to Soviet Ukraine and their distribution under international supervision."[61] Indeed, the Canadian Red Cross Society was made aware of that willingness on more than one occasion, for its national commissioner, J. L. Biggar, mentioned such readiness in a letter to the International Red Cross Committee in Geneva. In the letter, dated December 11, 1933, Biggar wrote that a "number of former Russian citizens now living in Canada have asked me on several occasions whether the Canadian Red Cross Society could assist them in arranging to send food supplies to their relations in Russia." Many of the people making these enquiries belonged to the "farming classes and have surplus supplies of wheat and flour" but little in the way of "actual money." If the arrangements could be made, continued Biggar, then a "certain amount of grain and flour would no doubt be contributed."[62]

Mowinckel persuaded the Council of the League of Nations to discuss the famine behind closed doors, but could not convince it to act.[63] Ukrainian Canadian newspapers, citing the weekly *Tryzub* of Paris as the source, reported on a "noble" address by Mowinckel days before his mandate as president had come to an end. According to the *Tryzub* article, the general secretary of the League of Nations had stated formally that the matter of the famine could not be discussed because the USSR was not a member. Therefore, Mowinckel decided that he would summon his colleagues and confer with them about the famine on September 29, 1933, at the end of the session; representatives of fourteen members of the Council of the League of Nations thus discussed the famine at a secret meeting. The meeting, the article said, lasted no less than an hour and the discussion was very heated. Those who knew the affairs of the league, the article continued, said the matter was accorded importance. Members of the league, while not denying the essence of Mowinckel's proposal, apparently could not see a practical way out and objected to the idea of drafting an official statement by the League of Nations. Some delegates were said to have supported Mowinckel's position, including those from Ireland, Germany, and Spain. Mowinckel himself, according to the article, took the floor four times. Speaking on behalf of his entire nation, Norway, he said that his small and poor country was ready to make the sacrifices necessary to assist Ukraine—and he appealed to the larger countries to do the same. In the end, it was decided to defer the issue to a nonpolitical body such as the Red Cross. Some in attendance suggested that Ukrainians themselves turn to the Red Cross—"as though we do not [already] do this!"—but Mowinckel said he considered it an obligation, as the head of the Council of the League of Nations, to go to the International Committee of the Red Cross himself. The article then referred to Henry de Korab, described as an employee of the French newspaper *Le Matin*, who stated that the existence of the famine had been affirmed at the Seventy-Sixth League Council Session.[64] Thus, even if only for an hour, the situation in Ukraine had become the centre of world attention, the article said. It then asked whether there would be any real results from the act by Mowinckel. While it did not put high hopes on it, the article nonetheless considered the moral effects as colossal and undisputed, closing by praising Mowinckel and declaring that Ukrainians would forever have deep sympathy for Norway.[65] Later, *Kanadyis'kyi farmer* published the letter of gratitude that was sent to Mowinckel from the Civic Committee for the Salvation of Ukraine in Czechoslovakia.[66]

The decision of the League of Nations not to intervene directly in the matter of the famine was also reported in the mainstream Canadian press.[67] The International Committee of the Red Cross did direct a letter to the Soviet government; on October 12, it wrote to the Alliance of the Red Cross and Red Crescent Societies soliciting information about the famine. The reply from Moscow came more than two months later, in a letter dated December 26. In it, the alliance's president, Abel Enukidze, asserted that Mowinckel had retracted his statements about the famine. In fact, Enukidze claimed that the Norwegian statesman had publicly expressed regret at being misled by elements hostile to the Soviet Union.[68]

A Rally in Winnipeg

The Ukrainian community in Canada already knew from experience that the Red Cross had limited influence, referring time and again to the Red Cross and Red Crescent Societies of the USSR's refusal in 1932 of an offer of aid from Ukrainian farmers in Canada. The refusal was recalled during a meeting of several hundred people at the Ukrainian Greek Orthodox Cathedral in Winnipeg on Sunday, September 17, 1933, at which speakers denounced the Soviet regime for "a determined, planned annihilation of the Ukrainian peasants." The resolution passed at the meeting mentioned the 1932 offer of grain for the starving people in Ukraine.[69] That same month, in a letter to the editor of the *Toronto Star*, Rev. Dmytro D. Leschishin also mentioned the approach made to the Canadian Red Cross and the lack of cooperation on the Soviet side.[70]

"Hot Cables" to Canada from the USSR: Pierre van Paassen

The same newspaper that published Leschishin's letter to the editor had begun to feature articles by Pierre van Paassen about the Soviet Ukrainian countryside. For Cromie was not the only Canadian associated with a newspaper who had travelled to the Soviet Union in 1933. That year, van Paassen was sending to Canada "hot cables" on his "Russian trip," and thus Canadians also read about the famine in the dispatches he remitted.[71] Van Paassen, born in the Netherlands and educated in a Calvinist parochial school, had studied for the ministry at Victoria College in Toronto; he had also served as an assistant pastor in a Ukrainian mission for the Methodist Church. During his career as a journalist, he wrote for several Canadian and American newspapers and travelled to various parts of the world. Beginning in 1932, van Paassen spent three years in the Soviet Union as a correspondent for the *Toronto Star*. In August 1933, he was assigned to investigate reports of the famine, specifically in Ukraine. Apart from the *Star*, his reports were also published in other Canadian newspapers. The *Edmonton Bulletin*, for example, in announcing van Paassen's impending trip, noted that because the journalist spoke "both German and Yiddish, he will be able to converse freely with the natives."[72]

An article published in September 1933 placed van Paassen in Kremenchuk, Poltava Oblast. In it, van Paassen reported that witnesses from all walks of life—some of whom had lived through the 1921 famine on the Volga—"tell me that the privations in the Ukraine did not quite reach the proportions of that earlier catastrophe when ten millions died of hunger and typhus." But, he continued, everyone agreed that from January 1933 until a few weeks earlier, the situation had been calamitous. There was little evidence of that situation at present, van Paassen went on to say, and so he could not give an eye-witness account. Yet he added, "The grain collectors were ruthless last year. There was a drought. There was a campaign to bring the government to a fall or at least to embroil it in grave difficulties. There was a bitter social and political conflict." The bad times, van Paassen said, lay behind, which he took to be "the simple explanation for the general reticence. People [would] rather talk of the future than of the past, except historians."⁷³

In another dispatch, titled "Future of Soviet Depends on Successful Harvesting," van Paassen related that he had spoken to a prominent Bolshevik official who had just returned from an inspection tour of a railway system in Ukraine. The official spoke of a "stampede" away from the countryside when hunger came, so urban workers were mobilized to cut grain. The kulaks, van Paassen was told, had such an influence on poorer peasants that "the whole rural Ukraine became the scene last winter of a most bitter phase in the class struggle. There is no question but the Ukraine is the most reactionary region in the Union. Besides the well-known causes of drought and a bad crop last year, the peasants of Ukraine have not taken kindly to the collective farm idea."⁷⁴

The *Edmonton Bulletin* ran no editorial similar to the *Journal*'s "Russia's Famine," but it did comment on Ukraine in light of van Paassen's accounts. "In the Ukraine, Mr. Van Paassen writes, there is a good crop of wheat: but the peasants are not reaping it and will not eat it," a *Bulletin* editorial began. "The reaping is being done for the Government, by labor-saving machinery operated by a few hands," it continued, adding that the families "who formerly won their living from the land are wandering the roads." The editorial went on to note that the USSR had in large measure accomplished in a few years the level of industrialization that took generations to achieve in other countries—but the achievement seemed to have landed them all in the same place: "where 'wealth accumulates but men decay.'" The editorial then remarked, "Humanity is about the least wanted commodity on earth today, whether in Soviet Russia or in the countries where the citizen is allowed to accumulate private capital and employ it."⁷⁵

Back in 1932, van Paassen said in the *Globe* that he conceived "the newspaperman's task one of telling the truth, objectively and sincerely, without being stampeded by sensations or being out for hollow thrills."⁷⁶ But when it came to the famine, he fell short of fulfilling that task. In an unfinished biography of van Paassen, Hugh Whitney Morrison, who worked as a reporter for the *Toronto Star*, wrote that van Paassen had "reported in generally favourable terms on the energy and spirit of the Russian people" but that "his observations on the famine in the Ukraine got him in temporary trouble." The famine had apparently "disturbed him but did not wholly dissuade him of the laudable aims of the Bolshevik revolution." Van Paassen acknowledged the famine's existence, but had been able to see "a quite different face of Communist behavior."[77]

Articles and Editorials in *Ukraïns'ki visty*

In Canada's Ukrainian community, van Paassen's reports were treated with some skepticism, particularly in light of other information that editors of periodicals were receiving from disparate sources including the Ukrainian-language press in Galicia under Poland and in London, Paris, Vienna, Berlin, and Prague.[78] In August and September of 1933 the pages of *Ukraïns'ki visty* were replete with stories about the famine, and more editorials were written. At the start of August, an article based on the western Ukrainian religious weekly *Khrystos Nasha Syla* referred to stories of defenceless children in Kuban being set upon and their flesh sold. It then addressed the difficulties of providing relief. Some months prior, the article said, it had been possible to send a five-kilogram parcel, which did not cost much to mail and was a big help to its recipients. But now, it continued, the only way to send parcels with produce was through a firm in Warsaw, which was quite expensive, and one had no control over the process. The article then noted that one could help family and friends in Ukraine by sending money, but this process, too, was difficult, as illustrated by the case of a Soviet citizen who had written to a relative in western Ukraine. The Soviet citizen, once at the post office, would receive not the dollars but rubles at the exchange rate of two rubles to a dollar. Upon request of the dollars only, the relative in western Ukraine was told, the post office would write the number of dollars issued, and then every month a financial inspector would check on how many dollars the recipient still possessed. If the recipient were to exchange the dollars on the black market at a rate of four to five rubles per dollar, then this would result in punishment with jail.[79] In the same issue of *Ukraïns'ki visty*, a letter from a worker in Soviet Ukraine to his brother in Canada related the difficulty of buying bread, which, he said, was probably available in the Torgsin stores in exchange for foreign currency. Some fifty people a day had been dying of hunger and weakness in his locality. The letter writer asked that two to three dollars be sent to the Torgsin store.[80] In another August article, *Ukraïns'ki visty* cited a letter pointing out that "about our life the Bible puts it best: 'Those killed by the sword are better off than those who die of famine.'" The same article referred to writings about the famine in London's *Fortnightly Review* (by Malcolm Muggeridge), Berlin's *Vossische Zeitung* (by Wilhelm Stein), and Berne's *Der Bund*.[81]

Other articles published in *Ukraïns'ki visty* that month concerned the suppression of scholarship in Soviet Ukraine, the establishment in western Ukraine in July of the Ukrainian Civic Committee for the Salvation of Ukraine, the appeal about the famine by Cardinal Innitzer, travel bans experienced by foreign journalists, and the writings of Walter Duranty and William Chamberlin.[82] In September, several stories referred to the establishment of a relief committee in Czechoslovakia and to articles about the famine published in Paris's *L'Ami du peuple*, London's *Daily Telegraph*, Lviv's Ukrainian Catholic weekly *Meta*, and a Swedish newspaper.[83] Other items included an account from the Russian émigré newspaper *Vozrozhdenie* (Paris) about cannibalism, the acknowledgment of deaths through privations by Soviet official Alexander Asatkin, and an article about the German relief organization Brüder in Not.[84] That organization, reported *Ukraïns'ki visty*, had in two weeks gathered 500,000 Reichsmarks to assist twelve thousand German families who mainly inhabited Soviet Ukraine. The obligation "with our brethren is far larger," said the Edmonton newspaper, which urged readers to be ready for the day when the signal would come to start collections for starving Ukrainians. "When there is a relief action for our starving brethren let us not, each one of us, fail even with a daily earning to give it up with Christian love. We must tear away the deadly claws from the necks of our brethren," *Ukraïns'ki visty* advised.[85]

In September the newspaper published several editorials and commentaries about the famine as well as a pastoral letter issued by the head of the Ukrainian Catholic Church in Canada, Bishop Basil (Vasylii) Ladyka. In an editorial titled "In Defence of a Ukraine That Is

Dying Out," *Ukraïns'ki visty* said that Ukraine's occupiers were turning it into ruin and mass murdering its population. The editorial continued with a number of statements: that those occupiers were destroying Ukraine not only culturally but also physically; that religion and family life were being obliterated; that people were being executed or deported to the Soviet north and, especially, the population was being subjected to starvation; that even the cautious newspapers of Britain and the United States had asserted that, from the autumn of 1932, three million people had died of starvation in Ukraine and Kuban; and that Ukraine was dying in the literal sense of the word, for after the murder of its intelligentsia (*po vymorduvanniu inteligentsiï*), the turn of the masses had come. Meanwhile, the editorial said, Moscow had declared at a world grain conference that it would give the world fifty million bushels of wheat. The tragedy of Ukraine was known the world over; yet, the editorial asked, had the world lifted a finger in defence of its dying population? Had a single minister of any state called upon Moscow, or perhaps even a former minister who then did not have to represent his state formally? The editorial asserted that the protests of "cultured people" were heard when Hitler's government limited the rights of six hundred thousand Jews, or when in Iraq the Kurds had slain six hundred Assyrians. *Ukraïns'ki visty* named one exception and that was the Catholic Church, which did voice its protest. The editorial cited the example of Pope Pius XI's objections on behalf of the "captive nations" under "the Bolsheviks" and over the destruction of religion, Catholic as well as Orthodox. It also mentioned the appeals of the church in Galicia and the efforts of Cardinal Innitzer, whose appeal was for the victims of all nationalities in Ukraine and Kuban. The editorial commented disapprovingly that countries had recognized the "bloody" regime in Moscow and then traded with it. Only the Catholic Church, in the view of *Ukraïns'ki visty*, stood with moral fortitude against "the anti-Christ" during a materialistic age. The paper noted that Lenin had understood in 1922 that the biggest battle for the destiny of humanity was between Moscow and Rome, adding that this was indeed borne out in the Catholic world's plea.[86]

Bishop Ladyka's pastoral letter, issued on September 13, spoke of the suffering of the Ukrainian people under the "tyrannical regime" of the "godless Communists" that had been imposed by "Muscovite invaders." Pope Pius XI had for the previous three years vigorously protested the anti-Christian policy of the Soviet regime, the spiritual leader of the Ukrainian Catholic Church in Canada said, but since then the situation had become worse. People who were able to flee the Soviets provided stories of starvation and cannibalism. Bishop Ladyka called on all believers to help with prayer and protest and to announce to the world the calamity that had befallen "Greater Ukraine."[87]

The pastoral letter was published in an issue of *Ukraïns'ki visty* that featured yet another editorial about the famine. This editorial declared that even with Communists trying to suppress the truth, people who had fled spoke of the famine and of the incidence of cannibalism. It noted that Ukrainians abroad were acting on the appeals of the church and the Ukrainian Civic Committee for the Salvation of Ukraine in Lviv, and that famine relief committees were being set up across Canada. The question, the editorial said, was whether "the Bolsheviks" would allow for relief to pass through. *Ukraïns'ki visty* expected the committee in Lviv to report on that matter, but in the meantime it emphasized to readers the importance of organizing mass rallies and other actions to draw public attention to the situation in Ukraine. Then, following a signal from the old country, relief could be gathered. The editorial closed with a call to Ukrainians in Canada to organize mass meetings and help "dig the grave of Bolshevism."[88]

Deportations to the USSR

While the famine was happening, the Soviet Union became a destination for deportees from Canada. One possible deportation to the Soviet Union, announced in May 1933, was of Sam Cohen, who with seven others had been convicted of belonging to an illegal organization.[89] Another case, that of Doukhobor leader Peter Verigin, was given considerable coverage in the Canadian press. Although threatened with deportation to the USSR, Verigin was ultimately not deported. But others during the course of 1933 were, including the Ukrainian Labour-Farmer Temple Association organizer John [Ivan] Sembay. In late December 1932, *Ukraïns'ki visty* had mentioned that three Ukrainians held in Halifax were ordered deported: Sembay, "the well-known agitator in Alberta"; Dan Holmes [Danylo Homitsky], the former foreman of the pro-Soviet newspaper *Ukraïns'ki robitnychi visty* in Winnipeg; and Stepan Vorozhbet.[90] In July 1933 came an announcement that Sembay was soon to be evicted from Canada.[91] Although he was born in an area of Poland that had hitherto been part of the Russian Empire, Sembay was refused entry to Poland. The USSR, though, was ready to admit him in view of "services in the cause of international labor."[92] Other people ordered or recommended deported from Canada to the USSR included Isaac Braun, a Mennonite from Saskatchewan;[93] John Neufeld of Warren, Manitoba (jailed for the theft of eight chickens);[94] and Sophia Sheinon of Calgary, described as a "Red" agitator.[95]

Chapter Five

"WHAT ARE 1,000,000 IN A POPULATION OF 162,000,000?"
Autumn 1933

Mrs. H. Satanove Returns from a Visit to the Soviet Union

Two accounts published in the *Edmonton Journal* in October 1933 further corroborated the existence of a famine. One was provided by Mrs. H. Satanove, who had recently returned to Edmonton after leaving in February for a tour of the USSR and Palestine. Satanove, who had immigrated to Canada from the Russian Empire in 1911, described the USSR as "a success" but asserted that "her people have been caught in the wheels of their own progress." Disease, she said, was "rampant, terrible. I saw heartrending scenes." The *Edmonton Journal* informed its readers that as Satanove "stood talking to a banker in Romna, Russia [Romny, in northeastern Ukraine]," she felt "something beneath her heel. She turned, looked down....It was a child—dead of starvation."[1]

Marie Zuk

The second account drew from the first-hand testimony of Marie Zuk. In September 1933, *Kanadyis'kyi farmer* had published a story about three newcomers from Soviet Ukraine. Its author, Dmytro Mykytiuk, reported that a woman and two children were at the Immigration Hall by the Canadian Pacific Railway station in Winnipeg on September 4 and 5. They were on their way to join their husband and father, a farmer in one of the western provinces of Canada, who had spent more than half a day with the family in the Immigration Hall. Thanks to her husband, who had come to Canada in 1928, the woman was able after much effort to leave the USSR with her twelve-year-old daughter and eight-year-old son. In August 1933, the three travelled from their southern Ukrainian home to Canada via Kyiv, Moscow, Lithuania, Hamburg, and New York. The journey cost seven hundred dollars.[2] Although the woman was not named in *Kanadyis'kyi farmer*, Mykytiuk was more than likely relating the story of Marie Zuk, whose account was published soon afterward in the *Edmonton Journal* and in other mainstream Canadian newspapers. In October 1933, the *Journal* reported that Marie Zuk, of Kalmazovka in the Odesa region, on her way to Consort, Alberta, after landing in Canada, "told of a case last spring in which a young married couple...killed and consumed their two small children. The gruesome crime was accidently discovered when a pig was stolen from the Kolhosp [collective farm]...and the members of the militia organized a search of all the houses in the vicinity in an endeavour to locate the stolen 'treasure.'" The head of one child was apparently found in an oven. Cats and dogs had disappeared, Zuk related, and "people also consumed all the field mice and frogs they could obtain." The only food the people could afford was a "simple soup prepared of water, salt and various weeds."[3]

The Ukrainian National Council in Canada, based in Winnipeg, wrote to President Franklin D. Roosevelt on October 2, 1933, "with an urgent request to take the necessary steps to arrange for an immediate neutral investigation of the famine situation in Ukraine." The council also submitted its bulletin (dated September 15, 1933) to the American leader. The issue featured the testimony of Zuk containing additional details.[4] Most of the markets in Ukraine were closed, Zuk said. She also referred to the "many cases of suicide, mostly by hanging, among the village population, and also many mental alienations." There was no escape, Zuk said, because no one could obtain "permission to leave the boundaries of Ukraine." The grain fields were "watched day and night by armed guards"; after threshing, the grain was "immediately removed to the government storehouses, or to the nearest port." She described the village schools as empty—children were "too hungry to attend to learning"—and hospitals as "bare of all medicines." Zuk had been expelled from her family home in 1931 by the "chairman of the collective farm who took the house for himself." She then lived in a small shack until she was expelled from there, too, and afterward moved from house to house. "It was only owing to the fact that her husband sent her money from time to time through the 'Torgsin,' which was paid out to her in foodstuffs and other goods, that she was able to avoid the lot of her less fortunate compatriots," the bulletin noted. Zuk's mother and a married daughter still resided in the village.[5]

The Ukrainian National Council

The formation of the Ukrainian National Council (UNC) in Winnipeg was announced in May 1933. Some fifty delegates representing fourteen organizations attended the founding meeting, held at the Ukrainian Reading Association "Prosvita" (on the corner of Flora Avenue and Mackenzie Street). The organization set out the following objectives: "Fostering of the principles of better citizenship, the advancement of the cultural activities of the Ukrainian population in Canada and to provide material and moral support for the Ukrainian people in Europe."[6] The UNC planned a mass meeting for Sunday, July 16, at which there would be a "special declaration condemning the Bolshevik rule in Ukraine and the Communist activities in Canada."[7] The meeting—held only days after the Ukrainian Labour-Farmer Temple Association hall in Winnipeg had been raided by the police[8]—was disrupted by pro-Soviet sympathizers and the ensuing "riot" became the subject of much press attention.[9] In August, M. Mandryka delivered a speech on the famine at a mass meeting called by the UNC, held at the Ukrainian Institute Prosvita.[10] In addition to the council's appeal to Washington, DC, it reached out beyond North America on other occasions—directing a letter to British prime minister Ramsay MacDonald and even sending one to Italy's "Il Duce," Benito Mussolini.[11]

A Play about the Famine

In addition to covering local famine-related protests,[12] the Winnipeg daily press reported on a local play about the famine that was staged in the city and later elsewhere.[13] The play, titled *The Death of Commissar Skrypnyk, or Famine in Ukraine*, was produced by the playwright P. Pylypenko (the pseudonym of Pylyp Ostapchuk). The *Winnipeg Tribune* discussed the performance of Wednesday, November 8, by the drama group Rusalka at the Ukrainian Institute Prosvita. The play depicted in "vivid colours the present ... suffering of millions in the Ukraine." The item in the *Tribune* mentioned the Soviet policy of the confiscation of grain and described the play's central figure, Nicholas [Mykola] Skrypnyk (played by Ostapchuk), as "the late acting prime minister of Soviet Ukraine, who recently committed suicide in protest against the persecution of Ukrainian culture."[14] *Kanadyis'kyi farmer* provided further details about the well-attended performance. The play's first act, it said, was set in the office of a village council and included scenes of a dying elderly man, who had come to seek relief; women asking for something to eat; and announcements of orders that had been sent from Moscow. There was nothing to eat and no one available to dig graves for the starvation victims. The officers at the council, drinking vodka and munching on an onion, did not know what to do. The second act depicted a dialogue between Skrypnyk and USSR leader Stalin. Skrypnyk gradually came to understand what the Third International and world revolution meant for Ukraine. The third act showed Skrypnyk in his office in Kharkiv, the Soviet Ukrainian capital, where a portrait of Ukraine's bard Taras Shevchenko could be seen hanging on the wall. Pavel Postyshev (sent in early 1933 from Moscow to Ukraine by Stalin) called on Skrypnyk; the latter, who was removed from his post, showed Postyshev the door. The play closed with Skrypnyk, having seen the ruin brought to Ukraine, taking his own life.[15]

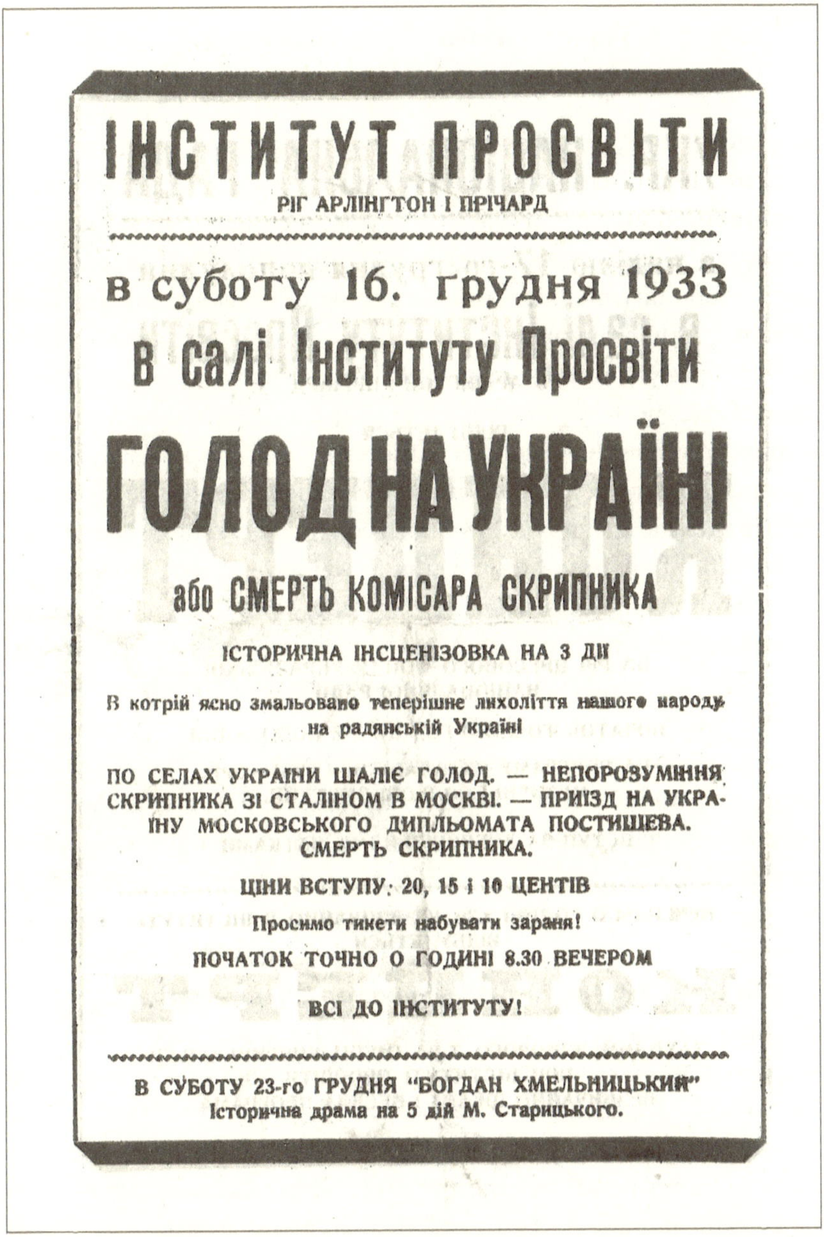

"What Are 1,000,000 in a Population of 162,000,000?" 97

ІНСТИТУТ ПРОСВІТИ
РІГ АРЛІНГТОН І ПРІЧАРД

в суботу 16. грудня 1933
в салі Інституту Просвіти

ГОЛОД НА УКРАЇНІ
або СМЕРТЬ КОМІСАРА СКРИПНИКА

ІСТОРИЧНА ІНСЦЕНІЗОВКА НА 3 ДІЇ

В котрій ясно змальовано теперішнє лихоліття нашого народу на радянській Україні

ПО СЕЛАХ УКРАЇНИ ШАЛІЄ ГОЛОД. — НЕПОРОЗУМІННЯ СКРИПНИКА ЗІ СТАЛІНОМ В МОСКВІ. — ПРІЇЗД НА УКРАЇНУ МОСКОВСЬКОГО ДИПЛЬОМАТА ПОСТИШЕВА. СМЕРТЬ СКРИПНИКА.

ЦІНИ ВСТУПУ: 20, 15 і 10 ЦЕНТІВ

Просимо тикети набувати зараня!

ПОЧАТОК ТОЧНО О ГОДИНІ 8.30 ВЕЧЕРОМ

ВСІ ДО ІНСТИТУТУ!

В СУБОТУ 23-го ГРУДНЯ "БОГДАН ХМЕЛЬНИЦЬКИЙ"
Історична драма на 5 дій М. Старицького.

Figure 4. Handbill announcing the December 16, 1933, performance of the play *The Death of Commissar Skrypnyk, or Famine in Ukraine* at the Ukrainian Institute Prosvita, on the corner of Arlington Street and Pritchard Avenue, Winnipeg. Demetrius Elcheshen fonds, Ukrainian Cultural and Educational Centre (Oseredok), Winnipeg.

Peter J. Lazarowich Writes on the Famine in the *Edmonton Journal*

In October 1933, the *Edmonton Journal* turned over space to Peter Lazarowich to discuss the famine. The article was important because it synthesized much of the news that had been made available in the preceding months and demonstrated the extent to which prominent community members were informed of developments in Soviet Ukraine. "While the press of Europe, and the American continent is, quite properly, devoting much space to Germany's treatment of the Jews," Lazarowich began, "it is surprising that so very little interest or sympathy is shown in the matter of the terrible famine now raging in the Ukraine." Lazarowich traced the origins of the famine to the beginning of 1932 and said that it had "now been conclusively established in spite of the official denials of the Russian Soviet government." News about the conditions in Soviet Ukraine had come from foreign press correspondents, refugees, and "countless letters written by the Ukrainians and others to their friends and relatives in Canada and other parts of the world." Lazarowich drew readers' attention to Alexander F. Kerensky's letter about the famine that was printed in the London *Times*. During the spring and summer of 1933, he continued, the famine had reached such proportions that "even the friends of the Soviets like Walter Duranty, correspondent of the New York Times, are no longer able to conceal the terrible conditions pervading in the Ukraine." Lazarowich cited a report by the W. Sanford statistical service in Winnipeg (March 29, 1933) to show that, in spite of the famine conditions, "during the period between August 4, 1932, and March 23, 1933, the Soviet government shipped 17,312,000 bushels of wheat out of Ukraine." The government in Moscow had, Lazarowich stated, denied all reports of famine "and refused to allow any direct investigation into the existing conditions by an impartial committee thereby precluding all possibilities of assistance to the famine-stricken area." He then mentioned the 1932 offer of grain by the Ukrainian community, through the Canadian Red Cross. Lazarowich went on to note that in spite of Soviet denials, the "whole world" was aware "of the most terrible famine in history." Journalists, statesmen, tourists, students, and peasants, who had recently returned or fled from Ukraine, confirmed the famine, he said, including people in Edmonton: "There are several people in this city of Edmonton whose names and addresses are in the possession of the undersigned who have arrived from the Ukraine in the course of the last few months and who may be interviewed and the facts ascertained." There were also others in the city in possession of letters from relatives and friends that, Lazarowich said, told of conditions in Ukraine: of people reduced to eating grass, weeds, tree bark, and insects; of the incidence of cannibalism; and of villages losing two-thirds of their population.

Lazarowich then turned to the question of the total number of fatalities caused by the famine. The "consensus of opinion," he maintained, was that "it will exceed the famine in 1921–22, which was officially placed at about 5,000,000 people." In spite of this, Lazarowich noted, the Soviet government had not desisted from forcible requisition of grain. Officials had "invaded the country under the personal direction of [Pavel] Postyshev" and were "draining the last drop of blood from the dying population of Ukraine." Lazarowich came to the conclusion that the government in Moscow was "deliberately determined to starve most of the population of Ukraine in order to beat it into complete submission to the principles of Communism which the Ukrainian peasant masses have hitherto vigorously resisted and repudiated."

Lazarowich then mentioned efforts by Ukrainian organizations in western Europe to establish "an international relief committee for Ukraine for the purpose of devising ways of sending immediate relief to the famine stricken areas of Ukraine." Ukrainians from Romania (Bukovyna) and Poland (Galicia), he reported, had met with "representatives of the leading humanitarian institutions of London, England, and steps have been taken towards the establishment of a relief committee in London composed of both English and Ukrainian representatives." Lazarowich pointed out that Ukrainians in Canada had also formed relief committees; moreover, they were conducting "a Canada-wide action of vigorous protest against the present inhuman policy of the Russian Soviet government in the Ukraine" and hoped "to arouse the civilized world from its apathy towards the impending disaster of the Ukrainian nation and to enlist its co-operation in the effort to send relief to the famished area."[16]

U.S. Recognition of the Soviet Union

Over the course of 1933 there was much speculation in the Canadian press on whether the United States would recognize the Soviet Union. Franklin Delano Roosevelt, the Democratic Party leader who assumed the presidency several months after the Republicans were defeated in November 1932, moved steadily in that direction. Roosevelt viewed recognition as an opportunity to amplify trade between the two countries.[17] At the same time, the USSR had been working toward recognition by other states as well and was forming nonaggression pacts.[18]

Ukrainian groups in North America petitioned the American president to have the situation in Ukraine investigated before initiating diplomatic relations with the USSR. No encouraging responses came from such petitions. Thus, after the UNC in Canada had written to President Roosevelt on October 2, 1933, the U.S. consul general in Winnipeg was requested, "unless he perceives objection to such action, to inform [the UNC] that, as the conditions ... do not appear directly to affect American citizens or interests, the Department is not in a position to take any action."[19] After receipt of a resolution about the famine that the Ukrainian community in Oshawa, following a meeting on October 13, had forwarded to the U.S. State Department, the American consulate in Hamilton was "directed merely to acknowledge receipt of the communication and nothing further."[20]

On October 28, the *New York Times* reported that the United Ukrainian Organizations of the United States planned to send a delegation to President Roosevelt. The purpose was to draw attention to the famine, which had claimed the lives of "several million inhabitants of the Soviet Ukraine," and to propose "an impartial investigation of conditions in the Ukraine before recognition is accorded Soviet Russia."[21] The delegation were told, according to *Kanadyis'kyi farmer*, that the U.S. president could not find the time to receive them. However, Roosevelt's secretary, Marvin H. McIntyre, assured the delegation that their concerns would be taken into consideration.[22] In spite of such efforts, on November 16, the United States recognized the Soviet Union. Roosevelt knew about the famine[23]—so too did his predecessor, Herbert Hoover, who was not in favour of recognition.[24]

The recognition of the USSR by the United States was welcomed by the *Ottawa Citizen*, which mentioned the famine in an editorial. When Soviet commissar for foreign affairs Maxim Litvinov came to Washington, DC, the editorial said, people were surprised by how he looked. Indeed, the *Citizen* claimed newspaper reporters appeared "disappointed." It continued: "Even they [the press] have been fed on stories of Russian hardships, and so when M. Litvinov showed no sign of wearing a lean and hungry look, they possibly felt themselves fooled." The editorial went on to say, "It may be, of course, that Comrade Stalin ordered a special wardrobe for the natty commissar. But that sounds far-fetched." The *Citizen* editorial suggested it was "just possible, after all, that most of the yarns about famine and disaster in Russia are exaggerated."[25]

After Litvinov had concluded his business in the United States, he stopped in Italy upon his return to Europe. Montreal's *La Presse* noted in early December that "just when the Russian minister of foreign affairs Maxim Litvinov arrived in the Italian capital, [the Vatican newspaper] *L'Osservatore Romano* published a story in big letters titled 'Cannibalism in Russia.'" According to *La Presse*, the article in the Vatican newspaper cited testimonies that had appeared in the *Journal de Genève*, which seemed to indicate that cannibalism existed in remote areas such as Siberia and "even sometimes in Ukraine, because of the desperate condition of the population in several districts." People were "dying of starvation by the thousands," and parents were keeping their children "at home to prevent abductions."[26]

Demonstrations in the United States

The Ukrainian community in Canada also followed the famine-related protests in the United States. In November 1933, *Kanadyis'kyi farmer* announced that a demonstration would take place in Detroit, by Cass Park (at Second Boulevard and Ledyard Avenue), on the morning of Saturday, November 4.[27] Afterwards, New Jersey's *Svoboda* reprinted a *Detroit Free Press* report about the rally, which estimated that about 2,500 Wayne County Ukrainians had gathered in the city that morning. Robert E. Ireton of the University of Detroit addressed the group and drew a parallel "between the Ukrainian struggle against Soviet tyranny and Ireland's fight for freedom." He urged those assembled to send a copy of their protest resolution to President Roosevelt and to representatives of each member of the League of Nations. "Most of the Bolsheviks hate the limelight of publicity," Ireton was quoted as saying. "Send these resolutions and let the nations of the world know you are aware of the Soviet despotism in the Ukraine." Further, he advocated "a publicity campaign for similar demonstrations by Ukrainians in the United States and Canada."[28]

By that time Ukrainians in at least one part of Canada had directed a resolution to the League of Nations, although not to each individual member state. In October 1933, the *Calgary Herald* reported a mass meeting of Ukrainians in Hamilton, Ontario, and noted that appeals had "been made to the League of Nations in behalf of the famine-stricken population of Russian Ukraine." The report did not say who had organized the meeting, but it did note that several speakers had condemned the Soviet policy of grain confiscation. The speakers, the newspaper said, charged that the Soviet regime "was taking away grain from a starving people in order to add to its exportable surplus."[29]

The Ukrainian Canadian press reported other examples of American Ukrainian appeals to the U.S. government. On November 12, 1933, Fr. Mykola Kopachuk, of the Ukrainian Catholic parish in Ambridge, Pennsylvania, wrote a letter to President Roosevelt appealing to the U.S. government to come to the assistance of the starving population of Ukraine through the American Red Cross or other means. Kopachuk received a reply, dated January 5, 1934, from Robert Kelly (eastern European affairs officer, Washington, DC) stating that there was no possibility of any action, because there was no matter of American citizens or interest directly involved. The American Red Cross could not set up a station in Ukraine without a request by or the agreement of the USSR.[30]

Both before and after the U.S. government's recognition of the USSR, Ukrainian organizations were mobilizing their members for mass demonstrations on the streets of a number of American cities. Some of these street demonstrations, which drew attention to the famine, were covered by the mainstream Canadian press. For example, the

Toronto Telegram covered a November 1933 demonstration in New York that, it said, involved ten thousand people and resulted in injuries after demonstrators were attacked by Sovietophiles.[31] The *Winnipeg Free Press* reported on a December demonstration in Chicago that included three thousand individuals and ultimately led to a clash in which about fifty marchers and attackers were injured, twenty of whom were treated for injuries at hospital. The three thousand demonstrators, said the *Free Press* (citing an AP dispatch), had "been set upon by 500 rioters, said by police to be Communists." Police took from the attackers—men and women alike—"pieces of gas pipe, lengths of loaded rubber hose, brass knuckles and clubs." Following the attack, the demonstrators reassembled and marched on with police protection.[32] Canadian newspapers such as the *Border Cities Star, Toronto Star, Edmonton Journal,* and *Star-Phoenix* also carried accounts of the demonstration in Chicago.[33] The Ukrainian-language press in Canada also covered the protests there and in other U.S. cities.[34]

Assassination of a Soviet Consular Official in Lviv

By the time the *New York Times* had reported the concerns of the United Ukrainian Organizations, it had already announced the assassination of a Soviet consular official in the city of Lviv. In addition to the protests against the famine and the appeals to assist the starving inhabitants, Canadian newspaper readers also came to learn of the assassination of the Soviet official. On October 21, 1933, Aleksandr Mailov, an official with the Soviet consulate in Lviv, was slain by a member of the Organization of Ukrainian Nationalists (OUN), Mykola Lemyk. The assassination was reported by the *Calgary Herald*, which said that the assassin's identity was being kept secret by the police. The assailant, according to the *Herald*, had asked to see Mailov. "When Mailov asked him his reason the man drew the revolver and fired," the *Herald* explained, adding that another consular official (Ivan Dugai) had been wounded in both hands.[35]

The killing affected Soviet-Polish relations. According to the *New York Times*, the "Soviet Government sent a rather angry note to Poland accusing her of tolerating anti-Soviet propaganda conducted in Eastern Galicia by Ukrainian émigrés." In reply, the Polish foreign office noted that anti-Soviet outbreaks had occurred "even in Soviet Ukraine." The Polish police, meanwhile, arrested over fifty people in connection with the assassination, including Lemyk, described as the son of a wealthy peasant and a student at Lviv University.[36] Poland hoped to maintain good relations with its powerful neighbour, and its relative silence on the matter of the famine during 1933 has been attributed to that desire.[37]

The mainstream press did not say what had prompted the assassination of Mailov, but the Ukrainian-language press in North America linked it to conditions in Soviet Ukraine. The motive was described in Edmonton's *Ukraïns'ki visty* as a "protest against Soviet policies in Ukraine."[38] The periodical informed its readers on developments in the case. It noted that eight lawyers had planned to defend the eighteen-year-old, but the court considered that idea to be tantamount to a demonstration and thus permitted only two legal representatives; one other person could serve as a deputy. Although the death penalty was sought, Lemyk received life imprisonment for the assassination—the case of the wounding of the other Soviet employee was to be heard separately—on account, the periodical surmised, of his age.[39] *Ukraïns'ki visty* also cited a telegram that stated that a demonstration (resulting in the injuries of two persons and ten arrests) had taken place in Lviv against the death sentence for Lemyk.[40] In fact, the assassination was cited as grounds for the cancellation of demonstrations altogether. According to *Ukraïns'ki visty*, the Ukrainian Civic Committee for the Salvation of Ukraine stated that on October 24, 1933, the head of the security branch of Lviv province had advised the committee that the authorities could not allow public meetings and gatherings about the famine that had been slated for October 29; the reason given was the assassination of the Soviet consular official in Lviv. *Ukraïns'ki visty* saw this as an act of collaboration between two occupiers.[41]

The Mailov assassination was not the only death connected with the Soviet consulate in Lviv during the time of the famine. In September 1933, *Ukraïns'kyi holos* announced the suicide of consular employee Mykola Stronsky. He had left the office one Wednesday morning, the Winnipeg periodical said, and was not seen thereafter. Stronsky was then discovered dead with a bullet in his head in a forest by women villagers who were bringing milk to the city. He had left a note concerning the disposition of his belongings, and two other letters were found in the consulate for his colleagues Havrylo[?] Mandzii and Ivan Dugai, but no reason was given for the suicide. However, *Ukraïns'kyi holos* interpreted Stronsky's suicide as a reaction to the anti-Ukrainian policies wrought by the "Bolshevik dictatorship"; Stronsky was to be summoned to Moscow but, the paper suggested, not wishing to go there he chose suicide instead.[42] Another related death, reported some time earlier, was not a suicide but an execution. In September 1932, *Ukraïns'ki visty* (citing "a telegram from Berlin") had announced the killing in Kharkiv of a former Soviet consul in Lviv, Lanchynsky (no first name given).[43]

Ukrainian Canadian Press Coverage in Autumn 1933

Ukrainian newspapers in Canada continued to follow the course of responses to the famine outside Canada. In early October 1933, *Ukraïns'ki visty* reprinted an editorial published in the Lviv-based *Nova Zoria*, the organ of the Ukrainian Catholic People's Party. This editorial suggested that any protest actions against the Soviet Union should be as widespread and sonorous as possible. The Soviets paid no heed to Western protests about religion; they paid more attention, according to the editorial, to forms of protests other than verbal ones, as witnessed in the United Kingdom trade embargo over the trial of the British engineers and the Japanese threat of war over Manchuria. Yet that did not mean that verbal protests were necessarily meaningless. That form of protest still held significance both for Ukrainians and for the wider "civilized world," the editorial averred.[44] Later in October, *Ukraïns'ki visty* announced that by September 24, Ukrainians in France had gathered 2,429.50 francs for the purpose of famine relief. The periodical called that fact an interesting one at a time when, it said, the response in Canada was still limited to writings, meetings, and protests.[45]

Stories published in November included the plan by Ewald Ammende, the head of the Congress of European Nationalities, to visit the United States in order to interest churches and charities in famine relief work in Ukraine. In Vienna, *Ukraïns'ki visty* noted, ten groups whose members lived under the Soviet system—Ukrainians, Germans, Poles, Armenians, Romanians, Greeks, Serbs, Czechs, Jews, and Hungarians—had created an international relief committee for the famine. The committee was under the direction of Cardinal Innitzer.[46]

Canadian Politicians of Ukrainian Descent

During the first half of 1933, the famine was raised in the legislative assemblies of Saskatchewan and Manitoba. In the widely publicized Saskatchewan case, it was discussed by a number of MLAs, including the premier of the province, James T. M. Anderson (Conservative), and a former premier, James G. Gardiner (Liberal). In Manitoba, the issue was raised by Cornelius Wiebe (Liberal). The press apparently made no reference to a member of the Ukrainian community bringing forth the question of the famine in any of the elective assembles in Canada, and that absence did not escape the notice of *Ukraïns'ki visty*. In 1933, five individuals of Ukrainian descent held political office in Canada: one in the federal Parliament (Michael Luchkovich, United Farmers of Alberta/CCF, Vegreville, Alberta), two in the Legislative Assembly of Manitoba (Nicolas Volodymir Bachynsky, Liberal-Progressive, Fisher; and Nicholas Apoluner Hryhorczuk, Liberal-Progressive, Ethelbert), and two in Alberta (Peter Miskew, United Farmers/Liberal, Victoria electoral district; and Isidore Gorecky, United Farmers, Whitford). A June 1933 editorial in *Ukraïns'ki visty* had conveyed dismay at the lack of any discussion about the famine in the parliaments of countries inhabited by Ukrainians (specifically, Poland, Romania, Czechoslovakia, and Canada).[47] Now, in November, an editorial in *Ukraïns'ki visty* expressed frustration at the lack of action on the matter by the Canadian elected representatives of Ukrainian descent. They had neglected their obligations, the editorial reproved. While acknowledging past contributions by Luchkovich in the House of Commons on behalf of the Ukrainian community—he challenged remarks made about non-English-speaking newcomers by Anglican Bishop George Lloyd of Saskatchewan in 1929 and made statements about the repressive measures against the Ukrainian minority in Galicia (the "Pacification") in 1930—the editorial stated that the activities of the five serving elected representatives had fallen short of expectations. *Ukraïns'ki visty* reminded its readers that the Ukrainian press had supported the politicians when they were candidates, but now those politicians were ignoring the Ukrainian press. Among the complaints expressed in the editorial was the seeming indifference of these men to the famine, even though "it was the most important issue for all Ukrainians today." Where at the rallies were their voices? Where were their writings in the press? Had any of them given lectures about the current situation in Ukraine before an English-language audience? The editorial contrasted their seeming inaction with examples of other groups in Canada.[48]

As it happened, Luchkovich and Miskew had attended a rally about the famine just days before the editorial was published. On November 5, people in Willingdon, Alberta, and the surrounding area "packed to capacity" the local Ukrainian National Hall to hear several speakers denounce the Soviet regime. In addition to Miskew, the speakers included Mr. Yanda and Mr. Lazarowich of Edmonton (presumably Peter Lazarowich) and Mr. Pidruchney and Dr. Boykovich of Willingdon. "Hundreds of thousands of Ukrainian people are being starved to death in the once productive Ukraine," pointed out the *Vegreville Observer* in its report on the meeting. "In the meantime the Soviets blind the eyes of the world with their successful five year plan." At the close of the meeting, Luchkovich took the floor and addressed the gathering, "declaring that the eyes of the civilized world should be turned to the unfortunate situation that now exists in the Ukraine." Four "strong resolutions" condemning the "work of the communists in the Ukraine and in Canada" were passed at the meeting that Sunday.[49]

Day of National Mourning

Ukraïns'ki visty complained of a lack of coordinated action with regard to the famine on still another occasion—this time, in connection with a day of national mourning, prayer, and fasting that the pro-OUN Ukrainian National Federation had proclaimed for November 24. *Ukraïns'ki visty* asserted that the Ukrainian Catholic Church had already issued a pastoral letter setting aside October 29 as a day of mourning. Thus, to observe a different date could be perceived as putting the interests of a party first and foremost.[50] A similar point was made by *Ukraïns'kyi holos*. On September 5, 1933, the Ukrainian Greek Orthodox Church of Canada had issued a request for its priests to conduct a *moleben* (service of intercession or supplication) for the suffering and a *panakhyda* (memorial service) for the victims of famine. The periodical also drew attention to a proclamation published around that time by the executive of the Ukrainian Self-Reliance League of Canada, titled "We Will Not Allow Moscow to Kill by Famine the People of Ukraine."[51]

In November, *Ukraïns'kyi holos* announced that it had been informed of protest meetings held in fifty-nine localities (most likely under the auspices of the Ukrainian Self-Reliance League of Canada). Of these, twenty-four were in Manitoba, fifteen in Saskatchewan, twelve in Alberta, two in Ontario, two in British Columbia, and one in Quebec.[52] This figure may have included protest meetings against Communism (and Communist activity in Canada), of which there were many, as well as those focusing mainly or in part on the famine. Yet as the second half of 1933 progressed, *Ukraïns'kyi holos* would increasingly exhort its readers to action. "Do You Know What Famine Signifies?" read the title of one of its summons in late November. It suggested that readers try not eating for just a single day—and then imagine what it would be like to be deprived of food for a week, a month, or two to three months. After such privation, the exhortation continued, it would make no difference to the person starving whether something was fit to consume or tasted good; rather, the person would cease thinking about the world around them and think only about where and how to obtain something to eat. The front-page call in *Ukraïns'kyi holos* then went on to describe the process of dying of starvation through the swelling of the body. Millions of people of Ukraine were presently dying in this fashion, readers were told—dying because the Soviet regime was taking from them everything there was to consume for sale abroad. Not until the world reacted with indignation would Moscow desist from its practice, *Ukraïns'kyi holos* said, for Moscow was "afraid of world opinion." Readers were thus urged to cry out as loud as possible so that the public could hear them protest the famine.[53]

The Ukrainian National Federation also organized protests, albeit fewer in number than the Ukrainian Self-Reliance League of Canada. The *Edmonton Bulletin* reported in July 1933 that a meeting of the Ukrainian National Federation at Edelweiss Hall had featured Ukrainians who made a "strong protest against alleged inhuman treatment" in the USSR. The protesters also drew attention to the imprisonment and sentencing of a large number of Ukrainians by the Polish government. According to the *Bulletin*, the resolution passed at the meeting stated that "35 millions of Ukrainians are being persecuted, oppressed, starved and murdered by the Soviet government of Russia."[54] The *Edmonton Journal* also reported on the passage of a resolution "offering a protest alleging a conspiracy between the Polish and Soviet governments" to exterminate the people of Ukraine by "crucifying them on the Cross of Golgotha."[55] In an appeal published in the October 3, 1933, issue of its periodical *Novyi shliakh*, the national executive of the Ukrainian National Federation summoned its members to action, calling upon every Ukrainian and especially the branches of the organization to come to the assistance of the eastern Ukrainians. Members of the Ukrainian community in Canada must not allow infants to die the agonizing death that results from starvation, it said; otherwise, they would be forever covered with shameful disgrace. Each branch of the Ukrainian National Federation would receive the "necessary information"; in the meantime, the executive asked that anyone who had any information or letters about the situation in Ukraine forward such materials to them.[56] In addition to organizing its own protest actions, the Ukrainian National Federation, through *Novyi shliakh*, reported on activities taking place elsewhere outside of the USSR. In August, it announced the formation of the Ukrainian Red Cross by the general secretariat of the Federation of Ukrainian Organizations Abroad in Brussels. The stated objectives of the Ukrainian Red Cross were to analyze the situation in Ukraine, inform the public, and, in cooperation with other institutions, provide humanitarian aid.[57] Later, in December, it noted a crescendo of activities in Europe, including protests and other activities in Bulgaria, Luxembourg, France, Czechoslovakia, and Belgium.[58] The Ukrainian National Federation also received some funds for the aid of the starving in Ukraine.[59]

More than eighty protest meetings at which the famine was mainly or partly the focus were held in various locations across Canada, beginning with one in Saskatoon on February 26, 1933, and continuing well into 1934.[60] These meetings were organized by different organizations, which were mostly but not exclusively Ukrainian.[61]

The Family of Rabbi Isaac Haft Arrives in Canada

In November 1933, Canadian newspapers reported on the latest newcomers to Canada from the USSR: the wife, four daughters, and son of Rabbi Isaac Haft of Edmonton, from whom they had been separated for six years. In the USSR, the family's home was in Poltava, Ukraine. While in Saskatoon en route to Edmonton, Mrs. E. Haft told the *Leader-Post*'s local bureau of a shortage of bread and the high cost of passports back home (she and her children had paid US$283.00 for each of their passports). Her husband had left the Soviet Union because "of his attacks on the Communist government."[62] Other than the distribution of bread, Mrs. Haft considered the Soviet system of distribution to be functioning well; she noted that "prices were much the same as in Canada although slightly higher in some commodities."[63] The family's arrival in Alberta's capital was covered by the *Edmonton Bulletin*. That newspaper described the newcomers as the "first family to come to Edmonton with first hand information regarding conditions in southern Russia in the last five years." The *Bulletin* was told that conditions in winter 1932 and the summer of 1933 had been very severe; that there was hardly any crop in 1932 and even coarse bread was a luxury; and that there had been an outbreak of typhoid in the summer.[64]

A "Bountiful Harvest"

By the close of 1933, foreign correspondents in Moscow had been reporting successful harvests in the Soviet Union. Thus, when the archbishop of Vienna, Cardinal Innitzer, predicted that a famine would again occur in the winter, Canadian newspapers such as the *Edmonton Journal* and *La Presse* informed their readers of these positive reports from Moscow, which indicated that the crops were good and "gave assurance of adequate food supplies."⁶⁵ A spokesperson for the Soviet foreign office dismissed any talk of an impending famine: "I am happy to say, we have no famine and no cardinals."⁶⁶

Indeed, the impression given in reports in the final months of the year was that the Soviet leadership had been able to reexert control over the agricultural sector and effectively address problems in time for and during the harvest of 1933. A June 1933 report described the "extension of control by [the Communist Party's] 'political sections' to all collective farms."⁶⁷ An AP story that circulated widely in August concerned the children who had been used to "protect the Socialist crop" in North Caucasus, Ukraine, and "mid-Volga regions." The story gave several examples of their success; for instance, twelve-year-old Dmitri Gordeenko was "credited with trapping three grain thieves in a collective field," while eight-year-old Anastasia Omelchenko "caused the arrest of a supposed Kulak woman in whose home she saw a bucketful of grain."⁶⁸ Such developments reminded *Kanadyis'kyi farmer* of the Old Testament story about the enslavement of the Israelites in Egypt.⁶⁹ A United Press report carried by the *Montreal Star* asserted that people everywhere in the USSR were being mobilized for harvest work and that automobiles in Kharkiv and other cities were "being pressed into harvest service." The same article noted that many villages "reported illness and even deaths from overeating as peasants, after months of deprivations, devoured immense quantities of bread."⁷⁰

The American writer and editor William Allen White declared the famine over in a piece that was published in the *Toronto Telegram* in late October 1933.⁷¹ An AP report published in the *Border Cities Star* that month announced a favourable trade balance for the Soviet Union for the first time in years, a speedier flow of goods to the villages, and an end to rationing. "This year's bountiful harvest after two years of bad crops is regarded in official quarters as furnishing undeniable proof of the success of collectivization," the report said, adding that it was perhaps "a turning point in the country's difficulties in attempting to build a socialist state." The report claimed an assurance of adequate food supplies and mentioned the hope among the populace that rationing would be abandoned. In addition to all of this, there were plans to improve the quality of output and increase the productivity of labour. Successes in foreign policy were pointed out, including the establishment of friendlier relations with France and Poland, which was contrasted with Japan's lack of interest in signing a nonaggression pact with the USSR.[72] Indeed, reports around this time indicated not only that the United States was seriously studying the question of recognition of the USSR but that, after the resignation of Japan and the potential withdrawal of Germany, the League of Nations might move toward bringing the Soviet Union into its fold.[73] Both France and Poland—with whom the USSR had now improved relations—were members of the league. Stalin's invitation to Józef Piłsudski to visit Moscow in October was hailed as a "great political miracle."[74]

In spite of the many positive reports about the Soviet harvest, the *Border Cities Star* remained skeptical. Although a bountiful crop was reported, said the Windsor, Ontario, newspaper in late September 1933, the USSR was purchasing grain from Turkey. Turkish sources indicated that the wheat was to be used to "feed people in the famine-stricken areas of the Ukraine and the North Caucasus." People outside the USSR, the newspaper said, "cannot help wondering why it is, if the Soviet has had such a great harvest, that the Russians have to import grain from Turkey."[75] The *Border Cities Star* expressed this skepticism in an issue that also included an AP report stating, on the basis of a tour of Ukraine and the North Caucasus by its correspondent, that the grain crop was so prosperous it would preclude the recurrence of a food shortage. While Alexander Asatkin, head of the political sections of Ukraine, acknowledged mortality from undernourishment, the report said, he claimed that it was in numbers considerably lower than the millions stated abroad. Asatkin blamed the peasants for the troubles, alleging that they had believed that after they joined the collective farms the government would take care of them. Now, the AP report quoted him as saying, they had been taught the bitter lesson that "those who won't work won't eat."[76] Another AP report a few days later spoke of a disastrous spring and summer earlier in the year in Ukraine and the Northern Caucasus because of "peasant inertia," but assured readers that the situation would likely not be repeated because of the introduction of political sections in the collective farms, which would improve organization and educate the peasants in mechanized farming methods. By mid-September 1933, the

AP report said, Ukraine and the North Caucasus were "three months ahead of last year in grain deliveries to the government."⁷⁷ Alongside such reports was one that referred to an August amnesty for "many prisoners who participated in the construction of the newly-completed White Sea–Baltic canal." The amnesty decree reduced the sentences of 59,000 prisoners, unconditionally released 12,000 others, and restored another five hundred to "civil rights as a reward for outstanding work."⁷⁸

Meanwhile, an article in the *Border Cities Star* datelined "Moscow" pointed out that a law introduced by the Soviet government in August 1932—the law that made the theft of state property punishable by death—was still, more than a year later, in effect.⁷⁹ In the same issue, the newspaper reported the USSR's insistence on being allowed to export twice the amount of wheat that it had been allotted under the international wheat agreement.⁸⁰ The *Border Cities Star* deemed it "amazing" that the USSR was posing as a wheat exporter when it was importing grain from another country and "when her own people have not enough to eat."⁸¹

"I Never Saw So Many Healthy, Robust Men and Women as I Did There": George Palmer

The news in the autumn of a good harvest made it easier for Soviet sympathizers to dismiss any talk of famine. Thus, in November, George Palmer—a former resident of Macleod, Alberta, who had worked as a reporter for the *Moscow Daily News*—when asked about food shortages in the USSR, denied that there were any.⁸² "I never saw so many healthy, robust men and women as I did there," the *Edmonton Journal* quoted Palmer as saying. His remarks prompted an exchange in the letters page of the newspaper.⁸³ An exchange of letters also took place months later in the *Lethbridge Herald*, after Palmer had dismissed articles by someone identified as "Ukrainian" as a "conglomeration of bosh" and attributed "acute indigestion and mental constipation" to the author. Palmer's dismissiveness in turn elicited a response from Roy D. Bentley, who stated in his letter that on May 3, 1934, in a village that he did not name, he viewed two series of slides on the prewar Russian Empire and postwar USSR. The second series, Bentley wrote, showed "endless chains of haggard men and women ... seen waiting for food at ration stations and turning away empty-handed." Others showed scenes of famine, though Bentley did not identify the year in which these images were captured.[84]

Nonetheless, the *Lethbridge Herald* had already read sufficiently about the famine to be able to pen an editorial on the subject. The June 1934 editorial, titled "In the Ukraine," began by asking, "What is the truth about Ukraine?" It said that during the fall and winter the newspaper had received contributions from people who provided "indescribable scenes" of their former homes in Ukraine due to the harvest and the "heavy toll levied by the Soviets" to feed the people of the cities. "Along came one Palmer," who had contributed a series of articles of his own. He offered twenty-five dollars to any Ukrainian in Canada who could provide the name of one person who had died of starvation in Ukraine. The editorial went on to say, "Though letters were brought to the Herald written in the Ukrainian language, and which we were assured contained definite information, day and date and name of person who had died of starvation, no names were published because relatives here fear reprisals of the Ogpu on their friends when the news got back to Communist headquarters." Support for the Ukrainian position, said the *Lethbridge Herald*, came from the writings of William H. Chamberlin, correspondent for the *Christian Science Monitor*. The *Herald* noted that Chamberlin had eluded the attentions of the officials in the USSR and learned of the famine, which he stated had claimed 10 per cent of the Ukrainian population. Chamberlin was then quoted: "It was the general testimony of the peasants that the harvest of 1932, although not satisfactory, would have left them enough for nourishment, if the state had not swooped down on them with heavy requisitions.... [I]n 1933 the Soviet Government, quite conscious of what it was doing, was strong enough to wring out of the peasants enough foodstuffs to provide at least minimum rations for the towns and to turn the starvation weapon against the peasants themselves." The *Lethbridge Herald* closed its editorial by saying that there would still be people who would refuse to believe Chamberlin. But for its own part, "we have a great deal of confidence in the Christian Science Monitor as a newspaper which seeks to print the truth."[85]

Permission to Visit the Soviet Union Denied

The archives of the British Foreign Office confirm that a number of famine-related resolutions passed at meetings in Canada were received and commented upon by officials. They included the resolutions adopted and forwarded (to Washington, Ottawa, and Geneva, as well as London) at a rally held at St. George's Hall (Albert Street) in Oshawa, Ontario, on Friday, October 13, 1933.[86] The *Oshawa Daily Times* provided much detail about that event. The mass meeting had been organized under the auspices of the Central Committee of Ukrainian Churches and various other organizations, the paper said, to protest against "the fiendish plan of the Soviet government to exterminate the greater part of the Ukrainian population by means of famine and massed deportation to Siberia." A crowd of over three hundred men and women had filled St. George's Hall to capacity. Prominent among the speakers, according to the *Daily Times*, were Gen. V. Sikevich, Father Mykola Olenchuk of the Ukrainian Greek Catholic Church, and Rev. L. A. Standret of the Ukrainian Presbyterian Church. Olenchuk was the first to speak, and he read aloud the appeal that had been issued by the leaders of the Ukrainian Catholic Church in Lviv to the world. He mentioned that he had attempted to visit the Soviet Union, but was denied admission. Olenchuk expressed his conviction that the Soviet Union was determined to "destroy that part of the Ukrainian nation that was not readily surrendering its allegiance to God or to the nation." When Standret took the floor, he declared, "The crime that is now being committed against the Ukrainian people calls to heaven for revenge" and, further, it "should have no room in the present civilized world, and it could have been prevented." Millions of Ukrainians were starving, he said, because the Soviet government was taking their grain away for export. According to the *Oshawa Daily Times*, "Rev. Mr. Standret rapped some correspondents, like Pierre Van [Paassen], who had writte[n] fallacious accounts of the events in the Soviet Union." Standret was reacting to insinuations that Ukrainians were being swayed by Hitler and the Soviet regime was thus impelled to stamp out the pro-German movement. The Ukrainians were rebelling, Standret stated, but their movement was for self-determination.

"One cannot expect," the *Daily Times* quoted him as saying, "to hear facts from a correspondent who is feasted by the Moscow foreign commissar and who was sen[t] over to justify the stand his paper had taken in regard to the Soviet regime."[87]

The rally's main speaker was Sikevich, who had fought against the Bolsheviks during the Ukrainian war of independence of 1917–21. The Soviet government, Sikevich stated, had betrayed all the promises and agreements it had made to Ukraine. Sikevich also criticized the former French premier Herriot for "failing to see the calamity of the Ukrainians in his visit there." Canadian workers who went to the Soviet Union, he noted, would come back dissatisfied with the conditions there. After listening to two more speakers, the meeting's participants passed four resolutions, which were then to be sent to the governments at Ottawa, London, and Washington and to the League of Nations. The first resolution protested the policy of "ruthless grain collections from the starving population of the Ukraine [that] aggravates and prolongs the conditions of famine and starvation," and it appealed to "the civilized world in the hope that it will force the Soviet Union to cease this inhuman policy of starving out the population of Ukraine." The second resolution resolved that Ukrainian Canadians would "use all their powers to help their brothers to break away from the rule of the Union of Soviet Socialistic Republics, and assist them in the formation of the independent Ukrainian state." A third resolution was aimed against three Ukrainian-language periodicals in Canada—*Ukraïns'ki robitnychi visty*, *Farmers'ke zhyttia*, and *Robitnytsia*—"published in the interests of the Communist movement." The final resolution protested forced migration and deportation, which violated "the most cardinal right of the Ukrainian people to live on their own territory," and appealed to "the civilized world to create a strong public opinion to force the Soviet government to desist from this policy of the annihilation of the Ukrainian race."[88]

Earlier, Olenchuk had made known his intention to visit the Soviet Union in a letter to Bishop Ladyka in April 1933. He was planning at the end of that month to visit several places in Soviet Ukraine and the Crimea (Kyiv, Kharkiv, Dniprostroi, Odesa, Sevastopol, and Yalta) and had put down a deposit of one hundred złoty for the tour. He did not expect to stay in the Soviet Union for longer than thirty days. But in May, Olenchuk wrote to the Ukrainian Catholic prelate in Canada from Berlin, informing him that he had waited for more than a month in Galicia for a Soviet visa and, never getting to visit Soviet Ukraine, was heading back to Canada.[89]

Stories about foreign journalists experiencing travel restrictions in the USSR surfaced especially in the summer of 1933, though such limitations had already existed for several months.[90] But as the case of Olenchuk showed, such difficulties in travelling to Soviet Ukraine applied not only to journalists. Indeed, while one Pulitzer Prize winner, Walter Duranty, enjoyed the favour of the Soviet authorities, another, the American playwright Marc Connelly (author of *The Green Pastures*), was banned from entering the Soviet Union altogether in the summer of 1933 "for a reason that has not been explained."[91] A year later, another person denied permission to enter the Soviet Union was Canadian-born Hanka Romanchych, who in the summer of 1934 attended the Ukrainian Women's Congress in Stanyslaviv (Ivano-Frankivsk), western Ukraine. Before she departed for the congress, which convened in July 1934, she had obtained a visa to enter the USSR in London. Like Olenchuk before her, she had hoped to travel from Warsaw to Moscow and from there to visit Kyiv, Kharkiv, Dniprostroi, Odesa, and the Crimea. Romanchych was asked to stop at the Soviet consulate in Warsaw beforehand; she did this, after the congress, and was asked to wait. Romanchych waited for two weeks before being told that she could not enter the Soviet Union and that her visa was annulled.[92] The *Edmonton Bulletin* speculated, "Perhaps it was because she took a prominent part in the sessions of a women's conference which represented a minority race in a perturbed Europe; she doesn't know—but when she presented her carefully secured visa for Russia, she found she could not gain entrance to the Soviet." Romanchych, the *Bulletin* said, had spent nearly a hundred dollars in cables to the Soviet Union and London, but was given only the "noncommittal response 'Moscow decides; only Moscow knows,' and many shrugs from Russian officials."[93] Romanchych's participation in the international congress was noted by the *Manchester Guardian*. That newspaper listed the various subjects discussed at the well-attended congress and added that "strong and united condemnation was expressed of Soviet misgovernment of the Great Ukraine, with its resultant extermination of millions of Ukrainians by famine."[94]

As the examples of Olenchuk and Romanchych illustrate, tours of the Soviet Union, which included Ukraine, were offered at the time of the famine and while groups were requesting that large-scale relief or inspectors be allowed into the rural districts. Rev. A. E. Kerr of the Augustine United (Presbyterian) Church of Canada in Winnipeg went on one such tour in 1934. On June 12, he wrote to R. K. Finlayson, the prime minister's executive assistant, informing Finlayson that he and Rev. Clarke Lawson of the Greenwood United Church were planning a trip to Europe. Among other places, he noted, "We shall visit Russia, ... travelling from Leningrad through Moscow, to Odessa on the Black Sea." The two men expected to be on their own, "except for perhaps a week when we shall be with a C.P.R. tour conducted by Professor [John] King Gordon."[95] A travel brochure produced in April 1934 offered sixty days in Europe, including a thirty-five-day tour of the USSR, for $625.00. Departing Montreal on the SS *Montclare* on July 4, with a return date of September 1, the itinerary included stops in the United Kingdom and other European countries. In Soviet Ukraine and the Crimea, the tour would visit Kyiv, Kharkiv, Odesa, Sevastopol, and Yalta.[96] After his return, Kerr shared his impressions of the trip at his church. Among other things, Kerr mentioned to his audience in the church's packed auditorium that there had been a famine in Ukraine—"costing the lives of five to ten million persons"—and that "unless one had a ration card, foodstuffs were very expensive."[97]

Journalist Carleton J. Ketchum's Speaking Tour

The year 1933 closed in Canada with a series of lectures by a Canadian journalist who had recently returned from the USSR. Carleton J. Ketchum, who worked for the *Ottawa Citizen*, the *Vancouver Province*, and later the *Daily Express* of London, had brought back pictures, which he showed at his public lectures across the country.[98] In December, he spoke in Winnipeg at the Canadian Ukrainian Institute Prosvita. There he mentioned the famine, stating that at least five million and possibly ten million people had "died from starvation and malnutrition in the Ukraine"—though, oddly, he gave the years in which the deaths had occurred as 1931 and 1932. (There was indeed major hunger at that time, though not on the scale of 1932–33.) Ketchum added that the worst was now over. For the first time in three years, he said, "people will now have bread because of the good crop." But he cautioned that there were "still serious shortages of meat and other foodstuffs, and also clothing."[99]

Ketchum toured Canada as a guest of the Canadian National Council of Education. Before visiting Winnipeg, he had spoken at various venues in Toronto, including the Empire Club and the Arts and Letters Club, and had "twice broadcast his impressions of present-day Russia."[100] Ketchum had travelled to the USSR in the summer of 1933 at the "instance" of the council. He told his audience at the Empire Club on November 30, 1933, that he had been anxious "to ascertain to what extent the first five-year plan had triumphed [and] to ascertain the prevailing conditions on the farm lands, especially under the new collective farm system that obtains in every part of Russia for eighty per cent of the farm lands are now collectively owned." Ketchum spoke of successes in the industrial sector but mentioned deaths that occurred during the winters of 1931 and 1932. In the winters of those years, he said, at least five million persons perished of starvation. He stated that had it not been "for the turning of the tide this summer when they had the best wheat crop since 1913, combined with the factor of American recognition, I doubt very much whether the Soviet regime could have gone on very much longer without drastic action in various sections, so far as Communistic policy is concerned." It is not clear how the "factor of American recognition" had helped turn the tide, but Ketchum blamed "drought" for the "malnutrition and lack of food" in Ukraine and the North Caucasus. He also raised the spectre of the kulak; many had remained in Ukraine, he alleged, and they were causing all sorts of problems. Whether kulaks in Ukraine had "found that the drought had caused general disorganization among the peasants or not, anyway, they decided that the time had arrived for what was tantamount to a small sized rebellion." Ketchum continued that although "the world has never known the extent of the uprising, through the strangling of the press, the Kulaks came to grips with the Soviet power with very serious consequences." Buildings were burned, cattle slaughtered, and "thousands of Kulaks, I imagine, were killed, but the poor peasant, of course, was the man who really suffered in the end, for at the end of the harvesting seasons of 1931 and 1932, there was no grain in the Ukraine at all which meant that there was no bread and even a Russian can't live long without bread."[101]

In his speech Ketchum revealed that he knew Duranty of the *New York Times*. He and Duranty had discussed the exodus to the cities, which, according to Ketchum, the two journalists estimated had involved about two million souls. "They came to the cities and there the conditions were very bad, particularly in Odessa, which I visited in the summer." But the worst was now behind, according to Ketchum, and he described the most recent harvest as the best since 1913. "I saw evidences of a fine harvest everywhere I went," he told his audience in Toronto. "They certainly had the tractors and they had the organization. After the catastrophe of the holocaust in the Northern Caucasus they sent down shock brigades because they were determined at all costs to consolidate their forces there." The result was that everything was "back on terra firma, as far as the Ukraine and the Northern Caucasus are concerned. That means that for the first time in three winters, the average Russian worker and peasant alike will eat bread."[102]

The reference to the winters of 1931 and 1932 may have caused confusion among Ketchum's listeners across Canada and readers of the many newspapers that covered his lectures. Later, in early 1934, Ketchum visited Edmonton. At one forum, he was asked, "Did you see any actual starvation in Russia?" He replied, "I didn't see myself but there is no question that in the winter of 1931–32 between 1,000,000 and 1,500,000 persons in the Ukraine and the North Caucasus perished as a result of starvation, malnutrition and exposure." Ketchum repeated his thesis that it was all the result of drought, conflict between the land-owning kulaks and the peasantry, and a breakdown of collectivization, but he mentioned also Moscow's refusal to stop its export program in spite of the "SOS for aid." Ketchum claimed he had asked Moscow officials why they did not help; he was told, "What were these people when the interests of the entire Russian nations were at stake? What are

1,000,000 in a population of 162,000,000? We had to refuse to interrupt our export program in order to maintain our foreign credits."[103] Speaking in Calgary in February, Ketchum told his audience at the packed-to-capacity Central United Church of a current Soviet slogan: "He who wants to live must labor and he who would idle must perish." He noted that the Soviet government had tried to turn the agricultural population into skilled workers, but failed—though it did succeed in producing machines. He predicted that while the USSR had exported considerably to maintain its credit abroad, now that machinery had been produced it was not necessary to export as much as before. In Calgary, Ketchum again intimated that he had spoken to a Soviet official about the famine. He was given the "cold-blooded reply," he said, that even if "10,000,000 persons had died of starvation, would that matter greatly if Russian credit were established abroad?"[104]

By the time he was speaking in Calgary and Edmonton, Ketchum had broken with the Canadian National Council of Education. During the final weeks of 1933, newspapers across Canada reported that Ketchum had cancelled coast-to-coast speaking engagements sponsored by the council, and that the reason he gave was the council's attempt to "muzzle" him. Ketchum claimed that the council's secretary, Maj. F. J. Ney, had intimated to him that he would be expected to speak on the "Old Days of the Famine and the Terror in Russia"—but not on trading possibilities with the USSR—and that his photographs should be submitted in advance for inspection. Ney denied these claims. Regarding the pictures that Ketchum had brought back with him—a total of about fifteen hundred—Ney said the council could only bear the cost of making some five hundred of them into slides, plus the council wanted to have a say in the selection. The council had not dictated the subjects on which Ketchum should speak, Ney said, but had only expressed that they not be of a "controversial political nature."[105] Ney confirmed he had told Ketchum that, after his Winnipeg visit, the council had "no more [speaking engagements] for him in Canada."[106]

As a result, Ketchum continued to speak across Canada, but no longer under the auspices of the council.[107] Yet newspapers now commented less on his declarations about the famine and more on his complaints about being "muzzled."[108] Bob Bouchette, author of the column "Lend Me Your Ears" in the *Vancouver Sun*, concluded that Ketchum had been told "that in order not to embarrass Mr. Bennett he must talk about the old days of the terror and the famine in Russia." Bouchette went further, alleging a conspiracy: "By every conceivable means—press, radio and lecture—a campaign has been waged to keep Canadians from learning the truth about Russia. There has been a conspiracy to stultify the judgements of Canadians by preserving them in the ignorance of the facts."[109] The same columnist had earlier ridiculed a story about four million deaths from starvation; that had been the kind of story, he claimed, that surfaced time and again. The "starvation story" Bouchette was commenting on was, as he said, "dated 'Berlin'"—proof, Bouchette mocked, of the enterprising nature of the capitalist press. "It was pretty cute of the New York Times correspondent to get the facts of the food situation in the Ukraine while he was sitting in a b[i]ergarten in the Hooeystrasse."[110]

When Ketchum was scheduled to speak at the Ukrainian Institute Prosvita in Winnipeg, it was feared that his lecture there would be disrupted by pro-Communist hecklers. However, that failed to happen—reportedly because no one without an admission card was permitted to attend the lecture.[111] But perhaps there was not much cause for pro-Communists to be wary of the roving speaker. After all, Carleton J. Ketchum was not Humphrey Mitchell.[112] The Ukrainian community in Winnipeg followed with interest what Ketchum had to say about the USSR. The weekly *Kanadyis'kyi farmer* claimed that five thousand people had gathered around the Ukrainian Institute Prosvita on the evening of Wednesday, December 6, to hear Ketchum speak. Certainly the attendance was high, for *Kanadyis'kyi farmer* believed that never in the Institute Prosvita's history had so many Ukrainians and non-Ukrainians come together for an event on its premises. Its report on Ketchum's speech mentioned his assertions of a famine in 1931 and 1932 and a robust harvest in 1933, in addition to his statement that the recognition of the USSR by the United States would lead to improvements for the Soviet people. *Kanadyis'kyi farmer* noted that Ketchum showed over a hundred slides that portrayed life in the Soviet factories, cities, and collective farms. The author of the report commented on the poor appearance of people depicted in the slides, both physically (particularly in their faces) and in their dress. Youth looked impoverished and poorly fed and attired.[113] It is not clear from the report, though, which places in the Soviet Union these slides represented.

Ukraïns'kyi holos commented on Ketchum's three lectures in Winnipeg. Of particular interest in its coverage of the talks with respect to the famine were his statements on official declarations about the colossal number of deaths caused by starvation. "The government recognizes that two million perished," *Ukraïns'kyi holos* said, yet Ketchum had no doubt that the number was much larger, at least five to seven million. When Ketchum returned to Moscow from Ukraine, the periodical noted, he asked a Soviet official why the USSR was exporting grain when millions were dying of hunger. Ketchum quoted the official as replying, "What is five million in a population of 161 million? It is important for us to maintain our credit with other states, and that is why we send grain abroad." The report in *Ukraïns'kyi holos* also commented on the slides that were shown: even though the images had been sanctioned by the Soviet authorities, they did not paint a flattering portrait of labouring people.[114]

The pro-Soviet *Ukraïns'ki robitnychi visty* interpreted the slides differently, as inferred from the title of its article about the Ketchum lectures in Winnipeg: "The Pictures on Their Own Spoke the Truth about the USSR, and Not Mr. Ketchum." In other words, regardless of what Ketchum had to say, for *Ukraïns'ki robitnychi visty* the pictures he showed told their own story, and it was a favourable one. The article seized on the statements Ketchum had made about the years of the famine to discredit reports of starvation in 1933. Ketchum spoke about 1931 and 1932—not about the current famine in Soviet Ukraine, the article said, that was being claimed in the Ukrainian "bourgeois press."[115] When Ketchum and the Canadian National Council of Education later parted ways, *Ukraïns'ki robitnychi visty* provided much commentary on Ketchum's charges of "muzzling."[116]

The huge attendance at the Ukrainian Institute Prosvita must have impressed Ketchum. Later, when he was in the business of trying to persuade the prime minister of Canada to engage his services for the benefit of the Conservative Party, Ketchum referred to his 1933 visit to Winnipeg. "After I spoke before the Ukrainians in Winnipeg North," he told Bennett's private secretary, Arthur Merriam, "I was told I could win a seat there hands down for the Conservative Party against all comers by appealing, with my knowledge of the Ukraine, to those people in my own way."[117] Even before he had travelled to the USSR, Ketchum was endeavouring to interest the prime minister in employing him. On April 12, 1933, Ketchum informed Bennett that he was planning another visit to the USSR in order to update his knowledge of that state and to obtain "'action' pictures for a lecture tour." Because he envisaged the trip to be his final one to the USSR he saw no cause to speak favourably of the Soviet system. He would be available for speaking engagements upon his return and wondered whether the "Conservative Party might be interested in 'using me' in this way for their benefit."[118]

After the rupture between Ketchum and the Canadian National Council of Education, Ketchum complained to Prime Minister Bennett that rumours were circulating on the eve of his return to Fleet Street in London that he was "in the pay of the Russians." He blamed Ney for these rumours. Ketchum revealed to the prime minister that when he had received his visa from the Soviet authorities he had promised that he would do what he could to improve relations between Canada and the USSR. Now that he was free of the obligations of the terms, he could write as he pleased.[119] If there had ever been a "muzzle," it would seem that it may have been imposed by the USSR. In letters to the prime minister's office, Ketchum alluded to difficulties in obtaining a visa (and to a medical problem, too, for which there were expenses). Ketchum may have blamed Ney for the rumours, but it appeared that some pro-Communists, too, were of the impression that Ketchum was sympathetic to the USSR. In January 1934, he addressed a group at the Mount Royal Hotel in Montreal. The public meeting was held under the auspices of the Saturday Night Club, described as an organization that was "being used by the Communist[s] as an extension in order to attract people who otherwise would not associate or be seen at communist meetings." He apparently disappointed the organization.[120] On August 9, 1934, Ketchum disclosed to Bennett that he had been approached indirectly by the Oblate Fathers to see if he would lecture on Soviet religious policy. He had, Ketchum said, about a hundred slides depicting destroyed churches and antireligious museums, which Ney, he claimed, had not been interested in using.[121] The Conservative Party showed no official interest in Ketchum's propositions.[122]

While writing to Bennett during 1933, Ketchum also wrote to the prime minister's rival, W. L. Mackenzie King. In a letter written in August, on stationery from the Hotel Metropole in Moscow, Ketchum informed King that he was back in Moscow for a couple of months primarily to write articles for *Pearson's Magazine* but also to collect material for an educational lecture tour of Canada. He hoped "to have the opportunity of a few long talks" about the USSR with the leader of the opposition, and he intimated there was an "immense market" in the Soviet Union that was open to "Canadian exploitation." The Soviet Union, he said, was in need of agricultural implements and rolling stock and undoubtedly could offer Canada "favourable trading conditions." Ketchum criticized Bennett's "hostility" toward trade with the Soviet Union but believed that, from conversations he had had (it is not clear with whom), Moscow would be open to negotiations with Ottawa in the wheat market.[123] Later in the year, in October, Ketchum (now in London, England) wrote to Edward Pickering, King's private secretary, informing him that he had "1700 first-class pictures" and was getting ready to set sail for Canada on November 3. He expressed the view that, now that the United States had recognized the USSR, Canada— considering the business that could be available—"should waste no time now in revealing a less hostile attitude toward Russia." Ketchum had "no personal interest" but had "endeavoured to develop for myself a reputation in the last year of being a Canadian friend of the Soviet Union." He hoped, "some day when Mr. King returns to power, if not before, to serve Canada officially in some capacity in Russia."[124] And on October 25, Ketchum again wrote to the Liberal Party leader, for Howard R. L. Henry, King's private secretary, acknowledged receipt of a letter and thanked the journalist for his conveyance of "congratulations on the results of the three [recent] federal by-elections."[125]

After Ketchum had completed his Canada-wide lecture tour, the *Prince George Citizen* discussed what that journalist had said alongside statements by the British engineer Allan Monkhouse, who had just published his memoir *Moscow, 1911–1933*. Monkhouse appeared to be impartial in his account of the USSR, said the *Citizen* in March 1934, and pointed to accomplishments as well as mistakes made there. There had been great strides in industrial construction, but the price to pay for them was exorbitant. Millions of people had to suffer for the mistakes, Monkhouse reportedly said in his book, and "many hundreds of thousands have already died of malnutrition and its effects." Comparing Monkhouse with Ketchum, the Prince George paper considered the latter more optimistic than the former, surmising that this was probably due to Moscow having allowed the Canadian journalist to "see only what the Soviet authorities desired him to see." Nonetheless, the paper noted, Ketchum confirmed the "reports of the holocausts which engulfed the Ukraine and Northern Caucasus during the winter famine of 1931–32, when millions of people perished of starvation while the Russian government continued to export grain which could have been used to feed them." Ketchum's message was that the tide had changed and there was an opening for greater trade between Canada and the USSR. While doubting that expanded trade between the two countries was necessarily desirable for British Columbians seeking an outlet for their timber, the *Prince George Citizen* hoped that the situation in the USSR had indeed changed, for the sake of, especially, the people "who have been caught in the jaws of the experiment." For all that had been said about Communist progress and capitalist shortcomings, the newspaper suggested the Soviet achievements could hardly be judged "outstanding." For "no system of government," it said, "can be held to be desirable which permits people to starve so that food which maintains them may be available for export." A translation of a letter received by a Prince George district resident from his sister in Ukraine was then shared with the *Citizen*'s readers. The letter writer provided insight into the collective farm system. To keep a cow, the family had to pay to the state a tax consisting of ninety-six litres of milk and fifty-four kilos of meat. Four members of the family together contributed 500 working days (the mother 58 days, the father 62 days, the letter writer 116 days, and "Demyen" 264 days).[126] "We received for each working day 800 grams of rye, 1 kilo and 740 grams of wheat, 300 grams of barley, unshelled corn 1 kilo and 600 grams, rasps 100 grams,…hemp seed 40 grams, millet 15 grams, potatoes 1 kilo, beets 600 grams, straw and chaff 5 kilo." The letter's author then turned to the subject of the famine. "This year is very painful, many hungry people died," she wrote. The letter writer's family had not suffered as much as others "because we are close to the line" but "further in Ukraine there are many villages without people." The writer recalled a village meeting at which "it was advertised if anybody wants to go there for a living." No one from her family's village went, but some from other villages "went there to look. Nice villages, everything grown up with weeds and grass, and dead people were lying in the houses." The letter related the case of a boy from a place near Kyiv who came to the family's house asking for food. "In the village from which he came were [once] 430 families," but now "there are about ten families." The year 1933 "will be signed in history," the letter finished. This family hoped "to see a better time in the future, but the future looks to us very dark."[127]

V. Timoshenko Speaks in Canada

On December 23, 1933, J. M. Gilchrist of Winnipeg composed a letter to Murdoch A. MacPherson, the attorney general of Saskatchewan. The letter concerned mainly the amount of grain that might be shipped out of Argentina, but it ended with a remark about a professor who was visiting Winnipeg and was expected to speak about wheat in another part of the world, namely the USSR. "There is a very interesting Russian here in Winnipeg until Sunday," Gilchrist informed the attorney general. After Sunday, he would be going on to Saskatoon and Edmonton, but was due back in the Manitoba capital on January 2 in order to address the local Canadian Club. "His name is Professor Timoshenko," Gilbert told MacPherson.[128]

The Ukraine-born University of Michigan professor of economics and statistics had just the previous year published a book about agriculture in the USSR, *Agricultural Russia and the Wheat Problem*. Canadian newspapers had announced the publication of the book and provided coverage of his lectures during his Canadian speaking tour.[129] Although Timoshenko did not offer any details about the famine, he did provide insights into Soviet agriculture, which (in the form of collective farming) he considered a failure. "As a result of the passive resistance of the peasants, who resent wholesale seizure of their product for the state after a year of toil, the Soviet government was near a complete breakdown in 1931," he told the *Edmonton Journal*. Subsequently, in 1933, the Soviet government "decided on a policy of more intensive supervision of the collective farms." But this failed to have an impact on the world grain market. "I don't believe Russia is a factor in world wheat markets, despite reports to the contrary," Timoshenko concluded.[130] In Winnipeg, Timoshenko spoke briefly with Manitoba Premier John Bracken on the subject of the former's recent book.[131]

Chapter Six

"HUNGER BENNETT": THE PRO-SOVIET COMMUNITY IN CANADA

During 1932 and 1933, Canada was in the midst of the Great Depression. The Dirty Thirties, as the Depression years were dubbed, were characterized by widespread unemployment, a fall in exports, and a drop in farming incomes. A significant number of out-of-work immigrants were forced to leave Canada and others were deported to their countries of origin for one violation or another.

The Great Depression, which began in 1929, affected and was manifested in Canada in a number of ways. The global demand for various primary products fell precipitously from that year onwards, and by 1933, the prices for Canadian goods had dropped to 62.6 per cent of what they had been in 1929.[1] The country's economy had an "overcapacity" of products such as wheat, pulp, and paper, and Canada competed with several other states (Argentina, Australia, the USSR, and the United States) in efforts to market surplus crops. Prairie farmers were adversely affected by the economic downturn. In Saskatchewan, farmers—handicapped not only by the Depression but also by drought and grasshoppers—saw their income in 1933 average only 1.5 per cent of what they had earned in 1928. National unemployment rose sharply. Whereas 2.5 to 4.2 per cent of the labour force was out of work in 1929, between 19.3 and 27 per cent of all

Canadian workers were unemployed in 1933. By May 1933, "1.5 million Canadians, almost 15 per cent of the population, were dependent on direct relief for physical survival."[2]

The Communist Party of Canada was essentially outlawed for much of the 1930s, though it exercised influence indirectly through a number of leftist organizations. One such organization was the Ukrainian Labour-Farmer Temple Association (ULFTA), which had formally come into being in 1918. By the mid-1920s the ULFTA—which was inspired by the labour movement in Canada and by developments in the USSR—boasted sixty-eight branches, with 2,500 adult male members; thirty-five women's branches, with 807 members; and twelve youth branches, with 445 members.[3] Of the nine members of the Communist Party of Canada arrested in 1931 under section 98 of the Criminal Code, for membership in an "unlawful association," two were ULFTA members: John Boychuk and Matthew Popowich (a former alderman candidate in Winnipeg). The trial of the nine Communists, and the subsequent incarceration of eight of them including Boychuk and Popowich (seven were sentenced to five years in prison and an eighth to two years), generated considerable media attention across the country, and protests by sympathizers to have them released were legion.

Of course, the media coverage included the non-English/French-language press in Canada as well, particularly as 90 per cent of the membership of the Communist Party of Canada was of neither British nor French background. The ULFTA published the newspaper *Ukraïns'ki robitnychi visty*, which came out three times a week and was printed in runs of ten thousand copies (the number of pages was reduced from six to four in 1932 because of the Depression), as well as papers for its women's and youth sections and for farmers.[4] The ULFTA followed events in Soviet Ukraine closely and reacted accordingly. Most of the organization's members were from western Ukraine, but a few were eastern Ukrainians who had come to Canada before the 1917 Bolshevik Revolution.[5] When famine struck Ukraine and parts of neighbouring Russia between 1921 and 1923, the ULFTA was among the organizations that mobilized their members for the purpose of providing relief. It raised over $65,000 to put to that objective.[6] After the Bolshevik Revolution, the ULFTA established ties with the USSR.

Members received training at schools in Moscow or left Canada to found agricultural communes in Soviet Ukraine.[7] The ULFTA may have represented a minority in the Ukrainian community but it was a strongly organized group.

In the 1930s, the ULFTA was confronted with a series of challenges. The first was the anti-Communist actions of the Canadian government, exemplified by the incarceration of Communist Party leaders. In July 1933, the police raided the headquarters of the ULFTA's mutual benefit organization, the Workers' Benevolent Association.[8] Further challenges came with the turn of events in Soviet Ukraine: the famine, the suicide of Mykola Skrypnyk, the execution of Ukrainian intellectuals at the end of 1934, and questions surrounding the fate of former prominent ULFTA members in Soviet Ukraine, such as John Sembay and the writer Myroslav Irchan.

Domestic Pressure on R. B. Bennett and Relations with the USSR

While the ULFTA faced these pressures, the Canadian prime minister's strident anti-Communist policies and the practice of deportations came under criticism. In fact, it has been argued that it was not so much the Conservative government's lack of effectiveness in addressing the Depression that contributed to its demise in 1935, but more its inability to understand the "social milieu created by the depression" and the prime minister's "'paranoia' toward communism."[9] The Conservative government's refusal to expand trade with the USSR at a time of depression was unpopular not only among labour activists but also with business lobbyists. Bennett's aversion to Communism was expressed in a statement he made in response to the emergence of the CCF. In a November 1932 speech, he declared that "the swing to the left behind Mr. Woodsworth is towards a government soviet in its character.... [T]hey seek out to capitalize on the unrest that exists...and we know that throughout Canada this propaganda is being brought forward by organizations from foreign lands that seek to destroy our institutions. And we ask every man and woman to put the iron heel of ruthlessness against a thing of that kind."[10] The CCF became tagged by its critics as a Sovietophile movement;[11] at the same time, critics of Bennett cast the prime minister in the image of his "iron heel of ruthlessness" statement. The CCF leader James S. Woodsworth was a member of Parliament and had supporters in the House of Commons. Further to the left, the Communist Party of Canada exerted influence through such mass organizations as the Canadian Labour Defence League and the Workers' Unity League.

Between 1932 and 1934, leftist groups in Canada campaigned to have the convicted Communists released and to institute normal trade relations with the USSR. There was also opposition against deportations, which had been ongoing on a mass scale. Specifically, in the thirty months prior to December 1932, 15,368 people had been deported from Canada—more than three-fifths of them for "being public charges" or "not able to make the living Canada promised them when they came here."[12] A number of "hunger marches" were staged around that time to draw attention to the plight of the destitute in Canada.[13]

Typical of the pressure put on the Conservative government was the petition of the Russian Workers-Farmers' Club in Mountain Park (a coal-mining area in western Alberta) directed to Prime Minister Bennett for the release of five members of the Communist Party who remained imprisoned in July 1934. The petition demanded the "unconditional release" of the "political prisoners" held in the Kingston Penitentiary and insisted that the prime minister consent to a meeting with a delegation of the Canadian Labour Defence League "that will wait on you at the Palliser Hotel [in Calgary] on or about July 9th, 1934."[14] In a protest against the death of Montrealer Nick Zynchuk—who on March 8, 1933, was shot by the police during an eviction from his rented premises—the Women's Section of the ULFTA in West Fort William, Ontario, demanded (among other things) the immediate resignation of "Hunger Bennett" and vowed to "work relentlessly till the Iron Heel policy of the present murder Government has been stopped."[15] In March 1933 a resolution passed at a meeting of "workers and poor farmers" of the Kistow district in Saskatchewan demanded that a proposed "cattle-oil deal with the Soviet Union be consummated" and protested "the preparations for the Imperialist War on which the Canadian Government spends millions of dollars for the purpose of crushing the Soviet Union, while at the same time refusing to appropriate funds for adequate relief for destitute Canadians."[16]

The prime minister also received anonymous letters. One, written in Ukrainian and dated June 3, 1933, was of a threatening nature. The letter, from "Unknown Comrade" to "Comrade Bennett," instructed the prime minister not "to fire at my comrades any more, as they have already murdered many of my comrades." The prime minister was also told to "discontinue...Section 98 of the criminal Code in the month of June." The "Unknown Comrade" said he would "wait for my comrades in Winnipeg, and if they are not there on account of you not having released them, you may expect me soon at your quarters." He claimed to know "comrades not only in Canada, but outside of Canada also."[17] A second letter from "Unknown Comrade," dated June 30, 1933, referred again to section 98 of the Criminal Code and made the following claim: "Comrade Bennett, I know that your door will be open for me and then I will tell you the trouble. I need not look for your quarters as I was there already and made enquiry through one of your Ministers in the French language and who supplied me with all the information that I needed."[18]

In addition to such letters from individuals, the prime minister received communications from the Friends of the Soviet Union society. Bennett was clearly irritated by a particular telegram sent by that organization, for he responded to it. The telegram expressed its "sense of shame" that Canada had not drawn on its airplanes for the rescue of Soviet citizens "shipwrecked in [the] Arctic," considering that the USSR had repeatedly come to the aid of others in distress.[19] In his reply, Bennett pointed out that Canada had no aircraft west of the Great Lakes capable of flying to the Arctic region, but also noted, "Canada has never received any request to render assistance to the Soviet at any point." He then admonished the sender of the telegram: "I do not know whether you are a Canadian or not, but if you are you should have some 'sense of shame' for having made statements wholly without foundation, to the detriment of your fellow citizens in this country."[20]

The Friends of the Soviet Union was among the organizations that protested the Conservative government's partial embargo on trade with the USSR shortly after its imposition in 1931.[21] In addition to the many resolutions in favour of full trade relations between Canada and the USSR that were forwarded by organizations to the federal government during 1933–34, others were also directed to provincial governments.[22] The resolutions were often titled "In favour of Full Diplomatic and Trade Relations between Canada and the Union of Soviet Socialist Republics."

In spite of the considerable pressure to expand trade with the USSR, the government in Ottawa also received statements of support for its existing policy. Supporters included an individual in Toronto who objected to relations with the USSR on religious as well as economic grounds.[23] At the turn of 1933, there was much commentary in the Canadian press about Winnipeg lawyer G. G. Serkau's proposal of an exchange of 100,000 head of Canadian cattle for Soviet petroleum and coal products.[24] As historians Kirk Niergarth and J. L. Black have noted, the proposal came at a time of large inventories and depressed prices in the cattle industry in Canada and of food shortages in the USSR. The proposal, negotiated by a syndicate of Canadian business representatives led by Serkau, thus attracted much support. However, Bennett was opposed to the proposal for ideological and other reasons.[25] Opposition to the deal was also expressed by others on account of the situation in the USSR, including Ukraine. Joseph Dyk, a solicitor in Toronto, wrote to the prime minister in February 1933 expressing his opposition to proposals of such barter arrangements. No such agreement with the Soviet Union should be made, Dyk urged Bennett, "until and unless the conditions of Russia and Ukraine are investigated."[26] Canada's minister of public works, H. A. Stewart, received a letter that month from another individual in Toronto, O. F. Cummins of Dock and Dredging Contractors. Cummins told Stewart that in the fall of 1932 he had covered the width of the USSR "from Vladivostock to Poland" and compared it to a firm that had entered an uneconomic business venture and had gone too far to turn back. "They are shaky and are only keeping on by using ruthless force," he said in his letter of February 21.[27] Letters such as this one would hardly have dissuaded the government from its policy. The Quebec government may not have agreed with Bennett on some matters, but apparently "they at least agree with him in his attitude towards the Soviets."[28]

Insight into understanding the prime minister's approach toward Canadian-Soviet relations is afforded in his April 1934 letter to the Friends of the Soviet Union in which he pointed out that the USSR had made no formal representation to the Canadian government for aid. A similar point was made in respect to the question of trade. "This Government has received no intimation from the Russian Soviet Government nor from anybody on their behalf that any barter transaction is desired," Bennett wrote in January 1933 to Nova Scotia Conservative MP Finlay MacDonald. He dismissed the matter as "one of propaganda to create a condition of despair...all part of organized propaganda having for its object the destruction of the existing system of government in this country."[29] Moreover, the prime minister accused the Soviet Union of "dumping" practices in the world market. "Regardless of the wants of [the Soviet] people," he asserted in the House of Commons on February 13, 1933, "regardless of the necessity of the preservation of them from hunger and starvation, wheat which could be easily converted into money on the English market was rushed there and sold at a price that bore no relation to the cost of production, the result being that all the rest of the world suffered."[30]

Surveillance and Arrests

While Communist Party leaders were behind bars, Conservatives still complained of Communist activity in Canada. In the opinion of G. B. Nicholson, MP for Algoma East, the USSR was "at war with Canada" in addition to being "at war in her own country." "It has been proven in the courts," he declared in March 1932, "that the Soviet government sent money into Canada to pay Communistic organizers to disrupt this country." Russell Nesbitt, the member for Toronto Bracondale, charged that even though Communist Party leaders were imprisoned in Kingston, the aims of the organization were being furthered by "associations affiliated with the party." He singled out the ULFTA, the Jewish Labor League, and a Finnish club in Toronto. Children were "taught disloyalty to the country of their adoption," Nesbitt complained.[31] That same month, a concert sponsored by the Friends of the Soviet Union was given in the ULFTA hall in Winnipeg in "aid of the delegation which is to leave the city next month on a visit to the Soviet Union."[32] A large delegation planned to leave Winnipeg in September 1932 in time for an official Soviet celebration of the completion of the Five-Year Plan.[33]

On April 30, 1932, Stefan Worobeck was arrested in Montreal and tried in Halifax on charges that the ULFTA's TODOVYRNAZU (Association for Aid to the Liberation Movement in Western Ukraine)—an organization of which he was secretary—had received funds not only to aid the revolutionary movement in western Ukraine but also for the purpose of furthering the work of the Communist Party of Canada in western Canada.[34] In the midst of such trials the ULFTA held its thirteenth annual convention, in July 1932. Messages of greetings were read at the Winnipeg venue from different parts of North America as well as from Lviv, in western Ukraine, and from the Soviet Ukraine capital, Kharkiv. "The special message from the Ukraine," a news report said, "was given hearty and prolonged applause by the attending delegates." Growth in membership was announced: in the previous year, the ULFTA had gained 1,600 new members and added eighteen new branches. The combined membership of the ULFTA and its women's and youth sections now stood at 8,080.[35]

After the arrest of Communist Party of Canada leaders, the ULFTA came under pressure from opponents who called for its proscription. On June 9, 1933, the Canadian Finnish organization Suomi Local was declared to be Communist and banned from using a community hall at Wolf Siding, Ontario.[36] Later in June, in Manitoba the ULFTA was sued by members of the Ivan Franko Society, who asked that the Teulon Community Hall be restored to the society's ownership. In the statement of claim, the ULFTA was described as an "unlawful revolutionary society."[37] Then, on July 5, the RCMP raided the ULFTA headquarters in Winnipeg and seized the records of its fraternal wing, the mutual insurance organization Workers' Benevolent Association (WBA), which had refused to appear before a government auditor appointed to investigate it.[38] In condemning the action, the WBA characterized it as a general attack of the "Canadian capitalist class and their lackeys, the leaders of the Ukrainian Nationalist organizations, against the farmers' movement in Canada, against the workers who struggle for better living conditions."[39] Days later, a confrontation between ULFTA supporters and Ukrainian National Council members occurred at a meeting of the council in the premises of the Prosvita Reading Society. The *Winnipeg Free Press* described the incident as a "bloody riot." On the same page, it reported a story about the breaking up of a demonstration in Halifax by sympathizers of deportee John Sembay, who had been boarding a ship bound for the USSR.[40] Meanwhile, pro-Communists in Canada were responding to banning demands with some of their own; one of their targets was the Ukrainian War Veterans' Association in Saskatoon, which they charged was pro-Fascist.[41]

At the end of July and beginning of August, without waiting for the books to be returned to the WBA, the ULFTA held its annual convention. The association reported that it now had approximately 9,000 members (including the women's and youth sections) and owned seventy-five buildings.[42] Its WBA had registered an increase of 1,380 members over the 1932–33 year and had established four new branches.[43] The situation in western Ukraine (the territories in Poland, Romania, and Czechoslovakia) was the focus of another annual convention—that of the ULFTA-allied, 5,000-plus-member TODOVYRNAZU.[44] A speech delivered during the ULFTA's convention distanced this organization from the nascent CCF, which, since its founding, was often misleadingly associated with Communism and pro-Soviet tendencies by its critics.[45] By the close of 1933, the ULFTA had reviewed its development since its founding. Among the accomplishments of the Left that were highlighted was the election of Jacob Penner (born in Ukraine into a Mennonite family) to Winnipeg's city council and Andrew Belicki to the city's school board, "interpreted by the workers and farmers in the west as a great victory for the 'toiling masses.'"[46] A show of force by the pro-Communists had been displayed in the May Day celebration in Winnipeg "sponsored by the Communist Party of Canada." Some four thousand people were said to have taken part in the parade and demonstration on May 1, 1933.[47] At the close of the year, Jack Nakoff, a sympathizer of the Soviet Union and former coal miner in Alberta, took his Sovietophilism to such lengths as to name his Canadian-born son "Stalin," pack his family's bags, and, with his wife and son, board the liner *Duchess of York* in St. John, New Brunswick, destined for the "workers' paradise."[48]

It is not clear whether the delegation that intended to leave Winnipeg in September 1932 ever visited the USSR as originally planned.[49] Sam Patterson, who visited the USSR under the auspices of the Friends of the Soviet Union and spoke at various forums after his return, left the coal-mining town of Blairmore, Alberta, for the Soviet Union on October 14, 1932.[50] Another group, headed by Jack Cowan, visited the USSR in 1934. After the group's return, Cowan addressed five thousand people in Montreal on December 20, 1934, at a meeting held by the Friends of the Soviet Union, stating that "newspaper reports about starvation in the Ukraine which were circulated in 1932 were not true." According to an RCMP report, Cowan maintained that everyone in the USSR had "plenty to eat, that prosperity reigns everywhere."[51]

Jews and Communism

The RCMP in Canada increasingly paid attention to the growth of the radical right as well as the radical left. In 1932, Adolf Hitler's Nazi Party had emerged as the largest faction in the German Reichstag, and in January 1933, Hitler was appointed chancellor of Germany, gradually and ruthlessly establishing a dictatorship. Nazi ideology was both racist and anti-Communist—and both came together in a stereotype that twinned Jews with Bolshevism. The influence of that stereotype reached beyond the borders of Germany. In Canada, exchanges occurred in the letters pages of newspapers about the alleged predominance of Jews in the Soviet government. In Ontario, the *Kingsville Reporter* asserted in 1934 that "while the Jews in Germany were being persecuted and slaughtered, the Jewish rulers in Russia were perpetrating more hideous atrocities upon Russian peasants."[52]

Earlier, in April 1933, an unnamed minister of an unnamed Christian denomination visited Winnipeg and recounted to the *Winnipeg Free Press* a "strange tale of horror and persecution of Christians in Russia by Soviet commissars, mostly Jews." The minister, who had managed to leave the USSR for Germany in 1928, alleged that the Soviet Union was "today ruled by Jews, masquerading behind Russian aliases." Hitler, he asserted, had "saved Germany from the Communists and many of them are Jews."[53] The minister's statements were immediately challenged by A. N. Shinbane, president of the Canadian Zionist Organization in western Canada. He compared the minister's claims with the propaganda of the Black Hundreds of the Tsarist era and saw in them the influence of Nazi Germany. Shinbane believed that the minister intended to create more of an anti-Jewish than an anti-Soviet feeling. The Jewish religion, Shinbane stated, was persecuted in the USSR "as savagely as the Christian"; he disputed that the majority of Soviet "commissars" were Jews, countering that only about 5 per cent were Jewish—and that even they were "not professing Jews."[54] For his part, Rabbi Oscar Zilberstein of Winnipeg suggested that the Jews in the USSR suffered the most at the hands of the Communists. The largest number of them, he said, were former traders "declassed and doomed to starvation," while no Jew was "allowed to teach his children his religion, and the Hebrew language is prohibited altogether."[55]

Nonetheless, the claims of Jewish preponderance in the Soviet government persisted. A letter published in the *Winnipeg Free Press* in early June 1933 quoted unnamed German newspapers that alleged that of 503 members of the Soviet government, 406 were Jews. "What Soviet Russia does at present isn't the will of the Slavic people," the anonymous letter writer from Sturgeon Creek, Manitoba, declared, "but the will of a predominately foreign government."[56] Rabbi Zilberstein replied, admonishing the newspaper for publishing such a letter.[57] Discussion on the subject of Jews, and specifically of their status in Germany, also took place in the Legislative Assembly of Manitoba. A motion of protest against the persecution of Jews by the Hitler administration was carried in the house in a vote on April 25.[58]

The same themes and insinuations appeared in newspapers beyond Winnipeg,[59] and within Canada's Ukrainian community, too.[60] As noted by historian Orest Martynowych, in an essay about the attitude of Ukrainian war veterans in Canada toward Nazi Germany and Jews in the 1930s, "References to the disproportionately high percentage of Jews in the Communist Party and in the Soviet bureaucracy and political police, and criticisms of prominent Communists of Jewish origin ... appeared in a number of Ukrainian-Canadian weeklies during these years."[61] He notes that few "Ukrainian Canadians lent much credence to conspiracy theories about a Judeo-Bolshevik plot to dominate the world," though "some of the men who attained high office and represented Ukrainian Canadians on the national and international level shared such attitudes."⁶²

Jews and Russians were paired together with Communists in a pastoral letter about the famine issued by Ukrainian Orthodox Archbishop Ioann Teodorovych, who headed the Ukrainian Orthodox Church in both Canada and the United States. The American-based prelate wrote of Ukraine languishing "under the red Jewish-Russian occupation."⁶³ And, as noted by Martynowych, statements twinning Jews with Bolshevism were made at certain community rallies in 1933 and 1934.⁶⁴ At one of them (in Montreal, July 1933), a Sitch leader declared that "Jews have devised the diabolical stratagem of destroying Ukrainians."⁶⁵ An undated letter addressed to Bennett, written mostly in Ukrainian but partly in English by a self-described "Ukrainian Nationalist" and veteran, spoke of a "Russian Je[w]ish Government in Moscow" and purported to warn the prime minister about the international threat posed by "Jewish Communist propaganda."⁶⁶ While such anti-Semitic remarks were indeed uttered, Martynowych concludes that "even among the most jaded war veterans, anti-Semitism never became an obsession or a guide to action, as it was for [Adrien] Arcand's National Christian Social Party and [William] Whittaker's Nationalist Party."⁶⁷

The allegations of Jewish dominance of the Soviet government as well as the reaction to such accusations by Jewish Canadians were discussed in an *Ukraïns'kyi holos* editorial, after Ukrainian demonstrators in Boston were assailed by pro-Communists. "When someone says that the administration of the Soviet Union is in the hands of Jews," the editorial said, "many Jews in Canada and the United States are offended by this. They see in this anti-Semitic agitation." Jews, according to the editorial, would point out that they "also suffered much from the Soviet regime; the Soviet government ruined Jews materially, prohibited private trade, confiscated Jewish property, and, as it closed Christian churches so, too, has it closed Jewish synagogues." Yet it was strange that "among the Jews the organization of an anti-Communist movement was not visible." In Ukraine, the editorial continued, there was a famine, in which the number of victims was equivalent to either half of or the entire population of Canada (citing Ketchum as stating that five to ten million people had died of starvation). The editorial went on to say that it was for that reason Ukrainians had demonstrated on the streets of Boston. But there were attempts to break up the demonstration and the police arrested some of the culprits. Who had been arrested? The editorial proceeded to answer its own question, in part: Lillian Katz, Herman Stroiman, Victor Davidov, Abraham Baxer, Henry Aideman. "If these are not Jewish names," the editorial declared, "they are not Chinese." The editorial, which also listed the names of some arrested during a New York demonstration, then asserted that Jews were coming to the defence of the Soviet government, which was starving the Ukrainian people to death. *Ukraïns'kyi holos* would, of course, agree with the statement that the Communist Jews did not represent all Jews, continued the editorial, but what would happen if Ukrainians attacked Jews at a demonstration against Nazi policies? The question cued a discussion of Symon Petliura, the portrayal of Ukrainians vis-à-vis pogroms, and the 1917–21 Ukrainian war of independence.[68] Thus was the position of *Ukraïns'kyi holos*. Petliura had been assassinated in Paris in 1926 by Sholom Schwartzbard, who asserted that he had carried it out in vengeance for pogroms for which he held the UNR leader responsible. Ukrainians in Canada and elsewhere suspected Moscow's involvement in the assassination. As it happened, the editorial in *Ukraïns'kyi holos* was published before a 1934 visit to North America by Schwartzbard, who was acquitted after his trial in Paris. That visit prompted further public discussion.[69]

The *Ukraïns'kyi holos* editorial was published at a time when Ukrainians in Canada were voicing frustration that little was being done in the West in terms of applying pressure on the Soviet regime in regard to the famine. The Mennonite community felt frustrated, too. Decades later, Frank Epp wrote that after the conclusion of Western friendship pacts with the Soviet Union and the awarding of a permanent seat on the Council of the League of Nations to the USSR, the "Russian Mennonite community, at home (in Russia) and abroad (Canada and South America), could not understand this." To them, he said, "Germany had been their only sympathetic friends through the hours of darkest crisis," while "Hitler represented the world's only hope of stopping the spread of Communism." The indifference of the West, on the one hand, and "compassionate understanding in Germany on the other," Epp noted, drove "many of them to embrace the National-Socialist cause."[70]

The anti-Semitism expressed in various quarters may have led some to believe that the USSR was making positive strides in advancing the status of Jews. During 1933 and 1934, the *Western Jewish Bulletin* (Vancouver) announced the appointment of a Jew as the USSR's ambassador to Nazi Germany, pointed out that Maxim Litvinov ("one of the two Jewish members of the Soviet cabinet") was selected to go to the United States to negotiate recognition, and reported Moscow's invitation to German-Jewish refugees to settle in the Soviet Far Eastern region of Birobidzhan, where the "Soviet government is building an autonomous Jewish republic."[71] Referring to the Birobidzhan project and asserting that the Soviet regime had "removed all legal disabilities of the Jews," an article in the *Western Jewish Bulletin* in August 1933, attributed to the Organization for Jewish Colonization in Russia (ICOR), read: "We stress the fact that while the Jewish masses are being persecuted in Germany and many countries, and while anti-Semitism is rampant everywhere, it is only the Soviet Union that is demonstrating how the problem of the nationalities has been completely solved."[72]

In Canada, the famine was discussed less in the Jewish press than in the Ukrainian or Mennonite newspapers, but the various difficulties experienced by the far-flung and more urbanized Jewish community in the USSR were covered.[73] Jews from North America who travelled to the USSR brought back stories about the famine. In June 1934, the *Ottawa Journal* featured an account by Max Mosion of his three-month visit to Ukraine. Mosion, a resident of Canada since 1901 who was born in Odesa, had decided to visit his elderly mother in Ukraine. During his visit, he had travelled to "more than 100 Ukrainian villages," and "everywhere he found the spirit of revolt against the present system and the feeling that even the worst phases of the Czarist regime were infinitely to be preferred." Later in his account, Mosion wrote, "Canada is good enough for me. Why in the Ukraine during the famine they had to eat the cats and the dogs, and as a result you do not see either of those pets there."⁷⁴ The *Ottawa Journal* article was summarized in Ukrainian community papers in Canada.⁷⁵

As they gauged developments under the Stalinist regime, Ukrainians in Canada perceived that ethnic Ukrainians had become a minority in the governance of Soviet Ukraine—while they were beleaguered in western Ukraine, as Poland moved toward rapprochement with the USSR—and were losing complete control over their destiny. "When in Moscow the government is becoming more Russian," remarked *Ukraïns'ki visty* in late October 1932, "in Kharkiv the government [in Soviet Ukraine] is more and more ceasing to be Ukrainian."⁷⁶ Although many in the community considered the famine a deliberate attempt to debilitate Ukrainians, there was also awareness of efforts (such as the one coordinated by Cardinal Innitzer in Vienna) of bringing together various groups whose compatriots and coreligionists in the USSR were affected by the famine. Indeed, when Innitzer's delegate, Ewald Ammende, visited North America he emphasized in a memorandum that his committee comprised "all confessions: Catholics, Protestants, Orthodox, Reformed, Jews." Ammende's memorandum referred to deaths from starvation among the Jewish and German minorities in the USSR; it also noted that Harry Lang, the "correspondent of the 'Jewish Forward' of New York," had visited districts of Soviet Belarus and Soviet Ukraine and had stated that "40% of the population including a great percentage of Jews in those districts alone have died of hunger." Ammende went on to declare that "even the small German minority in Soviet Russia, now less than one million, has recently lost 140,000 members through death by starvation in the Ukraine, north of Caucasus, and in the Volga district."⁷⁷

In September 1933, *Novyi shliakh* published an eyewitness account by a Galician Ukrainian who had been able to flee the USSR. The fugitive asserted that it was incorrect to associate Jews with Communism and the Soviet secret police. While there were Jews in the OGPU, he maintained, the majority were Russians and Poles, and a very few were Ukrainians.⁷⁸ Jews had become hostile to the Soviet regime after the abolition of the New Economic Policy (a Lenin-era policy that allowed for a mixed economy, which was abolished by Stalin in 1928), and after 1929 their sympathy toward "Ukraine and its national interests" grew.

The Galician, who had worked in various Soviet public institutions, stated that among Jews in Ukraine, "especially Komsomol members," there "were many who considered themselves Ukrainians."[79] A month later, *Kanadyis'kyi farmer* reprinted a story that had appeared in the Philadelphia Ukrainian Catholic newspaper *Ameryka* about Jews dying of starvation in Ukraine. A Jewish resident of the city who was originally from Bila Tserkva in the Kyiv region had visited the *Ameryka* editorial office, where he explained that he had received a letter from a relative in Bila Tserkva; it was written in Ukrainian because she attended Ukrainian school there. In this letter, the relative had written that several members of her family had perished from starvation and that others would suffer a similar fate if they did not receive aid from U.S. relatives by way of the Torgsin store. The recipient of the letter, according to *Ameryka*, was about sixty years old, no longer healthy and strong. He had not been working for seven years already and was being supported by two of his daughters. One of the daughters received twelve dollars a week, and the other, only six dollars. He said with tears in his eyes that he could not help his family, who were, in Bila Tserkva, threatened with death by starvation.[80]

Ukrainians and Communism

The "canard of Judeo-Bolshevism," writes Martynowych, was "invoked mainly to discredit Ukrainian-Canadian communists rather than to foment hostility against local Jews (though that was an inevitable consequence)."[81] During exchanges about "Jews and Communists" in Winnipeg's mainstream press, a letter by L. Schoor was published in the *Winnipeg Tribune*. "Bolshevism is not a peculiar trait of the Jews in particular that I can see," he averred. "No race or creed could claim to be specially adopted for Bolshevism or Communism."[82]

In 1932 and 1933, "Communism" was also associated with Ukrainians in Canada. At the end of 1932 and beginning of 1933, the *Winnipeg Tribune* reported on a tax riot that had taken place in Arborg, a town in Manitoba's Interlake region. At the end of November 1932, a group of demonstrators, reacting against tax sales, demanded the resignation of B. I. Sigvaldson, the reeve of the Rural Municipality of Bifrost.

When he refused, "alien agitators leading the demonstrators" attacked him in Arborg and destroyed municipal records.[83] On December 2, the *Winnipeg Tribune* ran an editorial complaining that while Ukrainians and Icelanders lived side by side in the Interlake region, Ukrainians were "endeavoring to break up the only unit of ordered government they can reach—the rural municipality." Ukrainian community leaders were faulted for their "failure to make Canadians out of their Ukrainian compatriots." If such leaders did not rise to the task, the editorial warned, then "the very name of Ukrainian will become a term of reproach in this country." The editorial maintained that Canadians had to take some of the responsibility, too, because they had been "told time and time again that constructive work was needed to counteract Red propaganda among the Ukrainians."[84] The next day, the newspaper commented that "the Ukrainian rioters of Arborg have been made dupes," because "seemingly, nobody but Red agitators would take the trouble to talk with them."[85]

The *Tribune* editorial did not go unchallenged, but its general message hit a nerve.[86] Community leaders outside the ULFTA camp took pains to distance the group in Canada from Communism. Over the course of 1933, various organizations waged a campaign against Communism by staging mass meetings across the country and by adopting resolutions and then forwarding them to the federal government. One such resolution was passed at a mass meeting held in the Prosvita Hall in Windsor, Ontario, in January 1933. The meeting—jointly organized by the Prosvita Society, the Ukrainian War Veterans' Association, the Ukrainian Sporting Sitch Association of Canada, the local Ukrainian Catholic parish, and the Ukrainian Benevolent Association—called for "all the other Ukrainian national, cultural, educational and political organizations all over the Dominion of Canada, to establish a united front against the ignoble activities of those of Ukrainian descent who are prone to serve the Muscovite Bolsheviks, in order thus to wage a successful combat against those who are responsible for the present unhappy predicament of our fatherland, Ukrainia." The resolution passed at the meeting (reportedly attended by over seven hundred people) also appealed to "the administrative authorities of our adopted country, the Dominion of

Canada, that they assist us in our struggle against the Communist element, which by its activities endangers the happiness and welfare of all the loyal, upright and model citizens of Canada, the element which strives to raise our adopted country to the same moral and material pandemonium as it did in the case of our beloved Ukrainian lands."[87]

A resolution passed by two hundred people assembled in the town hall of Derwent, Alberta, was typical of the declarations against Communism forwarded to the federal government in 1933. The resolution, dated June 10, asked the prime minister to deport "Communist leaders, speakers, and all those actively occupied in spreading Communism." It also requested Ottawa to use its influence to counteract the "intended removal by Russia of 15,000,000 Ukrainians from Ukrainia, their native land, and settling it with tested Communists."[88] It is not clear to what this threat of deportation referred, but in late April 1933 a United Press (UP) dispatch published in the *Border Cities Star* had centred on two Soviet decrees intended to establish fixed zones of residence for the USSR population. The first decree divided the USSR into three main areas. The first of these—comprising Moscow, Leningrad, Kharkiv, and other centres—would be a restricted zone from which "the hostile classes and elements" would be expelled. In that zone alone, the syndicated UP story said, the "decree involved a revision of a population of more than 15,000,000 persons."[89] The London Ukrainian Bureau, too, had already alluded to the Soviet decree of December 27, 1932, on the compulsory passport system and the purging of undesirable elements from Kharkiv and other Soviet urban centres.

Ukrainians also joined with other groups in the campaign against Communism. In August 1933, *La Presse* reported that representatives of various Orthodox churches in Montreal had decided to meet to discuss cooperation in combatting Communism. The delegates met at the Yugoslavian consulate on Sainte Catherine Street, and the consul, M. N. Perazic, accepted their invitation to assume the role of patron of the joint movement.[90] In addition to mass meetings and resolutions, Ukrainian efforts included articles and letters submitted to, and published in, the mainstream press that aimed to disassociate the community from Communism. A letter in the *Lethbridge Herald*, by a writer identified only as "Ukrainian," bore the title "Ukrainians Are

Not 'Red.'" Its author began by stating that a doctor had once asked him the question, "Why is it that you Ukrainians show such red tendencies out here in Canada?" By way of an answer, the author asserted that the "Russian octopus" had its "tentacles'" in Canada, too, and tried its best to discredit Ukrainians in the eyes of Canada and the world. The letter writer then provided his perspective on recent Ukrainian history, which included the subject of the famine. "Our leaders and intelligentsia have been killed off," he wrote, and "now the whole nation faces extermination through deliberately planned starvation."[91] Toward the end of 1933, W. J. Black, director of the federal departments of colonization and agriculture, requested of the prime minister that he receive the leader of the Ukrainian Catholic Church in Canada, Bishop Ladyka, for an interview. "No one understands better than he does that a section of our Ukrainian people have conducted themselves in a manner disloyal to our institutions," Black wrote to Bennett. He expressed the hope that Bennett would receive Ladyka and give him encouragement in his work against "disruptive influences."[92] The prime minister was not able to meet with Ladyka, but the latter did speak with the minister of labour, Wesley Ashton Gordon.[93]

The campaign received the support of the Winnipeg mayor (and MLA), Ralph Webb. "Do you want starvation? Do you want murder? Do you want a man with a gun behind your back on your job? Do you want Moscow to run this city? Do you want your homes taken away?" These things would happen, Webb contended in November 1933 on the eve of municipal elections, if members of the left-wing Independent Labour Party and pro-Communists assumed control of the local city council.[94] Later, in March 1934, Webb wrote to Minister Gordon and complained about the federal government not being sufficiently diligent on the "Communist question" and asserted that the province lacked the necessary powers to deal with the problem. In his letter, Webb also pointed to efforts that members of the Ukrainian and other communities were making in their campaigns against Communism. "A few days ago the Ukrainians, Poles and Germans and other nationalities who have been labelled as Bolshevists *and who are not*, held a large meeting in this city" and they passed a resolution asking the federal government to do "something definite about matters," he informed Gordon. He

148 Chapter Six

was mentioning this, Webb told Gordon, because there was so much "misunderstanding, in the East particularly, and even here in Western Canada to some extent, that Bolshevism and Communism, and all their affiliations, are carried on entirely by the non-English speaking people."[95] During 1933, the *Winnipeg Tribune* ran a series on Manitoba's ethnic communities. When it came to the segment on Ukrainians, the article stressed that "loyalty to Canada is another factor which the Ukrainians clearly demonstrate. Only a very small percentage of Ukrainians have accepted the Communist teachings. The overwhelming majority are content to remain true to their adopted country."[96]

Ukraïns'ki robitnychi visty and the Famine

From 1932 to 1934, the ULFTA newspaper *Ukraïns'ki robitnychi visty* emphasized the achievements of the Soviet system in Ukraine while denouncing both Polish rule in western Ukraine and the Conservative government in Canada. The paper published pictures of Soviet Ukrainian factories, of women working in industrial plants, and of mobilized revolutionary youth alongside articles about the successes of the Five-Year Plan and the benefits of the Soviet system.[97] In late 1932, the newspaper commented on articles by Frederick Griffin and Pierre van Paassen, so as to counter the "fabrication of lies against the Soviet Union." The articles by van Paassen were described as "even more solid than those of Griffin."[98] When Sam Patterson and John Brown came to Winnipeg in January 1933, the newspaper encouraged readers to attend their lecture. "They will relate the life of the Soviet workers and their heroic completion of the Five-Year Plan in four years," assured the announcement in *Ukraïns'ki robitnychi visty*.[99] That same month, a drawing in the newspaper containing images of factories, cranes, buildings, an airplane, a railway, tractors, and a large sheaf of grain triumphantly proclaimed the completion of the Five-Year Plan in four years.[100] Canadian engineer John Calder's impressions of the USSR were also related, though it is not clear where they were originally published.[101] An article in June focused on the strides made in the city of Dnipropetrovsk, where in the last fifteen years, the article said, the population had tripled, from 130,000 inhabitants to 400,000.[102]

While the mainstream press and other Ukrainian-language periodicals drew attention to the attempts by refugees to cross the Dnister River to Romania, *Ukraïns'ki robitnychi visty* reported on the question of Chinese refugees from Manchuria in the USSR.[103] When the United States recognized the government in Moscow, the pro-Soviet camp applauded the move.[104]

In October, *Ukraïns'ki robitnychi visty* reported on a meeting, organized under the auspices of TODOVYRNAZU, that took place in Fort William, Ontario. Some 250 people were said to have attended at the local ULFTA hall on October 4. The organizers did not limit the invitation to ULFTA members, but also extended it to people in the rival camp in order that they may "learn the truth about the imagined famine in Soviet Ukraine and about the real famine in Western Ukraine." According to the report, a good number of people from the rival camp came to the meeting, including a person who had spoken about the famine recently at the local Prosvita hall. Unlike the Prosvita leaders, the report alleged, the ULFTA's speakers "proved by the very words of eyewitnesses, noted people in the bourgeois world, by the large bourgeois press, that there is no famine in Soviet Ukraine." The ULFTA speakers pointed to the Soviet harvest, which they described as the best in thirty-five years. Édouard Herriot's statements on the famine were also cited. The unnamed speakers "explained the actual situation in Soviet Ukraine and in the whole Soviet Union without covering up the shortcomings which, for the most part, appear as a result of 'laziness or wrecking.'"[105] In the autumn of 1933, *Ukraïns'ki robitnychi visty* drew its readers' attention to the aphorism "He who will not work, shall not eat"—an aphorism that, the newspaper said, was currently being supported in the Soviet Union.[106] Indeed, J. F. Fox of Vancouver had already uttered a statement along those lines back in November 1932. And in late June 1933, the *Calgary Herald* quoted George Palmer (the former staff reporter for the *Moscow Daily News* who was in the USSR from April to December 1932) as asserting that "work or starve" was a dictum in the Soviet Union. "The majority of those who preferred death to work were permitted to die off," claimed Palmer, a past *Calgary Herald* reporter.[107]

During 1933, *Ukraïns'ki robitnychi visty* followed with interest the evolution of United States–Soviet Union relations as those states gravitated toward rapprochement.¹⁰⁸ When that recognition finally came, an *Ukraïns'ki robitnychi visty* editorial called it a reply to the interventionists in Berlin and Tokyo. Nazi Germany, the newspaper asserted, aspired to separate Ukraine from the Soviet Union. The Ukrainian nationalist press, it declared, waged "a filthy defamation of the Ukrainian people in Ukraine, describing them as cannibals" and enlisted in their campaign "specialists even in cassocks" such as Cardinal Innitzer. No one listened to the campaigners, the editorial remarked, which hailed the American recognition as "another great victory of Red Soviet diplomacy."¹⁰⁹

During a time when other organizations were drawing attention to the famine in Soviet Ukraine, the ULFTA press published articles about hunger in western Ukraine. In October 1932, for example, *Ukraïns'ki robitnychi visty* reported that the population of Transcarpathia in Czechoslovakia was being threatened by a terrible famine.¹¹⁰ A month later, it reported on hunger in Transcarpathia, Romania, and Poland.¹¹¹ Stories about "famine" in territories outside the Soviet Union continued into 1933.¹¹² The newspaper criticized the rival camp for focusing their protests on (and spreading "lies" about) Soviet rule in Ukraine rather than on conditions in western Ukraine.¹¹³ In its view, it was the people in the western Ukrainian territories who were in need of help.¹¹⁴

Conditions in western Ukraine, rather than those in Soviet Ukraine, were thus the focus of public protests by ULFTA supporters. On April 16, a group meeting at the Ukrainian hall of South Porcupine, Ontario, drafted a resolution about "mass starvation and poverty of the toiling masses" in western Ukraine, where the "Polish Fascist regime" was "suppressing the cry for bread," and forwarded it to Prime Minister Bennett and the Polish and Romanian governments.¹¹⁵ It was in 1933 that a ULFTA activist, a miner who had settled in South Porcupine and was blacklisted for attempting to organize a union, "packed up the kids and returned to the Soviet Union."¹¹⁶

Letters from the Soviet Union

The very fact that the government in Moscow did not appeal for aid may have suggested to many ULFTA supporters that all was fine in

Soviet Ukraine. Reinforcing that impression were the many letters published in *Ukraïns'ki robitnychi visty* that came from individuals who had hitherto resided in Canada and then resettled in the USSR. In the early 1920s, a number of Ukrainians in Winnipeg and Montreal had departed Canada and established communes in Soviet Ukraine.[117] By the end of 1923, some nine communes had been founded in the Ukrainian SSR by former residents of Canada and the United States. In July 1925, their membership totalled 1,260, including those drawn from local sources.[118] One of the Canadian communes was named for Lenin in Myhaievo, in the district (*okruh*) of Tyraspolskyi, Odesa Guberniia. Two others (both called "Khliborob") were in the southeastern Kryvyi Rih district of Katerynoslav Guberniia. That guberniia was also the site of a commune founded by Doukhobors from Canada.[119] In 1923, some 364 Doukhobor families from Canada resettled in the Saratov, Don, and Crimea regions of Russia. Also in Russia, a group that called itself the Independent Canadian Doukhobors established itself in a commune in the Yekaterinburg region.[120] With the passage of time, some members abandoned the communes and then the USSR altogether.[121] But others remained. The communes were described in *Ukraïns'ki robitnychi visty* by the writer Myroslav Irchan, who had in 1929 resettled in Soviet Ukraine from Canada.[122]

In December 1932, in a letter to a friend in Toronto, T. P. Kalyniuk—formerly of Hamilton, Ontario, and now working for a printing press in Makiivka in the Donbas, Soviet Ukraine—expressed satisfaction with his employment conditions and hailed the success of the Five-Year Plan. Projects were finished ahead of schedule, he reported.[123] Also in December, D. Harasymchuk shared a letter he had received from his sister in a *kolhosp* (collective farm) in the Podilia region, Soviet Ukraine. (An earlier letter he had received from her had already been published in the ULFTA's women's periodical *Robitnytsia*.) Harasymchuk's sister, he explained, was born in Galicia but in 1916 had moved further east. "Now she writes that she is living the free life and is working for herself and for the good of her class." In her letter, O. Harasymchuk-Artamenko expressed surprise that there was widespread unemployment in Canada and conveyed sympathy. "I invite [our unemployed workers] to our Soviet Ukraine, where there is no unemployment and landlord oppression." She described the "commune" as a place where one worked happily and had "no fear of starvation."[124]

Letters also came from regions in the USSR outside Soviet Ukraine. T. Fedyk in Gorkovsky krai (today Nizhegorodskaya Oblast), Russia, wrote disapprovingly of the workers who had resettled in the USSR, failed to adjust, and then returned to Canada and there joined the "counterrevolutionaries" who spread lies about the USSR. The bulk of the lies about the Soviet Union, Fedyk said, originated in Riga, Latvia. He worked in a paper factory and described his working conditions in positive terms.[125] Dmytro Gryzhak, who had gone to the USSR in the summer of 1932 and was now digging tunnels for the Moscow Metro, also wrote to correct some "misconceptions" about the life of Soviet workers.[126] Yet another positive portrayal came from Mariika Myroniuk, formerly of Ansonville, Ontario, and now of Leninsk, Kuzbass, western Siberia.[127] A letter from A. H. Trofymovych, who had left Canada in 1931 and now lived in Leningrad (St. Petersburg), to I. Makovsky in The Pas, Manitoba, was published in an early September 1933 issue of *Ukraïns'ki robitnychi visty* under the heading "Tell Our Enemies That There Is No Famine Here, and All Is Going Better by the Day."[128]

A letter sent from the Lenin Agro-Commune in Myhaievo was published in *Ukraïns'ki robitnychi visty* in May 1933. Its author, whose surname was Hulin, spoke not about the commune but on the USSR in general. There was no unemployment in the Soviet Union, Hulin said, and as factories were closing in Canada, new ones were being built in the USSR.[129] A letter dated September 22, from members of the Khliborob commune, spoke of the progress made in building socialism. A reference was made to individuals who, during that time, had carried out damaging actions against the commune and were now in "America" helping the "counterrevolutionary" camp. In overcoming obstacles, the members said, the work that had been done was for the "benefit of our soviet socialist fatherland, ourselves, and our children." They had grown and strengthened with each passing year, the group said, as had the entire Soviet land. The letter sounded a particularly militant note when it spoke of a struggle with a "class enemy." The "class enemy of our country is broken, but not completely destroyed," the letter asserted. "The remnants of the kulaks, Petliurites, and other counterrevolutionary scum" were still out there, sensing their inevitable end. But their days were numbered, while the socialists were going from strength to strength; Comrade Stalin had assured that this would be the final year of difficulties. The letter went on to report a successful harvest and the progress made in the commune. It bore the names of more than sixty members.[130] Another letter that came in the late summer of 1933, from a village in Kharkiv Oblast, echoed the claim of a successful harvest, describing it as "one of the best."[131]

A smaller number of Ukrainians belonged to another pro-Soviet organization in Canada, the Russian Workers' and Farmers' Clubs (RWFC). Founded in 1930, it had branches across Canada that embraced Belarusians, Russians, and Ukrainians (the latter seem to have been largely from the regions of Volhynia and Polisia, which were part of the Russian Empire before World War I but incorporated into Poland afterward). The RWFC published the newspaper *Kanadskii gudok*, which—much like *Ukraïns'ki robitnychi visty*—contained articles that were favourable to the Soviet Union. In one, a special correspondent wrote about productivity in a meat plant in Leningrad.[132] Another featured greetings from miners in the Donbas.[133] An editorial criticized Prime Minister Bennett's anti-Soviet policy.[134] An article by Grace Wilson in the newspaper's "Children's Corner" said, in part, "While in Canada and all the rest of the capitalist lands the lot of the workers' children is hunger and cold, the Soviet children are well fed and looked after since they come always first."[135] There were letters from the North Caucasus[136] and Pravdinsk in Gor'gorskii krai.[137] Skrypnyk's suicide was reported, as were his "national-chauvinism tendencies."[138] A member of the RWFC in Winnipeg, F. Klimchuk, complained of "White guards and enemies of the working people" who "slander the Soviet Union in Canada. In their words, there is famine and distress." Klimchuk proceeded to relate his own experience in the USSR, which he had visited as a tourist between November 14, 1932, and February 4, 1933.[139] Other articles focused on the Soviet Union statements of Cromie and Ketchum.[140]

It is clear that ex-residents of Canada now in the USSR were asked to confirm whether or not there was a famine in Ukraine. In a private letter (date unknown), Alexander Porayko, a member of the Myhaievo commune, replied to a question put to him by his brother-in-law in Alberta, on whether there was a famine in Ukraine.[141] Porayko wrote that there was "no famine on a massive scale. Here and there, there are some instances through all sorts of reasons." He then elaborated. There were villages with "counter-revolutionary sentiments." In 1931, residents in those villages did not want to give to the state the quota of grain that was required of them. Their grain was then taken from them by force, and the following year, the peasants refused to sow the fields; they thought they themselves could buy the grain to sustain themselves, not knowing that a decree would forbid the free sale of grain. Porayko described a situation somewhere in the Chernihiv region, in 1933–34, where, after fulfilling the state quota, little or no grain remained due to a poor harvest. The peasants there were promised help from the state and an authorization was signed; according to Porayko, all that remained was for the carloads of grain to arrive. But owing to confusion, the delivery was delayed. Meanwhile, people fled to where they could or perished in their village. Many people came to where Porayko lived. He then explained that in his own district, too, there were "cases" in separate households for "various reasons." It was either because the people in question "never sowed anything" and did not join the collective farms, or because they had sold grain at a time when the prices were high, and afterward there was nowhere to buy or borrow it. People had only so much grain to last them until the new crop, Porayko said. He recounted that in "the fall of 1930–31," when the state was collecting the crop, the people overseeing the process tried to seize as much grain as possible for certain incentives (*shchoby zarobyty udarnytstvo*). They searched for grain whenever they could. They even took seeds, Porayko said, and falsely assured the people affected that the state would supply seeds when the time came. Some cases were investigated, and some of the culprits were sentenced and put behind bars, he told his brother-in-law in Canada, but the investigations and sentences were not done thoroughly.

Porayko then described his own personal experience. A year earlier, he—and presumably his family—had harvested the grain, and it was all taken as part of the state grain-collection obligation. Afterward, seeds, horse feed, and so on, as well as advances from the state for those who had little grain left, were brought in by rail or by carts through the marshes. He, too, had to borrow some grain before harvesting, Porayko wrote, and he expected that the situation in the present year would not be better, for the harvest was worse. Had there been no obstacles, whether ill-intentioned or not (*zloumshlenykh i ne zloumshlenykh*) and placed unconsciously or consciously, then the achievements of the Soviet Union would have been much greater, in Porayko's view. One may think that when the state was loaning grain to those organizations that experienced a poor harvest, everyone would receive as much as they needed—but, he told his relative in Canada, it was not like that. Porayko wrote that the administration board would take into account the number of days worked by members of the collective farm and then make monthly or fortnightly distributions accordingly, of five hundred grams of flour per workday. The distributions were made only to individuals who actually worked, Porayko clarified. Thus, in a family of five in which two people worked and the others were minors, the distributions for the two workers would have to be shared with the three not working. If a worker fell ill and could not go to work, then that person also received no ration, barring a special dispensation—an exception, said Porayko, that could provoke "anti-Soviet sentiment." Porayko considered the daily allotment of five hundred grams of flour sufficient if other products were available, such as borscht, potatoes, and beans. But, he noted, it was more often the case that only flour was available. The impression given in Porayko's letter was that when there was nothing but flour for food, one should not hope for baked bread; the flour would instead be used to prepare *zatyrka* (a gruel made of flour). But there was nothing extraordinary about this, he declared, for people had grown accustomed to that kind of life. By the same token, he felt it should not come as a surprise that gardens would often be the target of much theft.

Porayko cautioned that what he was describing could not be applied to other collective farms, for the quality of life varied from place to place, depending on the number of workers, the size of the farm, the administration, and the agricultural activities. In his case, during 1933—which he called a good harvest year—each workday was worth 2.7 kilograms of grain and 3.5 rubles in cash. Yet in other nearby collective farms, a workday was worth 7 kilograms of grain, and in others still, 16 kilograms—and these amounts did not count vegetables and fruits, which Porayko's group did not receive as these were converted into cash.[142]

Although Porayko's letter alluded to events from 1933, it was written after the major famine had passed. Readers of letters such as those published in *Ukraïns'ki robitnychi visty* were thus given the impression that there really was little cause for worry. Any difficulties that existed had passed and the harvest of the summer of 1933 was bountiful. The rival camp may have been quoting from letters originating in Soviet Ukraine, but the letters published in *Ukraïns'ki robitnychi visty* sent by friends who had lived in Canada gave little hint of dissatisfaction and praised the Soviet system. Socialism was being built. Counterrevolutionaries were being defeated. The names appended to the letter from the Khliborob commune suggested that no one among the people bearing those names had fallen victim to famine. Indeed, if none of them was pleading for help, readers could reason, what was all the fuss about?[143]

In spite of such contradictory information, it was clear that reports about the famine and Soviet policies in Ukraine prompted some Sovietophiles to question their sympathies toward the USSR. One such person was P. Baida. *Ukraïns'kyi holos* described him as "a former member of the Bolshevik organization," who was among the speakers at a meeting about the famine in Saskatoon on November 26, 1933.[144] "The liquidation of the kulaks, collectivization and the artificially created famine in Ukraine in 1932–1933 gave birth to certain reservations in the minds of some members regarding Soviet policies in Ukraine," writes John Kolasky. These reservations were reinforced by the suicides of Skrypnyk and Khvylovy, the execution of twenty-eight Ukrainian intellectuals in December 1934, and the arrests of Sembay and Irchan. Eventually, a group broke away from the ULFTA to found the Ukrainian Workers' and Farmers' Educational Association.[145]

The arrests in Soviet Ukraine of the former ULFTA leaders Sembay and Irchan had been announced in *Ukraïns'ki robitnychi visty* in August 1934. An RCMP report paraphrased the newspaper story: "When Irchan was working for the proletariat, he was held in high esteem," but "when he rolled into the counter revolutionary mud, he must be treated accordingly."[146] The news of the arrest of the two former leaders, according to the RCMP, was "causing much talk among the rank and file members of the Ukrainian Labour Farmer Temple Association and the Ukrainians in general." Irchan's sister in Winnipeg had "received a letter from the Soviet Ukraine informing her that her brother had been sentenced to 10 years and Sembay to three years' imprisonment for their nationalistic tendencies."[147] Questions about the fate of the two men were also raised in the Ukrainian community beyond ULFTA circles.[148] An unidentified Canadian Communist organizer, in Moscow undertaking a three-year training program around the time of the famine, was disillusioned by Stalinist policies in Ukraine. The activist distanced himself from the Communist Party after his return to Canada and criticized Soviet cultural policies in Ukraine.[149]

Chapter Seven

"A BLESSING FROM HEAVEN": AID AND APPEALS
January–June 1934

Sophie Slusarenko Addresses the Community

While much was being written at the turn of 1934 about what Carl Ketchum had to say about the Soviet Union and the famine, members of the Ukrainian community were also listening attentively to the first-hand account of Ukraine-born Sophie Slusarenko. On December 6, 1933, a letter to the editor from a "Ukrainian Canadian" appeared in the *Edmonton Journal* in response to journalist George Palmer's statements about the famine. The letter mentioned H. Satanove (whose address was given as 10158 – 114 Street), whose revelations had been published earlier in the *Journal*; a Mrs. Hawryluk of Beverly, Alberta; and a Mrs. Bilkowska of Granada, Alberta, who, the letter writer said, could corroborate Satanove's disclosures. The letter also named Sophie Slusarenko (of 10325 – 95 Street), who had "lectured recently at the Ukrainian hall in Edmonton."[1]

Slusarenko spoke at the Ukrainian National Federation's day of national mourning, prayer, and fasting observed on November 24, 1933. Some time later, in January 1934, *Novyi shliakh* published her speech. In it, Slusarenko remarked that the fields of Ukraine that had once been replete with ripened wheat were now covered with weeds and thistles.

Canadian Communists claimed that only those people who did not want to work were starving, she said. Slusarenko countered that people were dying not because they were indifferent to work and preferred death through starvation, but because the Communist regime had created an artificial famine for the purpose of destroying the Ukrainian nation. The regime was aware, Slusarenko maintained, that Ukrainian society would not always tolerate its harmful policies. Slusarenko described herself as a person who had experienced the famine but was able to survive it thanks to help from abroad. She presented an overview of the preceding two decades, during which Ukrainians had proclaimed their independence but efforts to maintain it had failed. The practice of taking bread from Ukraine had begun from the first years of Soviet rule, Slusarenko asserted, making reference to the famine of 1921–23. The village economy improved after the initiation of the New Economic Policy, she said, but Stalin's regime changed matters as heavy industry was developed at the expense of the agricultural sector.[2] Slusarenko also described the process of collectivization. At first, she said, there was little enthusiasm for the system, and because of this a decree was issued in 1930 for complete collectivization. From that time on, "a real hell began in Ukraine." The collectivization drive entailed a dekulakization process and deportations to the Solovetsky Islands; in this brutal fashion, Slusarenko affirmed, 70 per cent of farms were collectivized. She went on to describe an order in which the farmer was deprived of autonomy and could not leave the village without permission of the collective farm. Farmers could be contracted for work outside of agriculture, for the factories or coal mines of the Donbas, according to perceived economic needs of the state. Slusarenko then spoke on the subject of grain-procurement quotas. Moscow set unrealistic quotas, she said, without regard to the harvest, but still insisted the plan be fulfilled and used force. According to Slusarenko, activists would stress the need to build up heavy industry and feed a large proletariat, export grain, and fund world propaganda, with no regard to the sacrifices. To procure foodstuffs from the collective farm was not difficult, Slusarenko maintained, because it had its own administration which enforced rules. There was a famine, she noted, from the end of 1931.[3]

Because the regime refused to believe that nothing remained after their requisitions, Slusarenko declared, it set up search commissions that would look for anything edible—a practice that brought the villages to famine. Dead horses were consumed, as were dogs, cats, and mice. When the weeds were emerging in the spring, they, too, were used, Slusarenko related. People sought fish and frogs in the rivers and turned to molasses, chaff, flowers, and the bark of trees. No one was spared the hunger, not even the poorer peasants in the collective farm. There were times when fifteen to twenty deaths from hunger would occur in even the smallest villages. One's first concern was not for others but for one's own survival. Readers of Slusarenko's account were informed of cases where a person would set out on a journey to the next village, to see if he or she could find a dead horse, but never reached that village, falling dead on the way there. The deceased would often lie in a dwelling for a week, she continued, until the decomposing body was discovered. Then the people charged with collecting the corpses would go from house to house, picking up the bodies, and dig a common grave for them—a shallow one, Slusarenko pointed out, for those digging no longer had the strength to create anything deeper, and with no ceremony. This is how the famine unfolded in the Kyiv region, she said, in such villages as Rohova, Ostrivets, Nebelivka, Nerubaika, Pidvysoke, Kopenkovata, Perehonivka, Pokotylova, Holovanivske, Buznykovata, Semyduby, Verbova, Krutenke, and Stepkivka. In those villages, said Slusarenko, up to a third of the population had died. She also noted that entire families had fled to the Caucasus or Turkestan, where the Soviet measures were not as drastic. Valuables were exchanged for bread in the industrial centres of Russia by villagers who belonged to the collective farms and could send one of their members to make the trade. Slusarenko went on to relate how children were abandoned, how they would wander to the railway stations, and how they would die in the absence of care. She challenged the view that she said was maintained by members of the pro-Soviet camp in the community: that if anyone was dying from hunger, it was kulaks and people who refused to join the collective farms. She related the case of a poor villager who was the father of eight children. A former agricultural labourer, he became active in the collective farm. One day she saw him covered with blood. He had brought meat from a dead horse of the Karl Marx sugar refinery (in the collective farm, she said, even dead horses were no longer to be found). The man had been picking at the horse's corpse, and he died the next day.

As for the survivors, they were not spared punishment, for they were still expected to go to work, hungry, in the collective farms. Their diet, according to Slusarenko, consisted of water with a bit of sour fodder beets and corn flour. The OGPU, army, and party officials, meanwhile, all had access to closed cooperatives. Slusarenko then turned to the subject of cannibalism, providing several cases as examples: a family in Sokolivka, Kyiv region, who were arrested for slaying thirteen people; a man and his wife in the village of Sychivka, arrested for killing and consuming their four children; a girl in the village of Perehonivka who was killed with the object of being eaten; and a woman in the town of Uman, tried for putting her own child to death, who confessed that she had consumed seventeen individuals. In Uman, said Slusarenko, corpses were brought from the prisons, hospitals, and the orphanage to a cemetery where, in the absence of a pit, they were piled up. Few corpses from the pile remained the next day. Slusarenko went on to quote a poem by Taras Shevchenko: "A village, and the heart is at peace, a village in our Ukraine, a village like a pysanka."[4] The villages in Ukraine no longer resembled Shevchenko's description of them, she asserted; one could no longer hear a rooster crow or a dog bark, or see a gleam of light from the window of a house at night. In her opinion, the village was lately more akin to the Sahara Desert. The houses were half-ruined.

The speaker from Perehonivka also addressed press censorship. All talk of the famine occurred in the newspapers of Paris, Berlin, and New York, she pointed out; nothing appeared in the Soviet press about the millions in Ukraine who were dying of famine, the thousands who were deported to the Solovetsky Islands and Siberia for forced labour, or the horses that were almost wiped out from hunger. To utter a word against the regime would mean banishment to the Solovetsky Islands or prison—and jail meant death from hunger. While much construction was going on, Slusarenko said, it included the building of prisons. As for the workers, they subsisted on rations. And the army, she added, served only Moscow's interests. Slusarenko said that before she departed Ukraine on April 10, 1933, she could sense the thoughts of insurrection in the minds of villagers—even though they were feeebled by hunger—and in the minds of workers, army personnel, party members, and Komsomol youth. She expressed the belief that if the destruction of Ukraine were allowed to continue, in a matter of a couple of years there would be no school-age children in parts of the republic. Slusarenko commented on Moscow's pacts with Bucharest, Warsaw, Paris, and Washington. One could not be fooled into believing that there was any humanitarianism or civilization in the world, she noted disapprovingly. Her speech, as published in *Novyi shliakh*, ended with the statement that Ukrainian statehood could only be attained with a weapon in hand and by observing the spirit of the nationalist slogan "The nation above all!"[5]

Slusarenko was probably one of the three unnamed people, all women, mentioned by *Ukraïns'kyi holos* in January 1934 as having recently come to Alberta from Soviet Ukraine—one from the Podilia region, the second from the Kyiv region, and the third from the Poltava region. The three, who had come to join their husbands in Edmonton or in rural Alberta, had provided information about the famine. A summary of their accounts was presented in *Ukraïns'kyi holos*, covering several topics. One concerned the question of travel. It was difficult to leave the USSR, the summary said, because the Soviet regime did not allow it, except for a few exceptions where payment for an expensive passport was required. A woman joining her husband would generally have to pay US$284 for a passport, but the cost rose to US$500 if her husband came from the so-called kulak class. On top of that was the expense of travelling from the USSR to Canada. After the husband of the woman from Podilia had left for Canada in 1928, the Soviets had confiscated all the property and ejected the woman from her home, in winter. She went to a town where she worked hard for some bread. Bread steadily became more expensive and harder to obtain. The woman from Podilia, according to the item in *Ukraïns'kyi holos*, also believed that she would have died of starvation had she not obtained financial assistance from her husband in Canada.

What else was mentioned in this summary of the three women's experiences? Its claims included the following: that the Five-Year Plan had become an assault against the freedom of the Ukrainian peasantry; that many Ukrainians were against the collective farm system and did not want to surrender their property to the state and thus become "slaves" to the commissars; that the response of the regime was to deport rural leaders and Ukrainian national-conscious elements to the Solovetsky Islands and Siberia and confiscate their property (therefore destroying the rural leadership); that property was seized also from those who remained; and that some, through intimidation, joined the collective farms. The summary then asserted that, following unrest in 1931 and 1932, the regime had adopted another tactic to impose its will; namely, a famine was initiated at the end of 1931, which lasted until the present. In the autumn of 1931, the regime had requisitioned the grain from the peasants and nearly all other products as well. The farmers were forced to join the collective farms, according to this summary, otherwise their very existence was threatened by hunger. The women informed *Ukraïns'kyi holos* that the Soviet regime was well prepared for any potential insurrection: troops would come in to take the produce, and any resistance could lead to an execution on the spot or to deportation. The woman from Podilia related that in a village neighbouring hers, people realized that if they gave up their produce they would be condemned to death by starvation in the winter. Thus, when the collectors came to take their produce, the villagers resisted with their spades, rakes, and any other implement that could be used as a weapon in order to protect their grain. The next day, the government's armed militia came; some of the villagers were executed, and eighteen families were deported to the Solovetsky Islands. Some fled.

The summary affirmed that the major famine had begun at the end of 1932 and lasted through the spring. Even seeds for sowing in the collective farms, it noted, were insufficient or were supplied late. The woman from Podilia reported that fifteen to twenty people in her village had perished daily during the spring of 1932, and twenty to thirty people per day in 1933. The woman from the Kyiv region had lived in a village of more than two thousand inhabitants; as a result of famine and epidemics, she said, fewer than eight hundred people remained. There were so many deaths, the summary continued, that the corpses needed to be buried in a large common grave. People would fall dead anywhere—in the houses, hedges, fields, streets. Of every hundred farmers who went to the fields for collective work, fifteen to twenty would die each day. The majority of those dying were men and children. The summary stated that children could die on their way to school or even at the school itself. There was hardly any milk for them, for cattle had become scarce either through seizure by the collectors or through neglect. People fed on beets, cats, dogs, and even on corpses, the summary continued. Mothers were afraid to send their children to school, as there were children who disappeared. There were even cases when mothers killed their own children so as not to have to watch them perish from starvation. Epidemics broke out and also claimed lives. In one village mentioned (but not identified) in the summary, collectors had brought corn into one big heap but failed to cover the crop; thus, when the corn got wet it began to rot. A seven-year-old boy who went to the heap to alleviate his hunger was shot dead by a guard. The summary also noted that a woman who was not a collective farmer had hidden a sack and a half of corn in a hen coop, for which she was sentenced to a year and a half in prison. A sixty-eight-year-old woman was sentenced to an eight-year term in jail for "demoralizing" people, after selling sunflowers without state permission.

This item in *Ukraïns'kyi holos*, in summarizing the accounts of the three women from Soviet Ukraine, also noted that in the autumn of 1932, farmers had begged the authorities not to take everything, for there had been deaths from starvation in the preceding winter and spring. When they defended their harvest as they could, they were fired upon. At the same time, no starvation was taking place in Russia (*Moskovshchyna*), as far as people who had gone there in search of bread were able to determine. According to the published summary, many in Ukraine held the view that the famine had been organized to destroy the Ukrainian nation and increase the settlement of Russians and Jews. There was much antipathy toward the Soviet regime, the summary continued, but terror and possible denunciations deterred open criticism. Even in the schools, children were taught to inform on what their parents said at home about the government. The schools were thoroughly Communist, and the subjects of Ukrainian history and literature were not taught. Churches in the districts where the three women had lived were said to be mostly locked; taxes were so high that they could not be afforded. The church buildings were said to have been taken over and converted to Communist offices, or to be sitting empty. The summary also made reference to a longstanding antireligious campaign and to censorship of the press and propaganda (films were produced that depicted hunger outside of the Soviet Union, including in Canada and the United States). Further, it said that Ukraine did not have its own army; that people lacked arms for resistance, were weak and terrorized, and had been murdered; and that the OGPU had a network of spies. The best chance for Ukraine was for help to come from abroad through a war. In conclusion, the summary noted that people saw the famine as a punishment of those who did not like "Bolshevism," and many Ukrainians who had formerly been "Bolsheviks" and worked for "Bolshevism" had now abandoned it.[6]

Another first-hand account, also reprinted in *Ukraïns'kyi holos*, provided more insights into local dynamics. A Ukrainian refugee in Romania declared that villagers were waiting for the day that the Russian yoke would be removed, but that the political situation was such that the local village authorities were in the hands of "traitors" and people sent by the Russians.[7] In a letter sent to his father in Winnipeg, a young lad related that after his mother had left for work one day, five men had come into the house, breaking and seizing things. The boy went to inform his mother, and the two of them headed to the "cooperative"—and there found the same men who had sequestered flour from their home. When the boy's tearful mother asked for an explanation for the seizure, she was denounced by a senior official as a "counterrevolutionary" and accused of possessing foreign contraband goods. The mother displayed Torgsin records (*pokvitovannia*), but to no avail.[8]

The Elizabeth Skoropadsky Committee to Aid Victims of the Famine in Ukraine

Meanwhile, Ukrainians in Canada were collecting funds to assist the starving in Soviet Ukraine through a coordinated action in Europe. In the summer of 1934, a letter to the editor of the London *Times* from Florence Mary Mackenzie of Foveran, Aberdeen, drew attention to ongoing relief efforts for those starving in the USSR. "A number of private individuals, with no other than purely humanitarian interests, formed an English branch of HH Elizabeth Skoropadsky's Ukrainian Relief Committee," she announced to readers in her letter. The small committee, Mackenzie said, had been "able to afford assistance to many of the people starving in the Ukraine, where, as stated by Lord Denbigh in the House of Lords, the starvation is greatest."[9] The Earl of Denbigh (Rudolph Fielding) was among the members of the House of Lords who spoke about the famine during its debate of July 25, 1934. His interventions that day became known to Ukrainians in Canada and were applauded by the USSAC.[10]

Ielysaveta (Elizabeth) Skoropadsky was the daughter of Pavlo (Paul) Skoropadsky, who, following a coup d'état in April 1918, had become "hetman" of Ukraine, until his conservative regime was toppled toward the end of the year. Afterward, Skoropadsky and his family moved to Berlin.[11] Only days before Mowinckel discussed the famine with other council members of the League of Nations, on September 22, 1933, Ielysaveta Skoropadsky founded the Committee to Aid Victims of the Famine in Ukraine (Komitet Dopomohy Holoduiuchym na Ukraïni) in Berlin.[12] The daughter of the hetman was aware of the difficulties in getting aid into the USSR. In a circular issued by the committee in November 1933, the Soviet regime was said to have refused "bread from abroad even when half of the shipment was to be given to the state for free," and the example was given of Mennonites in Canada who were in a position to arrange for the shipping of food to their coreligionists in Ukraine.[13] Indeed, that same month (November), a relief committee in Prague announced that Ukrainians in Canada were prepared to organize a grain cargo ship for succour of the starving.[14]

One of the first acts of the committee was to express its gratitude to Mowinckel for raising the matter of the famine with the League of Nations.[15] The British branch of the Berlin Committee also wrote to Mowinckel. In that letter, Volodymyr Korostovets (Vladimir de Korostovetz), head of the London Ukrainian Relief Committee, shared his conviction with the president of the league's council that notwithstanding the good harvest, many people were still dying from the famine and "cannibalism is rampant." Korostovets added that although the Soviet Union was a member of the Red Cross, in his view they were more interested in that organization for political than for humanitarian ends. He thus asked Mowinckel for his advice about the "best channel" for helping the people who were currently suffering in Ukraine.[16]

On October 28, 1933, Pavlo Skoropadsky wrote a personal letter to President Roosevelt in which he urged the American leader not to recognize the USSR but asked that if the United States were to extend recognition, then during the negotiations it might discuss "the right of the U.S. to organize a relief committee for the starving on Ukrainian territory."[17] In November, the Berlin Committee to Aid Victims of the Famine in Ukraine reinforced the hetman's letter to Roosevelt with one of its own. Dated November 5, the letter implored the U.S. president to make the cessation of export of "grain and victuals from a hunger stricken country" a condition for any recognition of the USSR.[18]

Meanwhile, the Berlin Committee busied itself with fundraising in Germany and abroad and with dispatching aid to Soviet Ukraine. The manner in which it was possible to send relief to individuals in Ukraine was explained in an appeal by the British branch of the committee, published in the *Catholic Times*. Money collected by the committee, the appeal said, would be sent to the "Central Fund" and then "passed on to the individuals in the Ukraine in the form of parcels of food."[19] In time, branches of the Berlin Committee were established in several countries. As Hetman Skoropadsky put it, "My daughter has several committees in different parts of the world and they, we are happy to say, in their own quiet way, give her considerable assistance."[20] Canada was one of those parts of the world where assistance was being rendered.

The formation of the Berlin Committee was announced in *Kanadyis'kyi farmer* in early November 1933. Two months later, *Kanadyis'kyi farmer* published an appeal by the Berlin Committee.[21] In mid-January 1934, *Ukraïns'ki visty* announced that a meeting in Edmonton had been held under the auspices of the local Hetmanite organization, the USSAC. The purpose of the meeting, held at the Ukrainian National Home on January 10, was to protest the famine and to organize relief for its victims. One of the speakers, Il. Mazurkevych, compared the "Bolshevik" actions in Ukraine with King Herod's aim of killing young children (the biblical "Massacre of the Innocents"). Common to both Herod and Stalin, Mazurkevych said, was the fear of the loss of power. Another speaker, M. Hetman [Hethman], noted the hypocrisy of the Soviet line of "struggle against capitalism" when they were engaged in friendship pacts with countries such as Poland, France, and the United States. The pacts, he said, were concluded at a time when thousands were dying of starvation. A resolution passed at the meeting was sent to Ottawa and London. An appeal by the Committee to Aid Victims of the Famine in Ukraine—headed by Elizabeth Skoropadsky in Berlin—was read at the meeting. The committee, the attendees were told, was sending aid to the starving through the state-run hard-currency Torgsin stores. The prices for goods at these stores (lowered, it was said, through external pressure and the fear of losing hard currency) were also read out. From the meeting, a total of $30.25 was collected for the starving.[22] Collections were also made in such Alberta localities as Mundare ($16.40) and Derwent ($14.50).[23]

A letter of gratitude that came from the Berlin Committee noted that the $14.50 received from Derwent was equivalent to 38 marks and 93 pfennigs in German currency. To illustrate how much of a difference such assistance could make, the letter said that a person could live for a whole month on 8 to 10 marks.[24] The Berlin Committee also mailed a number of postcards. The USSAC in Derwent had requested three to four hundred postcards to sell "for the purpose of assisting our starving brothers and sisters in Greater Ukraine."[25] The postcard that was sent depicted a woman holding a dead child, a victim of famine, over her with a man lying behind them, against the backdrop of a village. The creator of the illustration was Riga-born artist Vasily Masiutin, who had settled in Berlin in 1921.[26] From a letter that the Berlin Committee had mailed to Edmonton, it can be determined that the price fixed for a postcard in Canada and the United States was five cents.[27]

Ivan Fedorovich of Regina, Saskatchewan, was able to have the efforts of the Berlin Committee publicized in a local German-language weekly.[28] The committee also corresponded with individuals and groups in Calgary, Monitor, Mundare, Musidora, and Myrnam, in Alberta;

Morse, Saskatchewan; Rossburn and Winnipeg, in Manitoba; Kitchener, Ottawa, Sudbury, Toronto, and Windsor, in Ontario; and Montreal, Quebec.[29] In a letter to the USSAC in Kitchener, thanking it for its donation of 32.63 deutsche marks, the Berlin Committee acknowledged that "conditions even in Canada were not easy." Although the majority of people who donated had originally come from territories in western Ukraine (or were born in Canada), there was a case or two in which the Berlin Committee was a means of rendering assistance to relatives in Soviet Ukraine. The USSAC asked the committee if it could provide assistance on behalf of two members in Winnipeg who had relatives in the Kyiv and Vinnytsia regions, supplying the pertinent addresses.[30]

The Berlin Committee generally sent money and food parcels to people in Soviet Ukraine through Fast and Company. It chose that firm because it was well-organized, it provided evidence of receipt of aid, and the Soviets recognized it. In addition, because the firm was large and dispatched tens of thousands of parcels and money orders—which would go through the Torgsin in Moscow—it was difficult for the Soviet authorities to determine from where the aid was coming. The addresses given to Fast would be "lost in a great number of other addresses and in Moscow it is impossible to know where they are."[31] It also seems that the Berlin Committee targeted women: in an explanation for the documentation of a receipt, it said that "our Committee tries to send help through women because it is less suspicious in the eyes of the bolshevics [sic] who see politics everywhere. It is not the woman alone that profits by it, but the whole family."[32]

The Elizabeth Skoropadsky–directed Committee to Aid Victims of the Famine in Ukraine was one of many relief initiatives among Ukrainians outside Soviet Ukraine that was established in response to the famine. The already mentioned Ukrainian Civic Committee for the Salvation of Ukraine, in Lviv, set up branches across western Ukraine in Poland in July 1933.[33] Committees were also founded in Romania, Czechoslovakia, Argentina, Austria, Belgium, Bulgaria, China (Manchuria), France, Italy, Luxembourg, Yugoslavia, and the United States—in addition to Canada, Germany, and the United Kingdom.[34] In the United Kingdom, the branch of the Berlin Committee came to be one of two devoted to the matter of famine relief.[35]

Figure 5. Postcard of the Elizabeth Skoropadsky Committee to Aid Victims of the Famine in Ukraine. Designed by Riga-born artist Vasily Masiutin, the postcard circulated in Canada. Demetrius Elcheshen fonds, Ukrainian Cultural and Educational Centre (Oseredok), Winnipeg.

An obstacle that the Berlin Committee encountered was the perception that its aims were "political" and that it discriminated in the disbursement of aid. In response to the characterization of "the committee over which my daughter presides" as political, Hetman Skoropadsky—in a letter to Sir Paul Makins of the London, England, branch of the committee—exclaimed that this was "an outright lie." In regards to the people whom the committee targeted, Skoropadsky responded as follows: "It is true that she helps any one in need, and those most in need are those who have not the benefit of the Soviet ration card, they are priests, professors, doctors, former bourgeoisie, farmers and peasants—but is this really political?"[36] In reply to the issue of political affiliation, Makins wrote to the hetman that while he fully believed "that the work over which Princess Elizabeth presides is fully philanthropic," the British "Foreign Office are not favourably disposed towards it."[37]

The branch in London declined, but even as it did, the Berlin Committee continued to maintain contact with groups and individuals in Canada and to send aid to addresses in Soviet Ukraine and elsewhere in the USSR.[38] Letters of gratitude received by the Berlin Committee were translated into English and given to anyone deemed interested, as evidence that the help was reaching those in need. A letter dated November 19, 1933, read, "We received your parcel in October. You must send us more as quickly as possible, for we are getting weak from hunger." Another, written or received in January 1934, said, "Your parcel came when we had nothing else in the house. Death was before us."[39] Extracts of such letters, in Ukrainian, were received by groups in Canada.[40] In a July 1934 letter, Elizabeth Skoropadsky described as successful the work that had been conducted to date by the committee branches in the United States and Canada.[41]

Later in 1934, *Ukraïns'ki visty* cited the *New York Times* to indicate that the Soviet regime was placing obstacles preventing the receipt of aid from abroad.[42] According to the *New York Times*, the Soviet government was refusing foreign aid on the grounds that "there is no famine or prospect of one, that the relief is not needed and that the campaigns themselves are a form of anti-Soviet propaganda." The *New York Times* correspondent noted that in the past some monies had reached the peasantry, though some was turned back "and some turned over by the peasants to the International Society for the Relief of the Revolutionary Workers and Their Families, a radical organization to succor imprisoned Communists in Germany, among other countries."43

The All-Union Company for Trade with Foreigners: Torgsin Stores

In December 1933 and January 1934, the amount of monies collected for famine relief purposes at three meetings in Alberta (in Edmonton, Mundare, and Derwent) totalled $61.15. This particular example suggests that community efforts to collectively raise funds for famine relief paralleled neither those undertaken in response to the 1921–23 famine nor those of the Mennonites at Rosthern, Saskatchewan. Several explanations for the smaller results are possible. One is the fact that a coordinated response to the famine in western Ukraine took shape in a major way only from July 1933. The committee Skoropadsky founded in Berlin came into being later, on September 22, 1933. By that time, many reports in the mainstream press indicated that the most recent harvest in the USSR was successful, which could be interpreted to mean that a famine no longer existed.

Another important reason may have been the fact that Moscow refused collective Ukrainian Canadian aid when it had been offered earlier, in 1932. This likely deterred the Ukrainian Self-Reliance League from mounting a major fundraising effort, instead emphasizing mass protests as the main strategy. In October 1933, the secretary of the league, V. Batytsky, explained the organization's approach to the famine as follows. When the league read in the newspaper *Dilo* of the formation in Lviv of the Ukrainian Civic Committee for the Salvation of Ukraine, the committee was contacted with the question of how best to help. The league shared with the committee its experience with the Red Cross. The Lviv committee, Batytsky said, was also of the view that the Soviet authorities would not permit aid, and so the course of action adopted by the league was to bring the world's attention to the famine, which it did through protest rallies.44

Ukrainian Canadians and other Canadians could and did make use of the Torgsin stores directly. Advertisements for these stores appeared in several Canadian periodicals. An advertisement in the April 5, 1933, issue of the weekly *Kanadyis'kyi farmer*, for instance, announced that four hundred larger and smaller urban centres in the Soviet Union already had Torgsin stores. The ad featured a list of food and clothing that could be bought, along with addresses of Torgsin representatives in New York and Chicago.[45] The Torgsin advertisement appearing in the July 5, 1933, issue of *Ukraïns'kyi holos* provided a New York address only.[46] But the one that appeared in the March 7, 1933, issue of the pro-Soviet *Ukraïns'ki robitnychi visty* gave the address of the Information and Financial Bureau on Selkirk Avenue, Winnipeg.[47] Information about the Torgsin stores was also published in the *Canadian Jewish Chronicle*. A September 1932 issue of that paper carried a notice that Torgsin in Moscow had announced that "money remitted by mail, cable or radio, by residents of the U.S.A. and Canada to beneficiaries in U.S.S.R.... will be placed to the credit of the named beneficiary at any one of the Torgsin stores." The beneficiary could "select at the Torgsin stores any article of food, clothing, or other commodities to the limit of his credit with Torgsin." If there was no Torgsin branch where the beneficiary resided, the Torgsin would send the commodities to the person. A list of companies authorized to receive money and issue merchandise orders was provided.[48] An announcement in a January 1933 issue of the weekly noted that rates for shipping parcels in the interior of the USSR would be reduced. To send within the USSR a forty-pound parcel to a place where there was no Torgsin store would now cost 75 cents instead of $1.25.[49] An announcement published in the *Canadian Jewish Chronicle* in October 1933 declared that, according to the General Representative of the Torgsin in the United States, prices of commodities in the Torgsin stores had been further reduced—on average by 50 per cent.[50] By that time—as can be inferred from an article in *Kanadyis'kyi farmer* titled "Torgsin Is the Largest Departmental Store in the World"—the number of these stores had proliferated. The number of urban centres in the USSR with a Torgsin store grew from 150 in July 1932 to a thousand in July 1933.[51] In 1934, at least one mainstream Canadian newspaper, the *Toronto Star*, also ran Torgsin advertisements.[52]

A letter sent from the village of Zarechie near the city of Proskuriv (since 1954, Khmelnytsky), Ukraine, written on March 1, 1933, and then mailed to Calgary, mentioned the Torgsin. The letter—from Maria Derus to her father, Peter Derus, and, it seems, her stepmother, too—arrived in Calgary on May 21. Maria Derus implored her father and stepmother "to send me any help you can, because I am dying of hunger." While she had been with her mother, "she was able to feed me, but mother has now died and I am alone and perishing from hunger." She cooked and lived off fodder beets. Her letter finished: "I go around to the store, the Torgsin, where they get flour from relatives in America. And they get all kinds of food products, but I can only look and cry and then go home....I sit at home and ask that you not ignore my request. I have written so many letters to you but have not received any reply from you."[53]

It is not clear what happened to Maria Derus, but while the Soviet Union allowed the Torgsin state-run hard-currency stores to operate, it continued to refuse offers of large-scale help from abroad. At a time of economic depression in Canada, it was not easy to support relatives in the USSR. Indeed, in at least one case, a person described as a "Russian" in Sault Ste. Marie, Ontario, had for five months "secured [Canadian government] relief... for a family of five children living in Russia," for which he was to be prosecuted.[54] Later, the *Star-Phoenix* noted the case of Feodor Sachynsky, whose parents had died of starvation in Ukraine. He had tried to help his parents as much as he could, but with the "exorbitant food prices and the scarcity of the same, could not save [them]." The *Star-Phoenix* then published a letter that Sachynsky had received from his brother in Ukraine. In it, Sachynsky's brother reported that "almost the whole part of our village has perished...mostly men. In a word, the suffering is unbearable, the people devour each other, mothers eat their own children. I do not know what will happen in the future." They existed, he wrote, "on the linden tree leaves. We pluck the trees, dry them and grind them into powder and eat them. We hardly exist and if you did not send me those four dollars [then] things would have gone very bad for me." He entreated his brother to "help me as much as you can to last out till August, as then the things might improve for us if we remain alive till the new harvest."[55]

Letters from Germans in Ukraine were also received by relatives in Alberta. Louisa and Robert Cerezke, who lived on a farm near Edmonton, received letters written in German from her mother, Luisa Wensel (Luiza Venzel), in the Kyiv Oblast of Ukraine. A letter Wensel wrote in July 1932 began with a quote from the Bible: "Blessed are those who hunger and thirst for righteousness, for they shall be satisfied." Wensel reported to her daughter and son-in-law that she had received their letter of the previous winter, had replied immediately, but to date had not obtained a response. "I don't know, are you still living or have you forgotten your old mother?" she asked. "So many people are sending letters from America and Germany to their friends here and also mail many gifts," she continued. Wensel then went on to describe food shortages. The situation, she said, had never been worse: "[as bad as] it is now with food, it never was before." The food she obtained was insufficient and the prices were prohibitive. "Many people from Canada have sent parcels to their friends here in our village [Wladimerufka] and they received it without difficulty," she noted. Wensel suggested that rice, flour, and bacon could be sent. "Dear daughter," she wrote toward the end of the letter, "be not angry that I have ask[ed] you for help."[56]

A letter to family members that Wensel wrote six months later from the village of Penki (possibly in the Zhytomyr area) sounded more desperate. "Especially this year we suffer very much," she wrote. Before the harvest had started, "we ate for at least one month leaves from the birch tree. This year it will be worse." Everything was expensive and the farmers had nothing. The "years had been very bad and nothing was growing and the Government confiscated the rest of the harvest. We had to hand in nearly everything." And in a section of the letter came the following chilling words: "Dear Aunt: I also send you heart-felt greetings. I cannot tell you very much only this: We live in distress. It is a dangerous and bad time here. Everything is arranged to kill us with hunger."[57]

A letter written on March 20, 1933, showed that some aid had by then reached Wensel. She acknowledged receipt of ten dollars that had arrived first in "Sitomir" (Zhytomyr) and had sent a telegram requesting transfer of the funds to "Mowograd" (likely Novohrad-Volynsky). With the ten dollars, "we bought ... 3 lbs millet seed, 2 lbs of flour, 2 lbs

Figure 6. Individuals in Canada received letters from relatives in the USSR. The *Saskatoon Star-Phoenix* published the translation of a letter sent from a man in Ukraine to his brother in Saskatoon, Feodor Sachynsky. The local merchant's parents, pictured, perished during the famine. *Saskatoon Star-Phoenix*, August 3, 1933, p. 4.

The above picture shows the parents of a local merchant, F. Sachynsky. His mother died of starvation in Russia four months ago, and only last week he received a letter, published below, notifying him that on June 21, 1933, his father died the same death. Mr. Sachynsky tried to help them as much as he could but with the exorbitant food prices, and the scarcity of same, could not save the lives of his parents.

The text of the letter presents a picture of the living conditions throughout Ukraine and Khuban.

My dear brother Feodor:

I am writing you a sad letter. We already have no parents, both old people have died—father and mother. Mother had died four months ago and father died on June 21. Both of them died from starvation. My brother, there is no death more terrible than the death from starvation. The dying person grabs anything within reach and carries to his mouth. To begin with the body of the starving person swells up very badly, then the victim falls into a great weakness and dies in a great agony. Almost the whole part of our village has perished in this manner, mostly men. In a word, the sufferring is unbearable — the people devour each other, mothers eat their own children. I do not know what will happen in the future.

The spring was quite cold, but the winter crops look pretty well but will mature quite late, probably not before August. But at the present we exist on the linden tree leaves. We pluck the leaves, dry them and grind them into powder and eat it. We hardly exist and if you did not send me those four dollars the things would have gone very bad with me. When I received the flour for that money I cried from joy. Now I thank you and your wife deeply and heartily and trust that God will repay you for it.

Now, I entreat you, help me as much as you can to last out till August, as then the things might improve for us if we remain alive till the new harvest. My brother, I wish to live yet but it is hard. My feet already begin to swell from starvation and I beg you to help me.

My brother, now I write you about father. When he received from you those eight dollars he lived on that money while it lasted, and after it was spent he had nothing to live on and we had no means to help him, so he died from starvation. And now try to save me by any means if only with two poods (72 pounds) of flour. Brother, I want to live, but it is hard, and I think you know everything.

sugar and 6½ metre Cotton." Wensel described the aid as "a blessing from heaven." Referring to what she had purchased, she stated that to pay for those items in Soviet currency "we [would have] needed at least Rubel 2,000.00." Until then, reported the eighty-year-old Wensel, "we hardly had anything to eat only a little jar of potatoes, that was all. All winter long we ate what cattle and pigs disliked to eat."[58] A letter in May 1933 thanked the Cerezkes for their gift. However, "everything is used up again and we are hungry again." If possible, Wensel asked, "please send me a few dollars. If you wish to send me something, please add one or two dollars. I would get it quicker. Then I go to Tor[g]sin and buy what I want. Here, many people get money put into letters and it arrives safely."[59] It is evident that the Soviet censors allowed such letters to go abroad and welcomed the foreign currency that was received. Indeed, the "resources gained from the Torgsin stores had contributed a whopping one-fifth of the total foreign currency resources used to fund Soviet industrialization."[60]

The USSR was not the world's only state in which regions experienced famine in 1933. During that year, Canadian newspapers had been reporting the existence of famine conditions in China and, importantly, the measures that Canadians were putting in place to assist the starving. In November, the *Toronto Star* reported that the Women's Auxiliary of the Chinese Church of Christ was planning an annual bazaar at the Toronto Chinese YMCA building. It added that proceeds from sales would be "entirely devoted for mission work and famine relief among their own people in China."[61] Later, in an article titled "Chinese Women Give $200 for Missions," the newspaper reported that some funds would go to the Chinese Foreign Famine Relief Committee in Shanghai.[62]

Michael Luchkovich's Speech in the House of Commons

By now, federal MP Michael Luchkovich was aware of the reports about famine in Ukraine and of the obstacles to succour. He had spoken about the famine at a November 1933 rally in his political riding as well as at a community hall in Fort William on January 11, 1934.[63] On February 5, Canada's first and (at the time) only MP of Ukrainian origin spoke in greater detail before a gathering of the nation's policy-makers. That day, Luchkovich rose from his chair to address his fellow elected representatives in the House of Commons. "Mr. Speaker, certain things that have emanated from at least two of the speakers tonight have brought me to my feet," stated the MP for Vegreville, Alberta. Those matters had to do with a CCF policy that was being debated and the subject of the famine in Ukraine.

The motion on the table that day, brought by the CCF, argued for a system "based on the principle of cooperative production and distribution in which human needs should be the first consideration." The CCF had only recently been founded, and Luchkovich, who was first elected to Parliament in 1926 as a candidate for the United Farmers of Alberta, was in 1932 one of its founding members.[64] How did the famine enter into debates about CCF policy? It was mentioned by John R. MacNicol, Conservative MP for Toronto Northwest, when he drew attention to the effects of socialism in the Soviet Union. "There is a cooperative commonwealth in Russia," MacNicol declared; he then proceeded to share a description of conditions in the Soviet Union made by Humphrey Mitchell after his visit there. Months earlier, Mitchell's observations had been reported in Canadian newspapers, and MacNicol quoted from the *Toronto Star*: "There are conditions in their factories which the Canadian people wouldn't stand for one minute. Girls walking around barefoot on iron filings, and that kind of thing. But worst of all is the shortage of food. It's not too bad in Moscow, it's a little worse in Leningrad. But out in the country, it's terrible—especially in the south, where much of the food is grown. I saw I don't know how many hundreds of people starving, in Kharkov and Kiev." MacNicol explained that the *Star* reporter (Matthew H. Halton) had then asked Mitchell a question: "How did you know they were starving?" Mitchell had responded: "I've got eyes. You don't need to be a scientist to know a person is starving. When white-faced men and women, and children with distended bellies, crowd around the train at every station begging for money or food—then it's a pretty sure guess they're starving. I saw hundreds of them in Kharkov and Kiev. They didn't even have the traditional dried fish and cabbage soup. They were down to bread and water—and sometimes less than that."[65]

Luchkovich challenged the equation of CCF agricultural policy with Communism. "When Canada is ever brought down to an agricultural system administered as it now is in Russia I will no longer give my support to a cooperative movement." He disagreed with the notion that the "policy of nationalization and planning advocated by this group [the CCF] would inaugurate a system of communism" such as that practiced in the USSR. "The ballot," he said, "not the bullet, will be our method." Luchkovich stated that he would not tolerate belonging to a group that was inclined to follow the Soviet model, and he gave the reason: the famine. "For many months rumors of extreme hunger have been rife in regard to what formerly was the richest, the happiest and the most fertile part of Russia, namely the Ukraine." The MP went on to say that he had read dozens of letters sent to Canada that described conditions in the USSR, and he referred to demonstrations that had been held in New York, Boston, and "other places in this continent against the hunger existing in the Ukraine." Resolutions passed at such meetings were sent to the president of the United States, Luchkovich noted, and he felt sure that "many have been sent to the prime minister of Canada." He also noted that the chairperson of one of the meetings, namely the rally held in Boston, "was a man by the name of Sullivan, an Irishman." Luchkovich read out to his fellow MPs one of the resolutions that had been sent to President Roosevelt as well as a letter about the famine that Whiting Williams had written to *Nation's Business* of Washington. He also referred to the appeals by Cardinal Innitzer on behalf of famine victims and the efforts made by Mowinckel to "put this matter on the agenda of the League of Nations, without success." Why were the Norwegian prime minister's efforts unsuccessful? In Luchkovich's opinion, it was because there were "too many axes to grind" and "too many impending non-aggression pacts." The MP for Vegreville concluded his speech by returning to the subject of farmers in Canada. It was his duty "as a farmer member to sit in eternal vigilance in behalf of the farmer interests of the people who sent me here," he said.[66]

Luchkovich's speech did not receive much coverage in the mainstream Canadian press, but for the Canadian government it served as yet another reminder of the matter of the famine. Gerald Schmitz wrote that the lack of coverage may have had something to do with

Luchkovich's political affiliation, since Canadian newspapers gave "a lot of space to the anti-CCF side."[67] Not even the *Vegreville Observer* in Luchkovich's home constituency, which often took an interest in affairs in Ottawa, mentioned the MP's statements in the House of Commons.[68] Schmitz noted that the Montreal French-language newspaper *Le Devoir* made a passing reference to the speech, and indeed *La Presse* did, too.[69] Windsor's *Border Cities Star* devoted three paragraphs to Luchkovich's statements—and its own commentary—in an article titled "Cannibalism in Russia," accompanied by a photograph of the Honourable Member for Vegreville. "There are many folks from Russia in the Vegreville section of Alberta," the article began, who "get letters from the homeland and sometimes they show these to Michael Luchkovich, U.F.A., M.P. for the constituency." The article then quoted Luchkovich on the content of the letters, some of which spoke of cannibalism. "Some day," the *Border Cities Star* said in its commentary, "we hope Mr. Luchkovich might get an opportunity to speak in Windsor and tell the contents of those letters."[70] The *Winnipeg Tribune*, in an article about the debates in the House of Commons concerning the CCF program, also noted that Luchkovich had described "starvation conditions among the farmers in the Ukraine under Soviet Russia."[71] In the Ukrainian community, *Ukraïns'ki visty* covered the speech, as did *Ukraïns'kyi holos* and *Kanadyis'kyi farmer*, in greater detail.[72] The speech received some notice outside of Canada, too. The bulletin of the Ukrainian Bureau in London, which was sent to various addresses around the world—including the Prime Minister's Office in Ottawa—commented on it. Among other things, the bulletin referred to the many resolutions that Luchkovich said had been sent to the U.S. president and the Canadian prime minister.[73]

Mayor Ralph Webb Speaks at a Meeting of the Ukrainian Famine Relief Committee

Also in February 1934, the mayor of Winnipeg was extended an invitation to speak at an "anti-communistic meeting" in the city. The meeting was being organized by a "committee" that was composed of "about 15 Ukrainian organizations in Winnipeg." Mayor Ralph Webb accepted the invitation. "I hope you will have a large turnout and a most successful meeting," he said in a letter addressed to D. M. Elcheshen of the USSAC.[74]

The "committee" was in fact the recently founded Ukrainian Famine Relief Committee, which had come into being at a meeting summoned by the USSAC on January 22.[75] The objectives of the committee, according to the *Winnipeg Tribune*, were to organize a series of lectures about the situation in Soviet Ukraine and to arrange for the collection of funds. The newspaper also noted that similar work was being carried out by the Ukrainian Self-Reliance League of Canada and the Ukrainian National Council.[76] The meeting to which the mayor had been invited, under the auspices of the Ukrainian Famine Relief Committee, took place as planned on Sunday, March 11, at the Rusalka Theatre, on the corner of Selkirk Avenue and Main Street. In his speech that afternoon, Mayor Webb called Ukrainians the only people in Canada fighting "Bolshevism and Communism" and challenged the press to cover the meeting. About half a dozen attendees were ejected from the premises when "they refused to stand in tribute to the victims of starvation in the Soviet Ukraine." Two resolutions were passed at the meeting. The first asked Ottawa to urge the Soviet government to "cease its inhuman policy of starving the people of the Ukraine" and to admit "external assistance for the starving." The resolution further stated that if Moscow rejected these requests, Canada should then discontinue trade relations with the USSR and cease importing "goods tainted with the blood of starving Ukrainians." The second resolution, proposed by Elcheshen and seconded by Webb, urged Ottawa to take a more vigorous approach against pro-Communist organizations. Copies of both resolutions were also forwarded to the British government.[77]

A second meeting convened a week later at the parish hall of the Blessed Virgin Mary Ukrainian Catholic Church (corner of Boyd Avenue and Artillery Street). Dr. T. Datskiw read letters received from Ukraine, "which told of famine and of millions of people dying due to starvation." The gathering adopted the two resolutions passed at the previous Sunday's meeting.[78] At a third meeting held under the auspices of the Ukrainian Famine Relief Committee, this time at the Ukrainian National Hall on McGregor Street and Burrows Avenue, those in attendance denounced Alderman Jacob Penner and Communist denials of the famine. A planned meeting by the committee in Elmwood, slated for April 9, was announced.[79] Other activities planned by the Ukrainian Relief Committee were also reported in the local press later in the year.[80] Coverage of the committee's activities was not restricted to Winnipeg. The *Calgary Herald*, via a Canadian Press cable, also ran a story about the March 11 meeting.[81]

Chapter Eight

"A GREAT RESPONSIBILITY": CANADA, THE USSR, AND THE LEAGUE OF NATIONS
July–December 1934

Godfrey Walter Phillimore (Second Baron Phillimore)

In 1934, Michael Luchkovich came to the notice of Lord Phillimore, of Henley-on-Thames, Oxfordshire, who on June 20 wrote a letter to the MP for Vegreville. In it, Phillimore told Luchkovich that he had heard indirectly of the latter's interest in conditions in Ukraine. The purpose of the baron's letter was to "suggest that we might work together to draw the attention of the very apathetic world to the terrible famine conditions in Southern Russia." He went on to say that in England it was a challenge to "make the English people believe that such appalling facts are true" in the face of the Soviet propaganda disseminated across the country. Phillimore stated that an effort was "now being made to get the Churches to pull together to draw attention to the calamity, and bring help if possible." The House of Lords member said that his committee, the Russian Coordinating Committee, believed that combatting the Third International necessitated publishing the truth.[1]

Luchkovich replied to Phillimore later that month, it seems, for Phillimore acknowledged receipt of a letter when he again wrote to the Canadian MP in July. This time, the baron thanked Luchkovich for "asking Mr. Humphrey Mitchell to give me his impression of his visit to the Ukraine last summer" and also for putting him in touch with Ukrainians in the United States. Luchkovich had furthermore given Phillimore articles by William Chamberlin, which it turned out the baron already possessed, and had referred him to the Ukrainian Bureau in London. Phillimore shared with Luchkovich his frustrations about the mood in Britain, and the world in general, regarding politics. As far as the USSR was concerned, "For the last five years our publicists have combined to express their faith in Soviet idealism, and in the success of the Five Year Plan, and are being led blindfold [sic] through Russia in troops of carefully shepherded tourists." It was the aim of his committee to "get the true facts published" and he thanked Luchkovich for helping the group.[2]

Luchkovich's proposal to ask Mitchell to share his impressions of the USSR should come as no surprise; of course, the two of them were together in the House of Commons at the time. Moreover, both had recently spoken on the topic of free speech at the Ottawa branch of the Canadian Legion of the British Empire Service, in Trafalgar House, on the same evening. Although Mitchell made no specific mention in the House of Commons of the famine, he did make a fleeting reference to Ukraine during the parliamentary debates on March 21, 1934. On that occasion, he mentioned Nazi Germany's designs on Ukraine, Stalin's overtures to Piłsudski, and Herriot, the "radical French socialist, going to Russia recently and saying to the Russian people all the nice things he could say and in my judgment making observations absolutely contrary to the facts, whereas only six months ago the attitude of the French government was directly the opposite in regard to the Russian government."[3]

In September 1934, Prime Minister Bennett also received a letter from Baron Phillimore. In that letter, Phillimore said he had been in correspondence with Luchkovich, "whom I think you know, and I have gathered from him and from other sources that the Canadian people are well informed as to the true aims of the Soviet Union and the actual state of affairs" in the USSR. He was hoping that the opposition of Switzerland to the entry of the USSR into the League of Nations would have some sympathy from the Canadian prime minister. After all, he said, Germany "was submitted to preliminary examination before entry." Phillimore, who recently had been to Berne, thought the USSR should not be admitted unconditionally. Even though he knew his view was not shared by the British foreign secretary, he assured the Canadian prime minister that a large number of people would support Canada's backing of the Swiss position.[4] In fact, only a couple of days after he had penned his letter to Canada's prime minister, Baron Phillimore wrote another, to the London *Times*, in which he outlined his views of the USSR's admission to the league. He again alluded to a recent visit to Switzerland, the seat of the League of Nations, where he had sensed that the Swiss people resented the unconditional entry of the USSR to the league and consequently a seat on its permanent council. It would mean more Communist propaganda in the country, he said. There was also the USSR's record of the treatment of minorities, and only a month previously, Phillimore added, the Archbishop of Canterbury had spoken about the famine that in 1933 had resulted in at least three million deaths.[5]

Indeed, after recognition of the Soviet Union by the United States, speculation mounted during 1934 over whether the USSR would be admitted to the League of Nations—and increasingly, it seemed that it would. The United States was never a member of the league. But Canada was, and its government was aware of the many famine-related protest rallies across the country from the resolutions directed to Ottawa. Indeed, Glazov argues that Canada's Soviet policy under the Bennett administration was to some degree influenced by the local Ukrainian community. "This policy," he writes, "resulted largely from the sentiments of Catholics in Québec and immigrants from the communist world (especially Ukrainians), both of whom abhorred Moscow's persecution of their political and religious compatriots."[6]

A Telegram from the Ukrainian Famine Relief Committee, Winnipeg

The debate over the admission of the Soviet Union to the League of Nations was scheduled to take place in Geneva on September 17, 1934. Planning to take part in the debate, Bennett boarded the *Empress of Britain*, which then set sail for Europe. On board the ship, the prime minister received a telegram from D. Yakimischak, president of the Ukrainian Famine Relief Committee in Winnipeg. Dated August 31, 1934, the telegram began: "The greatest tragedy in modern times is going on at present in Ukraine." Millions of people, Yakimischak said, were being exterminated by "the starvation policy of the Soviet government." Having failed to impose Communism after fifteen years, "this government has forcibly deprived peasants both individual and collectivized of all foodstuffs, leaving them to subsist on bark weeds rats mice etc, or else perish by starvation." Hundreds of villages had completely disappeared, the telegram continued, while the populations of others had decreased by 20 to 80 per cent as a result of the famine. Yakimischak referred to "thousands of letters" that had been received by relatives in Canada who had lost parents, brothers, and sisters. While the press acknowledged the seriousness of the famine, the Soviet government denied its existence and also prevented help from abroad. "We consider it high time that the civilized world take under its protection the victims of Communist madness and put an end to the horrid sufferings of millions of innocent people," he continued. The "350,000 Canadians of Ukrainian descent" requested that he use his "good offices" and "high influence" in "exposing the starvation policy practiced by the Soviet regime [in] Ukraine."[7] Once in Geneva, the prime minister was cabled another telegram, this time from the Ukrainian Self-Reliance League of Canada. This telegram, which also put at 350,000 the number of Canadians of Ukrainian origin, strongly protested the admission to the League of Nations of the USSR—"the inhuman monster which for several years is deliberately killing off millions of Ukrainians by an artificially created famine thus trying to compel them to submit to the [M]oscow slavery."[8]

Alexandre Choulguine (Shulhyn) of the Ukrainian Government-in-Exile

Among the prime minister's papers is a "Précis of the Memorandum of Alexandre Choulguine [Oleksander Shulhyn], Delegate of the National Ukrainian Government in Exile, etc., on the Candidature of the U.S.S.R. and the Ukraine." The précis argued that the "aggression of Moscow against Ukraine" from 1917 to 1920 and later was "irreconcilable with the Preamble of the Covenant of the League, reciting that each Member accepts certain obligations not to have recourse to war." It continued that the USSR was not a self-governing state in the meaning of Article 1 of the Covenant. Moreover, the précis maintained, the Soviet regime had practiced terror since its formation—executions, persecution of the church, and forced labour, all of which violated Article 25 of the Covenant. The précis underscored that Stalin had written a book at the end of 1933 that was very hostile to the league, and further, "the economic system is such that it has resulted and must result in misery and famine." The acceptance of the USSR to the league, the précis declared, meant the moral approbation of the Soviet government.[9]

The Paris-based Choulguine had earlier written to the Canadian delegation at the International Monetary and Economic Conference in London. In that communication, dated July 11, 1933, and written in French, Choulguine mentioned a letter he had directed to Ramsay MacDonald, president of the International Monetary and Economic Conference, on July 3, 1933, and a memorandum that "presents the Ukrainian point of view on the economic crisis in the USSR and the problem of economic recovery in Ukraine." The prime minister's private secretary, R. K. Finlayson, thanked Choulguine (then in Geneva) for the letters and the memorandum. "I am to add," Finlayson went on to say, "that Mr. Bennett very much appreciates your thoughtfulness in sending these matters to him, which he has read with very great interest."[10]

The Liaison Committee of Women's International Organizations, London

Also in the prime minister's papers is a copy of a letter from the London-based Liaison Committee of Women's International Organizations to Rickard Johannes Sandler, who had succeeded Mowinckel as president of the League of Nations Assembly. Dated September 13, 1934, the letter ventured to bring to Sandler's notice the "desperate plight of the population in Soviet Ukraine." In 1933, the letter continued, the Liaison Committee had succeeded in interesting Mowinckel in the matter. Having brought the question before the Council of the League,

Mowinckel had then "requested the International Red Cross to offer the Russian Red Cross the funds and the grain already collected by the devotion of the Ukrainian colonies in Canada and elsewhere." The Soviet government had refused the "friendly offer of help," the Liaison Committee—which comprised various organizations—went on to say. It continued: "In these twelve months famine has stricken down a great number of people, who are dying of hunger in the granary of Europe." The letter writers urged Sandler to use his "great personal and official prestige" (at that time, Sandler was also minister of foreign affairs for Sweden) to impress upon the Soviet government, if and when it became a member of the league, "to accept the help eagerly offered by fellow members of the League." The Soviet government should know that "there would be no loss of dignity" in accepting this aid; "on the contrary it would be a proof of international and humanitarian solidarity." The letter bore the names of Ishbel, Marchioness of Aberdeen and Temair, Mrs. Corbett Ashby, Mrs. Asch van Wjck, and Madame Clara Guthrie d'Arcis.[11]

Ewald Ammende

The prime minister also heard from Ewald Ammende, whom he met during the latter's visit to Canada in the summer of 1934. The honorary secretary of the Interconfessional and International Relief Committee for the Starving Districts of the Soviet Union, Ammende had credentials from Ukrainians in Lviv, London, and New York and desired to both engage the Canadian government in the matter of relief action and gain the support of Prime Minister Bennett. He had crossed into Canada from the United States. The *New York Times* informed its readers that Ammende had arrived in the United States on Thursday, June 28, 1934, on the *Bremen*. Ammende, who was representing Cardinal Innitzer, told the newspaper that he was not collecting funds but rather wanted to awaken the public to conditions that were being concealed by the Soviet government. Millions had died in Ukraine and elsewhere in the USSR in 1933, he said, while more than 1,700,000 bushels of grain were exported to obtain foreign currency. "There is no doubt whatever that the grain which was exported would have saved the lives of a few millions of human beings. Their lives were not saved and it is still being denied that there was a famine in the districts concerned," the *New York Times* quoted Ammende as saying. On the same page, the newspaper printed a denial by the Soviet ambassador to the United States, Alexander Troyanovsky, who declared that there was "no starvation in Russia today." Troyanovsky added that the existing conditions in the Soviet Union could not compare with those of Austria, and he contended that the aim of Ammende's committee was to discredit the USSR.[12]

Ammende replied to the Soviet envoy's statements. His committee, the Baltic German said in a letter to the *New York Times*, included representatives of Lutheran, Jewish, and other religious groups in Vienna, and he stressed that its aims were humanitarian and not political: specifically, to ensure that people threatened by famine obtained help in time. The belief that a famine loomed in the autumn and winter of 1934, he went on to say, came from official Soviet reports that the crop had been destroyed, owing to drought in some districts. Ammende pointed to a decree of May 27, 1934, which he said had caused the price of bread to rise by 100 per cent. He also quoted Columbia University professor S. P. Duggan, who had recently returned from the USSR. Ammende's committee had been in touch with the Archbishop of Canterbury, the Rabbi of London, and other groups on the matter of famine relief, and he was commissioned to do the same in the United States and Canada. Ammende urged that grain reserves in the West be used to help the starving in the USSR before it was too late for them.[13]

Ammende's Canadian itinerary included Winnipeg, a city that had served as the centre of the grain industry and contained a significant eastern European population. The *Winnipeg Free Press* commented on the disclosures Ammende made during his stay in the once-dubbed "Chicago of the North." The "point of Dr. Ewald Ammende's revelations during his recent visit to this city," the local newspaper remarked in July 1934, was "one far beyond any possible reaction which crop failure in Russia may have on world wheat markets. The point is the appeal to humanity." The story of "millions of human beings dying of starvation" was one, the *Free Press* continued, "which cannot lightly be put aside especially as Dr. Ammende in his own person and by the credentials he presents must be accorded a respectful hearing." Ammende said that at least five million people had died of starvation in 1933 even though the crop was a good one, and there were claims that drought had taken a heavy toll and that the price of bread had doubled. The Soviet ambassador in Washington had countered that since Ammende's committee was in Vienna, it should look after Austria first. The ambassador's statement, in the newspaper's view, was "a retort but not an answer." Meanwhile, noted the *Free Press*, the Moscow correspondent of the *New York Times* had estimated the current crop at 70 per cent of the 1933 harvest; according to the *Times*, this meant the USSR faced a winter and a spring of famine. The Winnipeg paper added that censorship had kept "the facts from being widely known and the millions who died of starvation were held by the Russians to have died for the cause." It then stressed, "In this part of Canada we must be doubly aware of it not only because of the thousands of our fellow-citizens to whom these provinces are not places on a map but connected by ties of association and of blood." Ammende, the newspaper concluded, had said his committee had nothing to do with political systems, but "it does have to do with the suffering of human beings."[14] The *Winnipeg Tribune* also covered the visit, quoting Ammende on the reason for his visit as follows: "Just as the aid committee recently got in touch with the Archbishop of Canterbury and other leaders of the church and humanitarian organizations in London, England, so has the [Vienna] committee sent me to do the same in the United States and Canada." Ammende added that the committee wanted to determine whether it was possible to make use of the large grain surpluses in the major grain-producing countries in order to help the starving people of the Soviet Union "before it was too late."[15]

Upon Ammende's arrival in Winnipeg, Luchkovich received a telegram from M. Stechisin (Stechyshyn), Dr. Novak, Dr. Dackiw, and Rev. Sawchuk. It stated, "Your help is imperative," urging the MP to "please come [to] Winnipeg immediately" to discuss the plans of the campaign, as Ammende would soon have to leave for Ottawa. The four men thought it might be necessary for Luchkovich to accompany Ammende to Ottawa, and they wrote that a Ukrainian "representation from New York" was ready to go to the Canadian capital as well. Any absence by Luchkovich, they cautioned, would do "great harm" to a "matter which is of great [importance]." They guaranteed to cover his travel expenses.¹⁶

Ammende himself wrote to Luchkovich on July 24, 1934. Writing on stationary of the Windsor Hotel in Montreal, he asked the MP to please "come to the boat for Quebec. It leaves at 7.30." But failing that, Ammende asked Luchkovich if he could meet with Rev. John Mackay of the United Church in Winnipeg and "tell him the details of our talk with Mr. Ben[n]ett and encourage him to be energetic and persistent in the matter of the organising the committee [sic] for the Starving Population of the Soviet Union." Luchkovich was urged to "support [MacKay] with everything you can." Ammende also requested that he "do everything you can to create in Winnipeg and in Alberta among the Ukrainians, Mennonites etc. a great popular movement in favour of the starving people in the Soviet Union" and "insist on Mr. Ben[n]ett to include you officially in the Canadian Delegation for the League of Nations and to come personally to Geneva in September." Luchkovich's presence in Geneva, in Ammende's estimation, "might pro[ve] for the Ukrainian cause this year of decisive importance."¹⁷

Toward the end of July, *Ukraïns'ki visty* also shared the news of Ammende's arrival in Canada. He had visited New York and Washington, readers were told, and through his efforts an aid committee had been set up in New York that comprised people of different faiths, including the chief rabbi. The Estonia-born general secretary of the Congress of European Nationalities also had managed to convince the *New York Times*—a newspaper "well-known for its sympathy to the Soviets"—about the famine, *Ukraïns'ki visty* said. The main aim of Ammende's visit was to familiarize the American public with the situation in Ukraine and other parts of the USSR, the paper continued. It drew its readers' attention to Ammende's refutations in the *New York Times* of the Soviet ambassador's denials about the famine, and it then provided details of Ammende's itinerary in Canada: He arrived in Winnipeg, from Chicago, on July 18. In Winnipeg, he visited the editorial offices of English-language newspapers and met with representatives of different confessions, who, on July 21, struck a relief committee. He received assurances from Ukrainian Canadians that the community could commit ten carloads of grain for the starving in Ukraine.[18] Ammende then left Winnipeg for eastern Canada. He was in Montreal on July 25. The *Montreal Star* noted that he had been travelling in the United States and Canada "getting the views of the clergy on the situation" in the USSR. The committee he represented, Ammende told the Montreal paper, "already has the endorsation of a large number of the clergy of Great Britain." It reported that Ammende had attended a meeting of interested religious representatives in western Canada and had organized a branch of his committee there; he hoped to do the same in Ontario and elsewhere in Canada.[19]

Ukraïns'ki visty remarked that, according to Ammende, the Soviets themselves had spoken of a collapse of the harvest, especially in the south, because of drought. There was thus a possibility of famine that could again threaten the lives of millions. *Ukraïns'ki visty* also informed its readers that Ammende had been granted an hour-long audience with the Canadian prime minister, though no date was given.[20] The *Toronto Star* noted that Ammende and a journalist, M. Popoff, met with Bennett on July 23 in the hope he would apply pressure on the Soviet government to relieve starvation in the USSR. Bennett had showed sympathy for their cause, the paper reported, but did not believe that Canada could be helpful. The *Star* then quipped that others had advised the prime minister's visitors that "Mr. Bennett's attitude toward the Soviets was such that a word from him to Stalin on behalf of the suffering would probably result in the prompt starvation of a few millions where none starved before."[21] According to *Ukraïns'ki visty*, Bennett had responded carefully on the matter of helping victims of the famine. He expressed the view that obtaining the consent of the Soviet government for relief of the starving would be difficult unless that consent could be bargained for during the deliberations on the USSR's admission to the League of Nations.[22] Around this time, there may have been a degree of speculation among the Ukrainian community over whether Ammende's wish for Luchkovich to accompany the Canadian prime minister to Geneva might indeed be realized in some fashion. In London, Kysilewsky recorded in his diary that he had received a "very interesting letter" from the editor of *Kanadyis'kyi farmer*, Teodor Datskiv (T. Datskiw), who informed him that Bennett had journeyed to Geneva and that Luchkovich might be going there, too. Kysilewsky added that Bennett had promised he would raise the matter of the famine in Geneva during the debate over the admission of the USSR to the League of Nations. Kysilewsky was asked by Datskiv to send the most recent information about the famine to Geneva. That he did, gathering up whatever material he could and forwarding it to Ostap Lutsky, a Ukrainian member of the Polish Parliament, who was in London and on his way to Geneva.[23] Ultimately, however, Luchkovich did not go to Switzerland.

New Jersey's *Svoboda* also provided some insight into Ammende's visit to North America. While in Canada, Ammende informed a representative of that newspaper that he had been able to meet with different religious leaders and begin the process of bringing them together in a committee. In Winnipeg, he spoke to representatives of the Mennonite, Lutheran, and Roman Catholic churches, but was unable to meet with Bishop Ladyka, who was ill. Many German immigrants in Canada had roots in the USSR, he said, and they were very interested in the matter, particularly as they already had received letters from brethren that attested to the catastrophic famine in the USSR. Ammende also intimated that he had been able to meet with the "head of the French Canadian" Catholics in Quebec. Although no name was given, he may well have been referring to Cardinal Jean-Marie-Rodrigue Villeneuve, the Archbishop of Quebec.[24] Indeed, Ammende considered his sixweek North American visit a success.[25] In one section of the Ukrainian community in Canada, however, the reaction to his visit was negative. The ULFTA's *Ukraïns'ki robitnychi visty* charged that Ammende was in fact a German and Japanese agent.[26]

Ammende's visit to North America revived interest within the Ukrainian community in the matter of aid for victims of starvation in Ukraine.[27] A July 1934 article in *Svoboda* by a person who identified herself as "Halychanka" (Galician Ukrainian) drew attention to the activities of the American Committee of Aid to the Starving in Ukraine. Although the committee had been founded in 1933 under the auspices of the Ukrainian National Women's League of America, the author stressed that the committee worked independently and that people who were not members of the league took part in its activities. The committee had performed a fair bit of work, publishing and distributing literature, but in the nearly ten months of its existence had raised only $375.00, she said. "Halychanka" added that the head of the committee, Neonilia Pelekhovych, maintained ties with the famine relief committees in Europe, in particular, the one headed by Cardinal Innitzer in Vienna and another in Prague. Noting that Ammende had come to the United States as a representative of Cardinal Innitzer, she wrote that "now there is hope that the campaign of aid to the starving under the Soviets will be better understood among Americans." When others expended so much effort in trying to rescue the starving in the USSR from death, continued the author, then one must expect Ukrainians to continue to be called to further action; Galicians often spoke about unity of the nation (*sobornist'*), and now here was a cause where that sentiment could be expressed. The reader might ask, she anticipated, how any aid could be dispatched—but there was no need for worry on that point, for the committee knew where to send the aid and to whom. "One sixth of the Ukrainian population died of starvation in Ukraine under the Soviets, and we in America and Canada have gathered up as much as $375.00 in order to save further millions from dying of hunger," remarked Halychanka. She closed with a question: "Ukrainians in America and Canada! Is this how we understand *sobornist'* about which we talk so much?"[28]

Ammende later wrote about his visit to Canada in his book *Human Life in Russia*. "At Winnipeg, the centre of the Canadian grain area, in whose neighbourhood are settled many emigrants from Russia belonging to the most diverse creeds (Ukrainians, Russians, Germans and Jews), all the local forces (Mennonites, Catholics, Lutherans, Orthodox Church, etc.) were united under the presidency of Dr. Mackay of the United Churches," he noted. The representatives of "all the Churches and religious sects in Winnipeg" addressed a joint manifesto to Prime Minister Bennett, "begging that Canada should give her consent to the admission of Soviet Russia into the League of Nations only on condition that measures were taken to save the victims in Russia." This manifesto, he wrote, proposed that Canada and other states petition the Soviet Union to allow an international commission of inquiry to travel to the famine areas and offer cooperation with the Soviets in "relieving the distress." Ammende observed that the "Canadian delegate did, in fact, declare that his country voted for the admission of Soviet Russia into the League in the expectation that it would in future be made possible for its citizens to assist their kinsmen and co-believers in the Soviet Union."[29]

The petition to which Ammende referred was forwarded to the prime minister at the end of August 1934. On August 31, John Mackay, chairman, and Rev. Luhovy, secretary, addressed a letter to "Prime Minister and Members of the Dominion Government," presenting a petition "signed by representatives of all the religious denominations of Winnipeg, after careful study of the problem of famine in Russia."[30] The petition, dated August 15, read as follows:

> In view of the fact that very disquieting rumours are reaching our fellow citizens who have relatives in Russia, and that reliable sources, which have hitherto shown no bias against the U.S.S.R., report that famine was widespread in certain parts of Russia last winter, taking a toll of from five million to ten million lives, a disaster almost as great as if the entire population of Canada had been wiped out, and that evidence from Soviet sources indicates that the total crop this year will be much less than last, making further appalling disaster likely;
>
> We respectfully appeal to the Prime Minister and the Government of Canada to co-operate with other Governments in asking the U.S.S.R. to provide facilities for the visit of an International Commission to the distressed areas, and at the same time offering to co-operate with the Soviet authorities in meeting the situation if it is anything like as serious as reports indicate. This would set at rest the minds of thousands of our fellow citizens, whose relatives live in the areas indicated.
>
> If the facts are as rumour suggests, no political or other consideration should keep the other nations from joining with the U.S.S.R. in a great and concerted effort to save the lives of these millions of men, women, and little children, already in the grip of slow starvation, while the bounty of a common Father has

filled the world with abundance so great as to be the cause of serious embarrassment in some places.

We, the representatives of the religious denominations of Manitoba, profoundly moved by the plight of our fellow human beings in Russia, do earnestly urge immediate and far reaching action, and pledge our wholehearted support to any steps which may be taken. Winnipeg, 15 August 1934.

The petition was signed by the Roman Catholic Archbishops of Winnipeg (Alfred Sinnott) and St. Boniface (Emile Yelle), the Anglican Archbishop of Rupert's Land (Isaac O. Stringer), the Greek Catholic Bishop of Canada (Basil V. Ladyka), the administrator of the Greek Orthodox Church of Western Canada (Rev. S. Sawchuk), Rabbi Solomon Frank of the Charey Zadek Synagogue in Winnipeg, and the authorized representatives of the Lutheran (Thomas Hurtig, president of the Manitoba Synod of the United Lutheran Church in America), Mennonite (C. F. Klassen for Bishop David Toews), Baptist (J. J. Ross), and United Churches (signature illegible). As well, it was signed by D. Yakimischak of the Ukrainian Relief Association, "which is offering ten car loads of wheat, as soon as safe conduct can be assured to the famine areas."[31]

Laurent Beaudry, Acting Undersecretary of State for External Affairs, issued a response acknowledging receipt of the petition but the rest of the letter was in the manner of a form reply. It said that a number of appeals for the relief of residents of Ukraine, or for investigation of conditions in that part of the USSR, had been addressed to the League of Nations in September 1933, and it was felt that "the only course open to the petitioners would be for them to address themselves to organizations of a purely non-political character such as the International Red Cross." His Majesty's government in Canada, Beaudry continued, "could not undertake to investigate conditions or to organize relief under the sovereignty of another government in the absence of any indication that such action would be acceptable to that government."[32] Later that month, Mackay again wrote to Ottawa, to reiterate the purpose of the petition. "The intention of the petition was not for the Canadian Government to investigate conditions or to reorganize relief, but simply to call the attention of the Soviet Government to the rumours to which reference was made," he explained, "and to ask for non-partisan investigation, which request would be coupled with the pledge of assistance if necessary."[33]

In a letter to the London *Times* written on September 12 but published on September 18 (a day after the vote in Geneva on the USSR's admission to the League of Nations), Ammende made a reference to interconfessional attitudes in Canada toward the question of the famine. "Religious circles of all denominations not only in Europe, but also in the United States and Canada fully supported the appeals of the Archbishop of Canterbury, Cardinal Innitzer, and other Church leaders, as my personal experience has proved," Ammende wrote. The honorary secretary of the Interconfessional and International Relief Committee for the Starving Districts of the Soviet Union added that "from the standpoint of elementary humanitarian duty it will be a very grave omission if on the eve of the entry of the Soviet Union into the League the question of relief for those unfortunate human beings is not considered in earnest." In closing, he expressed the view that it was a "great responsibility indeed which rests on statesmen of the world assembled at Geneva."[34]

A couple of days before penning that letter, Ammende, who was in Geneva, had written to the Canadian prime minister. "Your Excellency," he began, "A few weeks ago I took the liberty to send you the parliamentary Report containing the speech of His Grace the Archbishop of Canterbury on the Russian famine, delivered in the House of Lords on July 25th, and I hope that my letter has still reached you in Canada." Meanwhile, he continued, the leaders of other churches in the UK—most notably "Dr. Rushbrook, the present President of the Free Churches of England"—endorsed the Archbishop of Canterbury. They agreed, wrote Ammende, that the "question of rendering relief to the starving population of the Soviet Union must be cleared up and carried through in connection with the pending entry of the Soviet Union into the League of Nations." That standpoint now seemed more justified, in his view, because, as reported in the Soviet newspaper *Pravda*, only a comparatively small amount of the expected crop in the USSR had been collected, leading Ammende to believe "that this year again many millions of human lives in the Soviet Union are threatened by death from starvation." He referred to the conversation on the famine question "which I had the privilege of having with you a month ago in Ottawa" and turned the prime minister's attention to a convention of "the Congress of European Nationalities." The congress had just recently convened its tenth annual conference, he informed Bennett, where it had again discussed the question of the famine. "This was done because many of the nationalities who take part in the Congress have in the Soviet Union brethren who are victims of the famine and are in danger of dying from starvation." A resolution was passed that appealed "to the public opinion of the world, particularly to the League of Nations," to no longer ignore the matter of the famine and to have it brought to the attention of league members on the occasion of their debate over the entry of the Soviet Union. That resolution, Ammende said, was presented personally to Dr. Edvard Beneš of the Council of the League of Nations by a delegation of the congress. "On this occasion," he noted, "the Delegates of our Congress, representing the Ukrainian and Russian Minorities, appealed to Dr. Beneš in particular," asking him to act with regard to the famine in the same way as had Mowinckel in 1933, and "to support with all the powers at his disposal a fair and decent treatment of the question of a relief for the starving population of the Soviet Union." According to Ammende, Beneš (the Czechoslovakian foreign minister and one of the founders of the league) told the delegation that "if this question should be raised in a purely humanitarian manner and discussed by the League, he too will not remain silent and will do his best to see that the truth in this matter should be cleared up."

Ammende expressed regret over the state of affairs in Europe, which, in his view, resulted in many states being driven "only by their various opportunistic and political considerations" on the matter of the Soviet Union. Regarding entry of the Soviet Union into the League of Nations, he told Bennett, "they seem only to be interested in whether to say 'Yes' or 'No' to this question, without in most cases noticing the fact that maybe more important than the question of the entry of the Soviet into the League itself, is the question of the conditions under which the event ought to take place." Ammende noted, however, that he believed many delegates would "fully support an initiative for dealing with the question of the Russian famine in a purely humanitarian manner, should such an initiative be forthcoming." He expressed the hope that he could meet personally with the prime minister and also that Bennett could give "the privilege of a personal audience to Madame E. Rudnicka [sic], the prominent Ukrainian member in the Polish Parliament, who represents here in Geneva the Ukrainian Parliamentarians of Poland and Roumania and also fully enjoys the support of the Ukrainians living in Canada." The Ukrainian people, he stressed to Bennett, had no state of its own, and in the Soviet Union they were "living in most deplorable conditions." They were "deeply grateful to Canada that under the present unsatisfactory state of affairs in Europe only in Canada the Ukrainians are able to live a truly civilized and happy life."[35]

A reply came from J. J. Saucier, the private secretary to the prime minister, on September 15. Saucier wrote that Bennett was "suffering from a bad cold" and confined to his room for several days. Also, Saucier said he had spoken to Rudnycka on the telephone several times and explained to her that the prime minister was not well enough to undertake interviews. Saucier added that he would maintain communication with Rudnycka and notify her as soon as the prime minister had sufficiently recovered. "I presume that you will wish to meet with the prime minister at the same time," he continued, noting that he could be reached by telephone at room 14, Hôtel de la Paix.[36]

Two days later, on September 17, Ammende again wrote to Bennett from the Hôtel d'Angleterre in Geneva. He began his letter by thanking the prime minister for the message he had sent by way of Saucier and wishing him a speedy recovery. He would take the liberty, as was suggested, of getting in touch with Bennett that morning but "as time is very limited now and, as I hear at this moment, the discussion in the Sixth Committe[e] on the entry of the Soviet Union into the League will take place already this afternoon, I beg your permission to submit herewith in writing before you my considerations and suggestions on this matter."[37]

The Duchess of Atholl

The prime minister also heard from the Duchess of Atholl. The duchess had for some time publicly condemned Soviet practices, and she was one of the people Ammende met during his visit to the United Kingdom. Marco Carynnyk, Lubomyr Y. Luciuk, and Bohdan S. Kordan, the editors of a book about the British Foreign Office and the famine, describe the Duchess of Atholl as the "most persistent British lobbyist for the famine victims."[38] Indeed, as they point out, on July 5, 1933, she brought up the famine in Parliament and cited the reports of Gareth Jones and Malcolm Muggeridge.[39] That day, the Scottish MP spoke about British trade with the USSR and raised the question of "whether we are justified in importing into this country any of the foodstuffs and other necessaries of life which we have accumulating evidence to show are so acutely needed" in the USSR. She went on to mention the reports of Jones and Muggeridge and letters published in the London *Times* and then returned to the theme that Soviet exports of food and other products were actually needed at home.[40] Contrasting the famine of 1921–23 with that of the present, she stated that the earlier famine had been associated primarily with the Volga region, while now "authentic accounts are to hand that there is famine, not only in the Volga, but in the Ukraine, in North Caucasus, and in West Siberia—all the richest grain-growing areas." Moreover, in the previous famine "we were allowed to send help to those starving people," she pointed out. "The United States sent generous help, and we sent a good deal of help through the 'Save the Children' Fund from this country." But the reality now, she observed, was different. News of the "terrible disaster is being kept from us, and yet it is far more extensive than before, and, far from sending help, we have people who no doubt now that the embargo has been removed, are looking forward once more to making money out of importing Russian food, dirt cheap, and selling it again at higher prices." The duchess urged her government to ensure that any credits extended to the USSR come with conditions so that they "may inure to the benefit of the people...that would allow peasants to keep the product of their tilling of the soil—that people should be allowed to keep for their own use, to save themselves and their families from starvation, the food that they raise, without having it torn away from them, as we know has too often been the case." The member for Kinross and West Perth closed with a reference to the World Economic Conference that at that time was convening in London. She urged the British government to use its "influence to suggest to the Conference that an inquiry might be made into the conditions existing in Russia" and proposed that "no credit should be granted by our Government until reports have been received from an impartial commission of inquiry and they feel that they would be justified, from those reports, in making such a grant."[41]

The Duchess of Atholl's proposal was never adopted, but on another occasion, on March 1, 1934, she again brought the matter of conditions in the USSR to Great Britain's supreme public forum.[42] Months later, on August 25, the duchess wrote to the British foreign secretary, Sir John Simon. She said that over the previous three or four months she had been receiving particulars of the 1933 famine and "of conditions pointing to the probability of an equally terrible famine"—if not worse—"this coming autumn and winter." She and others who were concerned had not said anything publicly since they knew the churches would enquire and that any move would be better coming from them, the duchess explained. Now, she pointed out, they had made statements on the subject. The Archbishop of Canterbury had made a statement in the House of Lords on July 25, 1934, and the leaders of the Free Churches had a letter published in the London *Times* in early August. Because it did not seem that they would take any further steps, the duchess asked Simon if it were possible to make British consent to the USSR's entry into the League of Nations conditional upon the Kremlin's "taking steps to mitigate the famine" by keeping their foodstuffs at home and by allowing famine relief if such could be organized by churches or other bodies in other countries. She then mentioned the Vienna famine committee that sent parcels to individuals and noted that similar committees existed in the United Kingdom; however, she pointed out, "something is needed for the benefit of the unhappy people whose names and addresses are not known outside" the USSR, and it seemed terrible that the Soviet government should be allowed to take a place in the league "without a word being said." She believed it possible that the USSR, if pressed, would be more likely now to admit the matter of the famine than it was a year or two ago. Moreover, "Hitler's declared aim of securing expansion in Eastern

Europe and Russia must have a much greater chance of success than it otherwise would, with Russian agriculture largely in ruins and Russian peasants dying by the million." Consequently, she wrote, the USSR might be willing to take aid that was offered.[43]

Only a few days later, the Scottish MP wrote to the prime minister of Canada, reiterating her position that the USSR's entry to the league hinge on the condition that it stop food exports and allow relief to be organized from the outside. It would, the Duchess of Atholl stressed, be "a terrible act of hypocrisy if the League allows Russia to enter it and nothing is said as to the conditions of her people."[44] Prime Minister Bennett had by now heard much about the issue of the famine, but he still leaned toward voting for the USSR's admission to the league. He believed that Soviet entrance would be better for the international order. Nazi Germany had withdrawn from the League of Nations, and so, too, had Japan. Presumably, it might be more effective dealing with the USSR as a league member than as a state outside it and thus theoretically accountable to no one. On September 14, Bennett replied to the duchess. On the matter of the USSR joining the League of Nations, he expressed the belief that the majority of members of the assembly were in favour of it and that he personally shared that view. Bennett told the duchess that he had read the Archbishop of Canterbury's speech in the House of Lords before arriving in Europe.[45] On the question of making the USSR's admission conditional, Canada's prime minister wrote, "I am told that it is impossible to impose conditions upon Russia's acceptance of membership; that the whole matter will drop if any such effort is made." He nonetheless thought it "desirable to bring to the attention of Russia the present condition of her people." Bennett then intimated to the Duchess of Atholl that he was aware of the famine: "I know from first hand information received in Western Canada that very large numbers of people died from starvation last year in Russia." His own personal view was that there "has been too much haste in dealing with this matter." The prime minister did not explain his opinion further, nor what he meant by "haste," except to add that as a result of it a "difficult situation" had been created.[46]

The Earl of Denbigh and Ukrainians in Canada

On July 25, 1934, the day that the Archbishop of Canterbury had spoken in the House of Lords, the Earl of Denbigh also contributed to the discussion about the famine in the upper house. He drew attention to a resolution about the famine that Congressman Hamilton Fish of New York had introduced two months earlier, on May 28: "With regard to the reluctance of noble Lords opposite that this House should pay any attention to these matters, I do not know whether your Lordships are aware that in the House of Representatives in the United States in May there was a Resolution submitted which was ordered to be printed and referred to the Committee on Foreign Affairs." Lord Denbigh proceeded to quote the resolution, which noted that the Soviet government had "failed to take relief measures designed to check the famine or to alleviate the terrible conditions arising from it, but on the contrary used the famine as a means of reducing the Ukrainian population and destroying the Ukrainian political, cultural, and national rights." Lord Denbigh considered it "rather a striking Resolution to have been brought up in Congress in the United States, and it shows at all events that on that side there are not such delicate feelings as some people have on this side."[47] Although the resolution was referred to the Committee on Foreign Affairs, it never came up for a vote.[48]

Lord Denbigh's speech in the House of Lords came to the notice of Ukrainians in Canada. A letter of gratitude to the earl from the United Hetman Classocrats (formerly the Ukrainian Sporting Sitch Association of Canada) shared with Lord Denbigh the efforts that had until then been made in Canada on behalf of the starving in Ukraine. "Despite the numerous obstacles, our organization has been and is forwarding assistance, through private channels, to as many victims of the Soviet rule (misrule!) as it is possible under the circumstances," said the letter of August 18, 1934. "But all such assistance is insignificant—in view of the magnitude of the catastrophe—and will remain such until the Soviet Government is persuaded to admit external assistance, which could then be organized on a proper scale." The letter noted that, should the removal of barriers to relief efforts "be made to serve as a condition upon which the Soviet Union may be accepted to the

League of Nations," then "the result would be the saving from a tortuous death of millions of human beings." The letter wondered whether "the pleading of starving millions [would] take precedence over the established formalities and politics." Reference was then made to letters that had been received from Ukraine. "After receiving from our brethren heartrending letters describing their mental and physical suffering from the chicanery of the callous Soviet bureaucracy and the cruel famine inflicted upon them, letters in which innocent humanity in the agony of death is crying to heaven for help—Your Lordship's, so nobly manifested, deep concern over the fate of these seemingly forgotten souls is a source of inexpressible gratification to us!" The letter closed with the following statement: "All loyal Canadian citizens of Ukrainian origin are fully aware of Your Lordship's noteworthy act, and we beg to assure Your Lordship that their sentiments are also expressed in this humble letter."[49]

The League of Nations and the Admission of the USSR

On September 17, 1934, delegates of four dozen nations gathered in Geneva to debate and then vote on the question of admission of the USSR to the League of Nations. According to the *New York Times*, the deliberations that day included "severe denunciations of the Soviet political system and of Soviet actions in the recent past." The denunciations had come from Argentina, Belgium, Portugal, and "most bitterly of all," from Switzerland. M. Giuseppe Motta of Switzerland referred specifically to the famine in his speech. The Soviet Union, he said, was "afflicted with the somber curse of famine." Further, he stated, "Impartial observers wonder whether this famine is purely a natural phenomenon or whether it is a consequence of an economic and social system vitiated in its very roots."[50]

Switzerland was one of the three countries that voted against the admission of the Soviet Union; the other two were Portugal and the Netherlands. Seven others abstained: Argentina, Belgium, Cuba, Luxembourg, Panama, Peru, and Venezuela. Panama had apparently gone back on a "gentlemen's agreement" about voting for Soviet admission. The *Manchester Guardian* said it had done so under the influence of an article on Soviet Ukraine that had appeared in a Swiss newspaper.⁵¹ The *New York Times* elaborated: "The Panama delegate recorded with his abstention the statement that he did not feel justified in voting for Russia's admission after reading in the press about the condition of her starving masses."⁵²

Canada was among the thirty-eight members that voted to admit the USSR. But it did so mindful of the stories about the famine that the Canadian government had been hearing from people with relatives in the Soviet Union. The Dominion's position before the sixth committee of the assembly was voiced by Oscar Skelton, undersecretary of state for external affairs. Skelton expressed the belief that "under the present world circumstances" the USSR's entrance to the league was desirable, but that Canada had difficulty in accepting Soviet membership because of the gulf that existed between Canada's social and political principles and those of the Soviet Union. Skelton, too, mentioned the famine. He spoke of the "apprehension felt by many thousands in Canada who have relatives and friends" in the Soviet Union "as to the continuance of the sufferings and the famine which were reported in many districts of the Soviet Union last year [1933] and on previous occasions." He added that Canada believed the Soviet Union would, like other members of the league, be "prepared to do what is possible to relieve distress and will be prepared to sanction any assistance, devoid of political bias which individual citizens of any other Member of the League might desire to tender to those in distress, just as similar sanction would be given reciprocally."⁵³

Further insight into Canada's position on the question of the USSR's admission to the league is provided in a letter written by Skelton to his wife, Isabel, before the vote. In it, Skelton described a "difficult morning," during which he had discussed the subject with Bennett. While the prime minister's "head was convinced Russia should come in," his "heart wasn't and various telegrams he had from Canada and England hardened his heart." According to Skelton, Bennett had thus agreed only reluctantly to sign the invitation to the USSR to join the league.⁵⁴ Even after the prime minister signed, he—on the day the sixth committee was to meet—told Skelton that he wanted to take part and "take a whack" at the Soviets. Skelton replied that Bennett could not participate, as it was he, and not the prime minister, who was the Canadian member of the committee, and that in any case, the prime minister was to preside at the second (economic) committee. In discussing what would be said, Skelton said that he tried to "argue him out of some of his more extreme positions [and] succeeded in some measure." But the prime minister insisted that Skelton "lambaste [the Soviets] on propaganda [and the] famine." The two had now reached the committee rooms. Skelton "scribbled down some notes." He had "toned down" Bennett's points as much as he could and "embalmed them in some of my own ideas, so I didn't have to stretch my own conscience too much." Skelton described his own speech as "not long" and noted that it "seemed to go quite well." He added, "We had a great audience, and a tense debate, quite the highlight of the Assembly." Skelton thought that it "was quite amusing that on a question the [prime minister] had so much at heart" it should instead be he "who spoke for Canada."[55]

Skelton and Bennett were not particularly close. When Bennett's Conservatives were elected, Skelton had been "rather dismayed." While the two may not have always shared similar ideas, Bennett nonetheless retained the experienced Skelton in Ottawa.[56] If Bennett ever objected to Skelton's toning down of his points, he does not seem to have expressed it. In a letter to George I. Kurdydyk, Bennett described Skelton's statement in Geneva as one that "clearly defines our [the government's] position."[57]

In another letter to Isabel, Skelton noted that on Saturday, September 17, at noon, Walter A. Riddell, the Canadian advisory officer to the League of Nations, had a lunch for the prime minister and Skelton, with Soviet foreign minister Maxim Litvinov and the Polish foreign minister Józef Beck "as the star outsiders." Litvinov was seated between Skelton and the prime minister. "He [Bennett] got on quite well with Lit. [as the prime minister called Litvinov, according to Skelton], razzing him quite a bit." Sometime later, Skelton "was invited by the Soviet people to lunch at the Bellevue." The Canadian foreign minister recalled, "What struck me most was the lunch itself – caviar, lobster, pheasant, pate de fois gras etc, with Cordon Rouge champagne, Chambertin etc to say nothing of Vodka – quite the swankiest lunch I had seen in Geneva, and quite a striking commentary on proletarian principles and practices."[58]

Ukrainians in Canada may have petitioned the prime minister before and as he headed to Switzerland, but probably few expected a different outcome in Geneva. Of course, while the result may have been foreseen, it was not any more acceptable. An editorial in *Kanadyis'kyi farmer* summed up the common sentiment: "That people are guided in politics neither by ethics nor morals can be witnessed in the case of the acceptance of the Russian Bolsheviks to the League of Nations."[59] The same issue of the Winnipeg weekly reported the debate over admitting the USSR to the League of Nations, mentioning Skelton's statement about the apprehension felt by relatives in Canada concerning the famine. *Kanadyis'kyi farmer* thought, however, that the problem of dispensing relief to people who did not have relatives abroad had been overlooked.[60]

Almost a year earlier, and after receiving many appeals, the league had claimed it was unable to intervene to help the "famine-stricken populace of the Russian Ukraine." Johan Mowinckel, then president of the Council of the League of Nations, had brought up the subject of the famine at a secret session and urged that some action be taken. But the council had maintained that a country that was not a member of the league could not be approached on an internal matter. It was suggested that the issue instead be deferred to a nonpolitical body such as the Red Cross.[61] In 1934, members of the league voted to admit the USSR to its fold.[62] Presumably, then, the obstacle previously observed by the council had now been removed.

Admission of the USSR to the League of Nations: The Aftermath

Indeed, some observers expected practical results to follow from the League of Nations' vote as far as the matter of relief was concerned. On December 7, Canadian Mennonite Board of Colonization chair David Toews wrote to Prime Minister Bennett to inform him of the continued receipt of letters. Five million people had died from starvation in 1933, he wrote, and he expressed the fear that many more would perish owing to crop conditions. Toews mentioned that many thousands of dollars had passed through his board and other organizations in the attempt to save as many lives as possible. But now that the USSR was a member of the League of Nations, he continued, perhaps Canada's influence could be applied to make more effective the delivery of relief to those in need of it in that country. For that reason, he informed the prime minister, the Mennonite community was petitioning the Canadian representative in Geneva in the hope of "removing barriers that are placed in our way by various methods."[63]

On the same day that Toews wrote to the prime minister, another letter was sent to Geneva that included his signature and those of fourteen other Mennonite leaders. In 1933, millions of citizens of the USSR had died of starvation, "especially in the Ukraine, the North Caucasus, also along the Volga River, and in the exile camps in Northern Russia and Siberia," began the letter. And now, owing to crop failure, famine again loomed, which made urgent the matter of preparedness. "Trusting that by negotiations in the proper quarters of the League of Nations, arrangements can be made to fully open the way and make relief work as effective at all possible, we are representing the Mennonite people of Canada and the United States," the letter closed.[64]

Toews's letter to the prime minister was acknowledged by Skelton, who asked for further details on the obstacles to relief work to which Toews had alluded. That way, Skelton explained, "the Government would give further consideration to the question of approaching the Soviet authorities on the matter."[65] Toews promptly obliged. He began by complaining about the high tariffs; if grain, flour, and second-hand clothing could enter the USSR duty-free, it would then be possible to collect these items and send them to the people "who are starving." He then added that, according "to new regulations," it was possible only for individuals to send help as "no organized effort is permitted." Yet "since not only our people are starving, but a great number of others, we believe that the Russian authorities should welcome every organized effort to bring help to their people in as effective a way as possible." Toews believed sending clothing and food from abroad would be better, otherwise people would receive little for the money that was sent, and what they could obtain was likely of poor quality.

He then drew attention to the problems faced by people who received outside help: many were "put out of employment," and the amount of assistance they obtained was not sufficient "for them and their families to keep them reasonably comfortable." Moreover, Toews continued, there had been cases where people who obtained help from abroad were persecuted. He cited the additional problem of Soviet suppression of reports that showed "famine conditions as they really exist in Russia." If it were possible to arrange relief in an effective way, Toews believed, its distribution in the USSR should be supervised by a reliable committee from other countries. Indeed, he ended his letter to Canada's foreign minister, the best way to obtain a proper assessment of conditions in the USSR was for the League of Nations to send an independent delegation there.[66]

CONCLUSION

In December 1932, Andrew Cairns had explained to Alberta's premier that he preferred people to draw their own conclusions from the evidence contained in his reports. By the same token, readers can draw their own conclusions from the material presented in this book. However, one or two salient points may be developed for further discussion here. The first is that, as shown, considerable information about the famine was available in Canada. The second is that repeated calls were made to come to the rescue of the starving people in the USSR. Yet in spite of the abundant information about the Soviet Union and the appeals at various times and by different groups and individuals, there was no "widespread or sustained pressure for a federal response," as Gerald Schmitz observes in his own study of the famine. Indeed, Schmitz concludes that citizens of Canada and "of the industrialized West generally did not react with the outrage which might have been expected."[1] The question is why.

On the basis of the available data, attempts at providing an answer may be made. Upon hearing about the famine in 1932 and 1933, many Canadians may have remembered the one that had engulfed parts of the USSR ten years earlier. Indeed, the Canadian press drew parallels between the two famines. However, an important difference must be recognized. Whereas the famine of 1921–23 was characterized by Lenin's eventual acceptance of large-scale aid, that of 1932–33 saw his successor, Stalin, reject collective offers of relief. From the vantage point of Canada, Stalin's rejection could be interpreted in various ways. Perhaps the situation in the Soviet Union was not so serious if the government there was not seeking outside help. After all, it could be reasoned, what government would allow its own people to starve? While an occasional story about the famine was printed in the mainstream press, many others pointed to signs of progress in the USSR—attempts at turning the clock forward and transforming the USSR into an industrial society more quickly than the major capitalist states had been able to industrialize. The process was overseen by a man, Joseph Jughashvili, whose adopted surname—Stalin—signified "man of steel." News stories described the development of industrial plants, the Dnipro hydroelectric station, the official elimination of unemployment, the buildup of a mighty army, and strides made in education and the status of women. These and other examples of Soviet progress seemed to negate any possibility of a catastrophe in the order of a mass famine. Moreover, at the same time that news was being printed about advances in the Soviet Union, Canadian newspapers were replete with local stories associated with the Depression. In fact, pressure was applied on the Canadian government to lift its partial embargo on trade with the USSR to help alleviate some of the effects of the major economic downturn. The trend of Soviet rapprochement with capitalist countries, culminating with the U.S. recognition of the USSR in November 1933, may have made the notion of a catastrophic famine even less conceivable.

Not only did Stalin not welcome external help when it was offered, but, following British journalist Gareth Jones's disclosures about the famine, the Kremlin was quick to issue a denial that it even existed—a refutation that many Canadian newspapers reported at the close of March 1933. While the Soviet regime disapproved of the observations by Jones, and by others such as Rhea Clyman, it was more receptive to the writings of Pierre van Paassen and Robert Cromie. The regime seemed to like Cromie, the owner of the *Vancouver Sun*; he was quoted in *Pravda*, the official mouthpiece of the Communist Party of the Soviet Union. In July 1933, according to *Pravda*, Cromie spoke of the awareness of Soviet citizens vis-à-vis their achievements and commitments as well as of North America's huge unemployment rate, which he said produced much uncertainty for the future. Cromie acknowledged difficulties in the USSR, but apparently then asked whether it was possible for the achievements to be made without some sacrifice.[2] And Soviet officials viewed van Paassen as "friendly" toward the USSR. That was the adjective used by Soviet official Boris Skvirsky in Washington, DC, in a letter to the All-Union Society for Cultural Relations with Foreign Countries (VOKS) on May 23, 1933. "The liberal journalist Pierre van Paassen visited the Soviet Union last year and wrote a series of friendly articles upon his return," Skvirsky wrote. He added that van Paassen planned to again visit the Soviet Union in June and July in order to "collect materials for a new series of articles about the USSR" and that he would probably "ask about free or reduced price fares for his travel around the country." Skvirsky asked VOKS to accommodate van Paassen's request if possible.[3]

Van Paassen was among the journalists whose reports helped shape public perceptions about the Soviet Union. The lack of congruity in reports about the USSR in general, and the famine in particular, made the situation there difficult to understand. Just one published report denying the famine may have been sufficient to create an element of doubt. The potential for confusion was perhaps best expressed by the title of an August 9, 1933, editorial in the *Edmonton Journal*: "What to Believe about Russia?"[4] The famine coincided with the emergence of the Nazis in Germany, and the führer pointed to the incidence of mass starvation over which the *vozhd* at the helm of the USSR presided as a failure of Communism. Some commentators thus chose to interpret from the contradictory information presented that the famine was either an exaggeration or perhaps (as insinuated by columnist Bob Bouchette in the *Vancouver Sun*) even a yarn that emanated from Berlin. As even the *Ottawa Citizen* put it, "It is just possible...that most of the yarns about famine and disaster in Russia are exaggerated."

The fact that the government in Moscow opted not to seek international aid for famine victims seemingly reduced any responsibility on the part of Western governments to intervene. Canada was guided by a foreign-policy precept much like that of the United States or the United Kingdom: that if its citizens were not directly affected, then, unless invited to, it could not do anything. The Canadian government closely monitored the development of agriculture in the USSR, especially in light of the international competition for wheat exports. As the *Radisson Comet* in Saskatchewan observed, "agricultural development in Russia cannot but have a direct effect on agriculture in

Western Canada."⁵ The question of Canada's grain exports was often raised in Parliament, and trade with the Soviet Union was also a subject hotly debated both federally and provincially. Considering the government's interest in developments in the USSR, Ottawa would have been aware of the starvation by early 1933 at the latest. And before that, it had already been apprised of the situation in the Soviet countryside through the findings of agricultural specialist Andrew Cairns.

Whether the government fully comprehended the magnitude of the problem is another question. For the response even in western Ukraine (under Poland) seems to have come quite late. As Martha Bohachevsky-Chomiak has observed, the lateness of the response in western Ukraine to the famine can be explained by the fact that although news of it had reached the region in late 1932, "few realized the extent of the catastrophe."⁶ The Ukrainian Civic Committee for the Salvation of Ukraine was not established in Lviv until July 1933 and there does not seem to have been much discussion about the famine in the Polish Sejm during the first months of that year. Indeed, in view of all this, the actions of Saskatchewan's MLAs in March 1933 may seem remarkable. Remarkable, too, then, would be the offer of help by the Hafford, Saskatchewan, branch of the Ukrainian Self-Reliance League of Canada, already made sometime in the summer of 1932.

It was the Soviet rejection of that aid when it was offered that made people in the Ukrainian community in Canada apprehensive and inquisitive. Indeed, after the famine's existence was confirmed in the Saskatchewan legislature in March 1933, Ukrainians in Canada began to mobilize around the issue accordingly. There was no sustained centrally coordinated effort, though occasionally actions were conducted jointly among organizations. An attempt at a broader collective effort, transcending communities and faiths, does not seem to have been launched until the North American visit of Ewald Ammende. The many protests that took place—from Vernon, British Columbia, to Montreal, Quebec—during 1933 and 1934 may not have captured the international attention given to demonstrations in the United States, where the Ukrainian community was more urbanized and where many inhabited large cities such as Chicago and New York,⁷ but a good number of them were publicized in mainstream Canadian newspapers.

When reports about the mass meetings were published in Canadian daily newspapers, they generally included a national interpretation that was otherwise largely missing in the coverage of the Soviet Union. Ukrainians in Canada not only were troubled by the Soviet refusal of aid but increasingly came to believe that starvation was being used as a way to enervate the Soviet Ukrainian republic. The intent, as the Edmonton weekly *Ukraïns'ki visty* perceived it, was to ruin Ukraine physically and culturally. The suicide of the Soviet Ukrainian commissar and champion of Ukrainianization Mykola Skrypnyk reinforced such views. Why did Skrypnyk take his own life? Was it because he had seen the ruin that was brought to Ukraine by the regime he had supported, as suggested by a play in Canada, or because, as was painted elsewhere, he was associated with a nationalist plot that aimed with Germany's help to detach Ukraine from the USSR?[8] It is significant to observe here that the title of the play about the famine that was produced and staged in Winnipeg, *The Death of Commissar Skrypnyk, or Famine in Ukraine*, paired the two (famine and the minister's death). Significant, too, is the content of the play, for it shows how the Ukrainian community synthesized and interpreted information about the famine. Beyond the Ukrainian community, however, Skrypnyk's death was little commented upon in the mainstream press, whether English- or French-language. It ought to have attracted more attention than it did, but evidently the Canadian newspapers that did mention it were satisfied with the AP and UP articles they printed. An occasional article in an English-language newspaper outside Canada ascribed historical importance to the news of Skrypnyk's suicide. The *Times of India* remarked that it was the "first time that the suicide of one of the leading Bolsheviks has been announced" and called it a "momentous event in the history of the Ukraine." The newspaper went on to assert that it was "now an official doctrine at Moscow that any reluctance on the part of leaders to do their Bolshevik duty by getting grain away from the harassed Ukrainian peasants at all costs for the benefit of the industrial regions of Russia is always due to 'wrecking plots.'"[9] Though not often, the question of Ukraine's status within the Soviet Union was broached on occasion by a Western newspaper. In an editorial about the Soviet

Union and the League of Nations, for instance, the *Sydney Morning Herald* commented, "If the League cannot acknowledge the existence of [the Japanese-established state of] Manchukuo, might it not with equal consistency demand that the case of Georgia, and other dissatisfied provinces of Russia, notably Ukraine, be reopened."[10] The *Courier and Advertiser* of Dundee, Scotland, around the same time remarked that in "the Soviet Union there are half a dozen so-called republics which would not remain in the Union a week if they were free to act."[11] At the time of the famine, some in the Ukrainian community in Canada assessed the suicide of Skrypnyk in the context of questions and statements similar to these ones.[12]

In spite of the Ukrainian protests in rural and urban Canada and the resolutions that were forwarded to Ottawa, London, Washington, and Geneva, not everyone agreed with the protesters' interpretations of the famine. The ULFTA accepted the Soviet line on Skrypnyk. The accounts of Walter Duranty and van Paassen were preferred to the more alarming reports by others. The reaction to Carleton Ketchum's lecture in Winnipeg is revealing. Ketchum showed his audience a number of pictures; in none of them did there seem to have been any hint of a famine. It was thus easy to come away with the impression that the situation was not as terrible as some were depicting it. No photographs of starvation victims circulated in the Canadian press at the time.[13] Moreover, because Ketchum spoke of starvation in the years 1931 and 1932, rather than emphasizing 1933, the impression created was that any problems that had occurred had now abated. This was convenient, for when Ketchum embarked on his speaking tour the press was reporting a robust harvest, while any talk of famine was dismissed. The pleas of Cardinal Innitzer were given coverage, but so, too, was the Soviet retort.

Notwithstanding the retort to Innitzer, a Soviet official, Alexander Asatkin, made a semblance of an admission about the famine in September 1933—though avoiding the word "famine." He acknowledged there had been "mortality" as a result of "undernourishment," but claimed the losses were much lower than the millions reported abroad. And as the press reported a robust harvest, George Palmer in Alberta applied the adjective "robust" to the inhabitants of the USSR.

"I never saw so many healthy, robust men and women as I did there," said the former *Moscow Daily News* staff member (though he mentioned no specific places in the USSR). Thus, some ULFTA members may well have agreed with a letter to the editor published in the *Leader-Post* of Regina (and reprinted in the *Star* of Wainwright, Alberta) that expressed skepticism about a famine in the USSR, believing instead that the purpose of mentioning it was to undermine the "progressive" left movement. Reacting to the news of the Saskatchewan legislature's deliberations about the famine, the letter writer, William Raby of Regina, described the exercise of reading extracts of the letters as "pathetic." The extracts had "all the earmarks of a propagandist stunt by the knockers of the Farmer-Labor party in Saskatchewan and, in the Dominion, the C.C.F." The Mennonite community in Rosthern received from "their 'kulak' friends hundreds of letters," Raby scoffed, containing "melodramatic statements" and even cases of "people eating garbage (that is, in Russia, not Canada!)." Dismissing the statements as propaganda, Raby expressed his belief that nothing that the people of Ukraine were suffering in 1933 could compare to what they had experienced in 1919. He concluded, "One would imagine from the outpouring of the disciples of bossdom that Soviet Russia was the only country in the world where starvation abounded. These propagandists had better take off their long distance spectacles and look a little nearer." By nearer, Raby meant Depression-hit Canada. "Telling a hungry Canadian, living on a dollar a week relief about 'starving Russia' leaves him cold."[14] The *Wainwright Star* also reprinted a letter from the *Leader-Post*, written, in the same vein, by P. Mikkelson.[15] In another quarter, van Paassen was preferred over Jones on the matter of the famine. At the start of 1935, the *Edmonton Bulletin* serialized an account of the situation by Jones.[16] In response, a letter to the editor was printed expressing surprise that the newspaper had "published these articles without comment, for at the same time, your special correspondent Mr. Van Paassen in one of his articles mentioned the 'starvation in Russia that no one can find who goes there.'"[17] The series was also denounced by a speaker (T. E. Mountford) at a gathering of about four hundred people at the Odd Fellows' Hall in Coalhurst, Alberta.[18]

Ukraïns'ki robitnychi visty published letters from the USSR, but they gave no indication of any major problems. A letter from the Khliborob commune summed up a particular line, which went as follows: The Soviet Union was building socialism and making progress that would benefit the current generation and subsequent ones. Struggle was taking place with a "class enemy," who had been debilitated but not completely destroyed. The enemy was identified as the "remnants of the kulaks, Petliurites, and other counterrevolutionary scum."[19] While the Soviet leadership acknowledged some difficulties, it had vowed that 1933 would be the final year in which these would be experienced. This line was very close to Ketchum's descriptions (as quoted in the *Edmonton Journal*) of the reasoning of Soviet officials about the famine. "What were these people when the interests of the entire Russian nations were at stake? What are 1,000,000 in a population of 162,000,000?" An inference here could be that they were "counterrevolutionaries." When presented in that fashion, a million people—and counterrevolutionaries at that—out of a large population were "starving for the Five-Year Plan" (as van Paassen had once put it) for the greater good. Moreover, "we [the Soviet government] had to refuse to interrupt our export program in order to maintain our foreign credits."[20] In other words, industrialization was the priority for the Soviet regime, and if some people were to be left behind, so be it—they were people who were obstacles to progress, who resisted joining the collective farm. Starvation was justified with the axiom "He who does not work, neither shall he eat." To the starving peasants themselves was ascribed responsibility for the famine. One million in a population of 162 million may, to some, have sounded like not very many, particularly if the group dying was perceived as "reactionary." In Winnipeg, *Ukraïns'kyi holos* also quoted Ketchum, but differed from the *Edmonton Journal* in respect to the numbers: "What is five million in a population of 161 million?"[21] Lost in the fog of the figures is that however significant one or five million is in a population of 162 million, it is still more significant when applied to the areas that suffered most from the famine: Soviet Ukraine, the North Caucasus, and the Volga region. Demographers have arrived at a figure of four million deaths from the famine in Soviet Ukraine alone.[22] The rural population suffered the worst from the famine, accounting for nearly 93 per cent of direct losses in Soviet Ukraine. Rural Ukrainians numbered 24,639,100 in 1931 (the Soviet Ukrainian urban population was 6,582,100).[23] While Asatkin, the Soviet official, essentially attributed the blame for the famine (though he did not use the word *famine*) to the victims—"those who won't work won't eat"—UP correspondent Eugene Lyons saw matters differently, pointing the finger of culpability at the former Soviet commissar for nationalities, Stalin. Lyons, who was in Moscow at the time of the famine, said several years later that Stalin was "as directly responsible for each of those deaths as if he had killed them with his own hands."[24] In the absence of an international relief effort, people outside the USSR were restricted in their aid to options such as the Torgsin stores. Advertisements for Torgsin appeared in Canada in 1933 and/or 1934 in the *Canadian Jewish Chronicle*, *Kanadyis'kyi farmer*, the *Toronto Star*, *Ukraïns'kyi holos*, *Ukraïns'ki robitnychi visty*, and *Ukraïns'ki visty*. An unknown number of people otherwise doomed to die in Soviet Ukraine and elsewhere in the USSR were saved from starvation through the Torgsin option. Of course, millions of others in those areas would not have starved to death if people abroad had not been limited to that option. As the Duchess of Atholl noted, something more was needed for the many people whose names and addresses were not known outside the affected regions of the USSR. The Ukrainian-language press in Canada was aware that the Soviet authorities undertook relief measures of their own, but interpreted them as being selective and limited. One *Ukraïns'ki visty* article noted the concealed nature of relief disbursement and its limitation to twenty-eight cities. Travel from rural areas to those cities was made difficult with the introduction of the rigid passport system.[25] The option of travel abroad was even more constricted, as illustrated by the stories of people felled by the frontier guards' bullets when they tried to cross the Dnister.

Whether any of the people who managed to cross to Romania (or Poland) ever resettled in Canada is not known. But Canada deported people to the USSR as it received individuals from that country during 1933. The Canadian press provided examples of a handful of women who were able to be sponsored to come to Canada. They spoke of famine as well as the vulnerability of children. Their testimony did not square with the notion that in the Soviet Union children "come always first." Indeed, about a third of all victims of the famine in Soviet Ukraine were children.[26]

In his letter to Brownlee, Cairns wrote of the journalistic reporting on the Soviet Union. "I am sure the average reader in Canada, as well as the average reader in most countries, must be terribly confused as a result of all the conflicting reports which the press has published regarding current developments" in the USSR, he wrote; "I was very much struck, while in Moscow, by the fact that most of the foreign correspondents there are much more critical than their published reports would lead one to believe." He attributed this discrepancy in part to the journalists knowing what they could and could not get past the Soviet censors, but also to the practice of seeking news that was "readily saleable." Most of the correspondents, according to Cairns, were "in search of so-called popular news." He considered William Chamberlin an exception to the rule—in contrast to Walter Duranty, who emphasized Soviet progress but whose private views were "quite different from some of those he puts into print." Duranty, in Cairns's opinion, may have had the greatest reputation among the foreign correspondents, "as is clearly indicated by the fact that just recently he won the [Pulitzer] Prize for Journalism." Still, he considered Chamberlin worthy of "far more credit for his work than Duranty, yet I doubt if he has one-half of Duranty's reputation." The one mistake that Cairns, writing in December 1932, thought Chamberlin shared with the other foreign correspondents was the failure to venture outside Moscow.[27]

Eventually, Chamberlin did travel beyond Moscow and reported on the famine. Later, he asked whether the famine could have taken place had civil liberties prevailed in the Soviet Union, had newspapers been free to report the facts, had speakers been able to appeal for relief, and had the "government in power...been obliged to submit its policy of letting vast numbers of the peasants starve to death to the verdict of a free election." The answer is no.[28] In August 1933, the *Vancouver Sun* published a photograph of a Soviet parachute jumper—a woman—leaping out of a plane two miles over Moscow.[29] It was more evidence of Soviet progress. Many years later, Viktor Suvorov (a former Soviet military intelligence officer) recalled the Soviet parachute program thus:

> In order to appreciate the seriousness of Stalin's intentions, it must not be forgotten that the parachute psychosis reigned in the Soviet Union at the same time as did the terrible famine. Throughout the country, the bellies of children were swollen with hunger, but Comrade Stalin was selling grain abroad in order to buy parachute technology, to build great silk-producing complexes and parachute factories, to cover the country with a network of airfields and aero clubs, to put up parachute towers in every municipal park, to train thousands of instructors, to build drying rooms and storage depots for parachutes, to train one million well fed parachutists and to buy the arms, equipment and parachutes they needed.

The cost of training a million parachutists was expensive, Suvorov said, and "Stalin paid for the training of these parachutists and for their parachutes with the lives of Soviet children in great numbers." As for the purpose for which the parachutists were trained, he concluded, it was "certainly not to protect these children who were dying of hunger."[30]

Little sympathy was evident for survivors of the famine who were left parentless. In June 1933, the *Montreal Star* wrote of the plight of homeless children. The lot of children in the Soviet Union had long been "pitiable," it said. Homeless children from the previous famine were a common sight, but as "they died off or grew up or were organized and taken in homes in labor colonies, they disappeared for a time"—only to reappear in the autumn of 1932. The *Montreal Star* went on to assert that the "Riga correspondent of the London Times says that [Andrey] Vyshinsky, who prosecuted the British engineers, has held a special conference with the Ogpu and the police with the object of devising means to combat the 'new scourge.'" Further, it was the "ruthless determination of the new Communists" that was responsible for the so-called new scourge. The Montreal newspaper pointed out that the "children came to the towns in thousands from the villages in consequence of the eviction and banishment of their parents during the great grain drives last autumn."[31]

In 1934, the Soviet film *Road to Life* was brought to and shown across Canada. The film centred on the reform of children who had been orphaned by years of war and the 1921–23 famine.[32] As the film then toured North America, the ranks of the homeless and orphaned in Soviet Ukraine and elsewhere in the USSR were being joined by the children of the new Apocalypse.

APPENDIX

The following is a transcript of an address given before the Legislative Assembly of Saskatchewan by James G. Gardiner, leader of the Liberal opposition, on March 20, 1933, as published in "Text of Gardiner's Speech on Churches' Attitude to Russia," in Regina's daily *Leader-Post* (21 March 1933, p. 16).

The people of Saskatchewan are in the midst of a depression for which we are told by some that there is an economic cure. We may come to the conclusion sooner or later that we are travelling on the wrong road. Nothing will bring us to a more decided opinion on the matter than what we have been listening to this afternoon.

We have listened for some little time to letters read by Dr. Uhrich and the premier regarding conditions in Russia which cause our hearts to go out to the children of Russia even at a time when there is want in our own country. In other times we have been accustomed to hear such things through appeals from public bodies, particularly through church organizations. It is peculiar that in these times such things must be first revealed through appeals of starving relatives of those living in this country. I have no doubt that these stories are true in spite of the fact that they do not come through the regular sources.

The thought in my own mind which should be apparent from the context was that there was something wrong with religious conditions in Russia when there are no religious organizations in Russia appealing through religious organizations here until children and others are starving.

Get Appeal for Aid

We go to church Sunday after Sunday and never hear a word to the effect that people in one of the great countries of the world are starving. We hear glowing descriptions of conditions in Russia from speakers outside the pulpit. These, I presume, are for purposes of propaganda. I first had the condition in Russia as revealed in these letters brought to my attention two or three weeks ago by the minister of a non-English church in the east end of the city. He informed me that he had read a cablegram from his people in Russia the day before appealing for aid. He appeared to think there was something wrong somewhere when such things cannot get to the people of the world through the ordinary channels and told me of the conditions prevailing in his own church in Russia. Something is wrong that is of greater importance than reforming the banks and currency.

For a number of days we have been discussing before a committee the credit of our province and our people. Talk centred around credit. Where had all the credit gone? we were asked from time to time. Credit had disappeared for the time being for exactly the same reason as it had disappeared on previous occasions. Europe is in a state of fear. No world statesman ever mentioned these things. If he did it might bring the whole structure tumbling about him. But we can mention them here in the Saskatchewan legislature without our words causing undue alarm. Little attention is given to these matters by editorial writers or even by those trying to lead us in a spiritual way. Everyone in a position of authority seems afraid even to breathe the reasons.

Suggested in Articles

The reason for these conditions in Russia was suggested in Mr. Williams' articles when he returned from a trip to that country. He stated that the first entrenched boundary which he crossed in Europe was the Russian boundary. He also stated that there were red corners on every state farm and in the factory of every state industry. It is in these red corners that the young people from a population of 200,000,000 are educated in the arts of war.

The German people, the French and others seeing this preparation are moved by a fear for the future to produce their own food products. The leader of Russia tells his people that they must forego the five-year plan to take precautionary measures. That is, they must forego the production of food while they build up a military machine. This military machine is to be used to force upon the rest of the world doctrines which are being preached by some people in Saskatchewan right now.

Must Settle European Problem
With this condition where Europe is being threatened to be once more divided into two great military camps there is no credit in the world and there will be no credit no matter what reforms we have in our banking or currency systems until the European problem has been settled. There are only two alternatives. The first is the settlement for a similar condition which came in 1914. It is war. No one wants war. The second alternative is a better understanding among the nations of Europe.

The first tangible indication that we are approaching the latter rather than the first solution comes to us today in the form of a heading in the noon edition of The Leader-Post: 'MacDonald Trying to Stop Threatened Powers Regrouping.'

This is an indication that [British prime minister] Ramsay MacDonald is still working on the task of securing the peace of the world. After visiting Germany a few months ago, he returned to declare himself in favour of a National government, not for the purpose of keeping Britain on the gold standard, as some have stated, but for the purpose of establishing and maintaining the peace of the world. This state of peace can only be brought about and maintained when confidence based on understanding is re-established.

Cannot Ignore Conditions
It is almost inconceivable that the nations of the world can go on ignoring the condition which exists in Russia as described in the letters read here this afternoon. There are so many of them

from so many sources that we must recognize the condition as existing. Economics will not reveal the remedy. There is no better way for the Anglo-Saxon countries of the world to act than to provide 20,000,000 or more bushels of wheat for the starving millions of little children in Russia. There are those who would say: they will only plant it in the ground and grow more to compete with Canadian wheat.

Surely the great nations of the world can find a way to get this food to the proper place, in the proper way. In any case, we should bury our economics where the lives of women and children are concerned. We should bury all such ideas and act in the interests of humanity. We must say these people must not die. We must try to do the right thing, and the right thing in so far as the condition outlined in these letters is concerned, is to feed these girls and boys.

NOTES

Chronology of Major Events

1. James W. Heinzen, *Inventing a Soviet Countryside: State Power and the Transformation of Rural Russia, 1917–1929* (Pittsburgh: University of Pittsburgh Press, 2004), 52.
2. Bohdan Klid and Alexander J. Motyl, comps. and eds., *The Holodomor Reader: A Sourcebook on the Famine of 1932–1933 in Ukraine* (Edmonton: CIUS Press, 2012), xxxvi.
3. "New Passport System to Harry Starving Refugees," *Bulletin*, 15 Feb. 1933, 4, M-1317, 391401, R. B. Bennett Papers, Library and Archives Canada, Ottawa.

Introduction

1. "Special Soviet Stamp," *Irma Times*, 1 Jan. 1932, 6. According to the collectors' website Colnect.com, the stamp was issued on February 9, 1930, to commemorate the tenth anniversary of the First Cavalry Army. See http://colnect.com/en/stamps/list/country/2652-Soviet_Union_USSR/theme/2887-Army.
2. In later eyewitness testimony (originally published in Ukrainian in 1991), Havrylo Nykyforovych Prokopenko—referring to the village of Zhdanivka in Mahdalynivka raion of the Dnipropetrovsk region in 1933—recalled that "in the village and all around us an apocalypse was unfolding." Prokopenko, "Ukrainian Famine Memoirs: Eyewitness Testimony of Havrylo Nykyforovych Prokopenko," trans. Marta D. Olynyk, Montreal Institute for Genocide and Human Rights Studies, Concordia University, accessed 23 February 2017, https://www.concordia.ca/research/migs/resources/ukrainian-famine-memoirs.html.
3. "Disease, Famine Sweep over China following Battles," *Deseret News* (Salt Lake City), 22 Mar. 1932, 3; *Evening Record* (Ellensburg, WA), 22 Mar. 1932, 1. For a study that discusses famine in various contexts and different periods, see Rhoda E. Howard-Hassmann, *State Food Crimes* (Cambridge: Cambridge University Press, 2016).

4   Lancelot Lawton, "Russian Economic Realities," *Fortnightly Review* 135 (August 1934): 175–76. Lawton, the author of a two-volume economic history of the USSR, was among the founders of the Anglo-Ukrainian Committee formed in 1935, and his works were known in Canada. On November 13, 1934, the *Charlottetown Guardian*, without mentioning the author or title, quoted from a *Fortnightly Review* article about the famine (p. 4). For more on Lawton and Ukraine, particularly about the presentation of a collection of his articles at the British embassy in Kyiv, see Mykola Siruk, "A Book for Skeptics: 'The Ukrainian Question' 70 Years Later," *Day*, 23 May 2006, https://day.kyiv.ua/en/article/culture/book-skeptics.

5   Andrea Graziosi, Lubomyr A. Hajda, and Halyna Hryn, introduction to *After the Holodomor: The Enduring Impact of the Great Famine on Ukraine*, ed. by Andrea Graziosi, Lubomyr A. Hajda, and Halyna Hryn (Cambridge, MA: Harvard University Press, 2013), xv.

6   Olga Andriewsky, "Towards a Decentred History: The Study of the Holodomor and Ukrainian Historiography," *East/West: Journal of Ukrainian Studies* 2, no. 1 (2015): 19.

7   Stanislav Kul'chyts'kyi, "The Holodomor of 1932–33: How and Why?," *East/West: Journal of Ukrainian Studies* 2, no. 1 (2015): 93–116.

8   Nicholas Werth, "Keynote Address for the Holodomor Conference, Harvard Ukrainian Research Institute, 17–18 November 2008," in Graziosi, Hajda, and Hryn, *After the Holodomor*, xxxvi–xxxvii. The originator of the term genocide was Raphael Lemkin, who discussed Ukraine within the parameters of the United Nations definition of the same. For Lemkin, famine was one of the Stalinist regime's four destructive "prongs" against the Ukrainian nation (the other three being destruction of the Ukrainian national elites, destruction of the Ukrainian Orthodox Church, and the replacement of Ukrainian farmers with non-Ukrainians from Russia and elsewhere). See Roman Serbyn, "Lemkin on Genocide of Nations," *Journal of International Criminal Justice* 7 (2009): 123–30 (which includes Raphael Lemkin's 1953 essay "Soviet Genocide in Ukraine"). For other discussions relating to Lemkin, see Anton Weiss-Wendt, "Hostage of Politics: Raphael Lemkin on 'Soviet Genocide,'" *Journal of Genocide Research* 7, no. 4 (2005): 551–59; and Norman Naimark, "Genocide Isn't History—It's Part of the Long-Term Human Experience," *Conversation*, 16 July 2015.

9   Norman M. Naimark, "How the Holodomor Can Be Integrated into Our Understanding of Genocide," *East/West: Journal of Ukrainian Studies* 2, no. 1 (2015): 117. Scholars who do not consider the Holodomor a case of genocide include Mark Tauger; see Tauger, review of *After the Holodomor: The Enduring Impact of the Great Famine on Ukraine*, ed. Andrea Graziosi, Lubomyr A. Hajda, and Halyna Hryn, *Nationalities Papers* 43, no. 3 (2015): 514–18. In a review of the same book, Michael Gelb notes that he is not "completely comfortable with the concept of Holodomor—which implies a deliberate genocide." Stalin's "crimes were carried out everywhere in the Soviet Union," he writes, adding, "We need more comparative literature to ascertain whether social and

political repressions were in fact imposed with more intensity in Ukraine than elsewhere: studies of collectivization, industrialization, and Stalinist repression have made impressive strides over the last two decades, but the comparative aspect has lagged." Gelb, review of *After the Holodomor*, ed. Graziosi, Hajda, and Hryn, *Agricultural History* 89, no. 3 (2015): 447. See also Yana Pitner, "Mass Murder or Massive Incompetence?," review of *Hunger by Design: The Great Ukrainian Famine and Its Soviet Context*, ed. Halyna Hryn, *H-Russia / H-Net Reviews* (October 2010), http://www.h-net.org/reviews/showrev.php?id=30622. Reluctance to accept the Holodomor as genocide is thus in part based on the fact that deaths from famine also occurred outside Ukraine. Russian historian Viktor Kondrashin puts the number of deaths from famine in all the USSR in 1932–33 at a minimum of seven million. Further: "A comparative analysis of the 1926 and 1937 censuses shows the following level of decline of rural population in separate famine-affected areas: Kazakhstan 30.9 per cent, Volga region 23 per cent, Ukraine 20.5 per cent, North Caucasus 20.4 per cent. In the RSFSR [Russian Soviet Federative Socialist Republic] at least 2.5 million people died from famine in the early 1930s; adding Kazakhstan brings the total to some 4–5 million people." Kondrashin, "Hunger in 1932–1933: A Tragedy of the Peoples of the USSR," *Holodomor Studies* 1, no. 2 (2009): 20–21. Hiroaki Kuromiya notes some specificities to Ukraine and the North Caucasus at the time of the famine: "Only in Ukraine and the North Caucasus (thus not in Russia proper) were extreme measures taken against individual collective farms and villages for failures in procurement: a complete economic blockade (seizure of all foodstuffs, not merely grain but meat and other products, banning of import of foodstuffs to the villages); arrests of Communists in responsible positions; and wholesale deportations of peasants (collective and individual farmers).... In January 1933, Moscow ordered the closure of the borders with Ukraine and the Northern Caucasus in order to prevent massive migration of peasants out of these areas." He adds, "It is difficult to argue...that these orders were specifically directed against ethnic Ukrainians.... Ethnic Russians and Jews, more urban than Ukrainians, survived the famine more successfully than Ukrainians, but proportionately speaking, as many ethnic Poles or Bulgarians (most of whom lived in the countryside) as ethnic Ukrainians, died in the famine." Kuromiya, "The Soviet Famine of 1932–1933 Reconsidered," *Europe-Asia Studies* 60, no. 4 (2008): 668. Timothy Snyder writes of "approximately 3.3 million deaths by starvation and hunger-related diseases in Soviet Ukraine in 1932–1933. Of these people, some three million would have been Ukrainians, and the rest Russians, Poles, Germans, Jews, and others. Among the 1.5 million or so dead in the Soviet Russian republic were probably at least two hundred thousand Ukrainians, since the famine struck heavily in regions where Ukrainians lived. Perhaps as many as a hundred thousand more Ukrainians were among the 1.3 million people who died in the earlier famine in Kazakhstan." Snyder, *Bloodlands: Europe between Hitler and Stalin* (New York: Basic Books, 2010), 53.

10 The reversal of Ukrainianization extended to Ukrainian settlements elsewhere in the USSR, such as the Russian Far East. For a historiography of the Holodomor, see Andriewsky, "Towards a Decentred History." In the same issue of *East/West: Journal of Ukrainian Studies* (vol. 2, no. 1 [2015]), see also Frank Sysyn, "Thirty Years of Research on the Holodomor: A Balance Sheet," 3–16; Andrea Graziosi, "The Impact of Holodomor Studies on the Understanding of the USSR," 53–80; and Françoise Thom, "Reflections on Stalin and the Holodomor," 81–92. For other English-language studies since 2000, see Terry Martin, *Affirmative Action Empire: Nations and Nationalism in the Soviet Union, 1923–1939* (Ithaca: Cornell University Press, 2001); R. W. Davies and Stephen G. Wheatcroft, *The Years of Hunger: Soviet Agriculture, 1931–1933* (New York: Palgrave Macmillan, 2004); John-Paul Himka, "Encumbered Memory: The Ukrainian Famine of 1932–33," *Kritika: Explorations in Russian and Eurasian History* 14, no. 2 (2013): 413–38; David Marples, "Ethnic Issues in the Famine of 1932–1933 in Ukraine," *Europe-Asia Studies* 61, no. 3 (2009): 505–18; and David Marples, Eduard Baidaus, and Mariya Melentyeva, "Causes of the 1932 Famine in Soviet Ukraine: Debates at the Third All-Ukrainian Party Conference," *Canadian Slavonic Papers* 56, nos. 3–4 (2014): 291–312. For a collection of texts and source materials, see Klid and Motyl, *The Holodomor Reader*. For materials available online, see the homepage of the Holodomor Resource and Education Consortium, http://www.holodomor.ca/. For a bibliography that includes works in Ukrainian, see L. M. Burian and I. E. Rikun, comps., *Holodomor v Ukraïni 1932–1933 rr.: Bibliohrafichnyi pokazhchyk* (Odesa: Vyd-vo M.P. Kots, 2001). Important archival data are collected in historian Liudmyla Hrynevych's multi-volume series *Khronika kolektyvizatsiï ta holodomoru v Ukraïni, 1927–1933* (Kyiv: Krytyka, 2008).

11 Mykhailo H. Marunchak, *Natsiia v borot'bi za svoie isnuvannia: 1932 i 1933 v Ukraïni i diiaspori* (Winnipeg: UVAN, 1985), 30.

12 "Spanish Aristocrats Grab Cash, Leave for France," *Toronto Star*, 27 June 1936, 16.

13 "Freedom Means Food," *New York Times*, 5 Nov. 1934, 18.

14 Katharine Marjory Stewart-Murray, Duchess of Atholl, *Working Partnership: Being the Lives of John George, 8th Duke of Atholl, and of His Wife, Katharine Marjory Ramsay* (London: Arthur Baker, 1958), 188–89, 197. For more on the Duchess of Atholl, see Gordon Bannerman, "'Red Duchess' of Atholl," *Perthshire Advertiser*, 26 Feb. 2010; and Catriona Burness, "Count up to Twenty-One: Scottish Women in Formal Politics, 1918–1990," in *Women and Citizenship in Ireland in the Twentieth Century: What Difference Did the Vote Make?*, ed. Esther Breitenbach and Pat Thane (London: Continuum, 2010), 51.

15 Stanislav Kul'chyts'kyi, "The Holodomor of 1932–33: How and Why?" *East/West: Journal of Ukrainian Studies* 2, no. 1 (2015): 115.

16 Orest Subtelny, *Ukraine: A History* (Toronto: University of Toronto Press with the Canadian Institute of Ukrainian Studies, 1988), 386, 428, 447–48.

17 V. Ivanys et al., "Kuban," in *Encyclopedia of Ukraine*, vol. 2, ed. Volodymyr Kubijovyč (Toronto: University of Toronto Press, 1988), 693. The first all-union Soviet census of 1926 enumerated 31,194,976 Ukrainians by "nationality";

23,219,000 of these inhabited the Ukrainian SSR. Most of the remaining nearly eight million Ukrainians were inhabitants of the Russian SFSR. The total population of the Soviet Union in 1926 was 147,027, 915. See Vsevolod Naulko, Ihor Vynnychenko, and Rostyslav Sossa, *Ukrainians of the Eastern Diaspora: An Atlas*, trans. Serge Cipko and Myroslav Yurkevich (Kyiv: Mapa / Edmonton: CIUS Press, 1993).

18   Others in exile in the years after the Bolshevik Revolution included Ievhen Konovalets, who later became the leader of the Organization of Ukrainian Nationalists (assassinated in Rotterdam in 1938); the anarchist leader Nestor Makhno (who died in France in 1934); the Ukraine-born Bolshevik war commissar and politburo member Leon Trotsky; Russian Provisional Government leader Alexander Kerensky; and Russian White movement leader Anton Denikin.

19   Official counts may not confirm that figure, though unofficial estimates of the size of the U.S. Ukrainian community alone were as high as 600,000. "The Ukrainians in the United States," *Svoboda*, 29 Feb. 1916, 1.

20   Certainly, in western Ukraine there existed a perception that Ukrainians in Canada were a potential force. Hanka Romanchych of Edmonton (see chap. 5), upon visiting western Ukraine in 1934, was asked whether Ukrainians in Canada were planning and working toward obtaining the same rights as French Canadians. See Vladimir Kysilewsky, "Unedited Diaries," 245–46, MG 31, D 69, vol. 2, file 8, Vladimir Julian Kaye (Kysilewsky) Fonds, Library and Archives Canada, Ottawa (hereafter, VJKF).

21   Omelian Rudnytskyi, Nataliia Levchuk, Oleh Wolowyna, Pavlo Shevchuk, and Alla Kovbasiuk (Savchuk), "Demography of a Man-Made Human Catastrophe: The Case of Massive Famine in Ukraine 1932–1933," *Canadian Studies in Population* 42, nos. 1–2 (2015): 70.

22   "Newspapers Printed in Foreign Language in Canada Total 43," *Winnipeg Free Press*, 8 Oct. 1932, 6. Take the press in one prairie city as an example: Edmonton (population eighty thousand), the capital of Alberta, was home to, among others, the pro-Conservative daily *Journal* and the pro-Liberal daily *Bulletin*, and the weekly *Western Catholic* (the city was the seat of the Roman Catholic Archdiocese of Edmonton), all in English, in addition to the French-language weekly *La Survivance* and the Ukrainian Catholic weekly *Ukraïns'ki visty*, published in Ukrainian and distributed among readers both in and outside Edmonton. About 5,000 of the 225,133 Ukrainians counted in the Canadian census of 1931 lived in Edmonton.

23   *Canada Year Book 1933* (Ottawa: King's Printer, 1933), 118, 122. By 1926, 17,519 Mennonites had come to Canada from the USSR; another 847 came in 1927 and 511 more in 1928. Frank H. Epp, *Mennonite Exodus: The Rescue and Resettlement of the Russian Mennonites since the Communist Revolution* (Altona, MB: D. W. Friesen, 1967), 228. Among the 473,544 Canadians of German origin listed in the 1931 census, those of other faiths could also trace roots to the territory of the USSR.

24   For a discussion of demographic trends and social transformation in Ukraine during the twentieth century, see Bohdan Krawchenko, *Social Change and*

National Consciousness in Twentieth-Century Ukraine (Basingstoke, Hampshire: Macmillan, 1985).

25 Orest T. Martynowych, *Ukrainians in Canada: The Interwar Years*, bk. 1, *Social Structure, Religious Institutions, and Mass Organizations* (Edmonton: CIUS Press, 2015), 84–85. In a 1934 letter to R. K. Finlayson, private secretary to R. B. Bennett, the publisher Frank Dojacek asserted that the circulation of *Kanadyis'kyi farmer* was in excess of thirteen thousand. Dojacek to Finlayson, 26 January 1934, M-1278, 345393, R. B. Bennett Papers, Library and Archives Canada, Ottawa (hereafter, Bennett Papers). The Ukrainian Catholic Church had 350 parishes across Canada; the Ukrainian Orthodox Church had 160. Most of the parishes of the two churches were in the Prairie provinces. Martynowych, *Ukrainians in Canada*, bk. 1, 83. *Kanadyis'kyi farmer* was described as pro-Conservative in "Do spravy nashoï uchasty v politychnim zhyttiu Kanady," *Ukraïns'ki visty*, 15 Nov. 1933, 4. As historian Thomas M. Prymak explains: "Since 1912, the *Kanadiiskyi farmer* was not owned by a Ukrainian but, rather, by the Czech Frank Dojacek, who ran the paper as a business venture rather than as a political tribune. During the 1920s and 1930s, the paper inclined towards the Liberals, but by the 1930s T. Datzkiw, a strong supporter of the conservative Hetman Skoropadsky, was editor." Thomas M. Prymak, *Gathering a Heritage: Ukrainian, Slavonic, and Ethnic Canada and the USA* (Toronto: University of Toronto Press, 2015), 320n39. On the establishment of the Ukrainian Catholic Brotherhood in the winter of 1932–33, see Martynowych, *Ukrainians in Canada*, bk. 1, 465–74.

Chapter One

1 "Famine Feared in Russia; Grain Planting Neglected," *Edmonton Journal*, 6 Apr. 1932, 12.
2 "In Russia Today," *Edmonton Journal*, 2 June 1932, 4.
3 "Finds Workers in Russia Happy and Well-Housed," *Toronto Star*, 31 May 1932, 22.
4 The construction of the Dniprostroi hydroelectric power plant was the subject of the 1932 Soviet film *Ivan*, by Oleksandr Dovzhenko, which the *Vancouver Province* called the "latest and greatest Russian film" (13 Mar. 1933, 6).
5 "Russia's Wheat Supply," *Edmonton Journal*, 17 May 1932, 4. See also "Famine is Rampant, Peasants Murmur against Reds' Rule," *Globe*, 27 May 1932, 1.
6 "Ukraine Peasants Die of Hunger as Horses Go to Feed the Cities," *Toronto Star*, 27 May 1932, 1, 3.
7 "Author Red Constitution Predicts Failure Soviet," *Edmonton Journal*, 6 June 1932, 9.
8 J. L. Black, *Canada in the Soviet Mirror: Ideology and Perception in Soviet Foreign Affairs, 1917–1991* (Ottawa: Carleton University Press, 1998), 100.
9 Jaroslaw V. Koshiw, "The 1932–33 Famine in the British Government Archives," in *Famine-Genocide in Ukraine 1932–1933: Western Archives, Testimonies and New Research*, ed. Wsevolod W. Isajiw (Toronto: Ukrainian Canadian Research and Documentation Centre, 2003), 55. Cairns spent four months in the USSR

studying Soviet agriculture, from May to August 1932. See Black, *Canada in the Soviet Mirror*, 100.

10 For more on Cairns, see his research report *The Soviet Famine 1932–33: An Eye-Witness Account of Conditions in the Spring and Summer of 1932*, ed. Tony Kuz (Edmonton: CIUS Press, 1989). See also Marco Carynnyk, Lubomyr Y. Luciuk, and Bohdan S. Kordan, eds., *The Foreign Office and the Famine: British Documents on Ukraine and the Great Famine of 1932–1933* (Kingston: Limestone, 1988). A supplement to Cairns's letters and earlier reports appeared in May 1933—marked "SECRET." Cairns, *Agricultural Production in Soviet Russia: A Preliminary Report as at May 1st 1933*, M-1316, 391145–96, Bennett Papers.

11 "Famine Is Rampant, Peasants Murmur against Red Rule," *Globe*, 27 May 1932, 1.

12 S. J. Taylor, *Stalin's Apologist: Walter Duranty: The New York Times's Man in Moscow* (Oxford: Oxford University Press, 1990), 194–96.

13 Andrew Cairns (Empire Marketing Board) to John E. Brownlee, 8 Dec. 1932, Andrew Cairns Papers, Marshall Library of Economics, Cambridge University.

14 Ibid.

15 Ibid.

16 Ibid. Cairns worked as a statistician for the Wheat Pools of Winnipeg and then as head of the grain intelligence service of the Empire Marketing Board. In September 1933, he was appointed secretary of the International Wheat Advisory Committee. See "Appointment of Cairns Approved," *Star-Phoenix*, 20 Sept. 1933, 12; "Agreement on Wheat with Russia Sought," *Montreal Star*, 18 Sept. 1933, 1; and Carynnyk, Luciuk, and Kordan, *The Foreign Office and the Famine*, liv n17.

17 See, for example, "President of France near Death from Bullets Fired by Assassin," *Winnipeg Tribune*, 6 May 1932, 1.

18 "Paris Crowds, Stunned by Attack on Aged President, Await News on Streets," *Winnipeg Tribune*, 6 May 1932, 1.

19 "Mother Identifies Doumer's Assassin," *Vancouver Sun*, 27 May 1932, 1.

20 "Slayer of French President Hears Death Sentence," *Winnipeg Free Press*, 28 July 1932, 13. Gorguloff [Gorgulov] was a Kuban Cossack. See Robert H. Johnston, *"New Mecca, New Babylon": Paris and the Russian Exiles, 1920–1945* (Montreal and Kingston: McGill-Queen's University Press, 1988), 104. Gorguloff was portrayed by some as insane and by others as a former Bolshevik commissar or a former chief of the Cheka (secret police). See "Assassin Is Former Commissar," *Star-Phoenix*, 16 May 1932, 4; *Star-Phoenix*, 31 May 1932, 6; and "Assassin Faces Guillotine," *Star-Phoenix*, 3 June 1932, 5. His complaint of French policy toward the USSR was probably a frustration shared by other émigrés. Months later, former Russian premier Alexander Kerensky, during an interview in Paris, emphasized the Soviet agricultural sector, where, he said, the "revolutionary movement" had become "almost general" among the peasantry. He added that the situation was "particularly ominous" in Ukraine, the North Caucasus, the lower Volga region, and western Siberia. While not expecting assistance for any movement from the outside, Kerensky stressed that the West, by helping Moscow financially and economically, "intervene[d] in favor of the Soviet

regime," and he asked for a "cessation of this intervention." "Kerensky on Soviet," *Wall Street Journal*, 27 Feb. 1933, 8.

21 "Gorguloff's Mother Faces Fate as Son," *Toronto Telegram* (hereafter, *Telegram*), 19 Sept. 1932, 32. See also "La mère de Gorguloff exécutée en Russie," *La Liberté*, 28 Dec. 1932, 2. Gorguloff was executed on September 14, 1932. The *Prince George Citizen* (British Columbia) reported on the execution, which was witnessed by thousands: "There was no sympathy for his act. There was no protest against the justice of his sentence. But there was in the minds of hundreds of those who walked the streets of Paris that night...an infinite pity for humanity as a whole linked with some vague feeling of revolt against war, revolution, famine, disease and ruin, all of which had contributed to bring Gorguloff from the steppes of Russia to murder a decent old man whom chance had made president of the French republic" ("Thousands View the Execution of Paul Gorguloff," 6 Oct. 1932, 3).

22 Charles King, *The Moldovans: Romania, Russia, and the Politics of Culture* (Stanford: Hoover Institution Press, 2000), 54.

23 Alexandru-Murad Mironov, "And Quiet Flows the Dnister: Life and Death on the Romanian-Soviet Border, 1918–1940," *Arhivele Totalitarismului* 19, nos. 3–4 (2011): 32. The bridge was rebuilt in 1935, following the initiation of diplomatic ties between Romania and the USSR.

24 "40 Peasants Shot Swimming River to Flee Famine," *Toronto Star*, 24 Feb. 1932, 19. See also "Peasants Massacred by Soviet Soldiers," *Toronto Star*, 15 Mar. 1932, 17; "Fourteen Peasants Drown," *Toronto Star*, 18 Mar. 1932, 19; "Machine Gunners Kill Peasants Who Resist Attempt at Sacrilege," *Toronto Star*, 21 Mar. 1932, 19; "Peasant Women Shot Down by Soviet Machine Guns," *Edmonton Journal*, 21 Mar. 1932, 1; and "Ukrainians Shot Defending Village Cross," *Winnipeg Tribune*, 21 Mar. 1932, 1.

25 "Soviets Shoot Peasants Down on Sight," *Charlottetown Guardian*, 22 Mar. 1932, 1, 8.

26 "Rumanian Currency Ban in Effect," *New York Times*, 15 May 1932, 9.

27 "Rumuny viddaiut' utikachiv do ruk bol'shevykiv," *Ukraïns'ki visty*, 23 Nov. 1932, 2. See also "Bol'shevyky vydaly vtikachiv," *Kanadyis'kyi farmer*, 17 May 1933, 2. In London, England, the matter of the Ukrainian refugees was raised in Parliament. See 264 Parl. Deb., H.C. (13 Apr. 1932), 829. For a report about the matter being raised in the Romanian senate, see "Tragediia v Dnistri v rumuns'komu senati," *Ukraïns'kyi holos*, 18 May 1932, 3.

28 "Ukraine and Ottawa," *Svoboda*, 25 July 1932, 4; reprinted from a release of the Ukrainian Bureau (London), dated 7 July 1932. See also "Ukraïns'ka sprava na Imperial'nii Konferentsiï v Ottavi," *Ukraïns'ki visty*, 13 July 1932, 6. Meanwhile, the attempts to cross continued. In January 1934 *Ukraïns'ki visty* cited reports from Bucharest of renewed efforts to traverse the Dnister River after it had frozen. Not long before, the periodical said, seven villagers had tried to flee; two had been killed and the other five had made it across to the Romanian side ("Ukraïns'ki trupy na Dnistri," 17 Jan. 1934, 2). See also "Tragichna pereprava cherez Dnister," *Ukraïns'ki visty*, 5 Dec. 1934, 8.

29 Sir John Hope Simpson, *The Refugee Problem: Report of a Survey* (London: Oxford University Press, 1939), 413. An indication of how many people had managed to cross during the winter months before the spring of 1932 can be found in an April 1932 *New York Times* report: "More than 6,000 Russians are said to have found refuge in Rumania during the Winter months" ("Rumania Aids Russian Refugees," 16 Apr. 1932, 34).

30 Alberto Basciani, "From Collectivization to the Great Famine: Eyewitness Statements on the Holodomor by Refugees from the Ukrainian SSR, 1930–1933," *Holodomor Studies* 3, nos. 1–2 (2011): 26. Milena Rudnycka, a member of the Ukrainian parliamentary representation and president of the Union of Ukrainian Women who was active in trying to alert the world to the famine and in the efforts to organize relief, later wrote that between January 1 and March 13, 1933, 1,055 refugees crossed the Dnister. "Borot'ba za pravdu pro Velykyi Holod," *Svoboda*, 23 July 1958, 2. However, that figure most probably refers to the period from January 1 to March 13, 1932, and not the same period in 1933. In the middle of 1934 the *New York Times* reported that barriers on river trade between the USSR and Romania were going to be lifted. "There were days when fifty and more bodies of persons killed by Russian and Rumanian bullets were collected by Rumanians" along the Romanian-Soviet border, according to the paper ("Dniester Barrier to Be Lifted Soon," 17 June 1934, E2). In January 1932 the *Star-Phoenix* reported on Communists shot dead by Romanian guards while attempting to cross the Dnister River in the other direction, to the USSR ("Slain at Frontier," 11 Jan. 1932, 1). See also "Six Shot Trying to Enter Russia," *New York Times*, 11 Jan. 1932, 24. On crossings from Romania to the USSR and the motives, see Mironov, "And Quiet Flows the Dnister," 49–50.

31 Mironov, "And Quiet Flows the Dnister," 39. Refugees were interviewed about conditions in the USSR. The *Manchester Guardian* published an extract from a letter by a Ukrainian refugee who had crossed to Romania ("Famine in Soviet Ukraine," 2 Sept. 1933, 15). The Ukrainian Bureau received a letter from a Ukrainian refugee in Bucharest, dated August 25, 1933, and published an extract in its bulletin: *Ukrainian Bureau Bulletin*, no. 17 (Jan. 1934): 3. Refugee testimonies were collected by William Shirer and told in "Tribune Writer Hears Tales of Red Refugees," *Chicago Tribune*, 19 June 1932, part I, 15. A camp for refugees from the USSR was set up in Schneidemühl, Germany, reportedly housing 357 refugees, mostly from Soviet Ukraine and the Volga region. "Vtikachi rozpovidaiut' pro strakhittia holodu na Ukraïni," *Kanadyis'kyi farmer*, 16 Aug. 1933, 2. Moscow's *Izvestia* denounced the stories that appeared in the West about the attempted Dnister crossings: "This campaign of calumnies has been preceded by careful preparations on the part of the Roumanian Intelligence Service and 'Siouranza' [the Roumanian Secret Police]." Scores of secret agents were sent to the Soviet side, the Soviet newspaper continued, where they "carried on a vast propaganda campaign among the 'kulaks' of the autonomous Moldavian Soviet Republic…and offered to organize the Moldavians for illegal crossing of the frontier." Their "efforts met with no success among the proletarian elements

of the autonomous Moldavian Republic. But they succeeded in persuading some kulaks to flee." According to the *Izvestia* report, the agents "gathered the kulaks from various villages in one particular place, so as to have them cross the frontier in groups. ... Moreover, the Roumanian organizers of this group fired shots at the Soviet guards when the guards tried to prevent the kulaks from crossing the river." *Izvestia* charged that accounts in the Romanian and other press in connection to the Dnister events were proof of "a new international assault on the Soviet Union." "'Red' Massacre on the Dniester," *Literary Digest*, 7 May 1932, 14.

32 "Tragediia na Dnistri v Rumuns'komu Senati," *Ukraïns'kyi holos*, 18 May 1932, 3. The Ukrainian-language press in Canada also mentioned attempted crossings from the USSR into Poland; for example, *Kanadyis'kyi farmer* reported the case of four Soviet army officials who successfully traversed the USSR-Poland border on February 9, 1933 ("Masova vtecha voiakiv iz Sovitiv," 15 Mar. 1933, 2). According to Polish scholar Roman Wysocki, few of the people who attempted the crossing from Soviet Ukraine to Poland succeeded—and of those who were successful, some then faced the threat of deportation, prompting pressure on the authorities by Ukrainian community leaders to cease the evictions to the USSR. Wysocki, "Reactions to the Famine in Poland," in Graziosi, Hajda, and Hryn, *After the Holodomor*, 56. In 1932, the *Vancouver Province* mentioned a camp in a place identified as "Krajka" that served as a "transit prison for Russians who are apprehended trying to cross the frontier into Poland"; the camp caught fire and seventy of the inmates were "burned to death," twenty-three others were "dying," and another sixteen were reportedly "insane" ("Seventy Prisoners Die in Russian Fire," 2 Apr. 1932, 1). For more on crossings into Poland, see Timothy Snyder, "Covert Polish Missions across the Soviet Ukrainian Border, 1928–1933," in *Confini: Costruzioni, attraversamenti, rappresentazioni*, ed. Silvia Salvatici (Soveria Mannelli: Rubbettino, 2005), 55–78.

33 "Conditions of Famine throughout Russia Admitted by Moscow," *Globe*, 10 Mar. 1932, 1–2; "Russian Peasants Facing Starvation," *Toronto Star*, 10 Mar. 1932, 25. On the fear of famine, see, for example, "Famine Feared in Russia," *Edmonton Journal*, 6 Apr. 1932, 12; "Shortage of Bread Affecting Millions," *Toronto Star*, 7 May 1932, 21; and "Soviet Slavery Described in Letter to Canadian," *Edmonton Journal*, 9 May 1932, 1.

34 "Party of 20 Ukranians [sic] Leave Drumheller for Don Basin Region," *Edmonton Journal*, 4 Mar. 1932, 5. In 1934, Tomas Maryglad, who described himself as an immigrant from Galicia and lived eleven years in Drumheller, told his story in *Ukraïns'kyi holos*. At the end of 1931 he had left Alberta (leaving behind his wife and three children) for the mines of the Donbas, Ukraine; from there, he had managed to flee to Poland, only to encounter difficulty in efforts to return to Canada ("Poïkhav do 'raiu', vtik, a teper do Kanady ne vpuskaiut,'" 14 Mar. 1934, 3).

35 "Emigrants Return to Russia, Happy," *Edmonton Journal*, 2 Aug. 1932, 5; "Emigrant Party Sails to Russia," *Star-Phoenix*, 2 Aug. 1932, 2.

36 For example, "Improved Living Standard Is Aim of Soviet Russia," *Winnipeg Free Press*, 23 Jan. 1932, 6; "Stalin—Man of Steel," *Winnipeg Tribune Magazine*, 16 Apr. 1932, 3; "Huge Soviet Hydro Plant to Be Opened," *Winnipeg Tribune*, 10 Oct. 1932, 1; [Eugene Lyons], "End of Five-Year-Plan Climaxes Biggest Revolt in Annals of History," *Winnipeg Free Press*, 23 Dec. 1932, 7. On U.S. journalist Eugene Lyons, see Teresa Cherfas, "Reporting Stalin's Famine: Jones and Muggeridge: A Case of Forgetting and Rediscovery," *Kritika: Explorations in Russian and Eurasian History* 14, no. 4 (2013): 783–84, 790, 793–95, 797. He published a memoir: Lyons, *Assignment in Utopia* (London: George G. Harrap, 1938).

37 "Ukraine Starves for Five-Year Plan," *Globe*, 6 Aug. 1932, 1–2. Among other Soviet-related stories that appeared that month were Pierre van Paassen's "Punishment for Zeal Bewilders Servants of Blundering Soviet," *Globe*, 8 Aug. 1932, 1–2; "Continued Sacrifices Urged on Delegation from Hungry Ukraine," *Globe*, 9 Aug. 1932, 1–2; "Hatred Pursues Innocent Children," *Globe*, 13 Aug. 1932, 1–2; and "No Liberty in Russia Is Studied Conclusion of Trained Observer," *Globe*, 16 Aug. 1932, 1–2. See also "Mr. Van Paassen Upheld," editorial, *Globe*, 12 Aug. 1932, 4; and Frederick Griffin, "School Attendance Doubles in Four Years in Russia," *Toronto Star*, 23 Aug. 1932, 1, 5. (In 1936, the pro-Conservative *Mail and Empire* merged with the *Globe* to form the *Globe and Mail*.)

38 "Peripatetic Van Paasen [sic] a Perplexing Puzzle," *Telegram*, 28 Sept. 1932, 6. See also "Van Paassen Off to Russia to Study Red Rule," *Globe*, 14 June 1932, 1 (announcing van Paassen's investigative trip to the USSR); and "Is Russia Not So Bad or What Is the Matter," *Toronto Star*, 27 June 1932, 6 (asserting that van Paassen had found a different USSR to the one the *Globe* expected he would find, including the absence of slave labour in the lumber camps). Several years later, in a letter to the editor reacting to an article about Ukraine by Harrison Brown ("People are Happy in Glorious Ukraine"), "Ukrainian Subscriber" asserted that Brown reminded him of van Paassen, "whose despatches were filling the columns of Canadian and American newspapers not so long ago." Where now was van Paassen, the letter writer asked; he then answered his own question: "Passed into oblivion and of the newspapers of this country probably only the columns of the *Toronto Star* are still open to him. It appears that Mr. V[a]n Paassen's misrepresentations of facts have caused most self-respecting newspapers to close their pages to his misinformations." "People Not Happy in 'Glorious Ukraine,'" letter, *Winnipeg Tribune*, 30 Nov. 1936, 9. Van Paassen and the *Toronto Star* eventually also parted ways. Van Paassen was sent to cover the Spanish Civil War, but when the newspaper was told that he prepared his dispatches from his apartment in Paris, not Spain, he was fired. See David Halton, *Dispatches from the Front: Matthew Halton, Canada's Voice at War* (Toronto: McClelland & Stewart, 2014), 113. Though the circumstances in which he was dismissed have been questioned—see Don North, *Inappropriate Conduct: Mystery of a Disgraced War Correspondent* (Bloomington, IN: iUniverse, 2013), chap. 10—van Paassen again ran into trouble during the World War II years. In one of his books, he charged that the Duke of Hamilton had colluded and collaborated with prominent Nazi

official Rudolf Hess. The Duke of Hamilton sued both van Paassen and the publisher of his book, and the former *Toronto Star* and *Globe* correspondent was forced to make a public apology. *Charlottetown Guardian*, 14 Apr. 1943, 4.

39 "Lyst z Vel. Ukraïny," *Ukraïns'ki visty*, 12 Oct. 1932, 6. The English translation, by Roman Yereniuk, acting director of the Centre for Ukrainian Canadian Studies, University of Manitoba, was made available during Holodomor—The Famine-Genocide in Ukraine 1932–33, a symposium at the Oseredok Ukrainian Cultural and Education Centre, Winnipeg, 8 Nov. 2008.

40 "Soviet Harvest Suffers Setback," *Edmonton Journal*, 11 Aug. 1932, 6; "Russian Wheat Crop Fails," *Globe*, 11 Aug. 1932, 4.

41 "Food Shortage in Russia," *Globe*, 9 Aug. 1932, 1.

42 The contents of Moir's letter were disclosed to readers of *Ukraïns'kyi holos* later, in a September 1933 editorial about attempts to provide aid for famine victims ("Holod na Ukraïni," 13 Sept. 1933, 4).

43 "Crops Are Abandoned by Russian Peasants on Important Areas," *Toronto Star*, 8 Sept. 1932, 23.

44 "Moscow's Iron Fist on Peasant's Grain," *Toronto Star*, 24 Sept. 1932, 2.

45 "Police Charge Crowd as Stores Are Looted Soviet Prisons Fall," *Toronto Star*, 27 Sept. 1932, 1.

46 "Toronto Man Back Pleased by Russia," *Toronto Star*, 14 Sept. 1932, 4. Thorton Purkis, at a meeting of the Toronto real estate board, criticized the prime minister for his policy of refusal to trade with the USSR. Purkis said there would be a desperate shortage of food in the USSR because of a drought in Ukraine, which was "an act of God," but that the USSR would still go on producing. "Bennett an Ostrich Realtors Are Told," *Toronto Star*, 20 Oct. 1932, 45.

47 "Visitor to Russia Marvels at Mighty Dnieper Works," *Toronto Star*, 27 Sept. 1932, 1, 4.

48 "How to Fight Bolshevism," *Toronto Star*, 3 Oct. 1932, 6.

49 "Reconstruction or Revolution," *Toronto Star*, 7 Oct. 1932, 6.

50 "Toronto Newspaper Girl Ordered Out of Russia as a 'Borgeois Provocateur,'" *Winnipeg Tribune / Winnipeg Free Press*, 21 Sept. 1932, 10. Clyman's articles also appeared in other Canadian newspapers. See, for example, "A Town of Living Corpses Is Kem in Soviet Russia," *Star-Phoenix*, 10 Oct. 1932, 7; and "Ce qui se passe en Russie," *La Survivance*, 28 Dec. 1932, 6.

51 "Girl from New Toronto Begs," *Telegram*, 15 May 1933, 3. For more on Clyman, see Jars Balan, "Rhea Clyman: A Forgotten Eyewitness to the Hunger of 1932," *Ukraïna Moderna*, 21 Nov. 2014, http://uamoderna.com/images/shafka-dok/Balan-Clyman/Balan_Clyman_bio_Engl.pdf. Balan also has published an article on Canadian press coverage of the Soviet Union prior to the famine. Balan, "The Gathering Storm: The Mainstream Canadian Press Coverage of the Soviet Union in the Lead-Up to Ukraine's Great Famine-Holodomor," *Canadian Ethnic Studies* 42, nos. 2–3 (2010): 207–46.

52 "Expulsion from Russia Faces Correspondent," *Redcliff Review*, 27 Oct. 1932, 5. Later, in February 1933, Stalin displayed his wariness of foreign correspondents

in an order that he issued to fellow politburo members Viacheslav Molotov and Lazar Kaganovich: "Do you know who allowed the American correspondents in Moscow to travel to Kuban? They concocted filth about the situation in Kuban (see their correspondence). We must put an end to this and stop these gentlemen from traveling throughout the USSR. As it is, there are enough spies in the USSR." Oleg Khlevniuk, "Comments on the Short-Term Consequences of the Holodomor," in Graziosi, Hajda, and Hryn, *After the Holodomor*, 158.

53   See Rhea Clyman, "Starvation Stalks the Land," *Daily Express*, 2 Dec. 1932, 8.
54   "A Soviet Setback," *Charlottetown Guardian*, 20 Jan. 1933, 4.
55   "Wife of Stalin Dies," *Toronto Star*, 9 Nov. 1932, 1. One of the few references to Alliluyeva in the Canadian press earlier that year included a report that she had been "cited publicly for cutting classes." See "Dictator Stalin's Wife Faces Charge of Truancy," *Winnipeg Tribune*, 1 Apr. 1932, 1.
56   "Tasted His Food to Foil His Assassins," *Toronto Star*, 10 Nov. 1932, 25.
57   "Among Ourselves," *Globe*, 15 Nov. 1932, 15. Frederick Griffin was a feature writer for the *Toronto Star*. See "Fred Griffin Dies of Heart Attack," *Maple Leaf*, 19 Jan. 1946, 1. Many of his stories about the Soviet Union were published in the book *Soviet Scene: A Newspaperman's Close-Ups of New Russia* (Toronto: Macmillan, 1932). As Kevin Plummer notes, Griffin was "generally impressed with the Soviet Union." Plummer, "Historicist: A Toronto Journalist Reports from the USSR in 1932," *Torontoist*, 22 Aug. 2015, http://torontoist.com/2015/08/historicist-a-toronto-journalist-in-the-land-of-the-soviets.
58   In May 1933, readers of the *Toronto Telgram* were presented with a different perspective on Mme. Stalin's death to the one suggesting her martyrdom by dying while taking poison intended for the Soviet leader. Rhea Clyman contended that Alliluyeva had died by her own hand. "My own belief," Clyman wrote, was that "Mme. Stalin chose death because she could no longer bear to witness the suffering of her people." She noted that "Peasants from all over the country appealed to her for intercession when their lands were being taken and livestock and goods confiscated." The appeals had to go unanswered, however, for she could not sway her husband. Clyman believed that Alliluyeva chose to die at the moment when Stalin and others were celebrating the anniversary of the proletarian revolution and wanted her death to be "a protest against the victimization of her people—the peasants." "Stalin's Wife a Suicide—Took Life with Bullet on Reds' Anniversary," *Telegram*, 9 May 1933, 1–2. Also on Alliluyeva's death, see "Zahadochna smert zhinky Stalina," *Ukraïns'ki visty*, 16 Nov. 1932, 1; "Misteriia z Zinovievom," *Ukraïns'ki visty*, 14 Dec. 1932, 7; and "Zhinka Stalina skinchyla samohubstvom," *Ukraïns'ki visty*, 9 May 1934, 2; "Zhinka Stalina skinchyla samohubstvom," *Kanadyis'kyi farmer*, 9 May 1934, 1; "Zhinka Stalina skinchyla samohubstvom," *Ukraïns'kyi holos*, 23 May 1934, 5; "Buvshyi sovits'kyi komisar pro sovits'ku vladu," *Novyi shliakh*, 1 May 1934, 1; and "States Stalin's Wife Took Her Own Life," *Toronto Star*, 10 Apr. 1934, 21. See also, much later, Alexander Orlov, "Stalin's Secrets: Part IV," *Life*, 27 Apr. 1953, 146; and "Stalin Understood the Russian People," *Sydney Morning Herald*, 7 Mar. 1953, 4.

59 "Teror ukraïns'koho naselennia proty komunistiv roste," *Ukraïns'ki visty*, 9 Nov. 1932, 1. See also "Protybol'shevyts'kyi terror v Rosiï," *Ukraïns'ki visty*, 16 Nov. 1932, 1. Dnipropetrovsk was also named as the scene of a protest in April 1933 in which workers demonstrated in the streets against "starvation for the five-year plan," among other things. More than 100 people were shot and 150 others were wounded. Several hundred demonstrators were arrested and "a large portion of them were shot." Also mentioned was the locality of Zviahel (now Novohrad-Volynskyi), in "Soviet Volyn," where at the collective farm "Zhovten'" workers had stopped work in protest against the nonreceipt of monies or food. Two of the leaders were executed and other protesters were banished to the Solovetsky Islands. "Rozrukhy na Ukraïni," *Kanadyis'kyi farmer*, 14 June 1933, 1.

60 "Liudoïdstvo na Ukraïni," *Ukraïns'ki visty*, 9 Nov. 1932, 4. A study by Hennadii Boriak on famine-related archival sources provides an indication of how widespread cannibalism was during the period of the famine. "The key documents of the State Archives of the Ministry of Internal Affairs are concentrated in the collections titled 'Protocols of Special Proceedings and Tribunals [troiky]' and 'Criminal Cases in Trial Courts and Extrajudicial Organs.' The criminal files reveal the shocking truth about the total social collapse in rural regions and the mental aberrations that led to the eating of cadavers and cannibalism. Of the 83,000 such cases launched by the NKVD in 1932–1933, we have a record of no more than 3,000 today (the rest were destroyed in 1956). More than 2,500 people were convicted of cannibalism. Documents for 1,000 of these cases have survived. In my opinion, the public is still not ready today to accept these grisly photo and text records." Boriak, "Resources on the Famine in Ukraine's State Archival System," *Harvard Ukrainian Studies* 27, nos. 1–4 (2004–2005): 124.

61 "Dohovir pro neagresno mizh Frantsiieiu i sovitamy," *Ukraïns'ki visty*, 7 Dec. 1932, 1.

62 "Iak vyhliadaie robitnychyi 'rai' u bol'shevit" and "Seliany masovo vtikaiut' z Ukraïny," *Ukraïns'ki visty*, 21 Dec. 1932, 2.

63 "Hoarders of Grain Warned by Russia," *Globe*, 6 Dec. 1932, 8; "Soviet Peasants Warned against Grain Hoarding," *Winnipeg Free Press*, 5 Dec. 1932, 6.

64 "Soviet Buys Silver at Bargain Prices," *Telegram*, 12 Dec. 1932, 16. It was reported that a kilogram of butter could be obtained for 137 grams of silver. "Peasants of Russia Going Silver Mad," *Toronto Star*, 25 Mar. 1933, 4.

65 "Forced Labor Valued Asset of Bolsheviks," *Telegram*, 28 Dec. 1932, 15.

66 "Food Scarcity in Russia," editorial, *Winnipeg Free Press*, 1 Dec. 1932, 13.

Chapter Two

1 "Prominent 'Reds' Get Death Terms," *Edmonton Journal*, 3 Jan. 1933, 12.

2 "Russia's 'Food-Battle,'" *Edmonton Journal*, 31 Jan. 1933, 4. *La Presse* reported that Professor Otto Hoetzsch, "director of the [German journal *Osteuropa*

and] known for his pro-Soviet tendencies," had been obliged in the journal's February issue to acknowledge a situation of food shortages in the USSR ("La disette en Russie," 13 Apr. 1933, 6).

3   "Russian Wheat Is Sufficient Says Col. Mackie," *Border Cities Star*, 3 Jan. 1933, 16.
4   "Doubts Russia in Need Wheat," *Edmonton Journal*, 3 Jan. 1933, 12.
5   See, for example, M. H. Halton, "It's Up to Canada Now Attitude of Russians," *Toronto Star*, 13 Jan. 1933, 1; "Others Seek Soviet Trade if Canada Is 'Too Proud,'" *Toronto Star* 13 Jan. 1933, 1–2; Wilfred Eggleston, "Bennett Hatred of Soviet Still Bar to Barter Plan," *Toronto Star*, 13 Jan. 1933, 1–2; "Churchmen Score Holier-Than-Thou Attitude in Trade," *Toronto Star*, 13 Jan. 1933, 1–2; "Would Lift Ban on Russian Trade," *Edmonton Journal*, 16 Jan. 1933, 2; "Ex-Soldiers Demand Trade with Russia," *Toronto Star*, 17 Jan. 1933, 1; "Better to Lose Office and Retain Self-Respect, Declares [sic] Westerners to Weir," *Toronto Star*, 8 Feb. 1933, 3; and "Recognize Soviet, Al. Smith Advises," *Telegram*, 28 Feb. 1933, 2.
6   "Conditions in Russia," *Montreal Gazette*, 16 Jan. 1933, 10. See also "Conditions in Russia Today Are Depicted by Research Bureau Work," *Winnipeg Free Press*, 19 Nov. 1932, 11.
7   "Say 'No' to Hunger Army," *Border Cities Star*, 18 Jan. 1933, 7.
8   Reference to Canadians resettling in the USSR was made in the Legislative Assembly of Ontario in early 1932. General D. M. Hogarth, the Conservative member for Port Arthur, mentioned in the legislature on March 17 that the Labour MLA Earl Hutchinson (Kenora) had "quoted from a letter from one man who had gone to the Soviet, in which the man told of how glad he was he left Canada." See "Gen. D.M. Hogarth Creates Sensation during Debate in Early Hours," *Winnipeg Free Press*, 17 Mar. 1932, 1. The story of the Wolchok family of Toronto, who resettled in the USSR (Orehovia, Ukraine) and then returned to Canada, was related in the *Toronto Telegram* (see "Toronto Lad in Russia Found Labor 'Paradise' Gruesome, Starving Land," 11 June 1932, 2nd sec., 1; "Toronto Family's Fate," 18 June 1932, 41; "Workers Starve on Soviet Diet," 25 June 1932, 16; and "Jailed for Speaking to Policeman," 2 July 1932, 17).
9   Carynnyk, Luciuk, and Kordan, *The Foreign Office and the Famine*, 221.
10 Dominion of Canada, Parliament, House of Commons, *Official Report of Debates [Hansard]* (hereafter, *Hansard*), 17th Parl., 4th sess., vol. 2 (1933): 2057 (debate on farm relief, 13 Feb. 1933). Motherwell returned to the subject in 1934. Commenting on surplus wheat in Canada, starvation, and the matter of barter, he wrote to his constituents, "Surely among the millions and tens of millions of starving people throughout the world we can dispose of our surplus *wheat* to some of them on *some* terms, of long credit or barter, that would prove more economically beneficial to the state than slowing down production and taking no interest whatever either in extending our markets or feeding the hungry." William Richard Motherwell to "friends and constituents," Ottawa, 29 Mar. 1934, V.2.D, 17774, Motherwell Collection, Premier James Garfield Gardiner Papers, Provincial Archives of Saskatchewan, Regina (hereafter, Gardiner Papers). Ralph Webb, the mayor of Winnipeg, also questioned the Soviet

practice of exporting grain while much of the population suffered. "There is no doubt that the world is coming to a wheat shortage and Russia is definitely out of wheat export," he remarked in March 1932 ahead of the summer Imperial Economic Conference in Ottawa. "As a matter of fact," he continued, "if Russia were to do the right thing by her starving masses, she would be importing wheat." "Webb Predicts Better Times by June," *Vancouver Province* (hereafter, *Province*), 29 Mar. 1932, 5.

11 "Success, Almost Triumph in Stalin's Survey," *Toronto Star*, 11 Feb. 1933, 1–2. In a joint public statement on May 25, 1933, Stalin and Viacheslav Molotov declared that victory of the collectivization policy was assured and that the kulaks were "being defeated." In January 1934, kulak independent farms were declared "wiped out" in a general report authored by Stalin and other Soviet leaders, which was translated into English. "Herding of Farmers Succeeds in Soviet," *Toronto Star*, 25 May 1933, 23; "Soviet Gives Report on 'Five-Year' Plan," *Toronto Star*, 27 Jan. 1934, 11.

12 "Soviet Russia Fascinates Young Lethbridge Couple," *Edmonton Journal*, 11 Feb. 1933, 6. Born in Alsace, France, Richert was employed by the Lethbridge Northern Irrigation Project before his departure to the Soviet Union. See also "Alberta University Student Adviser to the Russian Soviet," *Winnipeg Free Press*, 7 Dec. 1932, 15.

13 "Soviet Exiles 45,000 Cossacks as Undesirable," *Toronto Star*, 19 Jan. 1933, 21, 23; *Telegram*, 19 Jan. 1933, 23. See also "Banished from Home," *Globe*, 28 Jan. 1933, 4; "Entire Population of Three Russian Villages Reported Sent to Exile," *Winnipeg Free Press*, 20 Jan. 1933, 1; and "Tolstoi's Daughter Appeals to World to Help Russians," *Globe*, 4 Feb. 1933, 1. The Soviet military had for months reportedly been sending trainloads of Cossack farmers to "unknown destinations." In some villages, women and children remained "until immigrant peasants were brought in to take over the collective farms"; the "habitations in other villages were simply burnt down and fugitives shot." "Dealing with Cossacks," *Winnipeg Tribune*, 2 Oct. 1933, 9. The famine affected the territory of both the Kuban and the Don Cossacks in Russia's North Caucasus. For details on the national and political orientations of groups identified as Cossacks, see Paul Robert Magocsi, "Cossacks," in *Harvard Encyclopedia of American Ethnic Groups*, ed. Stephan Thernstrom (Cambridge, MA: Belknap Press of Harvard University, 1980), 245–46. In October 1933, readers of the *Globe* were told that the newspaper had received a journal titled "Free Cossacks," published in Czechoslovakia, which contained an appeal to the world. An article in the journal titled "S.O.S." said that "the Cossacks are now tried by famine that was consciously organized by the Red occupants." Cossack emigrants were prevented from "giving even the small help their means will permit" ("The Call of the Cossack," 13 Oct. 1933, 4).

14 "Appeals for Russ People," *Border Cities Star*, 4 Feb. 1933, 2nd sec., 2. In that report the words "famine" and "hunger" were not used, but the latter did appear in a later story about Countess Tolstoy in the Spanish newspaper *ABC*. Some weeks earlier, the newspaper explained in late April 1933, the European

press had published a letter from Tolstoy, in which she asserted, among other things, that "the peasants, ruined, dying of hunger, are fleeing by the thousands from Ukraine." "Para los amigos de la Union Soviética," *ABC*, 26 Apr. 1933, 3. For earlier statements by Countess Tolstoy about conditions in the USSR, see "Countess Tolstoy Asserts Russians Now in Slavery," *Winnipeg Free Press*, 26 Mar. 1932, 24; and "Declares Russia Worse Off Than Two Years Ago," *Winnipeg Free Press*, 12 Mar. 1932, 5.

15 "Iak vyhliadalo povstannia kubans'kykh selian-kozakiv," *Ukraïns'ki visty*, 15 Feb. 1933, 2. See also "Povstannia kubans'kykh kozakiv," *Ukraïns'ki visty*, 18 Jan. 1933, 2.

16 J. L. Black wrote that Woodsworth returned to Canada with "mixed impressions. He was optimistic about some things, but cautioned that the tsarist dictatorship had been replaced by a dictatorship of the CPSU and secret police." Black, *Canada in the Soviet Mirror*, 103.

17 Dominion of Canada, *Hansard*, 17th Parl., 4th sess., 3 (1933): 2421.

18 See Orest T. Martynowych, "A Ukrainian Canadian in London: Vladimir J. (Kaye) Kysilewsky and the Ukrainian Bureau, 1931–40," *Canadian Ethnic Studies* 42, nos. 2–3 (2010): 263–88; and Roman Krawec, "Ukrainian Bureau," in *Ukrainians in the United Kingdom Online Encyclopaedia*, accessed 23 Apr. 2014, http://www.ukrainiansintheuk.info.

19 It was also a place where Ukrainian Canadians might stop during a visit to London. In April 1932, the *Winnipeg Free Press* announced that Ivan Boberskyj intended to visit the bureau during a European trip ("Professor I. Boberskyj Left for Europe This Week," 30 Apr. 1932, 3). Ukrainians in Canada with whom Kysilewsky maintained ties included Peter Lazarowich and Hanka Romanchych, both of Edmonton, who travelled to Europe and helped at the bureau. See Kysilewsky's diary for the years 1933 and 1934, VJKF. A letter by A. J. Macdonald to the editor of the *Montreal Star* ("Suffering Russia," 12 Oct. 1933, 10) about conditions in the USSR, including the famine, cited a Ukrainian Bureau press release. Kysilewsky corresponded with the associate editor of the *Telegram*, Charles H. J. Snider, who covered the World Economic Conference for that newspaper in July 1933. He invited Snider to visit the Ukrainian Bureau. Kysilewsky, "Unedited Diaries," 87 (entry for 12 July 1933), VJKF.

20 "Ukraine and the Five Year Plan," *Bulletin*, 15 Feb. 1933, 3–4, M-1317, 391400, Bennett Papers.

21 "Dissention in the Ukrainian Communist Party," *Bulletin*, 15 Feb. 1933, 4, M-1317, 391401, Bennett Papers.

22 "Terrible Repression in Soviet Ukraine," *Bulletin*, 15 Feb. 1933, 4, M-1317, 391401, Bennett Papers.

23 "New Passport System to Harry Starving Refugees," *Bulletin*, 15 Feb. 1933, 4, M-1317, 391401, Bennett Papers. On the adoption of the passport system, see "Must Be of 'Class' to Reside in City," *Toronto Star*, 16 Jan. 1933, 39.

24 "Say Cannibalism Exists in Soviet," *Edmonton Journal*, 17 Feb. 1933, 8; "Toronto Speaker Charges Russians with Cannibalism," *Edmonton Bulletin*, 17 Feb. 1933, 3; "Shields Paints Vivid Picture of Soviet State," *Telegram*, 17 Feb. 1933, 33. Shields

was probably referring to the 1921–23 famine; preceding his statement about cannibalism, he had declared that "probably the greatest famine in human history swept across that land in 1920–21" during which "millions of people perished." "Children in Soviet Taught to Write 'There Is No God,'" *Globe*, 17 Feb. 1933, 9.

25 "Would Barter or Sell Canada's Surplus Wheat to Soviet Russia," *Empress Express*, 2 Feb. 1933, 3. See also "Western Pool Seeks Barter with Soviets," *Drummondville Spokesman*, 3 Jan. 1933, 1. In January 1933 the *Winnipeg Tribune* reported on a rumoured Canadian twenty-million-bushel wheat deal with the USSR and of a barter proposal (of Canadian cattle for Soviet oil). "Soviet Russia has been open to suggestions of that kind, in view of the difficulty of obtaining foreign exchange with which to pay cash for materials from the outside world. Russia is also said to be experiencing a shortage of wheat." "Soviet May Take Wheat from Canada," *Winnipeg Tribune*, 20 Jan. 1933, 15. The opening line of an editorial in the *Charlottetown Guardian*, published after the conclusion of the World Wheat Conference in August 1933, read: "While reports of starvation have come from Russia there are millions of bushels of unmarketable wheat in the world." "The Wheat Problem," editorial, *Charlottetown Guardian*, 29 Aug. 1933, 4. See also "Food Shortage during Wheat Glut," *Star-Phoenix*, 28 Aug. 1933, 7, which mentioned the famine and included pictures (of the 1921–23 famine) to illustrate its point.

26 "Canada Recognizes Russia, Refuses Trade," *Edmonton Journal*, 18 Nov. 1933, 7.

27 See "Legislature Adopts Address in Reply to Speech from Throne," *Winnipeg Free Press*, 24 Feb. 1933, 1–2. See also "Some Aid Needy of Russia," *Edmonton Journal*, 25 Feb. 1933, 3.

28 "Soviet Forced Feed People in Caucasia," *Telegram*, 10 Mar. 1933, 32.

29 Helmut Harder, *David Toews Was Here, 1870–1947* (Winnipeg: CMBC Publications, 2002), 274. Toews wrote the letter to Herbert Mackie on January 11, 1933. Ibid., 520n39. Stalin apparently was opposed to foreign aid during the 1921–23 famine. When external relief efforts were underway in the early 1920s, Stalin exhibited "near-paranoiac suspicions about foreign organizations" and had not a single favourable comment to make about the American Relief Administration. Benjamin M. Weissman quoted in Dana G. Dalrymple, review of *Herbert Hoover and Famine Relief to Soviet Russia, 1921–1923*, by Benjamin M. Weissman, *Soviet Studies* 27, no. 3 (1975): 506.

30 "In Terrible Plight," *Star-Phoenix*, 25 Feb. 1933, 5.

31 "Soviet State Impresses Two Western Men," *Leader-Post*, 18 Jan. 1933, 9. On Brown's talk at the Regent Theatre in Saskatoon, see "Declares Workers in Russia Enjoy Better Standards of Living," *Star-Phoenix*, 19 Jan. 1933, 3. Patterson and Brown were two of the five people elected by the National Office of the Friends of the Soviet Union to visit the Soviet Union in October 1932. The other three were J. Koski, a pulp and sulphite worker in northern Ontario, Stanley Hood, a building-trades worker in Toronto, and Leon Bilec, a railway worker in Montreal. A sixth person (railway worker) was to be elected in Winnipeg, and a representative of the Friends of the Soviet Union was expected to travel with the

32 "Passfield on Russia," *Leader-Post*, 18 Jan. 1933, 4.
33 "Russian Life Is Described," *Border Cities Star*, 7 Feb. 1933, 12. Later in the year, Clark showed his pictures to members of the Board of Trade Club in Toronto. The Soviet "bubble" was not about to burst any time soon, was the message conveyed. "Says Russian 'Bubble' Won't Burst for Years," *Telegram*, 12 Dec. 1933, 19. Sherwood Eddy undertook a tenth visit to the USSR in 1933. In a letter to the editor of the *Manchester Guardian*, he described the 1933 Soviet harvest as the "greatest in the entire history of Russia, greater even than in 1913." On Ukraine and the famine, Eddy wrote, "I am convinced that when all the facts are known it will be found that there was much suffering in the Ukraine and North Caucasus last winter and spring, but that this has been relieved and the whole country blessed by the largest harvest in its history." "The Harvest in Russia," *Manchester Guardian*, 8 Sept. 1933, 18.
34 "To Speak on Soviet Peril," *Border Cities Star*, 24 Apr. 1933, 10; "Sordid Tyranny of Soviet Shown," *Border Cities Star*, 27 Apr. 1933, 3, 15. Eddy's own statements also came under scrutiny. After Eddy's visit to Lethbridge, in early 1934, a person identified as "Ukrainian" contributed "a supplement to Dr. Eddy's Address" in the *Lethbridge Herald*, in which he discussed the famine and other topics ("The 'Evils' of Soviet Russia," 7 Feb. 1934, 5). Later, the bulletin of the Ukrainian Bureau mentioned a "Canadian engineer of Ukrainian extraction" who had passed through London "after having spent ten months as a locomotive fireman at Magnetogorsk." The unnamed engineer had informed the bureau: "There was a famine in the country when I left." "Ukraine under Soviet Russia," *Bulletin*, Jan. 1934, 2–3. In March 1933, Kysilewsky recorded in his diary a meeting with Semen Kufliuk, who spent ten months in Magnitogorsk. Kufliuk told Kysilewsky in London that he was encouraged to go to the USSR by "our Bolsheviks." Kysilewsky, "Unedited Diaries," 36 (entry for 17 Mar. 1933), VJKF. Kufliuk's efforts to return to Canada from London and the bureau's assistance are noted in subsequent diary entries: March 18, 20, 21, 23, 28 and April 3, 5, 27 (all 1933).
35 Myroslav Shkandrij and Olga Bertelsen wrote on the OGPU: "After a number of organizational changes, on 15 October 1923 [the Cheka] became the OGPU or GPU [United State Political Administration, 1923–34]. The NKVD [People's Commissariat for Internal Affairs, 1917–46] took over the secret police in 1934....On 13 August 1924 Moscow issued a law stipulat[ing] that the head of the Ukrainian GPU had to be a plenipotentiary [povnovazhnyi] of the OGPU in the USSR, and the agency's operational activities were then supervised and directed by the OGPU in Moscow." Shkandrij and Bertelsen, "The Secret Police and the Campaign against Galicians in Soviet Ukraine, 1929–34," *Nationalities Papers* 42, no. 1 (2014): 55n13.
36 "London Letter Gives Reply to Border Lecturer," *Border Cities Star*, 6 Apr. 1933, 2nd sec., 5. Later, after his return to Windsor, Willis elaborated in an interview with William Sharman of the *Border Cities Star*. Unlike George Bernard Shaw,

Willis told Sharman, he had seen victims of starvation lying dead on the streets, but considered the stories of starving families eating their children an exaggeration ("Picture of Russia by Windsor Man," 22 Dec. 1933, 8).

37 "Conditions in Russia Are Declared Terrible at Meeting in Vernon," *Province*, 3 Nov. 1932, 19. This assignment of blame to the kulaks for the famine by sympathizers of the Soviet Union persisted. Thus, Anna Louise Strong, an American journalist who helped found the *Moscow Daily News*, remarked in 1935 that the "dispossessed kulaks were much to blame [for the famine] because of their acts of sabotage" and that Stalin and the party had not "anticipated the gravity of the situation." "What Shall We Think of Russia Now," *Toronto Star*, 16 Sept. 1935, 6. In its December 1933 issue, *Soviet Russia Today* announced that Strong would be speaking in Toronto on December 2 at Hygeia Hall ("Twelve Years in the Soviet Union," Dec. 1933, 20). *Soviet Russia Today* was the pictorial monthly published by the Friends of the Soviet Union.

38 David Toews to W. L. Mackenzie King, 14 Feb. 1933, C-3675, 169166, W. L. Mackenzie King Papers, Library and Archives Canada, Ottawa (hereafter, King Papers).

39 A. C. March to W. L. Mackenzie King, 28 Feb. 1933, C-3674, 167834–167839, King Papers.

40 King to March, 13 Mar. 1933, C-3674, 167840–167843, King Papers.

41 Toews and Gerhard Ens to King, 11 Mar. 1933, C-3675, 169170–169171, King Papers.

42 "Terrible Picture of Life in Russia," *Winnipeg Tribune*, 2 Mar. 1933, 15. The letter to the editor, though published on March 2, 1933, was written on February 23.

43 "House Urges Canada Send Surplus Grain to Starving Russians," *Leader-Post*, 16 Mar. 1933, 1, 14.

44 For Gardiner's entire speech, see Appendix.

45 "House Urges Canada," *Leader-Post*, 16 Mar. 1933. See also Canadian Press, "Grain for Russia Proposed Charity," *Globe*, 16 Mar. 1933, 1; and "'We Die of Hunger,' Say Piteous Pleas from 'Red Paradise,'" *Globe*, 17 Mar. 1933, 1–2. In 1948, Uhrich (who was of Alsatian origin) became the lieutenant governor of Saskatchewan. Richard Jones, "French," in *Encyclopedia of Canada's Peoples*, ed. Paul Robert Magocsi (Toronto: University of Toronto Press, 1999), 536.

46 "Russia Barter Plan Approved," *Leader-Post*, 17 Mar. 1933, 13.

47 King to Toews, 16 Mar. 1933, C-3675, 169172–169173, King Papers.

48 Such mistrust had earlier been expressed elsewhere, in reference to American wheat and flour sold to China "at a low price on long terms for famine relief." Vancouver "grain men" following "receipt of word" from Shanghai believed that the wheat and flour could be diverted to the USSR. Apparently, China sold ten thousand tons of wheat and another ten thousand tons of flour to the Soviet Union. "Fear Relief Grain Resold," *Province*, 11 Apr. 1932, 1.

49 "Minister Hopes House Withdraws Church-Soviet Statement," *Leader-Post*, 20 Mar. 1933, 3. The topic of Rev. Farley's sermon—"Should Canada Feed Russia?"—had earlier been announced in the *Leader-Post*. He would preach on the subject at the evening service, according to the article in the newspaper, and members of the legislature were invited ("Russia Topic Rev. Farley Sunday

Night," 18 Mar. 1933, 8). Soon after, on March 24, Farley wrote to Gardiner to clear up a misunderstanding. The topic of his sermon for the following Sunday was "Christian Duty and Civil Government"; Gardiner was invited to attend: "If you can find it convenient to attend this service I think you will find your view-point and mine coincides very closely on the present critical situation." Samuel Farley to James Gardiner, 24 Mar. 1933, VI, Box 19, 15957, Gardiner Papers. Gardiner was unable to attend, but in his reply to Farley he expressed his appreciation for the efforts made to remove the misunderstanding. Gardiner to Farley, 19 Apr. 1933, VI, Box 19, 15956, Gardiner Papers.

50 "Text of Gardiner's Speech on Churches' Attitude to Russia." *Leader-Post*, 21 Mar. 1933, 16. See Appendix.
51 "He Wouldn't Trust Them," *Leader-Post*, 30 Mar. 1933, 4.
52 "Trade with Russia," *Star-Phoenix*, 18 Mar. 1933, 11.
53 "Letters from Russia," *Leader-Post*, 21 Mar. 1933, 4.
54 "Letters to Hand from Present-Day Russia," *Winnipeg Free Press*, 18 Mar. 1933, 10. See also "Do Famine Conditions Now Obtain in Russia," *Winnipeg Free Press*, 27 May 1933, 26.
55 "Deny Williams' Report on Russia," *Star-Phoenix*, 22 Mar. 1933, 13. The portrayal was not presented by George Williams personally, but by H. Greenwood of the United Farmers' of Canada, who, in William's absence and in response to a question, gave his views and the reasons for the visit to the USSR. "Corrects Rosthern Meeting Report," *Star-Phoenix*, 8 Apr. 1933, 8.
56 Harder, *David Toews Was Here*, 273.
57 "Facing the Facts," *Leader-Post*, 24 Mar. 1933, 4. The *Leader-Post* very likely had in mind an address by Holland in Victoria made after his return to the British Columbian capital. See also "Soviet Workers' Lot Termed Unenviable," *Calgary Herald*, 24 Mar. 1933, 11.
58 "People Who Like Soviet Rule Should Read This," *Border Cities Star*, 28 Mar. 1933, 7. See also "Saskatchewan Told about Russia," *Montreal Gazette*, 23 Mar. 1933, 12; and "Soviet Rule in Russia," *Kingsville Reporter*, 30 Mar. 1933, 5.
59 "This Is Russia," *Globe*, 18 Mar. 1933, 4. The *Globe* had announced the adoption of the passport system in January ("'Social Enemies' to be Eliminated by Soviet Russia," 23 Jan. 1933, 1).
60 J. M. Speechly to James Gardiner, 18 Mar. 1933, VI, Box 19, 15824, Gardiner Papers.
61 Gardiner to Speechly, 27 Mar. 1933, VI, Box 19, 15823, Gardiner Papers.
62 "Soviets Refused Wheat," *Edmonton Journal*, 20 Mar. 1933, 4.
63 "Masove viche v Heford, Sask.," *Ukraïns'kyi holos*, 7 June 1933, 7.
64 O. Lukianchuk and D. Korpan to Premier Anderson, 31 Mar. 1933, M-988, 93396, Bennett Papers. Both this letter and the one from Krydor were marked "Copy for Mr. Bennett" and "Copy for Honourable Mr. Bennett," respectively.
65 W. J. Sarchuk (Krydor, SK) to Right Honourable J. T. M. Anderson, 25 Mar. 1933, M-988, 93395, Bennett Papers.
66 Premier Anderson to Prime Minister R. B. Bennett, 12 Apr. 1933, M-988, 93394, Bennett Papers. Receipt was acknowledged by Andrew D. MacLean, secretary to

the prime minister, on April 19, 1933. MacLean to Premier Anderson, 19 Apr. 1933, M-988, 93397, Bennett Papers.
67 Jamie Glazov, *Canadian Policy toward Khrushchev's Soviet Union* (Montreal and Kingston: McGill-Queen's University Press, 2002), 6.
68 [Illegible] to R. B. Bennett, 17 March 1933, M-1282, 351067–8, Bennett Papers.
69 James Bryant to E. E. Perley, 21 Mar. 1933, M-1282, 351100–3, Bennett Papers.
70 F. H. Epp, *Mennonite Exodus*, 269.
71 Ibid., 271.
72 Ibid.
73 Harder, *David Toews Was Here*, 208. The Mennonite newspaper based in Rosthern, *Der Bote*, published considerable famine-related material. See, for example, the letters published on 22 Feb. 1933 (pp. 3, 5), 12 Apr. 1933 (pp. 3, 4), and 26 Apr. 1933 (pp. 3, 4); the lists of collections for the USSR published on 20 Dec. 1933 (p. 4) and 25 Apr. 1934 (p. 6); and the following articles: "Brich dem Hungrigen dein Brot!," 22 Feb. 1933, 1; "Die Rotlage in Rusland und das Provinciale Parlament Saskatchewans," 22 Mar. 1933, 3; and "Hunger in der Ukraine," 17 May 1933, 6. On letters and survival strategies during the famine, see Marlene Epp, "The Semiotics of Zwieback: Feast and Famine in Narratives of Mennonite Refugee Women," in *Sisters or Strangers? Immigrant, Ethnic, and Racialized Women in Canadian History*, ed. Marlene Epp and Franca Iacovetta (Toronto: University of Toronto Press, 2004), 314–40.
74 Harder, *David Toews Was Here*, 208.
75 Colin P. Neufeldt, "The Fate of Mennonites in Ukraine and the Crimea during Soviet Collectivization and the Famine (1930–1933)" (PhD diss., University of Alberta, 1999), 243.
76 Ibid., 244.
77 Ibid. Those proceeding without the required travel and employment papers risked incarceration and, in turn, the reduction of their families to beggary.
78 Torgsin is an abbreviation of the Russian *torgovlia s inostrantsami*, which means "trade with foreigners."
79 Neufeldt, "Fate of Mennonites in Ukraine and the Crimea," 247; for a discussion of visits by foreign delegations, see p. 244.
80 Ibid., 248.
81 "Anti-Jewish Pogrom on Huge Scale Reported to be Planned in Germany," *Winnipeg Free Press*, 3 Mar. 1933, 4. See also "Speech by Hitler Sent to Moscow," *Montreal Star*, 3 Mar. 1933, 1–2. Germany learned about the famine both through letters sent by rural Germans in the USSR and from its diplomats and the many German engineers stationed across the Soviet Union. In August 1933, Erland Echlin, described as a special correspondent for the *Globe*, wrote from Berlin on German attitudes toward the USSR. German firms, he wrote, conducted major business with the USSR, and engineers from Germany were "everywhere in the Union and bring back true accounts of today's conditions." The USSR, Echlin continued, was "said to be starving on a vast scale and looking forward with dread to the coming winter." Such conditions were seen as a poor advertisement

for Communism. Echlin, "Germany Hesitates in Deciding Choice of Political Roads," *Globe*, 2 Aug. 1933, 1.
82 Neufeldt, "Fate of Mennonites in Ukraine and the Crimea," 248.
83 Harder, *David Toews Was Here*, 208.
84 F. H. Epp, *Mennonite Exodus*, 276–77.
85 Ibid., 277. An example of fundraising efforts was reported in September: "An address on the famine in Russia was given in the Rosthern town hall by E. Hintz of Regina on Wednesday. The speaker asked that all those able to send donations to the poor in Russia do so." "Asks Donations," *Star-Phoenix*, 16 Sept. 1933, 17.
86 F. W. Turnbull to R. B. Bennett, 24 Mar. 1933, M-1031, 192312–3, Bennett Papers.
87 Colin P. Neufeldt, "The 'Zborni' of Khortytsia, Ukraine: The Last Stop for Some Kulaks En Route to Stalin's Special Settlements," *Journal of Ukrainian Studies* 35–36 (2010–2011): 207–223, esp. 222–23.
88 Neufeldt, "Fate of Mennonites in Ukraine and the Crimea," 255. Neufeldt adds that some Mennonite settlements in Ukraine suffered no deaths, or only a few, as a result of starvation (p. 256). An estimated one hundred thousand Mennonites lived in the Soviet Union in 1926. Emigration and the brutal collectivization drive reduced that number. Dekulakization, arrests, and deportations from 1929 to 1933 claimed ten thousand victims, while the famine in 1932 and 1933 claimed five hundred. Peter Letkemann, "The Fate of Mennonites in the Volga-Ural Region, 1929–1941," *Journal of Mennonite Studies* 26 (2008): 182. From April 1933 to April 1934, Ukraine Germans, who accounted for less than half of the total Soviet German population, received 487,825 gold rubles from abroad in financial transfers. See Terry Martin, "Collectivization, Famine, and Terror, 1926–1934," *Conrad Grebel Review* 20, no. 1 (2002): 37.
89 "Dal'she mrut' z holodu," *Ukraïns'kyi holos*, 5 July 1933, 5.
90 "The Soviet and the Peasantry," *Manchester Guardian*, 25 Mar. (p. 13), 27 Mar. (p. 9), and 28 Mar. (p. 9), all 1933.
91 "Russia in Grip of Great Famine, Millions Dying," *Toronto Star*, 29 Mar. 1933, 1–2. On Siberia, the *Winnipeg Free Press* quoted the Moscow correspondent of the *Manchester Guardian*, who, in December 1932, had reported "nearly a famine" in western Siberia. "The 'Plan' in Danger," *Winnipeg Free Press*, 19 Jan. 1933, 11. There was speculation that Lloyd George, too, might visit the USSR, in the second half of July 1932 or later. Stalin was prepared to receive him, and it was expected that the former British prime minister's itinerary would include Leningrad, Ukraine, and the Caucasus, in addition to Moscow. He never made the trip. See "Mr. L.L. George May Visit Russia," *Aberdeen Press and Journal*, 15 July 1932, 7.
92 "Hungry but Not Starving," *Border Cities Star*, 1 Apr. 1933, 8.
93 "Russian Famine," *Vancouver Sun*, 10 Apr. 1933, 8. A commentary on Shaw's visit to and attitudes toward the USSR appeared in "The Omniscient Bernard," *Vancouver Sun*, 19 Feb. 1932, 6. On March 2, Shaw and various other "recent visitors to the U.S.S.R." signed a letter, published in the *Manchester Guardian*, that characterized revived attempts to "present the conditions of Russian workers as one of slavery and starvation" as "particularly offensive and

ridiculous" ("Social Conditions in Russia," 2 Mar. 1933, 18). That letter drew a reply from V. Tchernavin, a former professor of ichthyology in Leningrad and a forced labourer in the Solovetsky Islands before his escape to Finland in the autumn of 1932. On forced labour, Tchernavin wrote: "Concentration camps contain only a small minority of those who do forced labour. Most of it is done by the deportees, chiefly peasants from Kuban, Ukraine, Caucasus, and Crimea; their position is often worse that that of the prisoners in the concentration camps." "Conditions of Life in Russia," *Manchester Guardian*, 17 Mar. 1933, 20. Another person who challenged the joint letter was Canadian Ella Smith, who also had visted the USSR. See Kirk Niergarth, "Gender and the Great Experiment" (unpublished paper, 2015), 21–22.

94 *Lethbridge Herald*, 31 Mar. 1933, 4. See also "Soviet Deny Reports," *Oyen News*, 5 Apr. 1933, 3.

Chapter Three

1 "Brak khliba v SRSR," *Ukraïns'ki visty*, 1 Feb. 1933, 8.
2 "Povernuv z Velykoï Ukraïny," *Ukraïns'ki visty*, 15 Feb. 1933, 2.
3 "Strashni peresliduvannia na Ukraïni," *Ukraïns'ki visty*, 1 Mar. 1933, 1.
4 "Holod i honennia v Ukraïni," *Ukraïns'ki visty*, 1 Mar. 1933, 2.
5 "Hard to Get Out of Russia Says Settler," *Winnipeg Tribune*, 21 Feb. 1933, 4. The same story appeared a month later in the *Edmonton Journal*, titled "Russian Woman Reaches Tisdale" (24 Mar. 1933, 11), and in April in the *Border Cities Star*, titled "Russian Woman Describes Soviet" (15 Apr. 1933, 8).
6 "Hard to Get Out," *Winnipeg Tribune*, 21 Feb. 1933.
7 "Exodus from Russia Prohibited by Cost," *Telegram*, 30 Nov. 1932, 3. See also "May Quit Russia," *Star-Phoenix*, 30 Nov. 1932, 1.
8 "Cannibalism Rampant in Ukraine, Meeting Hears," *Star-Phoenix*, 3 Apr. 1933, 3.
9 "Ukrainians Protest," *Edmonton Journal*, 4 Apr. 1933, 13.
10 "Charge Horrible Conditions Exist under Soviet Rule," *Edmonton Journal*, 13 Apr. 1933, 12. In May, a letter by "a well-known Toronto citizen," published in the *Telegram*, described instances of cannibalism in the USSR; the letter writer asked for anonymity because he or she had been told of a case "where information published in Toronto derogatory to Russia led to the sender of the information being shot" ("Cannibalism New Horror of Red Rule," 6 May 1933, 1).
11 See, for example, "Ukrainians Determined to Resist Red Influence," *Telegram*, 20 Mar. 1933, 5; and "Ukrainians Charge Bolshevist Menace," *Telegram*, 3 Apr. 1933, 19.
12 "Lysty z Ukraïny," *Ukraïns'ki visty*, 5 Apr. 1933, 3; "Bol'shevyky rozstriliuiut' selian," *Ukraïns'ki visty*, 26 Apr. 1933, 1; "Zhinky i mushchyny biutsia z chekistamy," *Ukraïns'ki visty*, 26 Apr. 1933, 1; "Holod v bol'shevyts'kii Rosiï," *Ukraïns'ki visty*, 17 May 1933, 4. On Jones, see also "Miliony naselennia v Radianshchyny vmyraiut' z holodu," *Kanadyis'kyi farmer*, 12 Apr. 1933, 2; "Miliony v Radianshchyni vymyraiut' z holodu," *Ukraïns'kyi holos*, 12 Apr. 1933, 1; "Sekretar Lloida Dzhordzha pro vidnosyny na Ukraïni," *Ukraïns'kyi holos*,

26 Apr. 1933, 5; and "Angliets' pro hriznyi holod na Radianshchyni," *Novyi shliakh*, 4 Apr. 1933, 1. Ukrainian Bureau director (and, later, recipient of the Order of Canada) Vladimir Kysilewsky attended the first public lecture by Jones at the Royal Institute of International Affairs, on March 30, 1933. After the lecture, Jones joined Kysilewsky and others for snacks at the Café Royal on Regent Street. Two days later, Kysilewsky spoke with Jones again. A Ukrainian-language press release from the Ukrainian Bureau, dated April 8, 1933, noted that a representative of the bureau had been afforded the opportunity of a long talk with Jones, who had spoken of the Kremlin's Russification policy in Ukraine aimed at erasing the Ukrainian national movement. Martynowych, "A Ukrainian Canadian in London," 276; Kysilewsky, "Unedited Diaries," 43 (entries for 31 Mar. and 1 Apr. 1933), VJKF. For more on Jones, see the website developed by his grand-nephew Nigel Linsan Colley, at http://www.garethjones.org.

13 "Letter from Russia Paints Sad Picture," *Calgary Herald*, 28 Apr. 1933, 24.
14 See also *Ukraïns'kyi holos*, 17 May 1933, 5; and "Ponevoleni Moskvoiu narody apeliuliut do Ligy Natsii," *Ukraïns'ki visty*, 24 May 1933, 2. It is not clear to which Swiss newspaper *Ukraïns'ki visty* was referring, but the appeal did appear in the *Journal de Genève*, albeit a day later. See "Un appel à la S. d. N. de la Ligue des Nations opprimées par Moscou," *Journal de Genève*, 29 Apr. 1933, 3.
15 "Shcho dietsia v SRSR," *Ukraïns'ki visty*, 31 May 1933, 1. In June 1933, the *Telegram* announced the issuance of passports in Moscow as a measure to halt "the alarmingly rapid growth of population in the Soviet capital" (24 June 1933, 33). That summer, typhus struck the Soviet capital in an epidemic that was considered unusual for that time of year. "Typhus Visits Soviet Capital on Big Scale," *Telegram*, 11 July 1933, 2nd sec., 1.
16 Walter Duranty, *I Write as I Please* (New York: Simon & Schuster, 1935), 323.
17 "Count to Address Women's Canadian Club, October 18," *Chilliwack Progress*, 12 Oct. 1933, 2. Ignatieff's father had been the Russian minister of education in 1915 (and before that, the deputy minister of agriculture). See "Russian Character is Danger to Soviet," *Winnipeg Free Press*, 4 June 1932, 14; Nicholas Ignatieff, *The Russian Emerges: A Native Assessment of the Soviet Experiment* (Toronto: Macmillan, 1932). It may be of interest to note that the scholar and former Canadian Liberal Party leader Michael Ignatieff is the nephew of Nicholas Ignatieff. See Michael Ignatieff, *The Russian Album* (Toronto: Penguin Canada, 2009), esp. chap. 1.
18 Nicholas Ignatieff, "Real Motives of the Russian Sabotage Trial," *Saturday Night*, 29 Apr. 1933, 2. The *Ottawa Journal* reprinted most of Ignatieff's piece ("Economic Motive of Soviet Trials," 4 May 1933, 6); the piece was also discussed in the *Leamington Post* ("Real Motive behind the Russian Sabotage Trial," 4 May 1933, 6). Other writings by Ignatieff on Soviet agriculture included "Russian Tells of Farming Types in Different Lands," *Winnipeg Free Press*, 30 Aug. 1933, 16; and "Russian Nobleman Scores Method of Communism under Soviet Regime," *Winnipeg Tribune*, 7 Dec. 1933, 6. See also "Russia's Hope Lies in Youth, Says Ignatieff," *Globe*, 25 Apr. 1933, 14. For opponents of the restoration of full Canadian trade relations with the USSR, the sabotage trial served as

a vindication of R. B. Bennett's Soviet policy. See, for example, "The Way of Moscow," editorial, *Almonte Gazette*, 5 May 1933, 2.

19 In 1933, Trotsky remained in exile and was the subject of much press attention. Fearing assassination by Russian White émigrés, he moved frequently from one place to another. See "Found Hiding in France," *Edmonton Journal*, 16 Apr. 1934, 1, 6. Reports do not seem to have included any public declarations on the famine. The closest appears to have been a statement issued by Trotsky from his refuge on the island of Prinkipo, near Istanbul, in which, according to A. C. Cummings, the founder of the Red Army "joyfully proclaimed" the failure of the Stalinist agricultural policy and remarked that the peasantry would prove too strong for the Kremlin to coerce. Cummings, "No Russ Wheat for Export This Year," *Province*, 16 Apr. 1933, 25.

20 Nicholas Ignatieff, "The Plain Fact about Soviet Wheat," *Saturday Night*, 28 Oct. 1933, 2. See also Nicholas Ignatieff, "Socializing Agriculture: Stalin's Chief Worry," *Saturday Night*, 27 May 1933, 2. In 1934, Ignatieff added: "Not only were the drastic collections of grain from the peasants calculated to feed the whole of the greatly increased industrial population both in the Ukraine and Russia proper, but food was exported to help pay for industrialization while the peasants were left short." Individualism in agriculture, he wrote, had developed more in Ukraine than elsewhere and so collectivization was more ruthless in that region. All this, in his opinion, was "bound to create animosity against Moscow and revive the separatist movement." Nicholas Ignatieff, "Russia and Japan," *Saturday Night*, 8 Sept. 1934, 5.

21 "Britain's Answer to Soviet Hate," *Daily Mail*, 20 Apr. 1933, 10.

22 "Relatives in Canada," *Winnipeg Free Press*, 10 Apr. 1933, 7; "Within Sights of St. Paul," *Winnipeg Tribune*, 5 May 1933, 5; Allan Monkhouse, "Present Position of the U.S.S.R.," 8 Nov. 1934, transcript, *The Empire Club of Canada Addresses*, 99–117, http://speeches.empireclub.org/60031/data. However, in July of the previous year, Monkhouse did mention the famine in an address to the Manchester Rotary Club: "At the present moment there are districts of Russia where famine is already in existence. Western Ukraine and the Caucasus are already in that position, judging by all accounts." "Mr. Monkhouse on Russia," *Evening Telegraph and Post* (Dundee), 14 July 1933, 9. See also Allan Monkhouse, *Moscow, 1911–1933: Being the Memoirs of Allan Monkhouse* (London: V. Gollancz, 1933).

23 In March 1933, the *Guardian* had published a three-part article written by (but not attributed to) Muggeridge, titled "The Soviet and the Peasantry" (25 March 1933, p. 13; 27 March 1933, p. 9; and 28 March 1933, p. 9). See "Famine Exposure Newspaper Articles Relating to Gareth Jones' Trips to the Soviet Union (1930–35)," *Gareth Richard Vaughan Jones: Hero of Ukraine*, accessed 21 Feb. 2016, http://www.garethjones.org/soviet_articles/soviet_articles.htm.

24 "Hunger in the Ukraine," *Winnipeg Free Press*, 8 May 1933, 13.

25 "Soviets War on the Peasants," *Winnipeg Free Press*, 14 June 1933, 11. Summaries also appeared elsewhere—for example, in the *Stony Plain Sun* (22 June 1933, p.

7)—and *Novyi shliakh* commented on the original *Fortnightly Review* article (22 Aug. 1933, p. 2).

26 For example, "Témoignage de M. Malcolm Muggeridge, publié dans la presse anglaise en juin 1933," *La Presse*, 2 Nov. 1933, 6; and "L'horreur du régime communiste," *La Survivance*, 8 Nov. 1933, 4.

27 "Kinets' ukraïnizatsiï na Ukraïni," *Ukraïns'ki visty*, 7 June 1933, 1; "Nebuvalo strashni visty," *Ukraïns'ki visty*, 7 June 1933, 2; "Nyshshat ukraïns'ku natsiiu," *Ukraïns'ki visty*, 14 June 1933, 1; "Ukraïns'ke protestatsiine viche v Filadelfiï," *Ukraïns'ki visty*, 14 June 1933, 1; "Liudoïdstvo na Kubani," *Ukraïns'ki visty*, 21 June 1933, 1.

28 "Ukraïna ryne!" *Ukraïns'ki visty*, 21 June 1933, 2.

29 "Famine Toll in Ukraine," *Province*, 4 June 1933, 1. A year later, another article by Donald Day about the famine appeared in the *Chicago Tribune*. In it, Day wrote that he had conversed with three unnamed foreign diplomats in Moscow who informed him that between five and six million people had died in Soviet Ukraine and North Caucasus in the previous autumn and winter from famine, typhus, and other "plagues attendant to famine." Their explanation for the famine, Day said, was that the government had used the Red Army to collect the entire grain crop and send it to Siberia, to be stored in case of a war with Japan. One of the diplomats, according to Day, met M. Florinsky, head of the protocol department of the Soviet foreign office, who told the diplomat that the Kremlin was unconcerned with the loss of lives of peasants whose individualism made them oppose the Communist regime. The Kremlin, Day reported Florinsky said, was busy planning the settlement of depopulated famine areas with collective-minded city dwellers. The USSR, Day said, had now become an importer of grain from countries including the United States and Canada, among others. "8,000,000 Is Cost of Soviet Farm Relief," *Chicago Tribune*, 6 June 1934, 8.

30 The abolition (1930) of the Ukrainian Autocephalous Orthodox Church is mentioned in I. Mazepa, "Ukrainia under Bolshevist Rule," *Slavonic and East European Review* 12, no. 35 (January 1934): 337.

31 "Strashni podiï v Ukraïni," *Ukraïns'ki visty*, 14 June 1933, 4.

32 "Great Privations in Russia Told to Legislature," *Winnipeg Free Press*, 4 May 1933, 3. Wiebe was the first Mennonite elected to the Manitoba legislature. See *Global Anabaptist Mennonite Encyclopedia Online*, s.v. "Klassen, Agatha Wiebe Thiessen (1887–1979)," accessed 11 May 2016, http://gameo.org.

33 "Holod na Ukraïni," *Ukraïns'kyi holos*, 17 May 1933, 5. A Ukrainian summary of "Hunger in Ukraine," *Winnipeg Free Press* (8 May 1933), was also provided.

34 "Na protybol'shevyts'kyi front," *Ukraïns'ki visty*, 21 June 1933, 4.

35 "Protybol'shevyts'ki rezoliutsiï ukraïntsiv v Kalgarakh," *Ukraïns'ki visty*, 21 June 1933, 6.

36 "Protybol'shevyts'ke viche," *Ukraïns'ki visty*, 28 June 1933, 6.

37 "Sufferings in Soviet Ukraine Are Described," *Winnipeg Tribune*, 19 May 1933, 3; "Tells of Suffering in the Ukraine," *Border Cities Star*, 3 June 1933, 2nd sec., 6;

"Ukrainians Suffer from Hunger," *Charlottetown Guardian*, 5 June 1933, 6; "Says Ukrainians Die of Starvation," *Edmonton Journal*, 7 June 1933, 9; "Strashnyi holod na Ukraïni," *Kanadyis'kyi farmer*, 14 June 1933, 9.

Chapter Four

1   Ivan Koshelivets, "Skrypnyk, Mykola," *Internet Encyclopedia of Ukraine*, accessed 12 March 2017, http://www.encyclopediaofukraine.com.
2   "Soviet Incensed at Word of Suicide," *Globe*, 10 July 1933, 4. See also "Suicide of Bolshevik Blamed on Bourgeois," *Telegram*, 8 July 1933, 30; "Former Leader of Soviet Dies by His Own Hand," *Winnipeg Tribune*, 8 July 1933, 1; and, in the Canadian French-language press, "La régime en Ukraine," *La Survivance*, 4 Oct. 1933, 6.
3   "Anhliiska presa pro smert M.A. Skrypnyka," *Ukraïns'ki visty*, 26 July 1933, 1. See also "Zainteresovannia angliis'koï presy smertiiu M. A. Skrypnyka," *Kanadyis'kyi farmer*, 26 July 1933, 1, which included excerpts from the *Daily Telegraph* in addition to the London *Times*. For other articles relating to Skrypnyk, see "Tragediï [illegible] v USRR," *Kanadyis'kyi farmer*, 9 Aug. 1933, 2; "Borba z natsional'nym rukhom na Ukraïni," *Kanadyis'kyi farmer*, 16 Aug. 1933, 1; "Do smerty Mykola Skrypnyka," *Kanadyis'kyi farmer*, 27 Dec. 1933, 2; "Vidkryttyi lyst b. posla Volyntsia," *Ukraïns'kyi holos*, 16 Aug. 1933, 4–5; "Supereshnosti mizh Moskvoiu i Ukraïnoiu," *Ukraïns'kyi holos*, 23 Aug. 1933, 7; and "Nasha tragediia," *Novyi shliakh*, 18 July 1933, 4. See also "Moskva nahorodzhuie svoïkh prysluzhnykiv na Ukraïni," *Kanadyis'kyi farmer*, 12 Apr. 1933, 2.
4   "Bolshevist's Plea for Peasants," *Times*, 10 July 1933, 13. The suicide received attention in the English-language press beyond North America and the United Kingdom. The Ukrainian-language *Kanadyis'kyi farmer* cited a French newspaper, *Journal* (19 July 1933), as stating that Skrypnyk wanted to apply the Soviet constitution to Ukraine's right to secede, and intended to kill Stalin, but took his own life when he was about to be searched by the latter's secretary ("Chy Skrypnyk khotiv ubyty Stalina?," 16 Aug. 1933, 9).
5   "Mykola Khvyl'ovanyi [sic] pomer v Kharkovi," *Kanadyis'kyi farmer*, 14 June 1933, 9 (though here it was reported that the cause of the death was not yet known). See "Pro smert' M. Khvyl'ovoho," *Ukraïns'kyi holos*, 14 June 1933, 4; "Nad mohylo Khvylovoho," *Ukraïns'kyi holos*, 11 Oct. 1933, 7; "Pomer pys'mynnyk Mykola Khvyl'ovyi," *Novyi shliakh*, 6 June 1933, 1; and "Tragediia ukr. pysmennyka," *Novyi shliakh*, 27 June 1933, 3.
6   "Russia as an Example," *Globe*, 22 July 1933, 4. Humphrey Mitchell's election as a delegate to the British Trades Union was announced in the *Lethbridge Herald* (17 Sept. 1932, p. 4). Mitchell, an electrician, was born in Sussex, England, and had come to Canada as a teenager. According to the *Border Cities Star*, the Hamilton labourite "knows the labor movement in England, [and] can call

most of the English labor leaders by their first name. He knows the laborites in Canada—and the Communists, too. He has known Tim Buck for years and knows, as well, those other Communists now in the Kingston penitentiary with Buck. All of which should explain that Mr. Mitchell did not go to Russia with the idea of knocking the five-year plan" ("Criticizes Soviet Plan," 23 Sept. 1933, 2nd sec., 1).

7   See "Life in Russia One of Suffering Says Labor M.P.," *Edmonton Bulletin*, 19 July 1933, 9.
8   *Globe*, 22 July 1933, 4. In the Ukrainian-language press, see "Shcho vydav kanadiis'kyi leiboryt u sovitakh," *Kanadyis'kyi farmer*, 2 Aug. 1933, 1.
9   "Mr. Mitchell Sees for Himself," *Border Cities Star*, 19 July 1933, 4.
10 "What to Believe about Russia," *Edmonton Journal*, 9 Aug. 1933, 4.
11 "Vancouver Publisher Says that Russia Like Anywhere Else," *Star-Phoenix*, 29 July 1933, 6. See also "Canadian Publisher Finds that Life Goes On in Russia Much the Same as in Canada," *Radisson Comet*, 10 Aug. 1933, 5, and *Stony Plain Sun*, 10 Aug. 1933, 3; "Chez les Soviets," *Le Devoir*, 5 Aug. 1933, 1; and "Publisher Enthusiastic on Return from Soviet," *Montreal Star*, 5 Aug. 1933, 4.
12 Richard Sallet held an appointment in the Department of Political Science at Northwestern University. In 1933, Sallet, who was also the editor of the *Dakota Freie Presse*, left the United States for Germany, taking a position at the University of Berlin. See LaVern J. Rippley, "F. W. Sallet and the *Dakota Freie Presse*," *North Dakota History* (1992): 2–20. Presumably, this was the same Sallet about whom Renate Bridenthal wrote: "As for Richard Sallet, he returned to Germany in 1933, became a legation counsellor in the Foreign Service a year later, and finally joined the Nazi Party in 1938." Bridenthal, "Germans from Russia: The Political Network of a Double Diaspora," in *The Heimat Abroad: The Boundaries of Germanness*, ed. K. Molly O'Donnell, Renate Bridenthal, and Nancy Reagin (Ann Arbor: University of Michigan Press, 2005), 217. Later, journalist Donald Day also came under the sway of Nazi Germany; see Philip J. Harwood, "Axis Radio Personalities," in *The Guide to United States Popular Culture*, ed. Ray Broadus Browne and Pat Browne (Bowling Green, OH: Bowling Green State University Popular Press, 2001), 53.
13 "10,000,000 Die of Starvation in Russia in Last Six Months," *Montreal Star*, 8 July 1933, 1.
14 "Soviet Russia as Seen By a Canadian," *Border Cities Star*, 26 Aug. 1933, 9.
15 Examples in French include "'L'expérience russe réussit assez bien,'" *La Presse*, 4 Aug. 1933, 24; and "La Russie en lune de miel économique," *La Presse*, 10 Aug. 1933, 6.
16 H. H. Stevens to Arthur Merriam, 31 Aug. 1933, M-1031, 192321, Bennett Papers; "Memorandum to the Prime Minister," 31 Aug. 1933, M-1031, 192322, Bennett Papers.
17 "The Real Russia," *Edmonton Bulletin*, 8 Aug. 1933, 4.
18 "Starvation Does Exist in Russia," *Calgary Herald*, 6 Sept. 1933, 4. (Kerensky's letter was published in the *Times* on June 24, 1933.) A summary appeared in

the Ukrainian-language press in Canada; see "Velyka Ukraïna hyne z holodu," *Kanadyis'kyi farmer*, 5 July 1933, 9. Kerensky's views on the national question (presented as that of a "one and indivisible Russia") were also discussed; see "Samostiinoï Ukraïny," *Kanadyis'kyi farmer*, 3 May 1933, 9. A year or so after Henry S. Gold's letter appeared in the *Calgary Herald*, the *Blairmore Enterprise* reported that "from the neighbouring town of Delia, [Gold] is going to debate against Russian Communism." His opponent, the newspaper from southwestern Alberta stated, had "travelled in Russia and apparently is enamored of the regime in that far country" ("Question for Communists," 12 July 1934, 4).

19 "Says Russia Holding Own," *Daily Colonist* (Victoria), 17 Aug. 1933, 4.

20 "I Cannot Be Silent," *Daily Colonist*, 17 Aug. 1933, 4. The editorial noted that Countess Tolstoy's letter had appeared in the British newspaper the *Morning Post*. On December 5, 1933, Victoria's *Daily Colonist* ran another editorial that mentioned the famine, this time citing E. Sabline, the former chargé d'affaires for Imperial Russia in London ("Conditions in Russia," 5 Dec. 1933, 4). The editorial prompted a letter to the editor by A. B. Sanders, published two days later, pointing to reports of a robust harvest and to the statements of Herriot and others, and remarking that "Russians at the present moment are better off for food than millions of our Canadian people" ("'Conditions in Russia,'" 7 Dec. 1933, 17). In 1934 the Vancouver branch of the Friends of the Soviet Union reacted to a "four-page folder" issued by the Russian Missionary Group, the contents of which included "the old stories of starvation, famine, in the Soviet Union...on the authority of no less a whiteguard than the ex-member of the Czarist diplomatic service, E. Sabline." "With the F.S.U.," *Soviet Russia Today*, July 1934, 15.

21 *Province*, 11 Aug. 1933, 6.

22 See, for example, Marco Carynnyk, "Swallowing Stalinism: Pro-Communist Ukrainian Canadians and Soviet Ukraine in the 1930s," in *Canada's Ukrainians: Negotiating an Identity*, ed. Lubomyr Luciuk and Stella Hryniuk (Toronto: University of Toronto Press, 1991), 190.

23 See "The Truth about Russia," *Manchester Guardian*, 20 Sept. 1933, 16.

24 "Famine in Russia Seen during Visit," *Montreal Gazette*, 14 Dec. 1933, 19. A lengthier piece discussing Boivin's visit appeared in *La Presse* ("La masque de la misère en Russie," 14 Oct. 1933, 24). In early 1934, Cromie visited Edmonton and spoke to the local chamber of commerce, at the MacDonald Hotel. "R.J. Cromie Speaks Here Wednesday," *Edmonton Journal*, 23 Jan. 1934, 13; "Cromie Urges Canada Awaken to Opportunities Russ Trade," *Edmonton Journal*, 24 Jan. 1934, 1, 17; "Cromie Says Bennett, King Able as Roosevelt, but with Difference," *Edmonton Journal*, 24 Jan. 1934, 13. In an editorial about Cromie's address to the chamber, the *Journal* noted that he had "put that country [the USSR] in a more favourable light, in many respects, than the average investigator had done," but that he had nonetheless furnished sufficient information to show that it would be foolish to suggest that conditions in the USSR were preferable to those in Canada ("Hardly to Liking of Canadians,"

26 Jan. 1934, 4). A challenge to the editorial came in a letter to the editor by A. E. Saunders disputing any notion that socialism in Canada would make this country similar to the USSR ("Russian Conditions," 5 Feb. 1934, 4). Another letter printed in the *Journal*, signed "Subscriber," praised Cromie's lecture in view of much "propaganda" ("Russian Conditions," 12 Feb. 1934, 4).

25 The French, noted the *Border Cities Star*, were stunned at Gorguloff's assassination of President Doumer. The question on their lips, the paper reported, was, "Why Doumer, of all people?" The Windsor newspaper went on to trace the sequence of subsequent French politics. Francois Lebrun became the new president. Premier Pierre Laval had earlier in the year lost the confidence of the French chamber, and after a short spell in office by André Tardieu, Herriot again became prime minister following a general election. "A more conciliatory policy in European affairs," commented the *Border Cities Star*, was discernible after Herriot's term in office commenced ("France," 31 Dec. 1932, 24).

26 "French Envoy Visits Russia," *Toronto Star*, 23 Sept. 1933, 1, 3. Herriot had visited the USSR earlier, in 1922. "M. Herriot in Moscow: An Interview with the Former Premier of France," *Soviet Russia Today*, Nov. 1933, 18–19. During 1933 and 1934, *Soviet Russia Today* not only fended off stories about the famine, but also fielded suggestions from readers that it change its name to *Soviet Union Today*. One reader, L. M., argued that to retain the periodical's present name was to play into the hands of "Ukrainian and other nationalist-fascists" who used the name of the magazine to "'justify' the argument that Soviet Ukraine is being 'starved' and 'expoited' by 'Russia.'" "The Name of Our Magazine," *Soviet Russia Today*, Feb. 1934, 6.

27 "Famine in Russia Denied by Herriot," *Montreal Star*, 20 Sept. 1933, 20. Such dismissive statements about the famine could still be detected years later in the Canadian press. For example, a "Mrs. F. Sunday," responding to a letter in the *Edmonton Bulletin* concerning the repatriation fears of Ukrainians, Poles, and others, wrote that "we have been hearing some pretty tall stories for the last 20 years" about mistreatment and terror under the Communist system, including "the story that circulated in 1932 that hunger was so severe in the USSR that people killed children and ate them" ("Move Is to Left," 23 Oct. 1945, 4).

28 "France Taking Steps to Check Activities of 'White' Russians," *Montreal Star*, 7 Oct. 1933, 1.

29 See "M. Herriot a Moscou," *Le Matin*, 2 Sept. 1933, 3; and "Il faut qu'une mission officielle aille voir ce qui se passe en Ukraine," *Le Matin*, 2 Sept. 1933, 2. The Tokarzewski-Karaszewicz appeal was also mentioned in *Kanadyis'kyi farmer* ("Zakhodiat'sia kolo perevedennia slidstva na Sov. Ukraïni," 20 Sept. 1933, 12).

30 "Un défi a Moscou," *La Presse*, 7 Nov. 1933, 6.

31 "Soviet Denies Foreign Aides," *Province*, 27 Mar. 1932, 10.

32 J. K. Calder, "My Four Years in Russia," *Maclean's*, 15 July 1933, 12.

33 Ibid., 12–13, 27. For the second installment, on Kazakhstan, see J. K. Calder, "My Four Years in Russia," *Maclean's*, 1 Aug. 1933, 13, 36. An additional segment, with

the same title, appeared in *Maclean's* on August 15, 1933 (pp. 12, 43). For more on Calder, see "Calder–Russia's Trouble Shooter," *Winnipeg Tribune Magazine*, 21 May 1932, 3; and "Russia Now Independent of World, Says Engineer," *Toronto Star*, 31 May 1932, 2. His obituary in the *New York Times* noted that "Mr. Calder was considered by some correspondents to have been more admired by the Russians than any other American engineer except the late Col. Hugh L. Cooper." It also quoted Duranty, who described Calder as "hard and tough as the steel he handled" ("J.K. Calder Dead; Noted Engineer, 65," 17 Nov. 1946, 70). Duranty mentioned Calder in several of his pieces about the USSR for the *Times*. The Canada-born engineer was also discussed in Margaret Rourke-White, "Where the Worker Can Drop the Boss," *New York Times*, 27 Mar. 1932, SM8. An October 1932 article in the *Toronto Star* noted the "great tribute" that was "paid to the American engineers under Col. Hugh Cooper" for their role in the construction of the Dniprostroi dam ("Soviet Power Plant Opened with Pomp," 11 Oct. 1932, 4).

34 "Warns against Trade with Russia," *Border Cities Star*, 27 June 1933, 2nd sec., 5.
35 "Letters Tell of Suffering in Soviet Russia: Border Group to Protest This Evening," *Border Cities Star*, 21 July 1933, 3.
36 "Police Called as Reds Stampede Meeting," *Border Cities Star*, 22 July 1933, 1, 6. Humphrey Mitchell himself does not seem to have given any public addresses on the USSR after his return from there, though he did speak on the general topic of "dictatorships," which included the Soviet Union. For example, having returned from visits to Germany, Italy, and the Soviet Union, Mitchell discussed the subject in addresses to the Jewish Young People's League and the Zonta Club of Ottawa. "H. Mitchell, M.P.," *Ottawa Journal*, 28 Feb. 1934, 15; "Humphrey Mitchell Speaks at Luncheon on 'Dictatorship,'" *Ottawa Journal*, 29 Mar. 1934, 10.
37 "Workers' Resolution Attacks Soviet," *Border Cities Star*, 29 July 1933, 3rd sec., 5.
38 S. Odoevzev to R. B. Bennett, 8 Aug. 1933, M-1031, 192286, Bennett Papers. (The clipping and acknowledgment of receipt are in M-1031, 192287 and 192288.) In the United States, the Russian-language newspaper *Rassvet* hoped for the consolidation of Russian groups at a convention where the famine and U.S. recognition of the USSR would be discussed. Invitations were to be issued to representatives of the Russian community in Canada. "About Our Convention," *Rassvet* (Chicago), 21 Aug. 1933, http://flps.newberry.org/article/5423967_4_0958.
39 Emma Goldman, *Living My Life: Two Volumes in One* (New York: Cosimo Classics, 2011), 568. Goldman herself visited Canada—specifically, Toronto—in December 1933; in an interview with the *Toronto Telegram*, she did not mention the famine ("Anarchist Awards Britain Dubious Palm for Liberty," 22 Dec. 1933, 1, 12). However, she did discuss it later, in an essay published in 1935: "There Is No Communism in Russia," *American Mercury* 34 (Apr. 1935), http://www.hartford-hwp.com/archives/63/227.html.
40 "Bolshevism Is Assailed," *Border Cities Star*, 12 Sept. 1933, 6.
41 "Proty Bol'shevyts'kyi protest," *Kanadyis'kyi farmer*, 20 Sept. 1933, 6. As an example of the activities of Russians in the United States, the *Globe* mentioned the All-Russian Evangelical Christian Union in New York. "The Russian Red

Cross recently issued a photograph of a starving child taken in 1933," the Toronto paper reported in October. "The emaciated form would move the heart of stone, and the Red Cross declares there are literally thousands of these starving, emaciated children in Soviet Russia. . . . The All-Russian Evangelical Christian Union, 156 Avenue, New York City are holding themselves responsible for Famine Relief Service, and an urgent appeal is sent out to all who can, to lend their financial aid to these great armies of hungry Russians" ("Outlook of the Church," 14 Oct. 1933, 13).

42 "Famine over Russia," *Winnipeg Free Press*, 2 Sept. 1933, 19. In August 1933, foreign journalists were summoned by the authorities and told they could not travel outside the Moscow area without a special permit. "Russian Famine: Alarm of the Soviet Authorities," *Nottingham Evening Post*, 11 Aug. 1933, 3; "The Ban on Journalist Travel," *Manchester Guardian*, 3 Sept. 1933, 10. See also "Our London Correspondence," *Manchester Guardian*, 22 Sept. 1933, 8. As well, the *Nottingham Evening Post*, citing the *Daily Telegraph*, said that Moscow was hoping to secure American diplomatic recognition, trade, and credits and could not afford negative publicity: "It happened recently that one of the foreign newspaper correspondents in Moscow took the initiative of making a personal tour in the Ukraine, the Northern Kuban, and the Caucasus to judge for himself of the economic situation there. His reports on the chaos, scarcity and famine prevailing in these regions caused acute distress and alarm in Soviet official circles, owing to their probable repercussion on public opinion outside Russia" ("Russian Famine," 11 Aug. 1933, 3).

43 "Soviet Secrecy: The Ban on Journalist Travel," *Manchester Guardian*, 3 Sept. 1933, 10. See also "Our London Correspondence," *Manchester Guardian*, 22 Sept. 1933, 8.

44 "Russian Famine Areas Closed to Observers," *Telegram*, 12 Oct. 1933, 44.

45 "Moskva zataiuie strashnyi holod na Velykii Ukraïni," *Kanadyis'kyi farmer*, 30 Aug. 1933, 1.

46 George P. Kulchytsky, "Western Relief Efforts during the 'Stalin Famine,'" *Ukrainian Quarterly* 49, no. 2 (1993): 154. For studies on western Ukraine and the famine, see Iaroslav Papuha, *Zakhidna Ukraïna i holodomor 1932–1933 rokiv: moral'no-polityčhna i material'na dopomoha postrazhdalym* (Lviv: Astroliabiia, 2008); N. Z. Prokip, "Reaktsiia Zakhidnoï Ukraïny ta mizhnarodnoï spil'nota na Holodomor 1932–1933 rr. v Ukraïni," *Visnyk Natsional'noho universytetu L'vivs'ka politekhnika* (Lviv), no. 993 (2011): 181–87; Robert Kushnezh [Kuśnierz], "L'vivs'ka ukraïns'ka presa pro Holodomor v USRR," *Ukraïns'kyi istorychnyi zhurnal* 3 (2006): 199–209; and Ia. Papuha, "Pozytsiia Varshavy shchodo Holodomoru 1932–1933 rr.," *Mandrivets*, no. 4 (2010): 38–42.

47 "Polish-Soviet Peace Worries Ukrainians," *New York Times*, 30 July 1933, 24. The report added: "Many Soviet Ukrainians have crossed the Polish border searching for food. They say former Red Army soldiers from the North are settling from the frontier to combat anti-Soviet agitation led by the Berlin [Ukrainian] group."

48 "Catholic Bishops of Ukrainia Appeal to World against Soviet Injustice," *Western Catholic*, 18 Oct. 1933, 1. The letter was also published (on August 25,

1933) by the *Catholic Times* in the United Kingdom. See Kysilewsky, "Unedited Diaries," 102 (entry for 28 Aug. 1933), VJKF. In response to the letter, readers of the *Catholic Times* sent donations to the newspaper. Ibid., 108.

49 "La persécution dans l'Ukraine," *Le Devoir*, 24 Aug. 1933, 8; "La persécution dans l'Ukraine," *La Liberté*, 6 Sept. 1933, 2.

50 Andrii Krawchuk, "Protesting against the Famine: The Statement of the Ukrainian Catholic Bishops in 1933," *Journal of Ukrainian Studies* 8, no. 2 (1983): 59–62.

51 See, for example, "Famine Grips Soviet Claim of Cardinal," *Toronto Star*, 19 Aug. 1933, 1; and "Archbishop Says Famine Sure to Come," *Edmonton Bulletin*, 2 Sept. 1933, 3.

52 "Pope Weeps as He Hears of Millions Starving in Russia," *Western Catholic*, 30 Aug. 1933. The Jesuit was almost certainly Michel d'Herbigny. For more on the Vatican and the famine, see Athanasius D. McVay and Lubomyr Y. Luciuk, eds., *The Holy See and the Holodomor: Documents from the Vatican Secret Archives on the Great Famine of 1932–1933 in Soviet Ukraine* (Kingston: Kashtan, 2011). A story on Michel d'Herbigny appeared in the *Montreal Star* ("Russia Is Visited by Jesuit Bishop," *Montreal Star*, 15 Dec. 1933, 43). At the start of November 1933, the *Western Catholic* carried an appeal by Russian Orthodox Bishop Seraphim, who "found a refuge in Vienna," to the international public to come to the assistance of the "starving population of Southern Russia." The bishop expressed gratitude for the efforts of Cardinal Innitzer but lamented that they had led to no "visible action"; he also urged a boycott of Soviet food imports. The bishop asked, Why were "whole villages dying out there? Why is almost the whole crop confiscated by force?" His answer: "It is because in spite of all propaganda the Bolshevistic dictators did not succeed in winning over the souls of the people." ("[Illegible] Asked to Help Starving Russia," 1 Nov. 1933, 1). On Pope Pius XI and Ukraine earlier in 1933, see also "Ukraine Uses Root Bread," *Times-Union* (Albany, NY), 7 Apr. 1933, 30.

53 "Mussolini discutera avec Litvinoff la question d'une complète liberté religieuse en Russie," *Le Devoir*, 28 Nov. 1933, 1. See also "Religious Liberty in Russia Sought," *Montreal Star*, 28 Nov. 1933, 4.

54 Kysilewsky, "Unedited Diaries" (entry for 6 July 1933), VJKF.

55 "War Certain Says Lawyer," *Edmonton Journal*, 30 Aug. 1933, 14. The *Calgary Herald* also mentioned Lazorowich's return from Europe ("Believes Europe War Is Inevitable," 1 Sept. 1933, 20).

56 "Russia's Famine," *Edmonton Journal*, 1 Sept. 1933, 4. See also the September 7 editorial in the *Western Globe* (Lacombe, AB) ("Russia's Famine," 7 Sept. 1933, 8). Quite possibly, the *Edmonton Journal* editorial writer had seen the wireless dispatch from Frederick T. Birchall in Berlin that was published in the *New York Times* and also appeared in Canadian newspapers. Birchall wrote of the German collection of funds for relief, the estimate of four million deaths, and of two "Russo-German fugitives" and an American (Walter Becherer of the First Wisconsin National Bank in Milwaukee). See "Russ Famine Equals 1921," *Border Cities Star*, 26 Aug. 1933, 10.

57 "Rumeurs de famine," *La Presse*, 22 Sept. 1933, 6. It was a Belgian source, the Socialist *Le Peuple*, that the Edmonton French-language weekly *La Survivance* cited when it reported that foreign journalists in Moscow were speaking more and more about a famine in the USSR. "La crise économique chez les Soviets," *La Survivance*, 5 Apr. 1933, 7.

58 "La famine en Russie," *La Presse*, 13 Sept. 1933, 6. See also "La Famine en U.R.S.S.," *La Survivance*, 20 Sept. 1933, 1. CILACC—described as "an anti-communist organization that is occupied not only with propaganda against communism, but whose action is primarily oriented toward the active struggle, the technical struggle against this danger"—was probably the "Centre international de lutte active contre le communisme." The August 15, 1933, issue of its publication (also called *CILACC*) was devoted to "La famine en U.R.S.S." Published in French, Spanish, and Dutch editions, no fewer than eighteen issues were planned for 1933. A copy of the one on the famine can be found in Ielysaveta Skoropadska Papers: Committee to Aid Victims of the Famine in Ukraine 1933-44, reel 11 (Newspaper Clippings), V. Lypynsky East European Research Institute Archives, Philadelphia (hereafter, Skoropadska Papers).

59 *La famine en Russie* (Montreal: L'Oeuvre des tracts / L'Action paroissiale, 1933).

60 "Petytsiia Zhin. T-v do Soiuzu Natsii v spravi holodu na Ukraïni," *Novyi shliakh*, 31 Oct. 1933, 4; "Obiednanyi komitet Mizhnarodnykh Zhinochykh Organizatsiï v spravi holodu na Ukraïni," *Ukraïns'kyi holos*, 17 Oct. 1934, 5. For a discussion of the role of the Ukrainian Women's Union (western Ukraine) in publicizing the famine, see Martha Bohachevsky-Chomiak, *Feminists despite Themselves: Women in Ukrainian Community Life, 1884-1939* (Edmonton: CIUS Press, 1988), 277-278. For more on the League of Nations and the famine, see Roman Serbyn, "The Great Famine of 1933 and the Ukrainian Lobby at the League of Nations and the International Red-Cross," *Holodomor Studies* 1, No. 1 (2009): 91-133; and Roman Serbyn, "Public Pressure on the International Committee of the Red-Cross as It Waited for the Soviet reply on the Ukrainian Famine," *Holodomor Studies* 1, no. 2 (2009): 101-41.

61 Serbyn, "Great Famine of 1933," 111 (my translation).

62 Serbyn, "Public Pressure," 133.

63 "Holod na Ukraïni i Liga Natsii," *Ukraïns'ki visty*, 25 Oct. 1933, 1.

64 Famine-related articles appearing in *Le Matin* were discussed in the French-language press in Canada—for example, a report by Suzanne Bertillon in *Le Matin* concerning an interview with an American couple, Mr. and Mrs. Stebalo, who had visited Soviet Ukraine: "La detresse de l'Ukraine," *La Survivance*, 4 Oct. 1933. A number of French-language sources on the famine are compiled in *50ème anniversaire de la famine-génocide en Ukraine, 1933-1983* (La Famine en 1933, ce que la presse en disait) (Paris: Club de Amis de l'Ukraine, 1983).

65 "Holova Ligy Natsii u spravi holodu na Ukraïni," *Ukraïns'ki visty*, 8 Nov. 1933, 2; "Holod v Ukraïni ta Liga Natsii," *Kanadyis'kyi farmer*, 8 Nov. 1933, 9.

66 "Serdechna podiaka pryiatelevy Ukraïny," *Kanadyis'kyi farmer*, 27 Dec. 1933, 2.

67 "Thousands Dying of Starvation in Russian Ukraine," *Calgary Herald*, 30 Sept.

1933, 9. The *Charlottetown Guardian* ran the story on its front page ("Thousands Dying of Starvation in Russian Ukraine," 30 Sept. 1933, 1). At that time, there were many reports of a good harvest in the USSR, including references to the statements by Édouard Herriot. For more on responses of the League of Nations and the International Red Cross Committee to Mowinckel's appeal, see Serbyn "Great Famine of 1933," 95–96.

68 Serbyn, "Public Pressure," 101–2, 107–8. On the subject of the Soviet reply to the International Red Cross, Ewald Ammende wrote: "When Dr. Mowinckel took up the question [of the famine] at Geneva he could reckon not only on Norway resigning from the League Council—in which case she would have had to pay less consideration to the other states on the Council—but also on his not remaining at the head of the Government on account of the expected change in the strength of the respective parties in Norway. He had good grounds for supposing that after the assembly of the newly elected Parliament another Norwegian party leader would take over the reins of government. But now fate willed it that the relative strength of parties after the elections compelled Dr. Mowinckel—although his political opponents were stronger than before—to take upon himself the burden of the Premiership for a further period. But that meant that in all questions affecting Russo-Norwegian relations he had to confront the Soviet Government as chief representative of Norway and all her economic and political interests. Moscow, as usual, had exploited this situation for its own ends in masterly fashion. Before it replied to the [October 12, 1933] letter from the International Red Cross, it asked in Oslo for a statement to the effect that Dr. Mowinckel's idea of the state of things in the Soviet Union had been based on information placed at his disposal by 'the other side,' and not on his own personal observations on the spot. It is said that Dr. Mowinckel's statement—which it could not be difficult to extract from him as Norwegian Foreign Minister and negotiator in all dealings between his country and the Soviet Union—figured in Moscow's reply to the International Red Cross as one of the main planks in its denial of the existence of a famine and rejection of any offer of help." Ammende, *Human Life in Russia* (London: G. Allen Unwin, [1936]), 302.

69 "Policy of Soviet Regime Scored by Ukrainians Here," *Winnipeg Free Press*, 18 Sept. 1933, 6.

70 "Ukrainian Independence," *Toronto Star*, 28 Sept. 1933, 6. A couple of years later the Canadian Red Cross story was recalled south of the border; Lesio Sysyn brought it to the attention of readers of the *Herald-News* in New Jersey. In the article, which was reprinted in the American Ukrainian-language periodical *Svoboda*, Sysyn said: "In 1932 the Canadian Red Cross, upon the request of Ukrainian farmers of Western Canada to send some flour and bread to Soviet Ukraine, asked from the Soviet government permission to do some relief work there"; the Soviet Red Cross, however, "denied any existence of famine and refused to admit any supplies of food stuffs to the Ukraine." Sysyn, "Soviet Russia's Crime against the Ukraine," *Svoboda*, 25 July 1935, 4.

71 For an announcement of the trip, see "Pierre van Paassen to Send Hot Cables on Russian Trip," *Edmonton Bulletin*, 14 Aug. 1933, 1. See also "On 10,000-Mile Trip," *Winnipeg Free Press*, 12 Aug. 1933, 7.
72 "Pierre van Paassen to Send Hot Cables," *Edmonton Bulletin*, 14 Aug. 1933, 1.
73 "Ukraine Practically Won Over to Soviet Farm Plan," *Edmonton Bulletin*, 13 Sept. 1933, 1, and *Toronto Star*, 16 Sept. 1933, 1, 3.
74 "Future of Soviet Depends on Successful Harvesting," *Edmonton Bulletin*, 12 Sept. 1933, 3.
75 See "The Human Surplus," *Edmonton Bulletin*, 19 Oct. 1933, 4.
76 "Van Paassen Off to Russia to Study Red Rule," *Globe*, 14 June 1932, 1–2.
77 "Biography of Pierre van Paassen," 7, file 2 of 3, MG 30, series E408, vol. 7, Hugh Whitney Morrison Fonds, Library and Archives Canada, Ottawa (hereafter, LAC). More than two decades after the famine, van Paassen wrote the book *Visions Rise and Change*, in which he mentioned early interactions with Ukrainians in western Canada as well as the famine of 1932–33. He seemed to portray the "Ruthenians" among whom he preached around the time of World War I as hospitable but not very enlightened. Van Paassen wrote that he would often spend the night in the home of a Ukrainian family, out of necessity, but the "idea of sponging on these poor farmers was repugnant to me." Besides, the medical missionary with whom he travelled "would not touch the food they set before us when we happened to be invited for a bite, because the moment the bread or soup or whatever food reached the table, it was instantly covered with a dense mass of flies. The straw bedding they slept on was infested with vermin while everybody, men, women and children, understandably enough, sat up half the night scratching or hunting by candlelight." Van Paassen was glad when he "found permanent lodging at last with a family of Moravian Brethren." Van Paassen, *Visions Rise and Change* (New York: Dial Press, 1955), 22–23. It is not clear what the Ukrainian settlers in Alberta (the one place mentioned is the village of Andrew) thought of van Paassen, but some of them may well have been among the participants in the local rallies of 1933 and 1934 protesting the famine. Later on in the book, van Paassen discussed the famine, which he said had claimed three million lives. "The last glimmer of resistance against collectivization was extinguished when in '31 and '32 the government ordered the stocks of grain seed shipped out of that area," he wrote. In doing that, "an artificial famine was produced." When the outside world became aware of the famine, according to van Paassen, the excuse given was that Stalin had "ordered Ukrainian wheat shipped to the Red armies in the Far East," where there was a Japanese threat after Japan's invasion of Manchuria. Ibid., 107–8.
78 On press coverage of the famine in western Ukraine, see Myroslav Shkandrij, "Ukrainianization, Terror and Famine: Coverage in Lviv's Dilo and the Nationalist Press of the 1930s," *Nationalities Papers* 40, no. 3 (2012): 431–51; and Kushnezh, "L'vivs'ka ukraïns'ka presa," 199–209.
79 "Holod na Ukraïni," *Ukraïns'ki visty*, 2 Aug. 1933, 4.
80 "Lyst z Velykoï Ukraïny," *Ukraïns'ki visty*, 2 Aug. 1933, 7.

81 "Kartyny holoduiushoï Ukraïny," *Ukraïns'ki visty*, 16 Aug. 1933.
82 "'Naukovi Chekisty' nysshchat ukraïns'ku nauku," *Ukraïns'ki visty*, 9 Aug. 1933, 4; "Ukraïns'kyi hromads'kyi komitet dopomohy strazhdal'nii Ukraïni," *Ukraïns'ki visty*, 23 Aug. 1933, 1; "Apel' Kardynala Innitsera v oboroni vymyraiuchoï Ukraïny," *Ukraïns'ki visty*, 30 Aug. 1933, 4.
83 "Na pomich umyraiuchii z holodu Ukraïni," *Ukraïns'ki visty*, 6 Sept. 1933, 2; "Frantsuz pro holod na Ukraïni," *Ukraïns'ki visty*, 13 Sept. 1933, 2; "Anhliiska presa pro holod na Kubani," *Ukraïns'ki visty*, 20 Sept. 1933, 2 (about Kuban); "Vsenarodnyi povstannia na Ukraïny," *Ukraïns'ki visty*, 13 Sept. 1933, 1; "Novi avtentychni visty pro Holodovi Muky naselennia Ukrainy," *Ukraïns'ki visty*, 20 Sept. 1933, 2.
84 "Liudoïdstvo na Ukraïni," *Ukraïns'ki visty*, 27 Sept. 1933, 2; "Vzhe sama sov. vlada pryznaie holod na Ukraïni," *Ukraïns'ki visty*, 27 Sept. 1933, 1; "Braty v Nechshastiu," *Ukraïns'ki visty*, 27 Sept. 1933, 2.
85 "Braty v Nechshastiu," *Ukraïns'ki visty*, 27 Sept. 1933.
86 "V oboroni vymyraiuchoï Ukraïny," *Ukraïns'ki visty*, 6 Sept. 1933, 4.
87 "U khvyli narodnoho horia," *Ukraïns'ki visty*, 20 Sept. 1933, 1. Toward the end of 1933, *Ukraïns'ki visty* also published a pastoral letter on the famine by the head of the Ukrainian Catholic Church in the United States, Bishop Constantine Bohachevsky ("Pastyrs'kyi lyst Preosv. Konstantyna Bohachevs'koho z pryvodu holodu na Velykyi Ukraïni," 20 Dec. 1933, 5).
88 "Ukraïntsi! Kopaite hrib bol'shevyzmovy!" *Ukraïns'ki visty*, 20 Sept. 1933, 4.
89 "Jailed Communist Faces Deportation," *Border Cities Star*, 5 May 1933, 10.
90 "Kanada deportuvala bol'shevyts'kykh agitatoriv," *Ukraïns'ki visty*, 21 Dec. 1932, 1.
91 "Men, Held at Halifax 14 Months, Leave for Russia Soon," *Winnipeg Tribune*, 1 July 1933, 3. See also "Supreme Court Dismisses Communists' Appeal," *Ottawa Journal*, 28 Nov. 1932, 1 and 10. The forty-year-old Sembay had come to Canada in 1923.
92 "Edmonton Communist Soon to Be Deported," *Telegram*, 12 July 1933, 30.
93 "Braun Leaves Montreal for Trip to Russia," *Winnipeg Tribune*, 27 Oct. 1932, 1; "Braun Has Departed for Russia; Denies Smuggling of Money," *Winnipeg Free Press*, 28 Oct. 1933, 9. Braun left behind in Canada his wife and two children and had "no idea when he would see them again." He expected to do farm work in the USSR. "Deportee Denies Death Awaits Him," *Telegram*, 27 Oct. 1933, 42.
94 See *Winnipeg Tribune*, 17 Aug. 1933, 2. On March 5, 1934, Michael Luchkovich asked a question about deportation in the House of Commons: "We have often heard Canada referred to as the mecca of the workingman, but I have also heard people in this country refer to Russia in this way. The hon. Member for East Hamilton asked with regard to the number of workmen in this country who have asked to be deported to Russia, and I was wondering if that number was large." Wesley Ashton Gordon replied: "We have very great difficulty in returning anyone to Russia because of the passport troubles." Dominion of Canada, *Hansard*, 17th Parl., 5th sess., vol. 2 (1934): 1179.
95 "Russian Woman Red, Released from Calgary Jail, May Be Deported," *Province*, 22 Sept. 1932, 12.

Chapter Five

1 "Marching War Legions, Starving Children, City Woman's Picture of Soviet Russia," *Edmonton Journal*, 5 Oct. 1933.
2 Dmytro Mykytiuk, "Naochnyi svidok holodu na Velekyi Ukraïni u Vinnipegu," *Kanadyis'kyi farmer*, 13 Sept. 1933, 4.
3 "Starving Parents Eat Own Children," *Edmonton Journal*, 10 Oct. 1933. See also "Visitor Tells of Cannibalism in the Ukraine," *Winnipeg Tribune*, 9 Sept. 1933, 12; and "Ukraine Couple Eat Children," *Charlottetown Guardian*, 14 Oct. 1933, 6.
4 M. Wayne Morris, *Stalin's Famine and Roosevelt's Recognition of Russia* (Lanham, MD: University Press of America, 1994), 193–96. The text of the bulletin featuring the testimony was published in *Svoboda* ("Conditions in Soviet Ukraine," 12 Oct. 1933, 3). *Ukraïns'kyi holos* conducted an interview with Zuk that it published on September 13, 1933. That interview, in English translation, was included in Klid and Motyl, *The Holodomor Reader*; see also Bohdan Klid, "Early Survivor Testimony on the Holodomor," *New Pathway*, no. 2 (2010): 6.
5 Morris, *Stalin's Famine*, 193–96.
6 "Skoblak Named to Head Council of Ukrainians," *Winnipeg Tribune*, 13 May 1933, 4; see also "Stephen Skoblak Is Elected President of the New Ukrainian Council," *Winnipeg Free Press*, 15 May 1933, 3. A copy exists of the statute for the "Provisional Committee of the Ukrainian National Council," prepared for discussion at a general meeting of "all Ukrainian organizations" at the Ukrainian Reading Association "Prosvita" slated for Friday, May 5, at 8:30 p.m.: "Concert Programs/Leaflets/Society of Volyn Cor.," Ukrainian Reading Association Prosvita fonds (3 of 4), E-507 3/3, Ba-3-5, Ukrainian Cultural and Educational Centre (Oseredok), Winnipeg (hereafter, Oseredok). Stephen Skoblak was reelected president at the annual meeting of the UNC held on May 29, 1934, at the Ukrainian Literary Society, 49 Euclid Avenue. Other members of the new executive included C. Andrusyshen, first vice-president; W. Kohut, second vice-president; J. Baydack, recording secretary; P. Matweychina, financial secretary; J. Cymbalisty, secretary-treasurer. The board of auditors included D. Rawlick, J. Kostyniuk, and J. Korolyk; the advisory board, L. Biberovich, H. Kuz, K. Andrusyshin, A. Gospodin, M. Mandryka, D. Budka, D. Ravlik, W. Lach, H. Mudry, T. Hubicki, K. Hrycyshin, S. Kwasnycia, and D. Mykytiuk. "Stephen Skoblak Heads Ukrainian Council," *Winnipeg Tribune*, 30 May 1934, 17.
7 See "Ukrainian Council Issues Call for Mass Meeting," *Winnipeg Tribune*, 10 July 1933, 5.
8 "Police Raid Ukrainian Labor Temple," *Winnipeg Tribune*, 5 July 1933, 1.
9 "Stones Fly as Two Ukrainian Factions Riot," *Winnipeg Tribune*, 17 July 1933, 3; "Ukrainians Meet to Advance New National Council," *Winnipeg Free Press*, 17 July 1933, 3; "Charges May Follow Ukrainian Hall Riot," *Winnipeg Tribune*, 18 July 1933, 14. See also "Angry Scenes Again Feature Ukrainian Meet," *Winnipeg Tribune*, 28 Aug. 1933, 1. For a ULFTA perspective, see "Biika na mitingu ukraïns'kykh

natsionalistiv u Vinnipegu," *Ukraïns'ki robitnychi visty*, 20 July 1933, 1.

10 "Famine Sweeps Ukraine, Says Dr. Mandryka," *Winnipeg Tribune*, 21 Aug. 1933, 4. As Andrij Makuch notes, the meetings of the UNC did not receive much coverage in the Ukrainian Canadian press. It was accorded scant attention by *Ukraïns'kyi holos* possibly because the council was associated with Mykyta Mandryka, a Ukrainian Socialist revolutionary and "a figure to whom they [*Ukraïns'kyi holos*] were unsympathetic." Makuch, "Ukrainian Patriots, Communist Sympathizers, and the Holodomor Issue in 1933 Canada" (unpublished paper delivered at the Annual Convention of the Canadian Association of Slavists, Fredericton, NB, 28 May 2011), 6.

11 Carynnyk, Luciuk, and Kordan, *The Foreign Office and the Famine*, 339–43; Giorgio Petracchi, "Il fascismo, la diplomazia italiana e la 'questione ucraina': La politica orientale dell'Italia e il problema dell'Ucraina (1933–1941)," in *La morte della terra. La grande "carestia" in Ucraina nel 1932–33. Atti del convegno, Vicenza, 16-18 ottobre 2003*, ed. Gabriele De Rosa and Francesca Lomastro (Rome: Viella, 2004), 277–78. The UNC's letter to Mussolini was dated October 2, 1933 (as was the one to President Roosevelt). It called for Italian denunciation of the Kremlin's policy of denationalization of Ukraine through an organized famine.

12 "Canadian Ukrainians Protest Soviet Rule," *Winnipeg Tribune*, 19 Sept. 1933, 4; *Winnipeg Free Press*, 13 Sept. 1933, 4 (about a meeting at the Ukrainian Orthodox Cathedral in Winnipeg); "Policy of Soviet Regime Scored by Ukrainians Here," *Winnipeg Free Press*, 18 Sept. 1933, 6; "Grim Conditions in Ukraine Are Cause of Worry," *Winnipeg Free Press*, 27 Sept. 1933, 3 (about a meeting in Edmonton).

13 On a day of fasting and mourning and the staging of a play about the famine, see "Ukrainians Pay Tribute to Victims of Starvation," *Winnipeg Free Press*, 25 Nov. 1933, 8. See also "Drama Showing Ukraine Famine Is Effective," *Winnipeg Tribune*, 9 Nov. 1933, 17. The play was published as P. Pylypenko, *Smert' komisara Skrypnyka, abo Holod na Ukraïni* (Winnipeg: Nakladom Ukraïns'koï knyharni, n.d.). For more about the play, see Alyssa Erin Schmidt, "After History: Famine Plays of an Gorta Mór and the Holodomor" (PhD diss., Tufts University, 2012), 208–9. Schmidt describes how Pylypenko "shows a mother, who carries her starved baby in her arms, appeal to Skrypnyk concerning her husband's banishment to Siberia." Ibid., 209. See also Iroida Lebid-Wynnyckyj, "Ukrainian Canadian Drama from the Beginnings of Immigration to 1942" (MA thesis, University of Waterloo, 1976). The playwright P. Pylypenko (the pseudonym of Pylyp Ostapchuk), from eastern Ukraine, came to Canada in 1929. See "Nacherk ukraïns'koï literaturnoï tvorchosty v Kanadi," *Ukraïns'ki visty*, 13 May 1941, 7.

14 "Drama Showing Ukraine Famine," *Winnipeg Tribune*, 9 Nov. 1933, 17. A handbill issued in 1934 promoting another play, Mykhailo Kostiuk's *Tam de volia kroavym kvitom zatvyla*, described the western Ukrainian drama as including the theme of starvation ("see defenceless dying children and women who are stricken with hunger"). Handbill for *Tam de volia kroavym kvitom zatvyla*, "Ukraïns'ki kul'turno, osvitni, suspil'ni, ekonomichni tovarystva, n.d., 1930–1973" file, Demetrius Elcheshen fonds I-5 (c) – 6(a) Fb.2–5, Oseredok.

15 "Ukraïns'ka drama 'Holod na Ukraïni,'" *Kanadyis'kyi farmer*, 22 Nov. 1933, 7. The belief in a link between Skrypnyk's suicide and the famine also found expression in a 1938 article in the *Ukrainian Weekly*: "M. Skrypnik had courageously protested that the bread produced by Ukrainians should be used, primarily, to safeguard their own lives....He was 'liquidated'—driven to suicide" ("Hitler Wants Ukraine," 18 June 1938, 2). In July 1933, the *Chicago Tribune* cited a "Baltic diplomat" who, in Riga, said that the Soviet executive committee, of which Skrypnyk was a member, discussed in early July the "growing seriousness of the famine." Skrypnyk, according to the diplomat, demanded that the "Stalin faction change its policy toward the peasants by using the government's so-called iron reserve fund of grain to feed the village population." Skrypnyk tried to arrange a meeting with Mikhail Kalinin, chair of the Central Executive Committee of the USSR, and peasants from Soviet Ukraine, but "they were refused permission to visit Moscow." "Ukraine Denied Food; Cause of Leader's Suicide," 10 July 1933, 14.

16 Peter Lazarowich, "Famine in the Ukraine," *Edmonton Journal*, 25 Oct. 1933, 4.

17 Morris, *Stalin's Famine*, 9, 130. Among the Americans who favoured recognition was Raymond Robins, who had visited the USSR and was able to interview Stalin. According to *La Presse*, Robins, who had also visited the area a number of years before (immediately after the Bolshevik revolution), said after his 1933 visit: "In 1918, 1 May, the people suffered from hunger, cold and poverty," but in 1933, "I saw the spectacle of an army of workers happy with their lot" ("Un citoyen américain qui est favorable aux Soviets," 19 June 1933, 1 [my translation]).

18 See, for example, "Russia and France to Sign New Pact," *Winnipeg Free Press*, 1 Oct. 1932, 5; "Poland Signs Peace Treaty with Russia," *Winnipeg Tribune*, 20 Nov. 1932, 1; "Russo-Italian Peace Pact Is to Be Signed," *Winnipeg Tribune*, 26 Aug. 1933, 1; "Germany and Russia Sign Extension of Their Treaty," *Winnipeg Free Press*, 8 May 1933, 5. "Vatican Seeks Agreement with Soviet Government," *Winnipeg Tribune*, 23 Sept. 1933, 26; "Rumania, Russia, Poland Sign Eight-Power Treaty Defining Aggressor Nation," *Winnipeg Free Press*, 11 Oct. 1933, 1; "Madrid reconnaît la Russie rouge," *La Presse*, 27 July 1933, 1; and "Soviet and Hungary Resume Relations," *Calgary Herald*, 7 Feb. 1934, 2. On Soviet nonaggression pacts with Afghanistan, Estonia, Latvia, Iran, Poland, Romania, and Turkey, see "Russia Signs Non-Aggression Pacts," *Calgary Herald*, 3 July 1933, 1.

19 Morris, *Stalin's Famine*, 197.

20 James Mace, "Collaboration in the Suppression of the Ukrainian Famine," *Ukrainian Weekly*, 3 Jan. 1988, 5.

21 "Litvinoff Stays Hour in Warsaw," *New York Times*, 28 Oct. 1933, 16.

22 "Ukr. Organizatsiï podaiut' Prez. Ruzveltomy memorial pro vyznannia Rosiï," *Kanadyis'kyi farmer*, 15 Nov. 1933, 9.

23 Morris, *Stalin's Famine*, 9. Roosevelt had seriously been studying the question of recognition already in March 1933. See "Russian Relations Question Studied," *Montreal Star*, 20 Mar. 1933, 5. Later, in October 1934, the first American ambassador to Moscow, William C. Bullitt, shared his observations

on Soviet conditions with the U.S. Secretary of State. "Stalin's agricultural policy, however appalling its cost in human suffering, has been successful," he wrote to Washington. The peasants had "been starved, shot and exiled into submission." Yet now the new harvest was adequate, the Soviet fear of an attack had diminished, industrial production was "increasing rapidly," and consumer goods were appearing in the market in "considerable quantities." Bullitt to the U.S. Secretary of State, 2 Oct. 1934, 2, Roosevelt Papers, series 3: Diplomatic Correspondence, box 49, Russia: 1934, Franklin D. Roosevelt Library and Museum, New York, http://www.fdrlibrary.marist.edu/archives/collections/franklin/?p=collections/collections.

24 Keith Pomakoy, *Helping Humanity: American Policy and Genocide Rescue* (Lanham, MD: Lexington Books, 2011), 102: "Both Herbert Hoover and Roosevelt knew about the crisis as it developed, but raison d'etat kept this event from becoming a focal point of either administration." See also Morris, *Stalin's Famine*, 33. Later, during a visit to Canada, Hoover mentioned the famine. Speaking at the Fifteenth Annual Dinner of the York Bible Class in 1938, the former head of the American Relief Administration emphasized how moral rearmament had come to be the world's vital need. Hoover told his audience, which included various Canadian politicians, "The world is now learning the truth, that the Russian government, in its attempt to force state industrialization, pitilessly left millions of its own people to die of starvation when that government had gold with which to have bought them food." "Asks Moral Rearmament," *Windsor Star*, 23 Nov. 1938, 16. For reports on gold production and discoveries, see "Russia Claims Rich Discovery," *Star-Phoenix*, 26 Apr. 1933, 14; "Russian Purchases Increased Gold Balance," *Calgary Herald*, 18 Mar. 1933, 22; and "Soviet Reports Big Gold Gains," *Telegram*, 6 Nov. 1933, 2.

25 "The Natty Commissar," *Ottawa Citizen*, 20 Nov. 1933, 20.

26 "Le cannibalisme se propage en Russie," *La Presse*, 4 Dec. 1933, 17. See also "Il Duce Obtains Russian Support," *Montreal Star*, 4 Dec. 1933, 1–2. Litvinov's planned stop in Italy after visiting the United States was announced by the *Winnipeg Free Press*, which noted that Italy had already recognized the USSR ("Commissar Litvinoff, of Russia, to Confer with Il Duce after U.S. Visit," 21 Nov. 1933, 1). The Vatican, however, had not.

27 "Pozir! Ukraïntsi v Detroit, Hemtremk i okolytsi!" *Kanadyis'kyi farmer*, 1 Nov. 1933, 7.

28 "Parallel of Struggle with Irish Fight for Liberty Is Drawn by Professor," *Svoboda*, 15 Nov. 1933, 4. The article appeared in the *Detroit Free Press* on November 5, 1933.

29 "Starvation in Russian Ukraine," *Calgary Herald*, 6 Oct. 1933, 4.

30 "Chomu Ameryka ne mozhe pomohty Ukraïny," *Ukraïns'ki visty*, 24 Jan. 1934, 1. Appeals were also sent to the American government by Russians in the United States.

31 "10,000 Ukrainian Marchers Warn New York against Reds," *Telegram*, 18 Nov. 1933, 2.

32 "50 Hurt as Alleged Communists Attack Chicago Ukrainians," *Winnipeg Free Press*, 18 Dec. 1933, 1. See the same day's issue of the *Charlottetown Guardian*,

where the story appeared on the first page ("Fifty Injured in Clash").

33 "Parading Ukra[i]nians in Chicago," *Edmonton Journal*, 18 Dec. 1933, 7; "Parade Starts: Chicago Riot," *Border Cities Star*, 18 Dec. 1933, 20; "Fifty Hurt in Fight," *Toronto Star*, 18 Dec. 1933, 29.

34 For the one in Bridgeport, Connecticut, see "Bol'shevyts'ka aktsiia proty ukr. demonstratsii proty sovitiv," *Novyi shliakh*, 5 Dec. 1933, 1. For other examples of coverage of American Ukrainian demonstrations and protests in the Ukrainian-language press in Canada, see "Pokhid i viche ukraïntsiv v Niu Iorku," *Kanadyis'kyi farmer*, 29 Nov. 1933, 9; "10,000 ukraïntsiv v Niu Iorku demostruiut'," *Ukraïns'kyi holos*, 29 Nov. 1933, 5; "Amerykans'ki ukraïntsi protestuiut' proty vyznannia SSSR," *Novyi shliakh*, 7 Nov. 1933, 5; "Napad komunistiv na ukraïns'kykh demonstrantiv," *Ukraïns'kyi holos*, 20 Dec. 1933, 1; "Kryvava proty bol'shevyts'ka demonstratsiia v Shykagu." *Ukraïns'ki visty*, 27 Dec. 1933; "Ukraïns'ke protestatsiine viche v Filadelfiï," *Ukraïns'ki visty*, 14 June 1933, 1; and "Protybol'shevyts'ka demonstratsiia ukraïntsiv v Niu Iorku, Zl.D.," *Ukraïns'ki visty*, 29 Nov. 1933, 1, 8. The demonstration in Chicago inspired Vasyl Chereshyia to write a poem: "Hromylam ukraïns'kykh demostrantiv u Shykagu," *Ukraïns'ki visty*, 10 Jan. 1934, 3.

35 Associated Press, "Soviet Consular Official Slain," *Calgary Herald*, 23 Oct. 1933, 5. See also "Soviet Official Shot and Killed in Poland," *Winnipeg Free Press*, 23 Oct. 1933, 1; "Soviet Official Assassinated," *Telegram*, 21 Oct. 1933, 1; and "Poland Shows Desire to Mollify Soviets," *Montreal Star*, 25 Oct. 1933, 17.

36 "Lwow Incident Closed," *New York Times*, 26 Oct. 1933, 10.

37 Wysocki, "Reactions to the Famine in Poland," 61.

38 "Pislia atentatu u L'vovi," *Ukraïns'ki visty*, 8 Nov. 1933, 2. The second line following the headline in the announcement in *Novyi shliakh* read "Ukrainian Nationalist Actively Protested against the Destruction of Ukraine" ("Atentat na sovits'koho prestavnyka u L'vovi," 31 Oct. 1933, 1).

39 "Nahlyi sud nad Lemykom," *Ukraïns'ki visty*, 22 Nov. 1933, 1. According to the *New York Times* (31 Oct. 1933, 13), the summary court in Lviv imposed the verdict of life imprisonment "on the grounds of Lemyk's youth, his sincere confession, and the fact that he gave evidence against his accomplices." Others were tried in association with the assassination; two were acquitted and thirteen were sentenced to between two and fourteen years in prison. "Zasud za atentat na sovits'komu konsuliati u L'vovi," *Ukraïns'ki visty*, 25 July 1934, 4.

40 "Demostratsiia u L'vovi," *Ukraïns'ki visty*, 22 Nov. 1933, 2. For additional coverage in the Canadian Ukrainian-language press, see "Pislia atentatu u L'vovi," *Kanadyis'kyi farmer*, 1 Nov. 1933, 1; and "Vbyshchyk sovits'koho uriadovtsia zasudzhennyi u L'vovi," *Ukraïns'kyi holos*, 8 Nov. 1933, 1. *Kanadyis'kyi farmer* covered *Izvestia*'s reaction to the assassination. See "'Izvestiia' pro L'vivsks'kyi zamakh," *Kanadyis'kyi farmer*, 15 Nov. 1933, 2. And for the reaction in the pro-Communist *Ukraïns'ki robitnychi visty*, see "Iak provokatory OUN posylaiut' khloptsiv na vbystva," *Ukraïns'ki robitnychi visty*, 16 Nov. 1933, 2.

41 "Pol's'ka politsiia zaboronyla vicha i zbory v spravi podiï na Vel. Ukraïni," *Ukraïns'ki visty*, 15 Nov. 1933, 2. Romania exhibited a similar attitude. Kysilewsky

recorded in his diary that a planned mass demonstration against Soviet policies in Ukraine and a memorial service for famine victims in the city of Chernivtsi were originally banned by the police. Kysilewsky, "Unedited Diaries," 107 (entry for 11 Sept. 1933), VJKF.

42 "Pislia samohubstva Stons'koho," *Ukraïns'kyi holos*, 27 Sept. 1933, 9. See also Shkandrij, "Ukrainianization, Terror and Famine," 436. Shkandrij notes that Stronsky had earlier fought for Ukrainian independence as a member of the Ukrainian Sich Riflemen and the Ukrainian Galician Army. A couple of years after the suicide, the Soviet consul in Lviv noted that Sovietophilism was diminishing in Galicia and that Stronsky's daughter was giving "slanderous, anti-Soviet speeches." Myroslav Shkandrij and Olga Bertelsen, "The Soviet Regime's National Operations in Ukraine, 1929–1934," *Canadian Slavonic Papers* 55, nos. 3–4 (2013): 446.

43 "GPU roztrilialo buvshoho sovits'koho konsulia u L'vovi," *Ukraïns'ki visty*, 14 Sept. 1932, 2.

44 "V oblychchi tragediï Velykoï Ukraïni," *Ukraïns'ki visty*, 4 Oct. 1933, 4.

45 "Na borot'bu z holodom na Ukraïni," *Ukraïns'ki visty*, 18 Oct. 1933, 1. In the same issue, the periodical reported the creation of a famine relief committee in Paris, in response, it said, to the appeal of the Ukrainian Catholic bishops. It noted the active part played by Archduke Wilhelm Habsburg (pseudonym Vasyl Vyshyvanyi), "former captain of the Ukrainian Galician Army" ("Mizhnarodnii komitet dopomohy holoduiuchii Ukraïni," 18 Oct. 1933, 1). The formation of the committee was also announced in "Mizhnarodnii komitet dopomohy holoduiuchym na Ukraïni," *Kanadyis'kyi farmer*, 18 Oct. 1933, 2. See also Kysilewsky, "Unedited Diaries," 147 (entry for 8 Dec. 1933), VJKF.

46 "Dr. Amende pryide do Ameryky," *Ukraïns'ki visty*, 1 Nov. 1933, 1. Later, *Ukraïns'ki visty* referred to a congress called by Cardinal Innitzer that convened on December 16 and 17, 1933. Citing the newspaper *Dilo*, representatives of Ukrainian, Russian, German, and Jewish relief committees were said to have taken part. Nykyta Budka, the former bishop of the Ukrainian Catholics in Canada, represented Metropolitan Sheptytsky at the congress. One delegate came from Elizabeth Skoropadky's relief committee, and another came from a London committee as an observer. See "Konferentsiia predstavnykiv komitetiv dopomohy holoduichym na Ukraïni," *Ukraïns'ki visty*, 10 Jan. 1933, 2; "Mizhnarodnia konferentsiia v spravi holodu na Ukraïni," *Ukraïns'ki visty*, 17 Jan. 1934, 1, 8; and "Konferentsiia dopomohovykh komitetiv," *Kanadyis'kyi farmer*, 17 Jan. 1934, 2. On Bishop Budka's role, see Athanasius D. McVay, *God's Martyr, History's Witness: Blessed Nykyta Budka, The First Ukrainian Catholic Bishop in Canada* (Edmonton: Ukrainian Catholic Eparchy of Edmonton and the Metropolitan Andrey Sheptytsky Institute of Eastern Christian Studies, 2014), 501. Bishop Budka was also mentioned in Kysilewsky, "Unedited Diaries," 151 (entry for 21 Dec. 1933), VJKF.

47 A statement about the famine made by Ukrainian deputies in the Polish Sejm did come to the notice of the *Manchester Guardian* ("The Harvest in Russia: Alarming Polish Reports," 12 Nov. 1933, 31).

48 "Do spravy nashoï uchasty v politychnim zhtyttiu Kanady," *Ukraïns'ki visty*, 22 Nov. 1933, 4. In 1934, another MLA of Ukrainian origin, Dr. George Dragan, was elected, this time in Saskatachewan. *Ukraïns'kyi holos* said of his election, "Just as the eyes of all Canada are now turned on Luchkovich as the only Ukrainian representative in the dominion parliament, the eyes of all Saskatchewan, and those of people outside Saskatchewan, will turn on Dr. Dragan as the single Ukrainian representative in the Saskatchewan legislature" ("Pershyi posol-ukraïnets v Saskachevani," 27 June 1934, 4).

49 "Willingdon Citizens Protest gainst Bolshevik Regime in Ukraine," *Vegreville Observer*, 15 Nov. 1933, 5.

50 "Anarkhiia chy spekuliatsiia: Chy odyn i druhe razom?" *Ukraïns'ki visty*, 29 Nov. 1933, 4. Wysocki noted that collective efforts in western Ukraine vis-à-vis the famine were stymied by the inability of Ukrainian political circles in Galicia and Volhynia to sufficiently "transcend their individual party politics." Wysocki, "Reactions to the Famine in Poland," 62. Even though the famine took place in a neighbouring territory, the fact that the Soviet regime did not seek aid and even denied there was famine, coupled with Polish silence (even though the "victims of the Great Famine included over twenty thousand ethnic Poles" [p. 55]) and local distractions in regard to Polish rule in western Ukraine, may have lessened the urgency to assist. Stanley Frolick, who was in born in Hillcrest, Alberta, but as a youth moved to western Ukraine, in 1932, shared the following recollection of that time: "The great famine that occurred in Eastern Ukraine in 1932 and 1933 made less of an impression on us. We heard rumours about it; the Western Ukrainian press published articles about it, and some people even managed to escape from the Soviet Union and to bring out their accounts. But the famine was happening in another country. Of course, that was Ukraine, too, but it was in the USSR, and whether you were next door to the USSR or across the Atlantic from it didn't matter because it was a controlled society and little information got out." Frolick, *Between Two Worlds: The Memoirs of Stanley Frolick*, ed. Lubomyr Y. Luciuk and Marco Carynnyk (Toronto: Multicultural History Society of Ontario, 1990), 64.

51 "Konia kuiut', a zhaba nohu nastavliaie," *Ukraïns'kyi holos*, 22 Nov. 1933, 8.
52 "Oborona holoduiuchoho naselennia Ukraïny," *Ukraïns'kyi holos*, 22 Nov. 1933, 1.
53 "Vy znaite, shcho znachyt' holod?" *Ukraïns'kyi holos*, 29 Nov. 1933, 1.
54 "Ukrainians Make Strong Protest," *Edmonton Bulletin*, 24 July 1933, 9.
55 "Alleged Persecution in Ukraine Is Scored," *Edmonton Journal*, 24 July 1933, 11.
56 "KE UNO klyche vsikh ukraïntsiv Kanady pomohty holoduiushchym na Rad. Ukraïni," *Novyi shliakh*, 3 Oct. 1933, 1.
57 "Organizuiut' aktsiiu dopomohy holoduishchii Ukraïni," *Novyi shliakh*, 22 Aug. 1933, 1.
58 "Protybol'shevyts'ka protestna aktsiia v Evropi," *Novyi shliakh*, 5 Dec. 1933, 6.
59 For example, *Novyi shliakh* published the names of the people who had together gathered $18.20—in the community hall in Delph, Alberta, on February 11, 1934—and sent it to the newspaper for the purpose of aiding the starving in

Ukraine ("Na holoduishchykh na Skhidnii Ukraïni," 6 Mar. 1934, 8). On other such collections, see "Zbirka na holoduishchykh na Ukraïni," *Novyi shliakh*, 16 Jan. 1934, 7 (Ladywood, MB); and "Zbirky na pomich holoduiushchym na Velykii Ukraïni," *Novyi shliakh*, 16 Jan. 1934, 8 (Smuts and Krydor, SK).

60 In Alberta, these protest meetings were held in Calgary, Chauvin, Derwent, Edmonton, Eldorena, Halich, "Kepon" [Carbon?], Mundare, Myrnam, Prut, Sich-Kolemea, Smoky Lake, Spedden, Stry, Vegreville, and Willingdon; in British Columbia: Vernon; in Manitoba: Angusville, Ashville, Brandon, Cloverleaf, Dauphin, Fisher Branch, Gimli, Meleb, Oakburn, Rossburn, Sarto, Sefton, Teulon, Vita, Ward, Winnipeg, and Zelena; in Ontario: Chatham, Fort William, Hamilton, Kitchener, Oshawa, Ottawa, Preston, Sudbury, Thorold, Timmins, Toronto, and Windsor; in Quebec: Norande and Montreal; and in Saskatchewan: Beckenham, Brooksby, Canora, Glen Elder, Hafford, Krasne, Krydor, Lady Lake, Moose Jaw, Rhein, Saskatoon, Sopoff, Wakaw, Wimmer, and Wroxton. Sources of information about these meetings include the publications *Border Cities Star*, *Edmonton Bulletin*, *Edmonton Journal*, *Kanadyis'kyi farmer*, *Montreal Star*, *Novyi shliakh*, *La Presse*, *Star-Phoenix*, *Svoboda*, *Toronto Telegram*, *Ukrainian Weekly*, *Ukraïns'kyi holos*, *Ukraïns'ki visty*, *Vegreville Observer*, *Winnipeg Free Press*, and the *Winnipeg Tribune*, as well as records housed at LAC (Bennett Papers), Oseredok (Demetrius Elcheshen fonds), and Public Record Office, London. Foreign Office records pertaining to Ukraine in the Public Record Office were copied for the Canadian Institute of Ukrainian Studies (CIUS) at the University of Alberta and deposited in that university's library. For a catalogue of the files, see J. V. Koshiw, *British Foreign Office Files on Ukraine and Ukrainians, 1917–1948*, research report no. 60 (Edmonton: CIUS Press, 1997).

61 For more on the activities of Russians abroad vis-à-vis the famine, see Serbyn, "Great Famine of 1933," 94, 97, 107–8. Resolutions continued to be directed to the Canadian government in 1935 by Ukrainians in Montreal (assembled at the Ukrainian Catholic parish hall), Winnipeg (at the Ridna Shkola hall on Euclid Avenue and the hall of St. John the Almsgiver, Flora Avenue), Elmwood, Manitoba (at the Prosvita Society), Ottawa (at a meeting of the Ukrainian Literary Society of Taras Shevchenko), and Transcona, Manitoba (at a meeting of the Ukrainian Literary Association of Ivan Franko). See the resolutions to the Canadian government and the form replies signed by Undersecretary of State for External Affairs O. D. Skelton in RG 25, vol. 1673, file 742 (1933) Treatment of Ukrainians in Russia, LAC.

62 "Travel from Russia, Join Family Head," *Leader-Post*, 8 Nov. 1933, 15.

63 "Bread Shortage in Soviet Russia," *Star-Phoenix*, 8 Nov. 1933, 7.

64 "Rabbi Haft's Kin Arrives from Russia," *Edmonton Bulletin*, 8 Nov. 1933, 13. See also "Wife and Family of Jewish Rabbi Arrive from Ukraine," *Edmonton Bulletin*, 8 Nov. 1933, 6; and "Rabbi's Family Here from Ukraine," *Edmonton Journal*, 8 Nov. 1933, 14. The *Winnipeg Free Press* included a picture of the family, who had sailed from the USSR on September 27, 1933 ("Family Arrives from Russia," 4 Nov. 1933, 6); a photograph of the family was also published in the *Winnipeg Tribune*. The

children were Freda, age 22; Eva and Kheved (twins), 21; Rebecca, 15; and Herschel, 10. See "Rabbi's Family Wins 6-Year Fight to Get Out of Russia," *Winnipeg Tribune*, 3 Nov. 1933, 3; "Arrive in Canada after Six Years of Anxious Waiting," *Vegreville Observer*, 15 Nov. 1933, 2. Rabbi Haft was born in Novgorod, Russia, and had served in Yorkton and Winnipeg prior to coming to Edmonton. The former rabbi of Edmonton's House of Israel synagogue died in Rochester, Minnesota. See "Rabbi Isaac Haft Dies in Rochester," *Edmonton Journal*, 7 June 1941, 15.

65 "Appeals for Aid Soviet's Starving," *Edmonton Journal*, 2 Dec. 1933, 19; "Des affamés par millions en Soviétie," *La Presse*, 2 Dec. 1933, 17. The appeal was also mentioned in *Le Devoir* ("Un nouvel appel au monde," 2 Dec. 1933, 1).

66 *Western Catholic*, 12 Feb. 1934. It was during February 1934 that the *Edmonton Bulletin* featured an editorial alluding to statements about an impending famine in the USSR. "Predictions are being freely made," the editorial said, "by those who ought to know what they are talking about, that famine will be widespread during the coming winter." It referred to the unfavourable "growing conditions" of 1921 after which there was a loss of life in the order of ten million and also to the six million deaths of "two years ago." The editorial posited that agricultural production in the USSR would be "much below normal" and concluded that Canada had no cause for fear from Soviet competition but that, "on the other hand, if the alarmist reports now in circulation prove to be correct, supplies from the outside world will in all likelihood have to be sent to relieve the famine victims" ("Russia's Agricultural Decline," 23 Feb. 1934, 4).

67 "Spy Grip on Soviet Farms Is Tightened," *Winnipeg Tribune*, 16 June 1933, 1.

68 "100,000 Child Spies Used in Soviet Harvest," *Winnipeg Tribune*, 21 Aug. 1933, 2. See also "La 'protection des moissons socialistes' en Russie," *Le Devoir*, 21 Aug. 1933, 1; "Hundred Thousand Kiddies Protecting Russian Crops," *Toronto Star*, 21 Aug. 1933, 9; and—for the picture that was widely circulated in the Western press—"Army of Children Fights Famine," *Winnipeg Tribune*, 31 Aug. 1933, 1. Also on August 31, 1933, a report (originally published in the *Washington Post*) appeared in the *Western Globe* (Lacombe, Alberta) about the inauguration of an air patrol to watch the peasantry in Ukraine and the North Caucasus. "It was discovered by the new agricultural police," the report stated, that peasants often concealed seed for food, and in some cases were "found boiling grain in the fields to make porridge for themselves." The number of police in place to guard barns was deemed insufficient, and the guards themselves "frequently stole grain for their own use" ("Spies Are Using Airplanes," 31 Aug. 1933, 3).

69 "Hirshe Ehypets'koho – Nevil'nytstva na znyvakh na Ukraïni i na Kubanshchyni," *Kanadyis'kyi farmer*, 6 Sept. 1933, 9. For other examples of Ukrainian-language press coverage on the topic in Canada, see "Bol'shevyky uzhyvaiut' ditei iak shpioniv," *Ukraïns'kyi holos*, 6 Sept. 1933, 5.

70 "Soviet Mobilizes Harvest Workers," *Montreal Star*, 30 Aug. 1933, 5.

71 "Toll of Stalin's Famine Three to 5 Million Lives," *Telegram*, 26 Oct. 1933, 5.

72 "Russia Cheers Up at Good Harvest," *Border Cities Star*, 20 Oct. 1933, 11. The Japanese linked the USSR's gravitation toward friendlier relations with Western

countries to Soviet reinforcement of its army in the Far East. See "Tokio Hears Russ Reinforcing Army," *Border Cities Star*, 30 Aug. 1933, 6.

73 "Russia Flirts with League," *Border Cities Star*, 19 Oct. 1933, 1; "Germany Quits League of Nations," *Winnipeg Tribune*, 14 Oct. 1933, 1 and 4. In spite of the many suggestions of a real threat of war between Japan and the USSR, at least one article cited a Japanese contention that the USSR was not in a position "to carry on any kind of war (except on its own civil population)." "Japan and Russia," *Montreal Star*, 21 Oct. 1933, 10 (summarizing an article from the *Nineteenth Century*, London).

74 "Poles, Russ are Friends," *Border Cities Star*, 19 Oct. 1933, 6.

75 "Russia Buys Grain," *Border Cities Star*, 22 Sept. 1933, 4. Earlier, in June 1933, there had been reports in the American press about the USSR's desire to purchase grain from the United States. That month, a former Iowa senator, Smith Wildman Brookhart, travelled to Moscow to negotiate the sale of American cotton. The scheme, though, was seen as a "camouflage hiding secret negotiations between Brookhart and Boris Svirski [Boris Skvirsky]," the head of Amtorg in New York, regarding "large credits for purchase of American grain." Apparently, Skvirsky had "received instructions to do everything possible to purchase grain with a minimum of publicity, since Russia has decided to keep the tragic news of the present famine hidden from the world." "Russia Seeks U.S. Grain to Halt Famine," *Santa Cruz Evening News*, 21 June 1933, 2.

76 "Shortage of Food Ended," *Border Cities Star*, 22 Sept. 1933, 14. See also "Rich Soviet Grain Crop This Year Precludes Possibility of Recurrence Famine Conditions," *Lethbridge Herald*, 22 Sept. 1933, 2; "Les mort par la faim dans l'Ukraine," *Le Devoir*, 22 Sept. 1933, 3 (which attributed authorship of the AP report to Stanley P. Richardson); and "Soviet Russia Is Not Facing Grain Shortage," *Ottawa Journal*, 22 Sept. 1933, 9.

77 "Soviet Wins Farm Fight," *Border Cities Star*, 27 Sept. 1933, 9.

78 "Soviet Frees Many Political Prisoners," *Winnipeg Free Press*, 5 Aug. 1933, 1. A number of OGPU officers in charge of the canal project received awards. Earlier in the year, an AP dispatch published in the *Winnipeg Free Press* had quoted Joshua Kunitz, a former professor of Russian in New York who had been visiting the USSR, on the "vast mushroom towns" that had sprung up in "'unexplored' wastes." Some 100,000 prisoners were "carving out a canal as big as that in Panama" ("Progress Made by Russian Kulaks in North Related," 6 Feb. 1933, 4). A *Toronto Star* article, quoting from the USSR's *Komsomolskaia pravda*, noted that a 152-mile-long canal—which made possible a shorter route for the export of lumber from the Soviet northern regions—was built in nineteen months, compared with ten years for the Suez Canal and eleven years for the Panama Canal. The convict labour used for its construction came from "Kulaks, bourgeois professors, thieves, engineers-wreckers, spies, speculators, bandits, counterfeiters, embezzlers, beys (i.e., the better-off peasantry of Central Asia), thieves of social property (i.e., peasants sentenced under the new decree for pilfering foodstuffs from the collective farms, a crime also punishable by

shooting), common-law criminals (murderers, etc.)." "New Russian Canal Dug in Record Time," *Toronto Star*, 30 June 1933, 4.

79 "OGPU Must Be Careful," *Border Cities Star*, 22 Sept. 1933, 7. Ethel Ostry, originally from Kyiv, recounted how she had been able to see a prison during a recent visit to the USSR. At the prison, she had spoken with a woman who was serving a sentence of seven years for murdering her husband. In another cell was a woman who had been sentenced to ten years' imprisonment for stealing grain; her husband, who had been implicated in the theft, had already been executed on account of it. "Theft Worse than Murder in Russia," *Toronto Star*, 6 Nov. 1934, 11.

80 "Russ Spurn Wheat Quota," *Border Cities Star*, 22 Sept. 1933, 12.

81 "Russia Bolts," *Border Cities Star*, 23 Sept. 1933, 4.

82 *Blairmore Enterprise*, 2 Feb. 1933, 8. This article also noted that S. Patterson of Blairmore had met Palmer during his visit to the Soviet Union.

83 See, for example, "Ukrainian Citizen's Reply," *Edmonton Journal*, 28 Nov. 1933, 4; and "Russian Conditions," *Edmonton Journal*, 20 Dec. 1933, 6. Palmer had already shared his impressions of the Soviet Union at a public forum in Calgary. In June, the *Calgary Herald* reported that he had delivered an address (under the auspices of the Central Council of Calgary Unemployed) titled "What I Saw in the Soviet Union," at the Legion Memorial Hall. He had been on an extended trip to Europe, the newspaper said, and had for eight months worked as a reporter for a Moscow paper (the report did not say which one) ("George Palmer Will Speak on Russia," 27 June 1933, 5). When the Canadian government assumed a new offensive against Communist propaganda, the chief publication that Ottawa was "determined to keep out" was said to be the *Moscow Daily News*. See "Ottawa Drives to Keep Red Reading Out of Country," *Winnipeg Free Press*, 7 Dec. 1933, 19.

84 "In the Ukraine," *Lethbridge Herald*, 10 May 1934, 6. That year, a lecture on the USSR by Rev. Louis R. Patmont of California was announced in the *Globe*. Patmont—slated to speak at the People's Church on Bloor Street East, Toronto—was going to bring slides to show his audience. He had visited the USSR in 1930 and 1931, but "instead of remaining in the large cities like most tourists, he roamed the country for months and saw the brutal, horrible, wretched conditions. He took many photographs of Bolshevic atrocities." The slides, presumably taken during 1930 and 1931, included depictions of "starving, diseased children, etc." Patmont would tell "of being offered human flesh on the train." He had spoken personally with President Roosevelt about the USSR, the announcement said ("The People's Church," 30 June 1934, 7).

85 "What of the Ukraine?," *Lethbridge Herald*, 19 June 1934, 4. Chamberlin's book, *Russia's Iron Age* (Boston: Little, Brown, 1934), was commented upon in the Canadian press. See "Millions Killed in Famine Soviet Planned, Book Tells," *Toronto Star*, 13 Oct. 1934, 1, 2.

86 Carynnyk, Luciuk, and Kordan, *The Foreign Office and the Famine*, 343–46.

87 "Ukrainian Mass Meeting Makes Strong Protest," *Oshawa Daily Times*, 16 Oct. 1933, reprinted in *Svoboda*, 6 Nov. 1933, 4.

88 Ibid. The phrase "starving out the population" (in quotation marks) was used in a *Globe* commentary about Ukrainian Canadian protests: "Canadian Ukrainians are protesting against the Soviet system of grain collection in their homeland, which is 'starving out the population.' These new Canadians are likely to have recent and authentic information as to what is going on in the land of the Communist experiment" (3 Oct. 1933, 4).

89 Fr. Olenchuk to Bishop Ladyka, 22 Apr. 1933 and 25 May 1933, Correspondence – Diocesan Priests, 1924–1948, MO77–79, Ukrainian Catholic Archeparchy of Winnipeg Archives.

90 See Marco Carynnyk, "The New York Times and the Great Famine: Part I," *Ukrainian Weekly*, 11 Sept. 1983.

91 "Soviet Russia Is Barring Writer," *Border Cities Star*, 22 July 1933, 2; "Americans Barred from Entering Russia," *Stouffville Sun Tribune* (Ontario), 3 Aug. 1933, 7.

92 "Moskva boit'sia ukraïns'koï divchyny," *Svoboda*, 29 Sept. 1934, 1.

93 "Alberta Girl Refused Admission to Russia; Tells Story of Europe," *Edmonton Bulletin*, 7 Jan. 1935, Michael Luchkovich Papers, Ukrainian Canadian Archives and Museum of Alberta, Edmonton (hereafter, Luchkovich Papers). Romanchych initially also experienced difficulty in obtaining a visa for Poland. See *Dilo*, 10 Aug. 1934, reprinted in "Zemliachka z Kanady znaiomyt'sia z Ridnym Kraiem," *Ukraïns'kyi holos*, 12 Sept. 1934, 2; and "Moskva boït'sia, aby H. Romanchych ïï ne zavalyla," *Ukraïns'kyi holos*, 29 Aug. 1934, 8.

94 "Ukrainian Women: A Successful First Congress," *Manchester Guardian*, 13 July 1934, 9. The story in the *Guardian* was covered in *Ukraïns'ki visty* ("Anglis'ka presa pro Ukr. zhinochyi kongres," 8 Aug. 1934, 2). The 1936 denial of entrance to the Soviet Union of the well-known U.S. cartoonist Robert L. Ripley was linked to his remarks about the famine. Ripley, whose panel series "Believe It or Not!" appeared regularly in many a Canadian newspaper, had planned to stop in the USSR on a "round-the-world" trip. He was informed "unofficially but authoritatively" that the refusal stemmed from a radio speech he had made in April 1935 about conditions in the Soviet Union as "he saw them in a previous trip." In that speech, "Ripley attributed the deaths of 4,000,000 peasants by starvation in the Ukraine and North Caucasus to the Soviet Government and called the country a 'gigantic poorhouse.'" *Windsor Daily Star*, 2 Mar. 1936, 1. Apparently, in 1933 Nicholas Ignatieff tried to go to the USSR in order to "effect a reconciliation between the Soviet Red Cross and the Old Russian Red Cross." His application for a visa was supported by the *Toronto Star*, but the Soviet foreign office refused to grant one. "Michael Ignatieff's Uncle Spied on Suspected Nazis, MI5 Files Show," *Toronto Star*, 23 Apr. 2014.

95 Rev. A. E. Kerr to R. K. Finlayson, 12 June 1934, M-1332, 410391–2, Bennett Papers. On John King Gordon, see Keith Robson Fleming, *The World Is Our Parish: John King Gordon, 1900–1989: An Intellectual Biography* (Toronto: University of Toronto Press, 2015). Both Gordon and Professor Eugene Forsey spoke at the Young Men's Canadian Club in Montreal in March 1933, where their interpretations of Soviet life were challenged by "one of the members at the meeting who had

lived several years in Russia." Among the statements attributed to Gordon, who had visited the USSR with Forsey in 1932, was the one that the Soviet government "put the care of human life before the industrialization of the country." "Interpretations of Soviet Life Doubted," *Montreal Star*, 21 Mar. 1933, 9. In 1934, Gordon wrote of having seen a beaming Stalin at the annual physical culture day parade in Moscow's Red Square, which he described as "the most impressive event which I have ever witnessed in the U.S.S.R.—or possibly anywhere else." "Moscow, July 24th, 1934," *New Outlook*, 5 Sept. 1934, 750–51.

96 Brochure, M-1332, 410393–4, Bennett Papers.

97 "Pastor Scores Social System of Soviets," *Winnipeg Tribune*, 30 Oct. 1934, 8. See also "Rev. Kerr Condemns Russian Situation in Address Monday," *Manitoban*, 2 Nov. 1934, 1, 4. An address about the USSR by Kerr before the League of Nations Society in Winnipeg was scheduled for November 1, 1934. See "Rev. Kerr to Address League of Nations Society on Russia," *Manitoban*, 30 Oct. 1934, 1. Willard Brewing, a minister at St. Andrew's-Wesley Church, Vancouver (which united Methodists, Presbyterians, and members of other denominations), also visited the USSR in the summer of 1934. His group "spent fourteen days in Russia. His Grace the Archbishop of Canterbury spoke on August 17, 1934, in the British House of Lords of the appalling conditions in Russia. Dr. Brewing saw things in an entirely different light, and when he returned, spoke in sermons and lectures over a period of several months of his perception of the Russian situation." *St. Andrew's-Wesley Church: Reflections, 1933–1993* (Vancouver: St. Andrew's-Wesley Church, 1993), 25. After his return from the Soviet Union, Brewing spoke about the USSR to an audience in Vancouver: "The liquidation of the Kulaks was one of the horrors. The Kulaks were given the opportunity to come into the collectives, but it was found that they were guilty of sabotage. They sowed inferior grain or none at all. They manipulated bookkeeping. They were enemies to the republic. There is no doubt that in the drought of 1931 and 1932 the Russians starved by the thousands. The Soviet was ruthless. They decided that if anyone was to starve their enemies would starve first. I had a communication on this subject from the Archbishop of Canterbury, but I hardly think that even the Archbishop of Canterbury, during the great war, would have allowed his sympathy for the enemy to stop the boycott of Germany. For it is a war to death in Russia. A class war, which is even worse than international war. We must consider, when we review the situation, first the fruits of Communism, not its roots to which we may object." "Lenin Rival of Christ for Devotion of World Bishop Brewing Holds," *Toronto Star*, 3 Oct. 1934, 9.

98 "Newspaperman Just Back from Russia to Speak in Winnipeg," *Winnipeg Free Press*, 1 Dec. 1933, 11.

99 "Plans to Disturb Ketchum Lecture Are Frustrated," *Winnipeg Free Press*, 7 Dec. 1933, 2. For further coverage of his Winnipeg lectures, see "Ketchum Says Russia Back on Economic Feet," *Winnipeg Tribune*, 4 Dec. 1933, 4; and "Conditions in Russia Better, Says Ketchum," *Winnipeg Tribune*, 6 Dec. 1933, 7.

100 *Toronto Star*, 4 Dec. 1933, 22.

101 Carleton J. Ketchum, "The Russia of Today," 30 Nov. 1933, transcript, *The Empire Club of Canada Addresses*, http://speeches.empireclub.org/60735/data.
102 Ibid. At the time of the 1933 harvest, Ketchum wrote to a former colleague at the *Province*. In the letter, written from Rostov-on-the Don on September 5, 1933, Ketchum described a visit to a collective farm in the North Caucasus at which ten thousand people were employed. He had travelled 1,350 miles down the Volga River and planned to go to Tiflis (Georgia) via the military highway and to Baku (Azerbaijan), Odesa, Kyiv, and Kharkiv. He was hoping to visit Vancouver in December 1933. "Ketchum Proceeding on Tour of Russia," *Province*, 29 Sept. 1933, 14.
103 "No Chance Early War between Japan, Russia, Says Carl J. Ketchum," *Edmonton Journal*, 27 Feb. 1934, 6. Earlier that year, in July, the *Sydney Morning Herald* referred to Soviet self-praise vis-à-vis the Five-Year Plan: "'We shall not allow,' said Stalin himself, 'the lives of a few peasants to stand between us and our aims.' For a 'few' read, if necessary, 'a few million.'" ("Russia's Self-Praise," 31 July 1933, 8). A year and some months later, the *Globe* referred to Oswald Garrison Villard's commentary on the Stalinist attitude. Describing Villard as the "contributing editor of the socialist New York Nation," the *Globe* quoted him as saying: "The question remains: Can we uplift humanity at the cost of human flesh and blood? And how many 'dastards' is an allegedly altruistic government to be allowed to kill anyhow? The Communists admit that no fewer than one million kulaks were torn from their homes and sent to Siberia, many of them to experience worse than death. I heard a Communist orator say the other day that this exile of the kulaks was a mere 'flea-bite of cruelty,' but I am sure that the million who suffered thought it something more than 'flea bite.'" The *Globe* then interjected that most Canadians would endorse Villard's view when he concluded that "The world does not progress by murder, by a violation of liberty, or by the vicarious suffering and death from persecution of multitudes." It is not clear when Villard had made these remarks, but the *Globe*'s editorial included them together with statements made by Ewald Ammende and William Randolph Hearst about the famine and Soviet conditions ("Where Murder Rules," 25 Jan. 1935, 4). The U.S. Hearst press had just begun an anti-Communist campaign, the credibility of which was undermined when it turned out that the evidence in some of its articles and photographs was questioned. According to Frank Sysyn, "The sensationalist Hearst press in the United States had taken up the issue of the famine, at times with specious evidence, and thereby actually undermined the credibility of more reputable reporting on the topic." Sysyn, "The Ukrainian Famine of 1932–3: The Role of the Ukrainian Diaspora in Research and Public Discussion," in *Studies in Comparative Genocide*, ed. Levron Chorbajian and George Shirinian (New York: St. Martin's Press, 1999), 184. See also Nigel Linsan Colley, "The 'Thomas Walker' Conspiracy (Or the Fraudulent Famine Photo Affair)," *Gareth Richard Vaughan Jones: Hero of Ukraine*, accessed 8 Feb. 2016, http://www.garethjones.org/soviet_articles/thomas_walker/thomas_walker.htm.
104 "Says Idlers Fare Badly in Russia," *Calgary Herald*, 27 Feb. 1934, 3. Later, in 1935, H. Rubin, a travel agent with Intourist, spoke to the *Toronto Star* about the

kulaks: "Many were killed," he admitted. "It was not murder. It was war." He contended that the situation could only be understood if one knew "the place held by the kulaks under the czarist regime." ("90 P.C. Russ Farms Collectivized Now," 21 May 1935, 9).

105 "Ketchum Says N.C.E. Tried to Muzzle Him," *Winnipeg Tribune*, 19 Dec. 1933, 1.

106 "Ketchum, Speak on Soviet, Charges Educational Council Sought to Impose 'Muzzle,'" *Winnipeg Free Press*, 20 Dec. 1933, 6. See also "Won't Be Muzzled," *Vancouver Sun*, 19 Dec. 1933, 1; and "Ketchum et le Conseil d'éducation," *Le Devoir*, 20 Dec. 1933, 1.

107 In January 1934, Ketchum spoke on Soviet women at the Ottawa branch of the Canadian Women's Press Club (see "Women's Press Club Has Enjoyable Dinner," *Ottawa Journal*, 8 Jan. 1934, 8) and on the Red Army at the annual meeting of the United Services Institute of Ottawa ("Carl Ketchum Addresses United Services Inst. Col. Melville President," *Ottawa Citizen*, 17 Jan. 1934, 4). He also spoke on the USSR and showed slides at a Kiwanis Club luncheon at the Chateau Laurier hotel (see "Carl J. Ketchum Kiwanis Speaker," *Ottawa Journal*, 8 Sept. 1934, 21); he returned to the hotel to address the 100 Club ("Carl Ketchum Speaks at 100 Club," *Ottawa Journal*, 30 Sept. 1934, 17). In Toronto, Ketchum was scheduled to speak at Massey Hall on January 31, 1934 (see "Carl J. Ketchum," *Toronto Star*, 27 Jan. 1934, 14, which noted that he had "assembled over 1,700 photographs"). Ketchum also spoke in Montreal in late January ("Trade with Soviet Russia Advocated," *Montreal Gazette*, 29 Jan. 1934, 6). He returned to Winnipeg in February 1934 en route to Calgary, Edmonton, and Vancouver, where he was to deliver lectures under the auspices of local branches of the Canadian Women's Press Club, Rotary Club, and other organizations (*Winnipeg Tribune*, 23 Feb. 1934, 5). For coverage of Ketchum's addresses in British Columbia, see "Russia Now on Up-Grade Says Noted Journalist," *Ubyssey*, 13 Mar. 1934, 1, 2 (which contains a lower number of famine deaths: "during last and the winter before fully 500,000 people perished of starvation in the Ukraine and Northern Caucasus alone, owing to crop failures" [p. 1]). Ketchum spoke on the USSR before the Political Science Club at the University of Alberta (see "Communistic Russia Outlined by Distinguished Journalist," *Gateway*, 2 Mar. 1934, 1). Later in 1934, Ketchum was interviewed in Calgary; a report on the interview focused on a "portable typewriter stolen from him on a Black Sea steamer" that "was returned in 10 days after he lodged a claim with the travel agency in Moscow, a few thousand miles away." *Gleichen Call*, 1 Aug. 1934, 3.

108 "Amazing 'Muzzle' on Carl Ketchum," *Vancouver Sun*, 27 Dec. 1933, 1–2. See also "Bias and Tolerance in Discussions on Russia," *Lethbridge Herald*, 20 Dec. 1933, 4; and "Soviet Trade," *Border Cities Star*, 21 Dec. 1933, 4. *Soviet Russia Today* commented on Ketchum's claims in an article by E. Cecil-Smith. According to the article, Ketchum asserted that Major Gibson of the Canadian Ordnance Corps, who was attached to the staff of the Canadian High Commissioner in London, had warned him to be careful because "everything he said in Canada

would be reported back." Smith then pointed to an editorial in the *Mail and Empire* that, he said, failed to substantiate a statement it had made about the famine. The editorial is quoted: "Communist agitators who prate about the advantage of Soviet rule ignore the official reports of famine and distress" in the Soviet Union. "$100,000,000—Will We Take it?," *Soviet Russia Today*, Jan. 1934, 5. *Soviet Russia Today* also implied that Robert Cromie had come under official pressure: in advertisements in the *Mail and Empire* he was now exhibiting an attitude that was "totally different" to his position after his return from the USSR ("Mr. Cromie Repents," Jan. 1934, 5). In February, E. Cecil-Smith again took exception with a *Mail and Empire* editorial—this time, one that relied on Carveth Wells as a source about famine in Ukraine. Cecil-Smith asked, Should one believe Wells, who claimed "to tramp through the Ukraine at a time when the roads...were absolutely impassable," rather than Stanley Hood or Saskatchewan farmer Florence Bowes, who had visited the USSR with a delegation of Canadian farmers? The "ruling classes" prevented people like Ketchum from telling the truth, asserted Cecil-Smith, while encouraging "troupes of Fascist Italian propagandists to tour the country" ("Who Is Kapoot?" Feb. 1934, 4).

109 "Lend Me Your Ears," *Vancouver Sun*, 28 Dec. 1933, 6.
110 Ibid. The article to which Bouchette was reacting was Frederick T. Birchall, "Starvation Takes 4,000,000 Russian Lives during 1933," *Province*, 26 Aug. 1933, 32. The article, copyrighted by the *New York Times*, was datelined Berlin. Bouchette quite possibly was also reacting to a column by J. Butterfield of the *Vancouver Province* that appeared to be about Cromie. It began: "My old friend and fellow world traveller, Bobski Cromieski, has spent nine days in Russia." *Province*, 5 Aug. 1933, 6.
111 "Plans to Disturb Ketchum Lecture Are Frustrated," *Winnipeg Free Press*, 7 Dec. 1933, 2.
112 Mitchell, who later became a federal minister of labour (appointed to the cabinet by Prime Minister King in 1941), pointed out the conditions in the USSR as he saw them, yet he remained an admirer of Lenin. In December 1934, the *Toronto Star* quoted him thus: "I am not interested in people who condemn Russia....Neither am I interested in those who speak of it as a heaven on earth. I visited the tomb of Lenin, Moscow, a man I believe will go down as one of the greatest figures of his century. Had he lived, conditions in that land would be vastly improved" ("Germany Menace to Peace, Hamilton M.P. Declares," 12 Dec. 1933, 34).
113 "Vyklad u Vynnypegu pro Sovity," *Kanadyis'kyi farmer*, 12 Dec. 1933, 4.
114 "Vidchyty pro Rosiiu," *Ukraïns'kyi holos*, 27 Dec. 1933, 2.
115 "Sami kartyny hovoryly pravdu pro SRSR, a ne pan. Kechom," *Ukraïns'ki robitnychi visty*, 12 Dec. 1933, 5.
116 For example, see "Iak Neshynel Kavnsel of Ediukeishen verbuie protyradians'kykh 'lektoriv,'" *Ukraïns'ki robitnychi visty*, 23 Dec. 1933, 2 (and other articles on the same page).

117 Ketchum to Arthur Merriam, 17 Aug. 1934, M-1322, 397390, Bennett Papers.
118 Ketchum to Bennett, 12 Apr. 1933, M-1322, 397340, Bennett Papers.
119 Ketchum to Bennett, 30 May 1934, M-1322, 397361, 397363, Bennett Papers. See also Ketchum to Bennett, 1 June 1934, M-1322, 397366, Bennett Papers.
120 J. L., "Re- Carl Ketchum, Memorandum to the Director, C.I.," 10 Oct. 1934, RG 13, vol. 404, file 9934-1008 Carl J. Ketchum, LAC. The author of the memorandum—identified only as J. L.—wrote of the break between Ketchum and the council: "It is alleged that the National Council of Education had cancelled his engagement on account of his pro-Soviet Russia tendencies."
121 Ketchum to Bennett, 9 Aug. 1934, M-1322, 397376, Bennett Papers.
122 See Arthur Merriam to Carleton Ketchum, 16 Aug. 1934, M-1322, 397391, Bennett Papers; Ketchum to Bennett, 30 Aug. 1934, M-1322, 39740, Bennett Papers.
123 Ketchum to W. L. Mackenzie King, 15 Aug. 1933, C-3673, 167074, King Papers.
124 Ketchum to Edward Pickering, 19 Oct. 1933, C-3673, 167076-167077, King Papers. In February 1934, Ketchum spoke before the University of Alberta's Political Science Club on the United States's recognition of the USSR. See "Russia's Morale Boosted by Pact," *Edmonton Journal*, 1 Mar. 1934, 13. The Canadian government maintained its trade policy toward the USSR in spite of American recognition of the USSR. Thus, in January 1934 the Soviet ambassador to Washington, DC, Alexander Troyanovsky, announced that he saw "no immediate expectation of increased trade between the Soviet Union and Canada." See "Russian Envoy Avoids Canada," *Edmonton Bulletin*, 11 Jan. 1934, 1. See also Frederick Griffin's article about Troyanovsky, "Our Relations with Canada Not Clear, Russ Envoy Says," *Toronto Star*, 11 Jan. 1934, 1, 3.
125 Henry to Ketchum, 7 Nov. 1933, C-3673, 167081, King Papers. He continued to write to King's office, and when the Liberal leader came to power. Ketchum made an unsuccessful claim against the Canadian government in connection with the "work that I did in 1933–34 at the instance of the so-called National Council of Canada and for the general benefit of Canada." Ketchum to C. P. Plaxton, Department of Justice, 21 Apr. 1939, RG-13, vol. 404, file 1934-1008, 397391, LAC; "J.R. 1008-34," 27 Apr. 1939, RG-13, vol. 404, file 1934-1008, LAC.
126 The time period in question is not identified in the letter, but these figures likely pertain to one year.
127 "Allan Monkhouse Concedes Success of Soviet Plan," *Prince George Citizen*, 22 Mar. 1934, 4. Later in the year, the *Prince George Citizen* mentioned the famine in its report on the switch of the capital of Soviet Ukraine from Kharkiv to Kyiv. The report said that the transfer back to Kyiv, on June 24, 1934, was seen as evidence of Soviet strength and the diminishing of any danger of uprisings in Ukraine. "It was in the Ukraine that the kulaks (individual farmers) waged their most desperate battle against collectivization, and it was here that famine exacted its heaviest toll." The report added that a major purge of the Communist Party of Ukraine had taken place in response to a "nationalist plot" in 1933 ("Switch in Ukraine Capital Evidence of Soviet Strength," 5 July 1934, 3). On purges and the reasons behind them, see Myroslav Shkandrij and Olga

Bertelsen, "The Soviet Regime's National Operations in Ukraine, 1929–1934," *Canadian Slavonic Papers* 55, nos. 3–4 (2013): 417–47.
128   J. M. Gilchrist to M. A. MacPherson, 23 Dec. 1933, M-1214, 137542, Bennett Papers.
129   "'Agricultural Russia and the Wheat Problem,' New and Valuable Publication," *Winnipeg Free Press*, 21 Dec. 1932, 15. The *Winnipeg Free Press* serialized some of the book's content as articles. For reports on Timoshenko's lectures, see, for example, "Winnipeg Ukrainians Honor Distinguished Countryman," *Winnipeg Tribune*, 25 Dec. 1933, 13; and "Farm Policy of Soviets Has Failed," *Star-Phoenix*, 27 Dec. 1933, 7.
130   "Russian Collective Farms Failure, Soviet Not Factor Wheat Mart Says Economist," *Edmonton Journal*, 30 Dec. 1933, 15.
131   "Soviet Methods Are Denounced by Ukraine Speaker," *Winnipeg Free Press*, 25 Dec. 1933, 1. For examples of items in Canada's Ukrainian-language press about V. Timoshenko, see "Prof. Tymoshenko u Vinnipegu," *Ukraïns'kyi holos*, 27 Dec. 1933, 8; "Prof. Volod. Tymoshenko u Vynnepegu," *Kanadyis'kyi farmer*, 27 Dec. 1933, 1; and "Try ukraïntsi maiut' doklady na vsesvitnii zbizhevii konferentsiï v Ridzhaini," *Novyi shliakh*, 1 Aug. 1933, 4. In a later article, Timoshenko discussed the famine thus: "In order to realize its dreams of large agricultural enterprises, the Communist Party had to undertake a real war against the peasantry in the early 1930s. The peasantry remained recalcitrant even after they had been forced into kolkhozes, particularly in the Ukraine and in the areas of Don and Kuban Cossacks where individual ownership of land was more common than in central Russia. The government deliberately starved these peasants into submission in 1932–33 by taking not only the surpluses from the kolkhozes but the food their members needed for survival." Vladimir P. Timoshenko, "Agriculture in the Soviet Spotlight," *Foreign Affairs* 32, no. 2 (1954): 246.

Chapter Six

1   Michiel Horn, *The Great Depression of the 1930s in Canada*, Historical Booklet No. 39 (Ottawa: Canadian Historical Association, 1984), 4–5.
2   Ibid., 10. The name R. B. Bennett became the stuff of folklore in Depression-era Canada. It has been pointed out, however, that in the midst of the immense hardships experienced across the country, the wealthy prime minister often would reach into his own pocket to donate personally to people soliciting his help. "Biography 1870–1947," *The Right Honourable Richard Bedford Bennett*, Library and Archives Canada, accessed 7 March 2016, https://www.collectionscanada.gc.ca/primeministers/h4-3281-e.html.
3   See "Great Depression," www.thecanadianencyclopedia.ca/en/article/great-depression/; Orest Martynowych, *Ukrainians in Canada: The Formative Years, 1891–1924* (Edmonton: CIUS Press, 1991), 497–98, 515n58; and Ol'ha Woycenko, "Community Organizations," in *A Heritage in Transition: Essays in the History*

of *Ukrainians in Canada*, ed. Manoly R. Lupul (Toronto: McClelland & Stewart, 1982), 187.

4   Ian Angus, *Canadian Bolsheviks: The Early Years of the Communist Party of Canada* (Victoria, BC: Trafford, 2004), 267; John Kolasky, *The Shattered Illusion: The History of Ukrainian Pro-Communist Organizations in Canada* (Toronto: PMA, 1979), 18.

5   Two examples are Michael Korol and Oleksander Mankowsky, who were among the ULFTA leaders. Kolasky, *Shattered Illusion*, 8.

6   Ibid., 12. Appeals to come to the rescue of the starving in Ukraine were also made in other quarters of the Ukrainian diaspora. In August 1921, an article in *Svoboda* pressed for direct aid to be sent to victims in Ukraine. See Roman Serbyn, "The First Man-Made Famine in Soviet Ukraine 1921–1923," *Ukrainian Weekly*, 6 Nov. 1988, 8. For documents and a larger discussion on the topic, in Ukrainian, see Serbyn, comp. and ed., *Holod 1921–1923 i ukraïns'ka presa v Kanadi* (Toronto: Ukraïns'ko-Kanads'kyi doslidcho-dokumentatsiinyi tsentr, 1992). Between July 1921 and September 1922, Canadian pro-Communist contributions for Russia totalled $95,596.99—and for Ukraine, $10,847.46. Ibid., 30.

7   Kolasky, *Shattered Illusion*, 8, 12. Ukrainians also left Galicia for the Ukrainian SSR. On their fate, see Myroslav Shkandrij and Olga Bertelsen, "The Secret Police and the Campaign against Galicians in Soviet Ukraine, 1929–34," *Nationalities Papers* 42, no. 1 (2014): 37–62.

8   "Police Raid Ukrainian Labor Temple," *Winnipeg Tribune*, 5 July 1933, 1.

9   J. Petryshyn, "R.B. Bennett and the Communists: 1930–1935," *Journal of Canadian Studies* 9, no. 4 (1974): 53.

10 Quoted in P. B. Waite, *In Search of R.B. Bennett* (Montreal and Kingston: McGill-Queen's University Press, 2012), 163.

11 In an editorial that mentioned Humphrey Mitchell's visit to the USSR, the *Toronto Telegram* labelled CCF-ism as "nothing better than thinly disguised Communism" ("C.C.F. Offers Canada Communism," 21 Oct. 1933, 6).

12 "Deportations," *Winnipeg Tribune*, 9 Dec. 1932, 15. Examples of stories covering protests against deportations include "Deportation of Workers Scored by Russian Club," *Winnipeg Free Press*, 3 Sept. 1932, 10; and "Voice Protest over Request to Deport Jobless Ukrainian," *Winnipeg Free Press*, 17 Apr. 1933, 16 (protest by James Grant, president of the East Kildonian Home Protection Association).

13 For example, see "Alberta Hunger March," *Winnipeg Free Press*, 1 Mar. 1932, 1; "800 in Hunger March on Alberta Legislature," *Winnipeg Tribune*, 1 Mar. 1932, 3; "Hunger March on Ottawa Urged by Jobless Veterans," *Winnipeg Free Press*, 27 June 1932, 3; and "Police Rout Hunger Marchers," *Winnipeg Free Press*, 21 Dec. 1932, 1–2. The Canadian press also carried many reports about "hunger marches" in other countries.

14 Petition of the Russian Workers-Farmers' Club, 6 July 1934, M-989, 94148, Bennett Papers. The Canadian government also received protests from abroad (George Bernard Shaw being among the signatories) for "repeal of a section of the Canadian criminal code which makes mere membership in the Communist

party a crime punishable by twenty years in prison." See "Protest Dominion Action Outlawing Communist Party," *Winnipeg Free Press*, 13 June 1932, 14.
15 Undated resolution to R. B. Bennett, M-989, 94402, Bennett Papers.
16 Resolution passed on 26 Mar. 1933, M-988, 93347, Bennett Papers.
17 Ukrainian original and English translation at M-988, 93428–30, Bennett Papers.
18 Ibid., 93435–7, 93444. Some months later, in January 1934, the prime minister received an anonymous letter in English in uppercase letters: "Dear Sir. This is to tell you that you have to resign by force. Because you are making the people suffer to[o] much. If y[ou] do not want [to] resign, you will be found dead in your office some day." Anonymous to Bennett, 14 Jan. 1934, M-988, 93715, Bennett Papers. Earlier, in February 1932, the *Winnipeg Free Press* reported that Bennett had received threats to his life unless the nine imprisoned Communists were released ("Communist Threats Received by Bennett," 26 Feb. 1932, 1).
19 Mrs. G. Wilson (secretary, Friends of the Soviet Union, Vancouver) to R. B. Bennett, telegram, 30 Mar. 1934, M-1031, 192289, Bennett Papers.
20 Bennett to Wilson, 9 Apr. 1934, M-1031, 192290, Bennett Papers.
21 Friends of the Soviet Union Conference to R. B. Bennett, 5 Apr. 1931, M-1032, 193134, Bennett Papers. See also "Resolution of Protest" passed by the gathering at the Labor Temple Association, 6 Apr. 1931, Crowland, ON, M-1032, 193135, Bennett Papers.
22 For examples of resolutions sent to the federal government, see A. Marsh (Workers Ex-Servicemen's League in Canada, Hamilton Branch) to R. B. Bennett, 16 Jan. 1933, M-1032, 193776, Bennett Papers; and the resolution of a gathering of the Farmers' Unity League at Lone Star, 3 Jan. 1934, M-1032, 193849, Bennett Papers. On a rally organized by Friends of the Soviet Union, see "Meeting Asks Russian Trade," *Border Cities Star*, 9 Jan. 1933, 3. For examples of those sent to provincial governments, see the resolutions from early 1934 of the UFA in Last Lake, Alberta; from a gathering at Lac Bellevue; from the Workers' Benevolent Association in Edmonton; from "workers" in Newcastle, Alberta; from the ULFTA in Calgary (with the claim that three hundred people were present); and from the Canmore Miners' Union: all in accession no. 69.289, file 281, roll 29 (file nos. 179-294A), Premiers' Papers, Provincial Archives of Alberta, Edmonton (hereafter, Premiers' Papers).
23 For example, see the January 1933 letter from R. L. Shiels of Toronto to R. B. Bennett. Referring to an article in the *Toronto Star* ("Russia Is Good Risk, Says Motor Executive," 10 Jan. 1933), Shiels wrote that the opinion expressed therein "was wrong; at this time Soviet Russia would 'step upon our economic corns' and very easily too. Especially if we exchange *food* for oil, or even gold:– Until the essence of all that is Christian which our countries' very foundations was originally built upon is recognized by Soviet Russia (which looks very improbable), it would be fool-hardy to deal in any such measures, which Soviet Russia proposes, at this time (and because of their full adherence to atheism)." Shiels to Bennett, 11 Jan. 1933 (emphasis in original), M-1032, 193705–13, Bennett Papers.

24 See Max Foran, "Hooves for Gallons: The Canada-Russia Barter Deal of 1932–33," *Alberta History* 49, no. 2 (2001): 12–19. See also "Winnipeg Men to Continue to Work for Cattle Deal," *Winnipeg Free Press*, 3 Feb. 1933, 10; "Believes Britain and Russia Will Cancel Embargo," *Winnipeg Free Press*, 28 Apr. 1933, 3; "Mullins Denounces Promoter of Russian Cattle Deal Scheme," *Winnipeg Free Press*, 16 May 1933, 1, 4; and "Serkau Goes to New York on Soviet Trade Deal," *Winnipeg Tribune*, 23 Sept. 1933, 26.

25 Kirk Niergarth and J. L. Black, "Revisiting the Canadian–Soviet Barter Proposal of 1932–1933: The Soviet Perspective," *International Journal* 71, no. 3 (2016): 409–32. The study is based on both Canadian and Soviet documents. The USSR pursued the deal for both economic and diplomatic reasons. In spite of Bennett's opposition to the deal, negotiations were terminated not by the Canadian side but by the Soviets, who in the spring of 1933 rejected a renegotiated proposal. Ibid., 2.

26 Joseph Dyk to R. B. Bennett, 23 Feb. 1933, M-1033, 193984, Bennett Papers.

27 Cummins to Stewart, 21 Feb. 1933, M-1031, 192258, Bennett Papers.

28 "Quebec's Viewpoint," *Winnipeg Free Press*, 31 Jan. 1933, 13.

29 R. B. Bennett to Finlay MacDonald, 13 Jan. 1933, M-1032, 193666, Bennett Papers. Later in the month, Bennett received a letter from his minister of trade and commerce; H. H. Stevens informed him of the significant agitation in western Canada "regarding the sale of a block of wheat to Russia." After some investigation, Stevens had come to the conclusion that there was "no definite evidence that the Russian Government is in the market for wheat." He noted that the USSR had bought some wheat in 1932, "presumably for seed, and largely through western ports," and thought it possible that the USSR would make "fairly large purchases for this purpose again" in 1933 but also "possibly some for food purposes." Stevens seemed to imply a need for caution by referring to an exchange between the United States and the USSR on the subject of overdue accounts. Stevens referred to a "very responsible person" who had told him that the United States was "sharply complaining at the failure of Russia to meet her payments in a proper manner" and it appeared that the USSR was "finding herself in an increasingly difficult position to meet these payments." Stevens to Bennett, 25 Jan. 1933, M-1032, 193821–2, Bennett Papers. In reply, Bennett intimated that "the more I understand the situation the more certain I am that the Serkau incident is propaganda for the purpose of making difficult the position of this Government." Bennett to Stevens, 26 Jan. 1933, M-1032, 193823, Bennett Papers.

30 Dominion of Canada, *Hansard*, 13 Feb. 1933, 2211, M-1314, 435807, Bennett Papers.

31 "Soviet Activity at Ottawa Is Alleged," *Winnipeg Free Press*, 17 Mar. 1932, 6.

32 "Delegation Is Planning to Visit Soviet Union," *Winnipeg Free Press*, 25 Mar. 1932, 5.

33 *Winnipeg Tribune*, 8 Apr. 1932, 2.

34 "Details of Secret Trial of Alleged Communists at Halifax Are Revealed," *Winnipeg Free Press*, 10 May 1932, 4.

35 "145 Delegates to Ukrainian Labor Body in Session," *Winnipeg Free Press*, 12 July 1932, 3.
36 "Finnish Organization Ruled Communistic," *Winnipeg Free Press*, 9 June 1933, 1.
37 "Ukrainian Labor Farmer Temple Society Sued," *Winnipeg Tribune*, 20 June 1933, 9.
38 "Police Swoop Down on Ukrainian Hall and Seize Records," *Winnipeg Free Press*, 6 July 1933, 3.
39 "Workers' Society Wants Return of Documents Seized," *Winnipeg Free Press*, 11 July 1933, 6.
40 "Scores Injured in Winnipeg Riot," *Winnipeg Free Press*, 17 July 1933, 1, 5; "Winnipeg Deportee Given Hot Farewell," *Winnipeg Free Press*, 17 July 1933, 1.
41 "Asks Saskatoon Organization Be Declared Illegal," *Winnipeg Free Press*, 27 July 1933, 3. See also "Deny Charges of Fascism against Saskatoon Body," *Winnipeg Free Press*, 28 July 1933, 3.
42 "Dominion Meeting of Ukrainian Association Here July 31-August 1," *Winnipeg Free Press*, 28 July 1933, 3.
43 "Benevolent Society Gains in Membership," *Winnipeg Tribune*, 5 Aug. 1933, 20.
44 "Ukraine Liberation Body Opens Convention Today," *Winnipeg Free Press*, 4 Aug. 1933, 4.
45 "C.C.F. Movement Attacked at Meeting of Ukrainian Labor-Farmer Association," *Winnipeg Free Press*, 1 Aug. 1933, 3.
46 "Ukrainian Labor-Farmer Temple's Work Reviewed," *Winnipeg Free Press*, 11 Dec. 1933, 4. For a biography of Andrew Bilecki, a former Ukrainian Labor-Farmer Publishing Co. employee, see *Winnipeg Tribune*, 16 Nov. 1932, 11. On Jacob Penner, see "Memorable Manitobans: Jacob Penner (1880–1965)," Manitoba Historical Society, last revised 5 Nov. 2016, http://www.mhs.mb.ca/docs/people/penner_j.shtml; and "A Glowing Dream: The Story of Jacob Rose Penner," A Scattering of Seeds, accessed 12 Feb. 2014, http://www.whitepinepictures.com/seeds/iii/33/.
47 "Communists of Winnipeg Stage Orderly Parade," *Winnipeg Tribune*, 2 May 1933, 10.
48 "Canadian-Born Child Named after Stalin," *Winnipeg Tribune*, 16 Dec. 1933, 1. *Svoboda* reported on another Soviet sympathizer who left Canada for the USSR in 1933: Andrii Pankiv, a Winnipegger, departed for the USSR with his wife and three children. It is not clear from the article where in the USSR he settled, but *Svoboda* noted that Pankiv wrote to a lawyer in Winnipeg, McCarthy, asking that the latter sell his house and help bring him and his family back to Canada ("Perekonavsia," 11 Sept. 1934, 1).
49 Although there is no reference to a delegation, a tour to the USSR in 1933 was advertised in *Ukraïns'ki robitnychi visty* (25 Feb. 1933, 6). According to the advertisement, the SS *Volendam* was to set sail from Halifax on April 3, enabling the tourists to witness the May Day celebrations in the Soviet Union. Ukraine is not specifically mentioned in the advertisement.
50 H. M. Newson (assistant commissioner, Commanding "K" Division) to Deputy Attorney General of Alberta, "Re: Confidential C.I.B. Monthly Report, 'K' Division – October, 1932," confidential report, accession no. 69.289, file 108, Premiers' Papers. An RCMP report about a celebration of the October

Revolution at the Rialto Theatre in Edmonton on November 6, 1932, which around fifteen hundred people were said to have attended, provides some glimpses into local ties with the USSR. One of the speakers, Dr. Crang (no first name specified), mentioned that his son, who was working in the USSR as an engineer, described the Soviet Union as the "best country in the world" from the perspective of workers—a place with no unemployment, good wages, and "no bread-lines." Another speaker who had visited the Soviet Union, Peter Kleparchuk of Mundare, described conditions there in positive terms. See Royal Canadian Mounted Police, "Division: 'K,' Sub-District: Edmonton, Detachment: C.I.B. Edmonton," report, 8 Nov. 1932, accession no. 69.289, file 108, Premiers' Papers. In early 1933, the town of Blairmore elected to its council members of the Workers' Unity League, an "alleged Communist organization." "Reds Defeated in One Alberta Mining Town but Win in Another," *Province*, 15 Feb. 1933, 11.

51 "F.S.U. Delegation Returns from Russia," *Weekly Summary Report on Revolutionary Organizations and Agitators in Canada* (RCMP Security Bulletin No. 738), 28 Dec. 1934, 470–71. Cowan was a contributor to *Soviet Russia Today*. In the October 1933 issue of that magazine he wrote about Soviet state planning ("State Planning in the Soviet Union: The Second Five-Year Plan," Oct. 1933, 7–8). A later issue published an enthusiastic letter submitted by Max Shur (described as a "Canadian Worker") from the USSR (it is not clear where) in which he challenged reports about starvation. "Despite what you read in the newspapers," Shur wrote to "Comrade Sidney," "we are not starving, we have plenty to eat, including meat and fish." There were hardships, he conceded, which he attributed to "class enemies of our own as well as outsiders, sabotagers." ("A Canadian Worker Writes," Jan. 1934, 18). Of note: "The Soviet University," published in the December 1933 issue of *Soviet Russia Today* (p. 18), was written by A. Shur—a former student of Harbour Collegiate Institute, Toronto, who had departed Canada in 1931 and, in February 1932, enrolled at the D. I. Mendeleev Chemical Technological Institute in Moscow.

52 *Kingsville Reporter*, 11 Oct. 1934, 4.

53 "Strange Tale of Horror and Persecution Told by Minister from Russia," *Winnipeg Free Press*, 13 Apr. 1933, 5. The minister declined to give his name for fear, he said, of repercussions against his wife, daughter, and son-in-law, who were still in the USSR. He told the newspaper it could call him "Fr. Teofilos." A photograph, however, was published.

54 "President of Zionist Says Minister's Story Is Maliciously Untrue," *Winnipeg Free Press*, 14 Apr. 1933, 1.

55 "Declares Jews in Russia Are Greatest Sufferers at Hands of Communists," *Winnipeg Free Press*, 15 Apr. 1933, 3.

56 "One German's Opinion of Jewish Activity," *Winnipeg Free Press*, 3 June 1933, 13. The letter is signed "M.A.F.V.B.P.B." See also "Urgent Problem of Germany and the Jews," letter to the editor, *Winnipeg Free Press*, 29 Apr. 1933, 25. The same number—406 Jews of 503 members of the Soviet government—appeared in an article in *Novyi shliakh*, which attributed the figure to the German newspaper "Anglif" [*Der Angriff?*] ("Zhydy i bil'shovyzm," 25 Apr. 1933, 1).

57 "The Jewish People in Recent World Events," *Winnipeg Free Press*, 10 June 1933, 13. Placed at the end of this letter was an editorial note defending the paper's decision to publish the anonymous letter. From that point on, the editorial note said, writers of letters on the subject would be required to sign their names for publication, unless there were "special circumstances." Letters on the subject also appeared in the *Winnipeg Tribune*, for example, "What about Russia? Asks a Correspondent" and "Why Pity the Jews, Asks Foreigner," both 17 Apr. 1933, 9.

58 "Persecution of Jews by Hitler Is Protested," *Winnipeg Tribune*, 26 Apr. 1933, 9.

59 For example, "Clergy Plead for Friendship and Forbearance," *Star-Phoenix*, 10 Apr. 1933, 3; "Still Unsettled," *Globe*, 30 Nov. 1934, 6; "Jews and Communism," *Globe*, 1 Oct. 1934; and "Russia, Canada and Communism," *Globe*, 28 June 1935, 4. In Germany, the scapegoating of Jews for the famine found sinister expression in a 1933 address by Otto Nippold, deputy gauleiter of Upper Bavaria, before five thousand people in Munich. Nippold "charged that Soviet Russian Jews were responsible for the starvation of thousands of German colonists in Russia" and threatened that a day may come "when the German people will declare that for every German citizen succumbing in Russia, ten Jews will be promptly hanged on German gallows." "Ten Jews Will Die for Every German Russians Kill, Nazi Retaliation Rate," *Jewish Telegraphic Agency* (New York), 9 July 1933, 9.

60 Marco Carynnyk, author of several works on the famine, states, "In 1932 and 1933, reports in Ukrainian Canadian nationalist newspapers about the famine in the homeland were accompanied by anti-Semitic insinuations." Carynnyk, "Chairman's Remarks," in *Multiculturalism and Ukrainian Canadians: Identity, Homeland Ties, and the Community's Future*, ed. Stella M. Hryniuk and Lubomyr Y. Luciuk (Toronto: Multicultural History Society of Ontario, 1993), 42.

61 Orest T. Martynowych, "Sympathy for the Devil: The Attitude of Ukrainian War Veterans in Canada to Nazi Germany and the Jews, 1933–1939," in *Re-Imagining Ukrainian-Canadians: History, Politics, and Identity*, ed. Rhonda L. Hinther and Jim Mochoruk (Toronto: University of Toronto Press, 2011), 190.

62 Ibid., 206.

63 Ioann Teodorovych, "Do virnykh Ukraïns'koï Pravoslavnoï Tserkvy v Amerytsi i Kanadi – Arkhypastyrs'ke poslannia," in Marunchak, *Natsiia v borot'bi za svoie isnuvannia*, 92–93. The letter was published in the religious journal *Vistnyk* (Winnipeg) on September 1, 1933. See also "Iz no. 91–92 religioznogo informatsionnogo biulletenia (Zheneva) o reaktsii pravoslavnoi tserkvi v SShA, Kanade i Frantsii na golod v SSSR," *Istoricheskie Materialy* [Historical materials], 12 Oct. 1933, accessed 30 Nov. 2015, http://istmat.info/node/43614.

64 See Martynowych, *Ukrainians in Canada*, bk. 1, 355–56 (for examples from Sitch-organized rallies), 419–20 (for rallies reported in *Ukraïns'kyi holos*).

65 Ibid., 355.

66 [Anonymous], "Glory Canada Wheat," M-1033, 194246–7, Bennett Papers.

67 Martynowych wrote that in weeklies edited by Ukrainian war veterans, "less than 2 or 3 percent of the material can be characterized as anti-Semitic" (in

contrast to Arcand's *Le Fasciste Canadien*: "More than 60 per cent").
Martynowych, "Sympathy for the Devil," 201.

68 "Dlia zhody treba dvokh storin," *Ukraïns'kyi holos*, 20 Dec. 1933, 4. See also Makuch, "Ukrainian Patriots"; and Andrij Makuch, "The Petliura Legacy in Interwar Canada" (paper presented at the annual convention of the Canadian Association of Slavists, University of Victoria, 27 May 2012).

69 Ukrainians in Toronto voiced opposition to a local public appreearance by Schwartzbard. "Ukraïntsi v Toronti ne dopustyly do publychnoho vystupu Sh. Shvartsbarta," *Ukraïns'ki visty*, 31 Jan. 1934, 1; "Scores Police Board for Ban on Meeting," *Toronto Star*, 20 Jan. 1934, 3. An article by Pierre van Paassen, in which he asserted that the "last czarist pogrom under the Hetman Simon Petlura cost 200,000 Jews their lives in Ukrainia in 1920" ("Investigate Nazi Pamphlet Ascribing Murder to Jews," *Toronto Star*, 1 Aug. 1934, 1, 7), was challenged by Rev. D. D. Leschishin in a letter to the *Star*'s editor ("Ukrainians and Jews," 8 Aug. 1934, 6). Van Paassen claimed to have known Petliura well. "Hatred of Jews Fades in Russia," *Toronto Star*, 8 Oct. 1932, 1, 3. He does not seem to have made similar claims (i.e., of personal acquaintance) regarding another Ukrainian leader during the war of independence period—the still-living Pavlo Skoropadsky—but did comment on the exiled hetman and the famine in Ukraine: "Ex-hetman Skoropadski made a brief appearance at [a secret congress held in Berlin on May 30, 1934, in which Alfred Rosenberg greeted two hundred Ukrainian delegates in the name of Hitler].... The usual harrowing litanies about perennial famine in Ukraine were recited. Seven million Ukrainians were said to have died of famine last year; six million the year before. People were eating human flesh, the electrification works on the Dnieper were said to be non-existent and the industrialization of Poltava existed only on paper. In short it looked like a walk-over for the boys. Reports from the Caucasus were even worse. Human flesh was not even available there. Stalin had it all confiscated for himself and his friends and shipped to Moscow." See "German Favor Greets Plan for Ukrainian Independence," *Toronto Star*, 11 Aug. 1934, 28. Earlier, an article by van Paassen implying Skoropadsky was supporting anti-Semitic activities ("White Russians Join Hitler against Soviet," *Edmonton Bulletin*, 15 July 1933, 3) prompted a letter to the editor by John Esaiw, a prominent member of the local Hetmanite movement ("Ukrainian Ideals," *Edmonton Bulletin*, 24 July 1933, 4, 5). On the belief of Soviet involvement in Petliura's assassination, see the letter by Rev. D. D. Leschishin, "Petlura [sic] and the Jews," *Toronto Star*, 1 Sept. 1934, 5. Quite conceivably, that suspicion may to some extent have emerged from the timing of the assassination; just days before (May 12–14, 1926), Polish leader Józef Piłsudski, with whom Petliura had formed an alliance against the Bolsheviks in 1920, had returned to power in Poland in a coup d'état.

70 F. H. Epp, *Mennonite Exodus*, 272–73. Anti-Semitic views from Germany were echoed within segments of the Mennonite community in Canada. See Alan Davies and Marilyn F. Nefsky, *How Silent Were the Churches? Canadian Protestantism and the Jewish Plight during the Nazi Era* (Waterloo, ON: Wilfrid

Laurier University Press, 1998), 108–16. Anti-Semitism also existed in Russian émigré circles, according to "Russia and the Jewish People," *Jewish Western Bulletin*, 13 Apr. 1933, 6.

71 "Russia," *Jewish Western Bulletin*, 7 June 1934, 1; "Maxim Litvinov, Special Envoy from Russia to the United States," *Jewish Western Bulletin*, 9 Nov. 1933, 1; "Russia Invites Refugees," *Jewish Western Bulletin*, 11 Jan. 1934, 1.

72 "ICOR News," *Jewish Western Bulletin*, 24 Aug. 1933, 3.

73 For example, a story in the *Jewish Western Bulletin* attributed the refusal to manufacture matze to the "agitation carried on in the Yiddish Communist press against Jewish institutions abroad for devoting so much attention to the condition of starvation of Russian Jewry" ("Soviet Refuses Permission to Manufacture Matze in Moscow," 6 Apr. 1933, 3). Articles in the *Canadian Jewish Chronicle* included "Zionist Socialist Delegation in Tel Aviv States Thousands of Jews in Russia on Verge of Starvation" (30 Sept. 1932, 10[?]) and, on the introduction of the passport system, "The Soviet's New Purge" (17 Mar. 1933, 7). Several pieces on the Soviet Union by van Paassen were also published in the *Canadian Jewish Chronicle*, including "Jews and the Soviets" (6 Jan. 1933, 5, 17), "Anti-Semitism in Russia" (13 Jan. 1933, 6, 18), and "The Birth of a Jewish Republic" (3 Feb. 1933, 6, 18).

74 "People in Ukraine Hopeful That War Will Free Them," *Ottawa Journal*, 1 June 1934, 5. While the article mentioned the famine, it offered few details about its causes beyond the following: "There had been a terrible drought in the Ukraine in the past few months and Mr. Mosion predicted that there was another famine in the offing. 'When the peasants found that they had to work for the Government they decided that it would be far better to die than to till the soil under such conditions, and as a result when the Soviet agents called to gather the crops they found it unharvested with thousands of people dead in the villages. A villager was unable to keep a horse, a cow, or a pig, without having it confiscated by the state and these conditions were intolerable.'" The article noted that while Mosion was in Odesa, "in deference to his mother's wish," he bought a two-acre plot and presented it to "one of the Jewish communities to be used as a cemetery." Ibid. On Mosion, see J. W. Guy Fortier, "Growing Up in Lower Town," *Heritage Ottawa Newsletter* 30, no. 2 (2003): 6.

75 "Liude na Ukraïni viriat', shcho nedaleka viina prynese ïm spasennia," *Kanadyis'kyi farmer*, 13 June 1934, 10; "Liude na Ukraïni nadiut'sia til'ky na viiny," *Ukraïns'kyi holos*, 13 June 1934, 1. Reprinted in English in "Press Reports on Ukraine and Ukrainians," *Svoboda*, 7 June 1934, 3.

76 "V uriadi Radians'koï Ukraïny ostavsia til'ky odyn ukraïnets'," *Ukraïns'ki visty*, 26 Oct. 1932, 1.

77 Ewald Ammende, "Memorandum on the situation in the starving districts of the Soviet Union by Dr. Ewald Ammende, General Secretary of the Inter-Confessional and International Aid Committee for the Starvation Districts in Soviet Russia," M-1033, 19414, Bennett Papers. The memorandum is marked "Received for file July 25/34." The question of how the famine affected different national groups in Ukraine is currently being examined by Oleh Wolowyna and

a team of demographers at the Institute of Demography and Social Studies of the National Academy of Sciences of Ukraine.

78 In an article about the Holodomor, John-Paul Himka states that "the actual participation of Jews in the communist movement, in the Soviet apparatus, and particularly in the organs of repression should be carefully studied empirically and clarified." Himka, "The Holodomor in the Ukrainian-Jewish Encounter Initiative" (paper presented at the meeting of the Ukrainian Jewish Encounter Initiative, Ditchley Park, England, 14–16 Dec. 2009), 3, http://www.academia.edu/499209/The_Holodomor_in_the_Ukrainian-Jewish_Encounter_Initiative. Some figures pertaining to the repressive apparatus are presented in an analysis of the western Ukrainian newspaper *Dilo* (1930s), by Myroslav Shkandrij. Shkandrij writes of a "growing anti-Semitic discourse in Galicia during the 1930s" but also notes "that the perception of Jews as active in the Soviet repressive apparatus was not a fantasy. There had been a substantial number of Jewish activists within the Cheka-GPU-NKVD in Ukraine from the organization's early years. Vadym Zolotarev [in *Z arkhiviv* 2 (2009)] has calculated that of the top ninety people in the Ukrainian NKVD in 1936, sixty were Jewish (66.67%), fourteen Russian (15.55%), six Ukrainian (6.67%), three Latvian (3.33%), two Belarusian (2.22%), and one Polish (1.11%)." Shkandrij, "Ukrainianization, Terror and Famine," 447–48n5. The role of Jews in the Soviet regime is discussed in Antony Polonsky, *The Jews in Poland and Russia*, vol. 3, *1914 to 2008* (Oxford: Littman Library of Jewish Civilization, 2012), 259–66. According to Polonsky, "Jews became more important in the security apparatus in the period of collectivization and the first Five Year Plan," and "when the OGPU was transformed into the NKVD [in 1934], people classed as Jews under paragraph 5 of the internal passport law made up thirty-seven out of the ninety-six 'leading cadres' of the organization, as against thirty Russians, seven Latvians, five Ukrainians, four Poles, three Georgians, three Belarusians, two Germans, and five others" (p. 261). Their prominence in the security apparatus, he added, "may well have reflected a deliberate decision by Stalin to use them in these unpopular roles in order to deflect hostility from himself and the Soviet state" (p. 262). From late 1933, the Soviet regime began to emphasize the Russians as the "first among equals" among the Soviet nations and periodically turned against its own adherents. Thus, "Jewish communists…suffered disproportionately in the purges of 1936–8 and remained highly vulnerable even when these were brought to an end" (ibid., 248, 273).

79 "Ochvydets pro polozhennia na ukraïns'kykh zemliakh pid moskovs'koiu zaimanshchynoiu," *Novyi shliakh*, 13 Sept. 1933, 2. For a discussion of *Novyi shliakh*, the Ukrainian National Federation, and the famine, see Martynowych, *Ukrainians in Canada*, bk. 1, 525–27. Martynowych notes that "*Novyi shliakh* and UNF leaders conceded that 'as co-creators and defenders' of the brutal Soviet regime, the most prominent and celebrated Soviet Ukrainian politicians and intellectuals, including Mykola Skrypnyk and Mykola Khvylovy, who both committed suicide in the summer of 1933, were at least partly responsible for the Famine."

Recognition of Ukrainian culpability in that tragedy may also have prevented the Nationalists and their weekly from scapegoating Soviet Jews as famine perpetrators" (p. 527). Attitudes toward Skrypnyk made apparent in *Ukraïns'kyi holos* are discussed in Makuch, "Ukrainian Patriots," 9. Skrypnyk's suicide, critics charged, did not make him a patriot (see, for example, "Samohubstvo ne robyt' zradnyka patriotom," *Ukraïns'kyi holos*, 16 Aug. 1933, 8). On nationalist debates on these and other questions, see Myroslav Shkandrij, *Ukrainian Nationalism: Politics, Ideology, and Literature, 1929–1956* (New Haven: Yale University Press, 2015).

80 "Chy nema holodu na Ukraïni," *Kanadyis'kyi farmer*, 18 Oct. 1933, 2. Myroslav Shkandrij wrote of the Jewish victims during the famine: "Jewish farming colonies were also collectivized, and there is evidence that they also starved in 1932–33." Shkandrij, *Jews in Ukrainian Literature: Representation and Identity* (New Haven: Yale University Press, 2009), 150. The majority of the 1,574,000 Jews in the Ukrainian SSR were urban dwellers. Of some of the towns and cities, Shkandrij writes, "In the spring of 1933 people were dying of hunger in Berdychiv, Zhytomyr, Uman, Bila Tserkva, Fastov, and Proskuriv, where there were large Jewish populations. According to official data, in February of that year 918 corpses of Jews who had died of hunger were picked up off the streets of Kyiv" (p. 150). Some 26 per cent of the Jewish population of Soviet Ukraine were rural dwellers. See Volodymyr Kubijovyč and Vasyl Markus, "Jews," in *Encyclopedia of Ukraine*, accessed 28 Dec. 2016, http://www.encyclopediaofukraine.com/. According to Harry Lang, who visited Ukraine in the autumn of 1933 and wrote about Jewish collective farms in the American Yiddish-language newspaper *Forward*, "By means of help from relatives in America, the Jewish kolkhozniki managed to somehow tide over the famine which during the course of the year struck the whole countryside." Lang, "A Trip to the Jewish Kolkhozy of Ukraine and White Russia," *Jewish Daily Forward* (New York), 30 Dec. 1933," reprinted in *Holodomor Studies* 2, no. 2 (2010): 237. Jeffrey Veidlinger states something similar: "While those shtetl Jews who lived through the famine all recall the sufferings that the Jewish community endured, many admit that conditions were worse in the villages.…Some Jews managed to survive because they still had relatives in America who could help provide for them." Further, he adds, "Although an untold number of Jews died of starvation during the Great Famine, the ability of some to survive on the basis of foreign currency and political clout has contributed to the false perception, often manipulated for political reasons today, that Jews were the instigators rather than among the victims of the Great Famine." Veidlinger, *In the Shadow of the Shtetl: Small-Town Jewish Life in Soviet Ukraine* (Bloomington: Indiana University Press, 2013), 50–54.

81 Martynowych, "Sympathy for the Devil," 201.
82 "More Regarding Jewish Persecutions," *Winnipeg Tribune*, 25 Apr. 1933, 8.
83 "Early Arrest of Ringleaders of Arborg Riot Likely," *Winnipeg Tribune*, 2 Dec. 1932, 1.
84 "A Task for Leaders," *Winnipeg Tribune*, 2 Dec. 1932, 13.
85 Untitled four-line comment in *Winnipeg Tribune*, 3 Dec. 1932, 17.

86 For examples of challenging responses to the editorial printed in the *Tribune*, see the letters by William Scraba ("Claims Ukrainian Leadership Is Adequate," 20 Dec. 1932, 9) and "ARGUS" ("Ukrainian Majority Resists Radicalism," 21 Dec. 1932, 13).
87 "Ukrainians Band to Fight Reds," *Border Cities Star*, 23 Jan. 1933, 3.
88 Resolution dated June 10, 1933, from Derwent to the prime minister, M-988, 93431-2, Bennett Papers. See also "Protybol'shevyts'ke viche," *Ukraïns'ki visty*, 12 July 1933, 6.
89 "Soviet Orders Huge Population Shifts," *Border Cities Star*, 29 Apr. 1933, 1. For an example of the story as it appeared in the Ukrainian-language press in Canada, see "Veselennia ukraïntsiv z Ukraïny," *Ukraïns'ki visty*, 17 May 1933, 4.
90 "Lutte de l'église orthodoxe contre les communistes," *La Presse*, 10 Aug. 1933, 13. See also "Colourful Ceremony Marks Union of Greek Orthodox Clergy Here," *Montreal Star*, 10 Aug. 1933, 8. In October 1933 a delegation of Russian Orthodox clergy met with the premier of Quebec, Louis-Alexandre Taschereau, and requested that the provincial government assist them in the establishment of two evening schools for the four Russian Orthodox parishes in Montreal. The delegation complained that Communist propaganda was "vigorous" in Russian circles in Montreal. "Pour les Russes orthodoxies," *Le Devoir*, 3 Oct. 1933, 3.
91 "Ukrainians Are Not 'Red,'" *Lethbridge Herald*, 26 Oct. 1933, 10.
92 Black to Bennett, 7 Dec. 1933, M-1329, 406137, Bennett Papers.
93 See the letters in M-1329, 406139-41, Bennett Papers.
94 "Webb Denounces Political Aims of His Opponents," *Winnipeg Free Press*, 20 Nov. 1933, 4. Webb spoke at the Ukrainian Institute Prosvita during a meeting held under the auspices of the St. Nicholas Mutual Benefit Society. See also "British Rule or Moscow's? Winnipeg's Mayor Asks," *Telegram*, 21 Nov. 1933, 3.
95 Webb to Gordon, 22 Mar. 1934, M-988, 93793-4, Bennett Papers.
96 "Manitoba Owes Much to Its Ukrainian Citizens," *Winnipeg Tribune*, 23 Dec. 1933, 7.
97 See, for example, *Ukraïns'ki robitnychi visty*, 7 Nov. 1933, 3 (photographs of factories in Luhansk, working women, and mobilized youth); and, on the Soviet health-care system, "Chy ie zapomohovi organizatsiï v Radians'komu Soiuzi," *Ukraïns'ki robitnychi visty*, 15 Oct. 1932, 2.
98 "Iak fabrykuiut' brekhni proty Radians'koho Soiuzu," *Ukraïns'ki robitnychi visty*, 17 Nov. 1932, 2.
99 Announcement in *Ukraïns'ki robitnychi visty*, 5 Jan. 1933, 4. On John Brown's lecture in Fort William, Ontario, on January 7, 1933, see "Kanads'kyi robitnyk vkazuiue na velyki dosiahnennia SRSR," *Ukraïns'ki robitnychi visty*, 10 Jan. 1933, 1; and in Saskatoon on January 18, 1933, "Ni, brekhni petliurivs'kykh vozhak ne spyniat' rozbudovy Rad. Soiuzu," *Ukraïns'ki robitnychi visty*, 7 Feb. 1933, 4. In early 1934, the newspaper announced a screening of one of the first Soviet sound films, *Putyovka v zhizn* [The road to life] (1931), about children orphaned by the upheavals of World War I and its aftermath. See "Radians'ka movna fil'ma 'Shliakh do zhyttia' bude vysvitliuvatysia v Edmontoni," *Ukraïns'ki robitnychi visty*, 24 Mar. 1934, 2; and

"Prykhod'te na radians'ku fil'mu v urd. poznaiomtesia z zhyttiam ditei v SRSR," *Ukraïns'ki robitnychi visty*, 6 Feb. 1934, 8. Vancouverite John Brown, together with Stanley Hood, Frank Busby (a papermaker from Kenora), and Albertan Sam Patterson, arrived back in Canada from their visit to the USSR on December 26, 1932. Soon after their return, Patterson told the *Winnipeg Free Press* that the cattle-for-oil deal being proposed by G. G. Serkau was a topic of much interest in Moscow ("Says Moscow Keenly Interested in Barter," 7 Jan. 1933, 3).

100 *Ukraïns'ki robitnychi visty*, 5 Jan. 1933, 3.

101 "Kanads'kyi inzhener Kalder pro radians'ke budivnytstvo," *Ukraïns'ki robitnychi visty*, 8 Nov. 1932, 4.

102 "Na mistsy staroho Katerynoslava roste velyke Dnipropetros'ke," *Ukraïns'ki robitnychi visty*, 1 June 1933, 2.

103 "Radians'kyi uriad kazhe Nankinovi zaopikuvatysia vtikachamy v SRSR," *Ukraïns'ki robitnychi visty*, 24 Dec. 1932, 1.

104 "Vyznaly," *Ukraïns'ki robitnychi visty*, 21 Nov. 1933, 2.

105 *Ukraïns'ki robitnychi visty*, 19 Oct. 1933, as translated in John Kolasky, ed. and trans., *Prophets and Proletarians: Documents on the History of the Rise and Decline of Ukrainian Communism in Canada* (Edmonton: CIUS Press, 1990), 221–22.

106 "Khto ne robyt', toi ne ïst'! Takoho hasla dotrymuiut'sia teper v Rad. Souizi," *Ukraïns'ki robitnychi visty*, 30 Sept. 1933, 5.

107 "Finds Russia Experiment in New Values," *Calgary Herald*, 30 June 1933, 21.

108 For example, "Kapitalystychna presa zatsikavlena perehovoramy mizh Spoluchenymy Derzhavamy i Radians'kym Soiuzom," *Ukraïns'ki robitnychi visty*, 4 Nov. 1933, 2.

109 *Ukraïns'ki robitnychi visty*, 21 Nov. 1933, as translated in Kolasky, *Prophets and Proletarians*, 237–38.

110 "Naselenniu Zakarpats'koï Ukraïny hrozyt' strashnyi holod," *Ukraïns'ki robitnychi visty*, 20 Oct. 1932, 4.

111 "Ponad polovyna liudnosty Zakarpats'koï Ukraïny – holoduie" and "V tsarstvi Rumuniï smert', holod i bezrobittia," both in *Ukraïns'ki robitnychi visty*, 29 Nov. 1932, 2; "Epidemiia, holod, i ruina sil's'koho naselennia Pol'shchi i pid Pol'shcheiu," *Ukraïns'ki robitnychi visty*, 29 Nov. 1932, 5.

112 For example, "Holod desiatkuie hutsul's'ke naselennia na Bukovyni," *Ukraïns'ki robitnychi visty*, 24 Jan. 1933, 2; "Na Zakarpats'kii Ukraïni strashnyi holod," *Ukraïns'ki robitnychi visty*, 8 July 1933, 4; and "Pozhvavim kampaniu nasennia dopomohy poterpivchym vid poveni," *Ukraïns'ki robitnychi visty*, 12 Sept. 1933, 2. In spite of such talk, no movement like the one of 1921–23—when tens of thousands of dollars were raised for alleviation purposes in the USSR—ever emerged for starvation relief in western Ukraine, and no alarming stories appeared in the mainstream press.

113 For example, "Za khvist i na sontse – OTUMANIIU," *Ukraïns'ki robitnychi visty*, 18 Apr. 1933, 3 (a reaction to the April 2, 1933, meeting at the Legion Hall, Saskatoon); "Usia ïkhnia pratsia ie – chorno brekhata na Radians'kyi Soiuz," *Ukraïns'ki robitnychi visty*, 13 July 1933, 4; "Lidery ukr. natsionalistiv vzhe ne

maiut' miry u svoïkh brekniakh," *Ukraïns'ki robitnychi visty*, 15 Aug. 1933, 6; and "Chomu vony ne dopomozhut' holoduiuchym Zakh. Ukraïny," *Ukraïns'ki robitnychi visty*, 5 Sept. 1933, 2. Conditions in western Ukraine were covered in Ukrainian-language newspapers abroad. An article in the *Ukrainian Weekly* about *Svoboda* coverage on the famine noted: "As news about the famine in Soviet-occupied Ukraine reached the pages of Svoboda, news about hunger in other Ukrainian territories was also covered on the pages of the newspaper." "The Great Famine: April 1932," *Ukrainian Weekly*, 6 Mar. 1983, 7.

114 See, for example, "Na dopomohu zhertvam poveni na Zakhidnii Ukraïni," *Ukraïns'ki robitnychi visty*, 26 Sept. 1933, 2.

115 H. Slupsky (chairman) and A. Radomsky (secretary), "Resolution of Protest," 16 Apr. 1933, M-988, 93393, Bennett Papers. A resolution addressed to the Polish minister of justice protesting the arrest of workers and peasants in western Ukraine was published in the *Edmonton Bulletin* as a letter to the editor ("Protest," 7 Feb. 1934, 4). A report about arrests of Communists in western Ukraine and central Poland was printed in "221 Reds Arrested in Polish Round-Up," *Montreal Star*, 29 Aug. 1933, 1.

116 Len Wallace, "Fanning the Flames," *Canadian Dimension*, 2 Sept. 2004, 19–24. As to the family's fate, Wallace wrote: "My grandparents were part of the Canadian/American contingent seeking opportunities in a land that was supposed to be the worker's state. The Soviet Union opened its doors and they worked in Siberia. By 1938 a change in the Stalinist party line forced them to leave. My grandparents journeyed to Poland. As the dogs of war sounded, my mother and her sister were allowed to return to Canada. She never saw her parents again."

117 Kolasky, *Shattered Illusion*, 12.

118 Olena Koval'chuk and Tamara Marusyk, *Holodomor 1932–1933rr. v USRR i ukraïns'ka diaspora Pivnichnoï Ameryky* (Chernivtsi: Nashi knyhy, 2010), 48.

119 Ibid., 49.

120 Black, *Canada in the Soviet Mirror*, 43.

121 Vadim Kukushkin, "Back in the USSR," *Beaver* 86, no. 4 (2006): 35. For insight into the fate of Doukhobors who remained, see the testimony by K. Petrus, who mentioned collectivization and arrests in 1934 in his unpublished memoir, "Soviets'ki areshtaty." Kolektsiia konkursu spohadiv, 1947–1948 rr. fond, Oseredok.

122 Kolasky, *Prophets and Proletarians*, 168–69.

123 "Robota ide povnym khodom v SRSR," *Ukraïns'ki robitnychi visty*, 31 Dec. 1932. The industrial city of Makiivka (Donetsk Oblast) is also where German-born Hans Blumenfeld found employment from 1932. Blumenfeld eventually emigrated to Canada and published his autobiography, in which he discussed the famine. See Myron Momryk, "A Western Communist Eyewitness to the Famine," *Holodomor Studies* 3, nos. 1–2 (2011): 123–31.

124 "Lyst selianky-kolhospnytsi z Radians'koï Ukraïny do brata v Kanadi," *Ukraïns'ki robitnychi visty*, 8 Dec. 1932, 3.

125 "Radians'ka vlada dbaie pro robitnykiv i selian v SRSR," *Ukraïns'ki robitnychi visty*, 26 Jan. 1933, 4. What in Riga was being referred to is unclear. Germany had an embassy there, the United States a legation, and the London *Times* an unnamed correspondent. Hiroaki Kuromiya has written of Riga as a place where anti-Soviet activities were planned: "In the 1930s, in the western borderlands as in the eastern borderlands of the Soviet Union, the Japanese and Poles as well as the Japanese and Estonians were secretly engaged in collaborative subversion against the Soviet Union.... Riga, Latvia, where Japan had a military attaché, was a major centre for such collaboration." Kuromiya, *The Voices of the Dead: Stalin's Great Terror in the 1930s* (New Haven: Yale University Press, 2007), 131.

126 "Kanads'kyi robitnyk pro polozhennia v Radians'komu Soiuzi," *Ukraïns'ki robitnychi visty*, 24 Jan. 1933, 4.

127 "V Radians'kim Soiuzi ia pobachyla zovsim inshe zhyttia," *Ukraïns'ki robitnychi visty*, 14 Feb. 1933, 4. Other letters included one from M. Pylypyk—who moved to the USSR in 1933 and was living in Stalinsk, Siberia—to "Comrade Paladiichuk" in St. Catharines, Ontario; and one from S. Kormylo—formerly of Falconbridge, Ontario, who in 1931 moved to the USSR and settled in Krasnouralsk (Sverdlovsk Oblast), Russia—to "Comrade Iahoda" in Sudbury, Ontario. See "Shcho pyshut' robitnyky pro zhyttia v SRSR," *Ukraïns'ki robitnychi visty*, 3 June 1933, 4. Comrade Maziar, who left Canada in 1932, wrote from the industrial city of Magnitogorsk (Chelyabinsk Oblast, Russia). "Shcho pyshe robitnyk pro SRSR," *Ukraïns'ki robitnychi visty*, 3 Oct. 1933, 5.

128 "Perekazhit' nashym voroham, shcho v nas nemaie holodu, i shchodnia ide do lipshoho," *Ukraïns'ki robitnychi visty*, 5 Sept. 1933, 4.

129 "Dopysuvachi pyshut' pro SRSR," *Ukraïns'ki robitnychi visty*, 16 May 1933, 4.

130 "Do zakhidno-ukraïns'kykh robitnykiv i selian, vyhnanykh zlydniamy na emigratsiiu v kapitalistychnu Ameryku," *Ukraïns'ki robitnychi visty*, 21 Sept. 1933, 3. The summer 1933 harvest was the main focus of a letter from Comrade Orydzhuk of the Khliborob commune to Comrade Patek in Winnipeg. "Shcho pyshe robitnyk pro SRSR," *Ukraïns'ki robitnychi visty*, 12 Oct. 1933, 4.

131 "Vrozhai ts'oho roku v SRSR – odyn z naikrashchykh," *Ukraïns'ki robitnychi visty*, 26 Sept. 1933, 4. A successful harvest was also stressed by Omeliian Kovaliv, who, in a letter to Canada, dismissed stories of a famine in Ukraine as a "fable." Kovaliv, a railway construction worker, said he resided about two thousand kilometres from Ukraine, in a place called Trubstroi. "Kazka pro 'holod' v Rad. Soiuzi," *Ukraïns'ki robitnychi visty*, 10 Apr. 1934, 5.

132 "Na Leningradskom miasom kombinate," *Kanadskii gudok*, 6 Apr. 1933, 3.

133 "Shakhtary Donbassa shliut privetstvie 4-mu S'ezdu RRFK Kanady," *Kanadskii gudok*, 22 June 1933, 5.

134 "Anti-Sovetskaia politika Benneta," *Kanadskii gudok*, 23 Feb. 1933, 6.

135 "November 7th," *Kanadskii gudok*, 1 Nov. 1933, 6.

136 "Pervomaiskii privet chlenam RRFK ot raboche krest'ianskoi militsii S.-Kavkazskogo Kraia," *Kanadskii gudok*, 1 June 1933, 4; "Chto mne prishlos' vydet' za shest' mesiatsev v Sovetskom Soiuze," *Kanadskii gudok*, 6 July 1933, 2–3.

137 "Pishut v Kanadskii gudok iz Sovetskogo Soiuza," *Kanadskii gudok*, 26 Jan. 1933, 4.
138 "Pokonchil samoubiistvom N.A. Skrypnik," *Kanadskii gudok*, 13 July 1933, 1.
139 "'Slukhi o golode v SSSR - giusnaia lozh' kulakov i vreditelei' pishut nam trudiashchiesia iz Sovetskogo Soiuza," *Kanadskii gudok*, 6 July 1933, 2.
140 On Robert Cromie, see "'SSSR mozhno zavidovat,'" *Kanadskii gudok*, 24 Aug. 1933, 4; on Ketchum, see "Fashchizatsiia obshchestvennogo mneniia i antisovetskaia propaganda kanadskogo pravitel'stva," *Kanadskii gudok*, 27 Dec. 1933, 2.
141 Alexander Porayko to Sofia Kyforuk, n.d., Kyforuk/Nay Fonds 2005.022/4, Bohdan Medwidsky Ukrainian Folklore Archives, Edmonton. Mention is made of Porayko (in earlier years) in "Sofia Kyforuk's Story," *Virtual Museum of Canada* (Ottawa: Canadian Museum of History, 2014–), accessed 11 Dec. 2014, http://www.virtualmuseum.ca/sgc-cms/histoires_de_chez_nous-community_memories/pm_v2.php?id=story_line&lg=English&fl=0&ex=464&sl=5523&pos=1.
142 Porayko to Kyforuk, n.d., Bohdan Medwidsky Ukrainian Folklore Archives. O. L. Leshchenko alludes to the fate of commune members before, during, and after the famine: "The fate of many Canadian communards became tragic. In the collectivization campaign all forms of agricultural associations were liquidated other than collective farms and state farms. The remnants of the former Canadian communards were persecuted. They were thrown into concentration camps, some died during the 1932–33 famine." Leshchenko, "Z istoriï sil'kohospodars'kykh komun kanads'kykh ukraïntsiv na Ukraïni," *Ukraïns'kyi istorychnyi zhurnal* 10 (1991): 69 (my translation). See also the interview with Stanyslav Lazebnyk in "Ukraïntsi za kordonom: ekskurs v istoriiu," *Personal Plius* 20, no. 282 (2008), http://www.personal-plus.net/272/3274.html; and O. S. Kramar, "Tovarystva tekhnichnoï dopomohy ta reemihratsiia zarubizhnoï ukraïns'koï hromads'kosti u politytsi komunistychnoho rezhymu (1921–1925 rr.)," *Hileia: Naukovyi visnyk* (Kyiv) 20 (2009): 70–79.
143 Members of the Bienfait "Red Hall" were aware of troubles in the Soviet countryside but believed that the scale of the disturbances was "exaggerated by critics of the Soviet experiment and that, in any case, they were really growing pains of a society that was refashioning itself along untrodden ways. They chose instead to pay attention to well-publicized examples of new collective farms that were mechanizing their production and working well." Stephen Lyon Endicott, *Bienfait: The Saskatchewan Miners' Struggle of '31* (Toronto: University of Toronto Press, 2002) 40.
144 "Informatsiine viche pro holod na Ukraïni," *Ukraïns'kyi holos*, 6 Dec. 1933, 2.
145 Kolasky, *Shattered Illusion*, 20–21. For more discussion on the association and related developments, see Andrij Makuch, "Fighting for the Soul of the Ukrainian Progressive Movement in Canada: The Lobayites and the Ukrainian Labour-Farmer Temple Association," in *Re-Imagining Ukrainian-Canadians: History, Politics, and Identity*, ed. Rhonda L. Hinther and Jim Mochoruk (Toronto: University of Toronto Press, 2011), 376–400.
146 "Irchan Reported Arrested in Ukraine, Charged with Counter-Revolutionary Activities," *Weekly Summary Report on Revolutionary Organizations and Agitators in Canada* (RCMP Security Bulletin No. 721), 29 Aug. 1934, 240.

147 "Arrests of Irchan and Sembay Cause Resentment among Ukrainians," *Weekly Summary Report on Revolutionary Organizations and Agitators in Canada* (RCMP Security Bulletin No. 728), 17 Oct. 1934, 340.

148 For example, "Irchan kontrrevoliutsionerom?," *Ukraïns'ki visty*, 13 June 1934, 1; and "Z Bol'shevyts'koï presy v Kanadi: Irchan 'kontrrevoliutsionerom,'" *Ukraïns'ki visty*, 15 Aug. 1934, 4. Excerpts of a letter written on June 19, 1934, by Olga Sembay to a brother-in-law, Julius Sembay (a farmer at Argyle, Manitoba)—in which she discussed the background to the death of her husband—were published in "Deported 'Red' Reported Killed by Soviet O.G.P.U.," *Winnipeg Tribune*, 30 Jan. 1937, 2. Myroslav Irchan was executed in 1937. On the challenges posed to the ULFTA leadership by the Soviet arrests of Irchan and Sembay, as well as by the famine, see Rhonda L. Hinther, "'Sincerest Revolutionary Greetings': Progressive Ukrainians in Twentieth Century Canada" (PhD diss., McMaster University, 2005), 68–70. Decades later, in the twilight of the Soviet Union's existence, a publication about Ukrainian Canadian relations with Soviet Ukraine—whose authors included members of the Association of United Ukrainian Canadians (a later successor to the ULFTA)—addressed the matter of the famine: It stated that ULFTA members "were victims of fraud." While millions of people died from famine in Soviet Ukraine, official propaganda "contrary to obvious facts" claimed that no such disaster existed—only "some food difficulties"; the ULFTA "took for granted this version and defended it." A. M. Shlepakov and N. M. Kravchenko, *Ukraïns'ki kanadtsi v istorychnykh zv'iazkakh iz zemleiu bat'kiv* (Kyiv: Dnipro, 1990), 113 (my translation).

149 See "I Was a Communist Agitator," *Ottawa Citizen*, 16 Nov. 1936, 20. The unnamed "agitator" worked in a meat-packing plant in Toronto and there met Ukrainians and even learned some Ukrainian words. One installment in the "I Was a Communist Agitator" series discussed Soviet Ukraine and Mykola Skrypnyk; it offered the following version of Skrypnyk's death: "According to one story, Skrypnyk, heart-broken at the action of the real Russians, committed suicide. That is the official story, but there are well-founded rumors that he was shot by Postyshe[v] during a heated argument." "I Was a Communist Agitator," *Winnipeg Free Press*, 3 Dec. 1936, 3. In 1953, S. O. Pidhainy recalled having met two miners who followed Myroslav Irchan from Canada at an "overcrowded transitory prison" in Kharkiv in 1933. Pidhainy, "Portraits of Solowky Exiles," in *Black Deeds of the Kremlin: A White Book*, ed. S. O. Pidhainy (Toronto: Ukrainian Association of Victims of Russian Communist Terror, 1953), 1:364.

Chapter Seven

1 "Russian Conditions," *Edmonton Journal*, 6 Dec. 1933, 4.
2 "Zhyttia nashoho narodu v sovits'kii nevoli," *Novyi shliakh*, 23 Jan. 1934, 2.
3 Ibid.

4 Translation from Orysia Paszczak Tracz, "Our Traditions in Literature: Shevchenko and Pysanky," *Ukrainian Weekly*, 4 Apr. 2004, 13, 26. A *pysanka* is a decorated Ukrainian Easter egg.

5 "Zhyttia nashoho narodu v sovits'kii nevoli," *Novyi shliakh*, 6 Feb. 1934, 3. Slusarenko was mentioned in a report in the *Edmonton Journal* about the annual convention of the Ukrainian National Federation held in Edelweiss Hall in February 1934, which condemned "Bolshevism." She was one of the speakers ("Says Bolshevism Menaces Canada," 1 Mar. 1934, 14).

6 D. E. Iandova, "Strakhittia holodu na Ukraïni," *Ukraïns'kyi holos*, 3 Jan. 1934, 4–5, and 10 Jan. 1934, 7. In April 1933, the *Toronto Telegram* announced the release of a Soviet film, titled *Prosperity*, about life in the United States ("Soviet Has Its Joke at Hollywood's Cost," 15 Apr. 1933, 39). Settlement in Ukraine from Russia was discussed in *Ukraïns'kyi holos*: a story in the paper said that in a period that stretched from before the harvest of 1933 to March 1934, 221,000 people plus their families had settled in Ukraine from Russia ("Kolonizatsiia Ukraïny moskaliamy," 11 July 1934, 12). According to Wsevolod W. Isajiw, from 1926 to 1939 the population of Ukraine increased by 12 per cent. The number of Russians in the republic rose by 67 per cent in that period, while the number of Ukrainians grew by less than 2 per cent. The Russian increase occurred chiefly in the cities. Isajiw, "The Impact of the Man-Made Famine on the Structure of Ukrainian Society," in *Famine in Ukraine 1932–1933*, ed. Roman Serbyn and Bohdan Krawchenko (Edmonton: CIUS Press, 1986), 143.

7 "Holod na Ukraïni," *Ukraïns'kyi holos*, 4 Oct. 1933, 2.

8 "Lysty z holodnyi Ukraïny," *Ukraïns'kyi holos*, 11 Oct. 1933, 5. Accounts providing specific details of enforcement at the local level are few, probably because it was believed that such details would not evade the censors or because letters containing such information may have been confiscated. The role of Mennonites and others in carrying out Soviet policies in Mennonite districts of Ukraine before and during the famine years is discussed in Colin P. Neufeldt, "The Public and Private Lives of Mennonite Kolkhoz Chairmen in the Khortytsia and Molochansk German National Raiony in Ukraine (1928–1934)," *Carl Beck Papers in Russian and East European Studies*, no. 2305 (Jan. 2015): 1–87.

9 "Starvation in the Ukraine," *Times*, 18 Aug. 1934, 6.

10 United Hetman Classocrats to the Earl of Denbigh (unsigned copy), 18 Aug. 1934, "Famine in Ukraine (Anti-Bolshevik Campaign, n.d., 1933–1934)" file, I-11 (b) – Fb.2-3, Elcheshen fonds. The letter expressed heartfelt gratitude on behalf of forty-two branches of the pro-Hetmanite organization in Canada.

11 Elizabeth Skoropadsky-Kuzhim, born in 1899, was a sculptor whose works were exhibited in the Netherlands, Finland, and the United States in addition to Germany. She died on February 16, 1976. See "Elizabeth Skoropadsky, Leader of Hetman Movement, Dies," *Ukrainian Weekly*, 28 Feb. 1976, 1, 3.

12 Committee to Aid Victims of the Famine in Ukraine (Berlin) to Committee to Aid Victims of the Famine in Ukraine (Warsaw), 30 Nov. 1933, reel 3 (Correspondence, General), Skoropadska Papers.

13 "Sprava dopomohy holoduiuchym v Ukraïni," Nov. 1933, Berlin, reel 10 (Other Documents), Skoropadska Papers.
14 "Canadian Ukrainians are willing to supply the starving in Ukraine with their grain and offered the Lviv Central Committee to send one cargo ship of wheat as soon as possible." "Ukrajinské a cizí pomocné výbory," *Hlad na Ukrajině*, nos. 1–2 (1933): 24 (my translation). The group from which this offer originated, and when, is not clear, but Milena Rudnycka mentioned the offer at a meeting in Stanyslaviv on October 28, 1933. According to a report on that meeting, prepared for the Stanyslaviv district governor, "In Canada, Ukrainian farmers have committed to sending one vessel with grain for Ukrainians in Russia." See document no. 165 ("30 October 1933, Stanyslaviv. Memorandum for the Stanyslaviv District Governor regarding the Proceedings of the Day of Ukrainian National Mourning in the District") in *Poland and Ukraine in the 1930s–1940s: Unknown Documents from the Archives of the Secret Services*, vol. 7, *Holodomor: The Great Famine in Ukraine 1932–1933*, ed. Jerzy Bednarek (Warsaw: Institute of National Remembrance, Commission of the Prosecution of Crimes against the Polish Nation, 2009), 438. It is evident that the role that surplus Canadian cereal stocks could play in famine relief was a recurring theme. For one such example, see document 182 ("6 lutego 1934 memorial Łewka Czykałenki poświęcony akcji pomocy glodującym zorganizowanej przez diasporę ukraińską") in *Hołodomor 1932–1933. Wielki Głód na Ukrainie w dokumentach polskiej dyplomacji i wywiadu*, comp. Jan Jacek Bruski (Warsaw: Wyd. Polski Instytut Spraw Międzynarodowych, 2008), 550.
15 Elizabeth Skoropadsky to Mowinckel, 4 Oct. 1933, reel 7 (Administrative Documents), Skoropadska Papers.
16 V. de Korostovetz to Mowinckel, 7 Oct. 1933, reel 1 (Correspondence, Official), Skoropadska Papers.
17 Hetman Skoropadsky to President Roosevelt, 28 Oct. 1933, copy, reel 2 (Correspondence, Official), Skoropadska Papers. On November 4, 1933, Oleksander Shulhyn (A. Choulguine), head of the Ukrainian Supreme Emigration Council, sent a telegram on behalf of Ukrainian emigrants in nine countries to President Roosevelt in support of the Ukrainian-American request that a mission be sent to Soviet Ukraine to investigate the famine. See "Emigratsiina rada vyslala telegramu do Ruzvelta," *Kanadyis'kyi farmer*, 6 Dec. 1933, 9. A telegram was also sent from the famine relief committee in Prague. See "Z Evropy pidtrymuiut' domahannia Amerykans'kykh ukraïntsiv," *Kanadyis'kyi farmer*, 6 Dec. 1933, 9. For other examples of groups that sent letters to the U.S. president, see Oleh Romanyschyn, Orest Steciw, and Andrew Gregorovich, comps., *Holodomor: The Ukrainian Genocide 1932–1933* (Toronto: League of Ukrainian Canadians and Ucrainica Research Institute, 2014), 98.
18 Berlin Committee to Aid Victims of the Famine in Ukraine to President Roosevelt, November 5, 1933, copy, reel 2 (Correspondence, Official), Skoropadska Papers. At least one other state leader may have also been contacted by the committee. A copy of a letter dated November 12, 1934, with

no signatures or names, was directed to Benito Mussolini. The letter, written in French, read in part: "Your Excellency, it is impossible that you, who have protected by special edict the life of birds in Italy, could turn a cold and impassive eye to the suffering and death of a whole generation of children in Ukraine!" Said to be enclosed were extracts of translated (presumably into French) letters received by the committee (presumably from Ukraine). Reel 4 (Correspondence, General), Skoropadska Papers. In December 1933 the USSR and Italy reached a cooperation agreement. "Reach Agreement on Soviet-Fascist Pact," *Winnipeg Free Press*, 4 Dec. 1933, 4.

19 "The Starving People of Ukraine," *Catholic Times*, 10 Mar. 1934, copy, reel 1 (Correspondence, Official), Skoropadska Papers.

20 Pavlo Skoropadsky to Sir Paul Makins, n.d., London, reel 1 (Correspondence, Official), Skoropadska Papers. From a letter that was sent to Edmonton in December 1933 it may be inferred that, in addition to Britain, the Berlin Committee had representatives in Switzerland, Lithuania, Czechoslovakia, and Romania. Committee to Aid Victims of the Famine in Ukraine (Berlin) to USSAC, 27 Dec. 1933, reel 2 (Correspondence, Official), Skoropadska Papers.

21 "Komitet dopomohy holoduiuchym na Ukraïni" and "Komitet dopomohy holoduiuchym na Ukraïni: Zaklyk," *Kanadyis'kyi farmer*, 17 Jan. 1934, 12; copy available in reel 12 (Newspaper Clippings), Skoropadska Papers. In addition to the Elizabeth Skoropadsky–led committee, there was a second committee in the German capital, which was "radical-democratic in orientation." Bohachevsky-Chomiak, *Feminists despite Themselves*, 277.

22 "Na pomich holoduiuchym na Velykii Ukraïny," *Ukraïns'ki visty*, 17 Jan. 1934, 6. See also D. Marcynuk to the Committee to Aid Victims of the Famine in Ukraine (Berlin), 12 Jan. 1934, reel 2 (Correspondence, Official), Skoropadska Papers. There is a reference to the recent formation of a "Sich Red Cross" within the USSAC, which was selling postcards of the Berlin Committee for the cause of famine relief, in "Visti z Alberty: Edmonton," *Kanadyis'kyi farmer*, 31 Jan. 1934, 6.

23 "Protestatsiine viche," *Ukraïns'ki visty*, 24 Jan. 1934, 6; "Na pomich holoduiuchym na Velykii Ukraïni," *Ukraïns'ki visty*, 31 Jan. 1934, 6. On the Derwent sum, see Petro Romaniuk to the Committee to Aid Victims of the Famine in Ukraine (Berlin), 18 Dec. 1933, reel 2 (Correspondence, Official), Skoropadska Papers. The funds in Derwent were probably collected at a public meeting in the district on December 17, 1933. Reference to a planned meeting on that date was made in USSAC (Derwent) to Committee to Aid Victims of the Famine in Ukraine (Berlin), n.d., reel 2 (Correspondence, Official), Skoropadska Papers.

24 Committee to Aid Victims of the Famine in Ukraine (Berlin) to USSAC (Derwent), 10 Jan. 1934, reel 2 (Correspondence, Official), Skoropadska Papers.

25 USSAC (Derwent) to Committee to Aid Victims of the Famine in Ukraine (Berlin), n.d., reel 2 (Correspondence, Official), Skoropadska Papers. In March 1934, *Ukraïns'ki visty* reported on collections that were sent to the Berlin Committee from Rossburn, Manitoba ($6.50), and Monitor, Alberta ($4.65). "Zbirky na narodni potreby," *Ukraïns'ki visty*, 7 Mar. 1934, 6. That month—at a talk titled

"Contemporary Bolshevism" (by L. Nakhvostach), in Skaro on March 10—$4.08 had been raised from the sale of postcards and sent to the Berlin Committee.

26 "MASIUTIN Vasily Nikolaevich, 1884–1955," *Internet Museum of Prints*, accessed 8 Feb. 2016, http://eng.printsmuseum.ru/artist/view/11.

27 Committee to Aid Victims of the Famine in Ukraine (Berlin) to USSAC, 27 Dec. 1933, reel 2 (Correspondence, Official), Skoropadska Papers.

28 See the letter and clipping from Ivan Fedorovich, Regina, 29 Jan. 1934, reel 2 (Correspondence, Official), Skoropadska Papers. Fedorovich referred to the newspaper as the "Der Courier Deutche" [sic], which may have been the Regina newspaper *Der Courier*.

29 See the letters in reel 2 (Correspondence, Official), Skoropadska Papers.

30 USSAC to Committee to Aid Victims of the Famine in Ukraine (Berlin), n.d., reel 2 (Correspondence, Official), Skoropadska Papers.

31 Undated document marked "Strictly confidential," reel 1 (Correspondence, Official), Skoropadska Papers.

32 "Receipt Nr. 4," reel 1 (Correspondence, Official), Skoropadska Papers.

33 Beyond Lviv, such branches existed in Berezhany, Bibrka, Bolekhiv, Buchach, Dobromyl, Horodenka, Horodok, Kalush, Kuty Lutsk, Peremyshl, Pidhaitsi, Rava Ruska, Rivne, Rohatyn, Sambir, Sniatyn, Sokal, Stanyslaviv, Stryi, Terebovlia, Ternopil, Turka, Volodymyr Volynsky, Zbarazh, and Zhovkva. See Kulchytsky, "Western Relief Efforts," 153n4.

34 Ibid. On the committees in Galicia and Czechoslovakia, see "Pomich dlia holoduiuchoï Ukraïny," *Kanadyis'kyi farmer*, 23 Aug. 1933, 1; and "Ukraïns'ki organizatsiï dlia holoduiuchykh na Ukraïni," *Kanadyis'kyi farmer*, 30 Aug. 1933, 12 (which noted that thirty-one organizations came together in Prague for the purpose of famine relief work). On Vienna, see "Chuzhyntsi organizuiut' dopomohovu aktsiiu holodnym na Velykii Ukraïny," *Kanadyis'kyi farmer*, 30 Aug. 1933, 1. In June 1934, the *Ukrainian Weekly*, noting that Ukrainian immigrants in Belgium had set up a committee in the summer of 1933, reported the formation of a similar "honorary committee" that included various Belgians in its ranks, including S. Terminde, a professor at Louvain University, R. Biard, an engineer, and General Helebot, a "former Minister of Belgium" ("Belgian-Ukrainian Relief Committee for Starving Soviet Ukraine," 8 June 1934, 1).

35 Kulchytsky, "Western Relief Efforts," 154.

36 Hetman Skoropadsky to Sir Paul Makins, 8 July 1934, reel 1 (Correspondence, Official), Skoropadska Papers. In a July 1934 letter, Elizabeth Skoropadsky wrote about priests as follows: "We have many letters from priests, but it would be dangerous to send them about too much. The priests are persecuted most dreadfully and...receive no help what ever [sic]. They belong to the category of people which are called 'Lishenzi' [*lishentsy*], that is to say they are superfluous. Those who help a priest also become 'superfluous.' Many priests were forced to divorce their wives because if not the children and wives also would belong to the 'Lishenzi.' It was the only means to save their families from starvation." Elizabeth Skoropadsky to "Auntie Ada," 29 July 1934, reel 5 (Correspondence

with Individuals), Skoropadska Papers. Elsewhere, Skoropadsky wrote of a family headed by a priest who had been exiled to the Solovetsky Islands. The seven children were also left without their mother, who had died. The children lived with friends who were not in a position to support them. The Berlin Committee sent twenty marks, for which were obtained 128 kilograms of rye flour and 30 kilograms of barley corn. "Nr. 5," reel 1 (Correspondence, Official), Skoropadska Papers. The *lishentsy* were mentioned in an Associated Press article published in the *Globe*—prior to the famine—with the title "Slow Starvation of Hated Kulaks to be Hastened." This article noted that according to *Izvestia*, three million kulaks in the USSR had been required to register with the police to prevent them from obtaining jobs in government departments and to induce them to perform manual labour "or cease to exist." Kulaks were accused of pretending not to be from their group and then taking government jobs and also of using these jobs as a means of committing sabotage. The article reported that the property of the kulaks had been confiscated, and thousands had been deported to the Soviet Arctic. The extermination of the kulak class was "looked upon by the Government as one of its most important policies." The article in the *Globe* concluded by stating that among the "outclassed" (with the kulaks) were "'nepmen,' or former merchants and traders, and the 'leshenitz' [*lishentsy*], or priests, former Czarist officers, Ministers of State, and others of their class" ("Slow Starvation of Hated Kulaks to Be Hastened," 23 Apr. 1931, 1).

37   Sir Paul Makins to Hetman Skoropadsky, 11 July 1934, reel 1 (Correspondence, Official), Skoropadska Papers. In June 1934, *Ukraïns'ki visty* reported that Pavlo Skoropadsky was visiting London ("Het'man Skoropads'kyi v Londoni," 20 June 1934, 7).

38   On ten dollars that had been sent from Winnipeg to the Berlin Committee from the sale of postcards, for example, see "Vynypeg holoduiuchym na Ukraïni," *Kanadyis'kyi farmer*, 25 July 1934, 8.

39   Extracts from letters in reel 1 (Correspondence, Official), Skoropadska Papers.

40   For example, see "Vypysky z lystiv z Ukraïny. Oryginaly znahotdiat'sia v Komiteti dopomohy holoduiuchym v Ukraïny. –Vannzee-Berlin, Al'zenstr. 17," "Komitet dopomohty holoduiuchym na Ukraïni (Vinnipeg) 1933–1934" file, I-II (b) – Fb.2-3, Elcheshen fonds. Receipt of a fifty-dollar donation was acknowledged and extracts of letters mentioned as having been sent in Berlin Committee to Fr. Gegeichuk, Ottawa, 4 Apr. 1935, reel 4 (Correspondence, General), Skoropadska Papers. Extracts of letters received by the Berlin Committee were published in "Chy holoduiuchym na Ukraïni doruchuiut' dopomohu," *Ukraïns'ki visty*, 11 Apr. 1934, 2.

41   Skoropadsky to Volodymyr Korostovetz, 3 July 1934, reel 1 (Correspondence, Official), Skoropadska Papers.

42   "Bol'shevyky ne puskaiut' pomochi dlia holoduiushykh," *Ukraïns'ki visty*, 7 Nov. 1934, 3.

43   "Soviet Bars Gifts for 'Famine' Relief," *New York Times*, 25 Oct. 1934, 15. According to the report, the main Soviet complaint was against the German

organization Brüder in Not. In the face of contradictory accounts—specifically, press reports of a bountiful Soviet harvest in the autumn of 1933 and subsequent denials of any presence of famine—people engaged in the famine-relief cause had difficulty in determining how to respond. In April 1934, Vladimir Kysilewsky wrote to the Ukrainian Civic Committee for the Salvation of Ukraine, stressing that a principal question that needed an answer was whether there "was a famine in Ukraine *now*" (emphasis in original), that is, after the harvest the Soviets were proudly proclaiming. "That there was a famine in the spring of 1933, the Soviet authorities have acknowledged," Kysilewsky wrote, but they were categorically denying there was one now. "Lyst Ukraïns'koho biuro u Londoni do Hromadians'koho komitetu riatunku u L'vovi vid 23.04.1934 roku," *Elektronnyi arkhiv ukraïns'koho vyzvol'noho rukhu*, accessed 4 June 2015, http://avr.org.ua/index.php/viewDoc/12897/. The famine continued to claim many victims in 1934, but on a much smaller scale than in 1933.

44 V. B. Batytsky to Vladimir Kysilewsky, 14 Oct. 1933, vol. 10, file 20, VJKF.
45 *Kanadyis'kyi farmer*, 5 Apr. 1933, 5.
46 *Ukraïns'kyi holos*, 5 July 1933, 7.
47 *Ukraïns'ki robitnychi visty*, 7 Mar. 1933, 6.
48 "Torgsin," *Canadian Jewish Chronicle*, 16 Sept. 1932, 8. The companies listed were Amalgamated Bank of New York, Am-Derutra Transport Corporation, American Express Company, Manufacturers Trust Company, Postal Telegraph-Cable Company, Public National Bank Trust Company, and Radio Corporation of America.
49 "Torgsin Reduces Rates for Transmission of Packages to Russia," *Canadian Jewish Chronicle*, 27 Jan. 1933, 9.
50 "Prices for Commodities in Torgsin Stores in the U.S.S.R. Reduced 50%," *Canadian Jewish Chronicle*, 13 Oct. 1933, 12.
51 "Torgsin naibil'shyi departamental'nyi stor v sviti," *Kanadyis'kyi farmer*, 9 Aug. 1933, 2. *Ukraïns'ki visty* featured a Torgsin advertisement on June 6, 1934, that included the following goods and prices: men's shoes, 3.7 rubles; men's suit (*muzhes'ki suty*), 7.5 rubles; women's shoes, 3.75 rubles; women's suit (*zhinochyi sut*), 7.3 rubles; children's shoes, 1.8 rubles; children's sweaters, 60 kopecks; coffee (2.5 pounds), 1.5 rubles; flour (2.5 pounds), 0.6 kopecks; sugar (2.5 pounds), 22 kopecks.
52 See, for example, the advertisement in the *Toronto Star*, 27 Feb. 1934, 9. Earlier, in 1932, in an article about the Torgsin stores, the *Toronto Star* had quoted from a Soviet description of the steps to be taken by local citizens and foreigners: "All you have to do is to ask your relatives and even acquaintances abroad to drop into the following banks and make out money transfers to the Torgsin. These remittances may be made for the account of any person and to any amount. Transfers are not subject to any limitation." A list of banks in twenty-five countries outside the USSR was provided ("Food, Bait of Soviet for Foreign Currency," 5 Oct. 1932, 37).

53 "Z poshty 1932–1933 za todishnyi holod," *Ukraïns'kyi Filatelistychnyi Visnyk* (Kyiv) 2 (2002): 26–27. The original letter is in the library of St. Vladimir's Ukrainian Orthodox Church, Calgary.
54 "Secured Relief for Five Children Living in Russia," *Winnipeg Free Press*, 30 Nov. 1932, 4; "Got Relief for Family in Russia," *Star-Phoenix*, 30 Nov. 1932, 8.
55 "Victims of Famine," *Star-Phoenix*, 3 Aug. 1933, 4. A picture of the parents appeared in the *Star-Phoenix* as well as in *Ukraïns'kyi holos*. The article that accompanied the picture in the Ukrainian-language paper referred to two letters that had been received from Bohuslava, Kyiv povit, in Ukraine. One, dated April 24, 1933, was from Sachynsky's sister, and the other, dated June 24, 1933, from his brother. In the former, Sachynsky's sister informed him that their mother had passed away on March 20. (The latter was the one translated into English in the *Star-Phoenix*.) "Zhertvy holodu v bol'shevyts'komu raiu," *Ukraïns'kyi holos*, 30 Aug. 1933, 5.
56 Luisa Wensel to Louisa and Robert Cerezke, 16 July 1932, English translation, accession no. 2008.0002, box 1, file 7, Luisa Cerezke fonds, Provincial Archives of Alberta, Edmonton (hereafter, Cerezke fonds). The address provided was Kolonia Pen'ki, Taukivski Silrada, Iemilchynskyi Raion, "Na Volyni," Kyiv Oblast. Today, Iemilchynskyi/Iemilchyne Raion is in Zhytomyr Oblast.
57 Luisa Wensel to Louisa and Robert Cerezke, 20 Jan. 1933, accession no. 2008.0002, box 1, file 8, Cerezke fonds. In the English translation, the words "We live in distress" are underlined. The words in German were "*Not Not*," meaning "distress" or "need."
58 Luisa Wensel to Louisa and Robert Cerezke, 20 Mar. 1933, accession no. 2008.0002, box 1, file 9, Cerezke fonds.
59 Luisa Wensel to Louisa and Robert Cerezke, 20 May 1933, accession no. 2008.0002, box 1, file 10, Cerezke fonds.
60 Martin, "Collectivization, Famine, and Terror," 38. Martin adds, in reference to Ukrainian Germans, that by April 1934 "the cost of allowing the transfers had become higher than the value of the foreign currency received. Transfers were now stigmatized as 'Hitler help,' and a wave of terror was launched against individuals said to have organized the movement" (ibid). For more on the role of the Torgsin stores in financing industrialization, see Elena A. Osokina, *Zoloto dlia industrializatsii: Torgsin* (Moscow: ROSSPEN, 2009).
61 "Silver Cross Women Bear Torches before Cenotaph," *Toronto Star*, 10 Nov. 1933, 30.
62 "Chinese Women Give $200 for Missions," *Toronto Star*, 2 Dec. 1933, 22. On China, see also "Famine and Death Follows Drought in Shensi, China," *Winnipeg Free Press*, 17 June 1933, 29; "Flood, Famine Threatening in North China," *Winnipeg Tribune*, 15 July 1933, 3; and "Millions Facing Famine Spectre in North China," *Toronto Star*, 15 July 1933, 15. Local Chinese government relief efforts were reported in "Strashnyi holod u Kytaiu," *Kanadyis'kyi farmer*, 15 Mar. 1933, 9.
63 "Posol Luchkovych bachyv 'bidnykh' didychiv v Halychyni, a ne bachyv bidnykh selian," *Ukraïns'ki robitnychi visty*, 6 Feb. 1934, 7. The author of the piece, critical of Luchkovich, noted that the MP was interviewed by a local "bourgeois" newspaper.

64 On the affiliation of the United Farmers of Alberta with the CCF, see "U.F.A. Joins New Third Party," *Winnipeg Free Press*, 19 Jan. 1933, 1. Luchkovich served as a member of Parliament from 1926 to 1935.
65 The article from which MacNicol quoted was "Russia Faces Crisis Year: Many Near Starvation," *Toronto Star*, 31 July 1933, 1, 5.
66 Dominion of Canada, *Hansard*, 17th Parl., 5th sess., vol. 1 (1934): 264–84. Nearly three decades later, Luchkovich wrote an open letter to Dean Rusk, the U.S. secretary of state. The letter concerned a decision to exclude Ukraine, along with Armenia and Georgia, "from the nations that were to have the support of the Department of State as being subjugated nations of Eastern Europe." The letter also mentioned the famine. When he became an MP, Luchkovich wrote from Edmonton, "it was shocking to me in the extreme how little regard was paid to the death of millions of Ukrainian peasants who died in the Communist-inspired famine of 1932–1933." It seemed to him then "that the death of an alley cat that had wandered into a park was cause for a greater commotion than the demise of such a colossal number of Ukrainian farmers." Where, he asked, "was our world conscience? Did any country speak out with righteous indignation against such genocide?" It was, he said, "extremely painful." Luchkovich, "An Open Letter to Mr. Dean Rusk," *Ukrainian Review* 9, nos. 1–2 (1962): 104–6.
67 Gerald Schmitz, *The Famine in the Ukraine, 1932–33: A Canadian Perspective after Fifty Years* (Ottawa: Library of Parliament, 1982), 44.
68 The *Edmonton Journal* and *Calgary Herald* discussed Luchkovich's contribution to the debate, but did not mention his references to the famine. "Both Liberals and Tories Flay C.C.F. in Parliament," *Edmonton Journal*, 6 Feb. 1934, 2; "Heaps Motion Is Accepted," *Calgary Herald*, 6 Feb. 1934, 2. The *Herald* also carried a report that day about an address on the USSR by Robert Cromie, before the Young Men's Canadian Club in Montreal ("Cromie Says Average Russian as Contented as Average Canadian," 6 Feb. 1934, 5).
69 "La résolution Heaps touchant la diminution des heures de travail au pays est adoptée," *La Presse*, 6 Feb. 1933, 8. For coverage of the debate in *Le Devoir*, see first and last page of February 6, 1934, issue.
70 "Cannibalism in Russia," *Border Cities Star*, 12 Feb. 1934, 2.
71 "Woodsworth Reveals C.C.F. Program Commons to Face Strong Criticism," *Winnipeg Tribune*, 6 Feb. 1934, 2.
72 "Posol Luchkovych hovoryv v parliament pro holod na Ukraïni," *Ukraïns'ki visty*, 14 Feb. 1934, 1; "Posol Luchkovych vidmozhovuies' vid bol'shyvyzmu," *Ukraïns'kyi holos*, 14 Feb. 1934, 8; "Z dominial'noho parliament," *Kanadyis'kyi farmer*, 14 Feb. 1934, 1. See also "Z sesiï dominial'noho parliamentu," *Novyi shliakh*, 13 Feb. 1934, 1, 4.
73 "Ukrainians in Canada," *Ukrainian Bureau Bulletin*, June 1934, M-1316, 391071, Bennett Papers.
74 [Unknown] to Ralph Webb, 16 Feb. 1934, unsigned draft, and D. M. Elcheshen to Mayor R. H. Webb, 3 Mar. 1934, and R. H. Webb to D. M. Elcheshen, 7 Mar. 1934, all in "Webb, R.H. – 1933–1936" file, I-9 (b) – F6 – 2–4, Elcheshen fonds.

Elcheshen was one of the founders of the Ukrainian Conservative Club and secretary of the St. Raphael Ukrainian Immigrants' Welfare Association. He ran as a Conservative in the Manitoba provincial elections of 1932. Both Elcheshen and Webb addressed a meeting held at the Ukrainian hall in Brooklands, Winnipeg. See "Elcheshen Named as Candidate by Ukrainian Group," *Winnipeg Free Press*, 22 Apr. 1932, 6; "Candidates in the Field for Provincial Election," *Winnipeg Free Press*, 6 June 1932, 18; and *Winnipeg Tribune*, 3 June 1932, 2.

75 "Stvoreno Komitet dopomohy holoduiuchym Sovits'kii Ukraïni," *Novyi shliakh*, 20 Feb. 1934. The delegates at the founding meeting included P. Baidak (Canadian Ukrainian Institute Prosvita), D. Hunkevych (Hunkevich) and O. Vabynets (Ukrainian National Home), Mr. H. Kuz and Mr. Iaremii (Markian Shashkevych "Ridna Shkola"), Mr. Vozniak (Prosvita Reading Association), M. Stechyshyn, editor of *Ukraïns'kyi holos* (Ukrainian Self-Reliance League of Canada), S. Kutnyi [Kutney] (Ukrainian War Veterans' Association), O. Malofii [Malofie] and V. K. Chyz (USSAC), Mrs. Kovbel (Mutual Aid Society, Branch 1), I. Melnychuk (Mutual Benefit Association of St. Nicholas, Branch 15), Mr. Pelekh (Mutual Benefit Association of St. Nicholas, headquarters), A. Zahariichuk [Zaharychuk] (Ukrainian School Teachers' Association), and D. M. Elcheshin and I. Pecheniuk [Petcheniuk] (St. Raphael Ukrainian Immigrants' Welfare Association). At a second meeting, on January 29, delegates from several other organizations took part, namely, the Ukrainian National Federation, the Ukrainian Young Women's League, the D. Vitovsky Ukrainian Sich Riflemen Society, and the Prometei (Prometheus) Ukrainian Students' Circle.

76 "Ukrainians to Assist Needy in Homeland," *Winnipeg Tribune*, 2 Feb. 1934, 6. The executive comprised A. Zaharychuk, presiding chairman; D. M. Hunkevich, vice-chairman; M. Kutney; A. Malofie, treasurer; Dr. T. Datskiw, D. M. Elcheshen, and J. Petcheniuk, editorial committee; and W. C. Chyz and J. Melnychuk, auditors. See also "Fund to Be Raised for Ukraine Famine Victims," *Winnipeg Tribune*, 25 Jan. 1934, 5.

77 "Anti-Radical Drive Started by Ukrainians," *Winnipeg Tribune*, 12 Mar. 1934, 4.

78 "Anti-Radical Meeting Held by Ukrainians," *Winnipeg Tribune*, 19 Mar. 1934, 16.

79 "Formation of Anti-Fascist League Scored," *Winnipeg Tribune*, 26 Mar. 1934, 6.

80 For example, the committee's intention to hold a special meeting at the Ukrainian National Home (corner of Burrows and McGregor), where delegates of "all Ukrainian organizations" would discuss plans to aid the starving in Soviet Ukraine. "Relief Committee," *Winnipeg Tribune*, 17 Aug. 1934, 2.

81 "Would Suppress Reds," *Calgary Herald*, 14 Mar. 1934, 5.

Chapter Eight

1 Lord Phillimore to Michael Luchkovich, 20 June 1934, vol. 2, file 24, Luchkovich Papers.

2 Lord Phillimore to Michael Luchkovich, 10 July 1934, vol. 2, file 24, Luchkovich Papers.
3 "Says Free Press Is Driving Force," *Ottawa Journal*, 8 May 1934, 20; Dominion of Canada, *Hansard*, 17th Parl., 5th sess., vol. 2 (1934): 1710.
4 Lord Phillimore (Coppid Hall, Henley-on-Thames) to Prime Minister Richard B. Bennett, 6 Sept. 1934, M-1091, 268880–1, Bennett Papers.
5 "Soviet and the League," *Times*, 8 Sept. 1934, 13.
6 Glazov, *Canadian Policy toward Khrushchev's Soviet Union*, 6.
7 D. Yakimischak to R. B. Bennett, telegram, M-1091, 268861–2, Bennett Papers. The Ukrainian Famine Relief Committee had drafted the telegram at a meeting held at the Ukrainian National Home Association on Burrows Avenue and McGregor Street. See "Ukrainians Protest Repression by Soviets," *Winnipeg Tribune*, 1 Sept. 1934, 2.
8 Ukrainian Self-Reliance League of Canada (M. Stechishin and W. Batycky, Winnipeg) to R. B. Bennett, telegram, n.d., M-1091, 268904–5, Bennett Papers.
9 "Précis of the Memorandum of Alexandre Choulguine, Delegate of the National Ukrainian Government in Exile, etc., on the Candidature of the U.S.S.R. and the Ukraine," M-1091, 268869–70, Bennett Papers. In October 1933, the Australian newspaper *Barrier Miner* (Broken Hill, New South Wales), without elaborating, asserted that the "Soviet is making frantic efforts to discredit the statements of M. Choulquine [sic], the ex-Foreign Minister…, who personally appealed to the Council of the League of Nations for assistance" ("Starvation in Russia," 2 Oct. 1933, 1).
10 R. K. Finlayson (Mayfair Hotel, London) to Alexandre Choulguine (Geneva), 26 July 1933, M-1031, 192285, Bennett Papers; A. Choulguine (Geneva) to the president of the Canadian delegation at the International Monetary and Economic Conference in London, 11 July 1933, M-1031, 192278, Bennett Papers. A letter about Ukraine that Choulguine wrote to the British prime minister, Ramsay MacDonald, on August 3, 1933, was published in *Ukraïns'kyi holos* ("Bez Ukraïny nema ekonomichnoï pidbudovy Evropy," 30 Aug. 1933, 5). Later, Choulguine published an article about Ukraine in a University of London journal: Alexander Shulgin [Choulguine], "Ukraine and Its Political Aspirations," *Slavonic and East European Review* 13, no. 38 (1935): 350–62, esp. 354–55.
11 Liaison Committee of Women's International Organizations (London, UK) to R. J. Sandler, 13 Sept. 1934, M-1091, 268935, Bennett Papers. Lady Aberdeen, president of the International Council of Women, was no stranger to the dominion. She was the founder of the Victorian Order of Nurses for Canada and her husband was a former Governor General of Canada.
12 "Wide Starvation in Russia Feared," *New York Times*, 1 July 1934, 13; "Envoy Denies Starvation," *New York Times*, 1 July 1934, 13.
13 "Famine in Soviet Union," *New York Times*, 11 July 1934, 16. See also the letter to the editor by Peter Khrisanfov (attaché, USSR embassy in Washington) titled "'Starvation in Soviet Union,'" *New York Times*, 14 July 1934, 12; and Duggan's

letter, titled "Mr. Duggan's Position," *New York Times*, 4 Aug. 1934, 10 (clarifying that when he spoke of famine, he was referring to famine specifically in 1932–1933).

14 "Famine over Russia," *Winnipeg Free Press*, 26 July 1934, 13. The *Charlottetown Guardian* quoted from the *Free Press* editorial in its own ("Famine over Russia," 1 Aug. 1934, 4).

15 "Millions of Russians Face Starvation, Says Geneva Investigator," *Winnipeg Tribune*, 20 July 1934, 1.

16 Stechisin [Stechyshyn], Novak, Dackiw, and Sawchuk to Michael Luchkovich, telegram, n.d., vol. 2, file 24, Luchkovich Papers. Luchkovich had been in Winnipeg not long before. On July 28 he had spoken at the Ukrainian War Veterans' Association's hall; a number of individuals associated with the Ukrainian Famine Relief Committee were present, including the lawyer D. Yakimischak, D. Hunkevych, and O. Malofii. "Vp. Posol Luchkovych hostem u Vinnipegu," *Novyi shliakh*, 7 Aug. 1934, 7.

17 Ewald Ammende to Michael Luchkovich, 24 July 1934, vol. 2, file 16, Luchkovich Papers. In a letter to Prime Minister Bennett, which focused on the Ukrainian question in Poland, George I. Kurdydyk raised the question of having a Canadian of Ukrainian background accompany the Canadian delegation to Geneva. See Kurdydyk to Prime Minister Bennett, n.d., M-1091, 268858, Bennett Papers.

18 "Holod na Ukraïni po zhnyvakh nemynuchyi," *Ukraïns'ki visty*, 25 July 1934, 1. For a study of Ammende's role as general secretary of the Congress of European Nationalities, see Martyn Housden, *On Their Own Behalf: Ewald Ammende, Europe's National Minorities and the Campaign for Cultural Autonomy, 1920–1936* (Amsterdam: Rodopi, 2014).

19 "Famine Certainty in Soviet Russia," *Montreal Star*, 25 July 1934, 1–2.

20 "Shcho skazav Benet Amendomu?" *Ukraïns'ki visty*, 12 Sept. 1934, 1.

21 "Hear Bennett Word Would Starve More," *Toronto Star*, 24 July 1934, 1.

22 "Shcho skazav Benet Amendomu?" *Ukraïns'ki visty*, 12 Sept. 1934, 1. The *Ottawa Journal* noted Ammende's presence in Ottawa: "Seen at the Chateau Laurier, Dr. Ammende placed the number of famine deaths in Russia last year as between five million and ten million" ("Millions of Russians Died of Starvation," 23 July 1934, 13). The *Ottawa Citizen*, which earlier had suggested that most of the "yarns" about the famine were possibly exaggerated, reacted to Ammende's visit to Canada by noting that the Save the Children Fund might once more be called upon to assist the destitute, in the Soviet Union but also in Germany. It then further linked the issue to Canada, where people also were in need: "But it is surely a mad world when there are many destitute in Canada similarly in need of relief, although Canadian storehouses are overflowing with food supplies" ("Famine," 24 July 1934, 18).

23 Kysilewsky, "Unedited Diaries," 242 (entry for 7 Sept. 1934), VJKF. Among the Canadian prime minister's papers in Library and Archives Canada is the (English-language) business card of "Ostap Luckyj, MP, President of the Alliance of Ukrainian Agricultural Co-operative Societies 'Centrosoyuz,' Poland"—very

likely given during the time that Bennett was in Geneva. See M-1091, 268747, Bennett Papers.

24 "D-r Amende pro dopomohovu aktsiiu dlia holoduiuchykh u Rosiï," *Svoboda*, 8 Aug. 1934, 3.

25 "Dr. Ammende Departs," *New York Times*, 5 Aug. 1934, N5.

26 "Eval'd Amende—ahent nimets'kykh ta iapons'kykh imperialisty," *Ukraïns'ki robitnychi visty*, 2 Oct. 1934, 3. Moscow's *Izvestia* attacked Ammende's activities as a Nazi provocation. "Holodova katastrofa u SRSR," *Kanadyis'kyi farmer*, 23 Aug. 1933, 9. For discussions related to the subject of Ammende's ties with Germany, see Colin Neufeldt, "Fifth Column? New Light on the Soviet Germans and Their Relationship to the Third Reich," *Journal of Ukrainian Studies* 24 (1988): 70 (describing Ammende as a "Nazi agent"); Walter Laqueur, *Russia and Germany: A Century of Conflict* (London: Weidenfeld & Nicolson, 1965), 186; and J. V. Koshiw, review of *Human Life in Russia* [reprint ed.] by Ewald Ammende, *Journal of Ukrainian Studies* 10, no. 2 (1985): 103. Ammende died in Beijing on April 14, 1936, before the release of the English edition of his book *Human Life in Russia*. "Dr. Ewald Ammende," *Times*, 24 Apr. 1936, 14. In announcing his death, *Ukraïns'ki visty* recalled Ammende's visit to North America and commented that Ukrainians would remember him with gratitude for his "courageous stand against Soviet policies in Ukraine" ("Pomer D-R Eval'd Amende," 6 May 1936, 1).

27 After Ammende's visit to North America, the subject of the famine remained in the news. On August 14, 1934, the *Montreal Star* reported that Berlin newspapers were attacking the Soviet Union on the matter of the famine. Moscow had recently prohibited the Brüder in Not from continuing its activities in the USSR, and the attacks from Berlin were considered a reply to that proscription. One newspaper asserted that 1,500,000 persons had "starved near Kiev this year" and that cannibalism was spreading daily. Soldiers were collecting bodies in Kyiv and burying them without coffins and "sometimes without clothing" ("Papers in Berlin Attacking Russia," 14 Aug. 1934, 5). See also "Berlin Newspapers Tell of Cannibalism in Russia," *Toronto Star*, 14 Aug. 1934, 19.

28 "Iak treba rozumity sobornist'," *Svoboda*, 21 July 1934, 3.

29 Ammende, *Human Life in Russia*, 305–6. A twenty-page report authored by Ammende, dated January 5, 1935—which warned of an impending famine in the USSR, mentioned groups in North America and referred to an appeal issued by the chief rabbi of France—is among the papers of Michael Luchkovich. "Extract from the Bulletin Issued by the Interconfessional and International Relief Committee for the Starving Districts of the Soviet Union, under the Presidency of Cardinal Innitzer, Archbishop of Vienna," in vol. 2, file 24, Luchkovich Papers. See also "Starvation in Russia," *Mercury*, 17 Aug. 1935, 3.

30 Mackay and Luhovy to Prime Minister and Members of the Dominion Government, 31 Aug. 1934, RG 25, vol. 1673, file 742 (1933) Treatment of Ukrainians in Russia, LAC.

31 [John Mackay (Manitoba College)] to the Rt. Hon. R. B. Bennett, P.C., K.C., and members of the Dominion Government, M-1091, 268934, Bennett Papers. The

joint letter was noted beyond Canada in "Bolsheviki i Liga Natsii," *Vozrozhdenie*, 16 Oct. 1934, 4. Although the *Western Catholic* published articles about the famine, little on the subject appeared in the pages of the United Church of Canada's *New Outlook* or the *Canadian Baptist*. However, the latter did mention the resolution on the famine passed by the World Congress of Baptists in the summer of 1934, which demanded "the formation of an international, non-political commission to devise ways and means to relieving distress [in the Soviet Union]." "Seventy Nations at Alliance," *Canadian Baptist*, 30 Aug. 1934, 7. *New Outlook* mentioned Ukrainian members in the United Church (see, for example, "The Non-Anglo-Saxon," 11 July 1934, 560), but did not report on their activities (if any) vis-à-vis the famine. The activities of Ukrainian Baptists in Saskatoon (whose church was on Avenue I South) were reported in the *Star-Phoenix*; for example, in September 1933, Ukrainian Baptists held a silver tea, committing any funds received to "the starving ones in Russia" ("Silver Tea Aiding Starving Russians," 18 Sept. 1933, 6; and "Silver Tea Will Provide Help for Needy Russians," 21 Sept. 1933, 7). On February 4, 1934, Ukrainian Baptists held a concert in the Biggar area, Saskatchewan. On the concert, *Kanadyis'kyi farmer* wrote that "although our farmers are poor this year and live on relief..., [nonetheless, $13.37 was raised] for the aid of the starving in Ukraine" ("Komitet dlia pomochi holoduiuchym," 21 Mar. 1934, 6).

32 Laurent Beaudry (acting undersecretary of state for external affairs) to Reverend John Mackay, D.D. (principal, Manitoba College, Winnipeg), 13 Sept. 1934, RG 25, vol. 1673, file 742 (1933) Treatment of Ukrainians in Russia, LAC. A copy of the form letter of reply can also be found at M-1031, 192291, Bennett Papers.

33 John Mackay to Laurent Beaudry, 27 Sept. 1934, RG 25, vol. 1673, file 742 (1933) Treatment of Ukrainians in Russia, LAC.

34 "Famine in Russia," *Times*, 18 Sept. 1934, 13.

35 Ewald Ammende to R. B. Bennett, 9 Sept. 1934, M-1091, 268937-9, Bennett Papers.

36 J. J. Saucier to Ewald Ammende, 15 Sept. 1934, M-1091, 268936, Bennett Papers. That day (September 15, 1934), the *Edmonton Bulletin* reported that the League of Nations had invited the USSR to apply for membership. It also reported that the assembly had received a memorial from "the Ukrainian group of the Polish parliament protesting against admission of Russia until the Soviet extends to the Ukraine the right of self-determination." From a Georgian group came the "demand that Russia evacuate" the Soviet republic of Georgia ("League Invites Soviet to Join," 15 Sept. 1934, 1). See also "Invitation to Enter League Accepted by Russian Government," *Calgary Herald*, 15 Sept. 1934, 1.

37 Ewald Ammende to R. B. Bennett, 17 Sept. 1934, M-1091, 268929, Bennett Papers.

38 Carynnyk, Luciuk, and Kordan, *The Foreign Office and the Famine*, xli.

39 Ibid., lviii n52.

40 280 Parl Deb HC (5th ser.) (1933), cols. 425-28 (UK). In April 1933, Edward Hilliard—in a letter to the editor of the London *Times*—described the British embargo on Soviet goods that had resulted from the trial of the British engineers in Moscow as a "merciful action." Peasants were starving

in many districts of the Soviet Union, Hilliard wrote; their crops had been "commandeered for use in the towns and export; and the animals are dying for lack of fodder." As foodstuffs were exported to Great Britain for much-needed foreign currency, he said, the United Kingdom "was obtaining cheap food at the expense of thousands of starving Russians" when it could be imported from elsewhere without increasing the cost of living. "Embargo on Russian Imports," *Times*, 25 Apr. 1933, 10.

41 280 Parl Deb HC (5th ser.) (1933), cols. 425–28 (UK). The Save the Children Fund decided against making an appeal in August 1933 because it had been advised by the Soviet ambassador in the United Kingdom that there was no famine. See Koshiw, "Famine in the British Government Archives," 64.

42 286 Parl Deb HC (1934), cols. 1319–32 (UK).

43 Duchess of Atholl to Sir John Simon, 25 August 1934, 371/1832 N. 5006, British Foreign Office.

44 K. Atholl to R. B. Bennett, 1 Sept. 1934, M-3144, 549241–3, Bennett Papers. The prime minister appears to have been familiar with the duchess's book about the Soviet Union, *The Conscription of a People* (1931); in 1932 he mentioned the publication, without naming it, at an annual convention of the Ontario Conservative Association, as follows: "Some [Socialists and Communists] are commending to you the history of Russia. If any of you have read the small volume of the Duchess of Athol[l], I do not think you will give it much support." "Bennett Raps Socialism, Communism," *Star-Phoenix*, 10 Nov. 1932, 5. Major Ralph Rayner was among the Britons who shared a view similar to the duchess. Quoting the Archbishop of Canterbury's figure of deaths from starvation in the USSR, Rayner remarked that while the government in Moscow relied on force and murder—which the League of Nations was set up to oppose—"we invite [the Soviet Union] to join up at Geneva." "Bitter Farce," *Devon and Exeter Gazette*, 28 Sept. 1934, 8.

45 The speech of the Archbishop of Canterbury (William Cosmo Gordon Lang) in the House of Lords is among the prime minister's papers, at M-1032, 192998–3314, Bennett Papers. The text can be found in 93 Parl Deb HL (5th ser.) (1934), cols. 1108–12 (UK). Both his speech and that of the Earl of Denbigh on the famine can be found online through "Lords Sittings in the 19th Century," *Hansard 1803–2005*, UK Parliament, accessed 21 Feb. 2016, http://hansard.millbanksystems.com/lords/.

46 R. B. Bennett to K. Atholl, 14 Sept. 1934, M-3144, 549245, Bennett Papers. Bennett's implication that the USSR's admission into the League of Nations might actually moderate the Communist regime was probably similar to the view expressed by the American writer and philosopher Will Durant, who had visited and lectured in Canada about the USSR. Durant described the USSR as a "gigantic prison" and its inhabitants as "prisoners" ("We looked back in horror and pity upon the land of our dreams and prayed that liberation might come soon to those 150,000,000 who we left behind"). He believed that U.S. recognition of the USSR would, among other things, "make for both the moderation of the Soviet and for the peace of the world." See "Russia, Where

Politicians Ousted the Dreamers," *Vancouver Sun*, 22 Feb. 1933, 2. In Great Britain, Conservative newspapers hoped that Bennett would oppose the admission of the USSR to the League of Nations. Much of the international opposition to its entry appears to have stemmed from aversion to the Soviet antireligious policy rather than the famine. "Stir Caused by Russian League Plan," *Calgary Herald*, 31 Aug. 1934, 1.

47 93 Parl Deb HL (5th ser.) (1934), cols. 1113–4 (UK).
48 Morris, *Stalin's Famine*, 160.
49 United Hetman Classocrats to the Earl of Denbigh, 18 Aug. 1934, Oseredok.
50 "League Committee Votes for Russia," *New York Times*, 18 Sept. 1934, 1; "Motta's Attack in League on the Soviet System," *New York Times*, 18 Sept. 1934, 10. In November 1934, *Ukraïns'ki visty* reported that a member of the Ukrainian community in the United States, Arkadii Mykytiak (a teacher at the Ukrainian Catholic high school in Stamford, Connecticut), had sent M. Giuseppe Motta a letter of gratitude for the Swiss's stand on the question of admitting the USSR to the League of Nations ("Deliegat Motta diakuie ukraïntsevi," 7 Nov. 1934, 7).
51 See "Russia Accepts Membership of the League," *Manchester Guardian*, 17 Sept. 1934, 14. In an additional vote, on whether to grant the Soviet Union a permanent seat on the League Council, forty countries voted in favour and ten abstained. "Moscow Takes Seat as Member of the League," *Globe*, 19 Sept. 1934, 2.
52 "Russia to Become a League Member with Council Seat," *New York Times*, 16 Sept. 1934, 36.
53 Report of the Canadian Delegates to the Fifteenth Assembly of the League of Nations, Geneva, 10–27 Sept. 1934 (Ottawa: Department of Foreign Affairs, 1935).
54 Oscar Skelton to Isabel Skelton, 16 Sept. 1934, MG 30, series D33, vol. 4, file 18, LAC. Two years later, on September 4, 1936, Skelton received a memorandum from Prime Minister King asking for details about the admission of the USSR to the League of Nations (External Affairs, T-1753, LAC). In his reply to the prime minister, Skelton clarified that the admission of the USSR was "of course the consequence of the growing fear of Germany." The USSR "desired to have League assistance against possible attack by Germany or by Japan, and France felt that the admission of Russia would facilitate and sanctify the proposals for a Franco-Soviet defensive alliance." It was thus France that took the initiative in driving the negotiations for the USSR's entry and to which the United Kingdom lent its support. In explaining Bennett's position on the issue, Skelton said that the then Canadian prime minister "concurred with reluctance in the proposal and particularly in the procedure which was eventually adopted, namely a round robin invitation from members of the League requesting Russia to join." Skelton mentioned the "somewhat obscure reference...to assistance to famine victims" in his League of Nations speech. He put it down to "an intervention by the late Dr. Ammende, head of an anti-Soviet organization." O. D. S., "Memorandum to the Prime Minister," 5 Sept. 1936, External Affairs, T-1753, LAC.
55 Oscar Skelton to Isabel Skelton, 18 Sept. 1934, MG 30, series D33, vol. 4, file 18, LAC.

56 Waite, *In Search of R.B. Bennett*, 95.
57 Bennett to [George] I. Kurdydyk (Winnipeg), 20 Sept. 1934, M-1091, 268860, Bennett Papers.
58 Oscar Skelton to Isabel Skelton, 20 Sept. 1934, MG 30, series D33, vol. 4, file 18, LAC.
59 "Z nahody pryniattia sovitiv do Ligy Natsii," *Kanadyis'kyi farmer*, 26 Sept. 1934, 4.
60 "Sovits'ku Rosiiu prynialy do Ligy Natsii," *Kanadyis'kyi farmer*, 26 Sept. 1934, 1.
61 "Council of League of Nations Unable to Intervene in Ukraine Famine," *Winnipeg Free Press*, 30 Sept. 1933, 31.
62 The USSR was expelled from the League of Nations on December 14, 1939, in response to the Red Army's invasion of Finland on October 30. (It was the only country ejected from the League of Nations.)
63 David Toews to Prime Minister R. B. Bennett, 7 Dec. 1934, C-15749, Mennonite Collection, LAC.
64 Rosthern to Canadian Representative at the League of Nations, 7 Dec. 1934, C-15749, Mennonite Collection, LAC.
65 Oscar Skelton to David Toews, 29 Dec. 1934, C-15749, Mennonite Collection, LAC.
66 David Toews to Oscar Skelton, 4 Jan. 1935, C-15749, Mennonite Collection, LAC.

Conclusion

1 Schmitz, *Famine in the Ukraine*, 38, 47.
2 V. V. Kondrashin, "Fenomen stalinizma v kontekste mirovoi i otechestvennoi istoricheskoi praktiki resheniia krest'ianskogo voprosa," in *Stalinizm i krest'ianstvo: Sbornik nauchnykh statei i materialov kruglykh stolov i zasedanii teoreticheskogo seminara "Krest'ianskii vopros v otechestvennoi i mirovoi istorii"* (Moscow: Izdatel'stvo Ispolitova, 2014), 104n8. The article about Cromie in *Pravda*, which cited the *News Chronicle* of London, appeared as "SSSR mozhno zavidovat'" (29 July 1933, 1). *Vozvrozhdenie* also reported on Cromie's statements in the *News Chronicle* ("Novyi bred o SSSR," 29 July 1933, 2).
3 Skvirsky thought that Intourist stood to gain from any articles. Vsesoiuznoe obshchestvo kul'turnoi sviazi s zagranitsei (All-Union Society for Cultural Relations with Foreign Countries) (VOKS) papers, *opis* 3, *delo* 386, State Archive of the Russian Federation, Moscow. I am grateful to Kirk Niergarth (Mount Royal University, Calgary) for sharing this item and the translation (from Russian) with me.
4 The *Winnipeg Tribune* said something similar in commenting about grain production in the USSR: "It is impossible to judge the Russian situation intelligently as official and private reports are utterly at variance. That Russia had a larger crop to harvest in 1933 than in 1932 may be admitted. That her harvest is greater than her actual needs is doubtful. Starvation killed 2,000,000 people in the Ukraine in 1932" ("Winnipeg Grain Prices End Year Considerably above Final 1932 Level," 1 Jan. 1934, 13).

5   "Real Light on Russia," *Radisson Comet*, 10 Aug. 1933, 2.
6   Bohachevsky-Chomiak, *Feminists despite Themselves*, 277.
7   The Ukrainian demonstrations in New York and Chicago also commanded the attention of the press in Europe. For example, see "Contre la reconnaissance des Soviets," *Journal de Genève*, 20 Nov. 1933; and "Les communistes et les Ukrainiens aux prises à Chicago," *Journal de Genève*, 20 Dec. 1933.
8   The *Literary Digest* mentioned Swedish newspapers that asserted Skrypnyk intended to go to the Kremlin to kill Stalin but having failed, took his own life. Further, "in Berlin, it has been rumoured that, in his attempt to separate the Ukraine from the Soviet Union, he sought the support of German Nazi leaders, but was found out by the Soviet Secret Police and so found himself obliged to kill himself" ("A Soviet Suicide Mystery," 26 Aug. 1933, 16). Members of the Ukrainian community in Canada were aware of Nazi aspirations vis-à-vis Soviet Ukraine, as the title of an article about a public talk by M. Mandryka suggests: "Hitler Would Colonize Ukraine with Germans," *Winnipeg Free Press*, 16 May 1932, 3. See also *Winnipeg Tribune*, 16 May 1932, 2.
9   "Bolshevik Chief's Suicide," *Times of India*, 4 Aug. 1933, 14. This article was very likely based on one that appeared earlier in London's *Daily Telegraph* with the same title: "Bolshevik Chief's Suicide," *Daily Telegraph*, 10 July 1933, 9.
10 "Russia and the League," *Sydney Morning Herald*, 11 May 1934, 10.
11 "The League and the Minorities," *Courier and Advertiser*, 14 Sept. 1934, 6.
12 In the months following Skrypnyk's suicide almost all of his staff in the ministry of education were arrested as part of the Soviet regime's counter-Ukrainianization campaign in Ukraine. See Shkandrij and Bertelsen, "Soviet Regime's National Operations," 427. During 1933 and 1934, Ukrainians in Canada were taking an interest in another prominent Ukrainian figure, the historian Mykhailo Hrushevsky. Elected head of Ukraine's parliament, the Central Rada, in 1917, Hrushevsky left the country after the victory of the Bolsheviks but returned in 1924. In January 1933, during a visit to western Ukraine, Vladimir Kaye met with the editor of the newspaper *Novyi chas*, Dmytro Paliiv, and asked him what he thought of the idea of paying for Hrushevsky's passage from the USSR. (In 1931, Hrushevsky had been forced to move from Kyiv to Moscow.) Paliiv replied that the matter was under discussion and that a Ukrainian judge was even prepared to pledge five hundred dollars of his own money for the cause. The question, though, was whether the Soviet regime would permit Hrushevsky's exit from the USSR. Kysilewsky, "Unedited Diaries," 7 (entry for 13 Jan. 1933), VJKF.
13 A Brüder in Not booklet was published that included photographs taken by the engineer Alexander Wienerberger in Kharkiv; no date is specified. A copy of the booklet is among the Ielysaveta Skoropadska papers (reel 11). On Wienerberger and photographs dating from the time of the famine, see Boriak, "Resources on the Famine," 131–33.
14 "Suspicious," *Leader-Post*, 27 Mar. 1933, 4; "Suspicious," *Star* (Wainwright), 19 Apr. 1933, 7.

15 "Stirring Up Antagonism," *Leader-Post*, 27 Mar. 1933, 4; "Stirring Up Antagonism," *Star* (Wainwright), 19 Apr. 1933, 7. Mikkelson reacted to "attacks on the private life of the leaders of [the Farmer-Labor Party and] attempts to connect such leaders with foreign revolutionary factions." He thought that the letters describing famine were a fabrication designed to undermine the cooperative movement. Thus, Mikkelson wrote of "the fabrication of letters of other parts of the globe describing stark starvation and suffering and the hope that a gullible public might connect such sufferings with the establishment of a co-operative state in this province and in our Dominion." Ibid.

16 "Stalin Butchery Laid to Hunger: Famine at Hand," *Edmonton Bulletin*, 19 Jan. 1935, 1, 3, and 21 Jan. 1935, 1, 8, and 22 Jan. 1935, 1, 8. In December 1934, Jones was travelling across the United States and delivered a speech at the Institute of World Affairs. The piece carried by the *Edmonton Bulletin* and other newspapers was written in connection with the recent Sergei Kirov murder. See "Famine Exposure Newspaper Articles relating to Gareth Jones' Trips to the Soviet Union (1930–35)," *Gareth Richard Vaughan Jones*, accessed 15 Nov. 2015, http://www.garethjones.org/soviet_articles/soviet_articles.htm. Jones was killed by bandits in Inner Mongolia on August 12, 1935. On the circumstances of his death, see "Overview 1930–33," *Gareth Richard Vaughan Jones*, accessed 15 Nov. 2015, http://www.garethjones.org/overview/mainoverview.htm. His kidnapping by bandits was reported in the Canadian press; see "Briton Captive by Chinese Reds," *Globe*, 30 July 1935, 1; "Former Secretary of Lloyd George Is Captive of Chinese Bandits," *Toronto Star*, 29 July 1935, 17; "Bandits Slay Gareth Jones Peiping Report," *Toronto Star*, 16 Aug. 1935, 17.

17 Walter Benn, "Says Russia Advances," letter to the editor, *Edmonton Bulletin*, 15 Feb. 1935, 5. An article by van Paassen—not on the USSR but on Morocco—appeared on the same page as a section of the first part of Jones's series about the famine. "Arabs Hurl Defiance with Bloody Attacks on French Invaders," *Edmonton Bulletin*, 19 Jan. 1935, 3. While Benn wrote that "Van Paassen in one of his articles mentioned the 'starvation in Russia that no one can find who goes there,'" in a newspaper south of the border van Paassen was writing about the famine in light of what others had said about it. On Édouard Herriot's visit he said that the former French prime minister could "speak with a certain degree of authority, for this is not his first visit to Russia since the Revolution. He saw the country when it was a huge chaotic confusion right after the great Volga famine and the civil wars." Van Paassen noted that while "it is true" that the USSR did not have the mass unemployment that the U.S. and Britain had, as people in the Soviet Union liked to point out, "there are spots with famine so bad that hundreds of thousands have died of hunger within recent months." This and other things, he said, "Herriot does not see, or if he catches a glimpse of them, he prudently doesn't say a word about them." Van Paassen then asserted: "And let it not be said that the famine is due to supernatural causes and that the authorities are therefore blameless." The famine was "in the main due to the ruthless enforcement of the collectivization of agriculture." "World's

Window," *Syracuse Herald*, 18 Sept. 1933, 16. Van Paassen again discussed the famine in the context of an exchange of letters on Soviet conditions—including views expressed by Sherwood Eddy—that appeared in the *Manchester Guardian*. "World's Window," *Syracuse Herald*, 23 Sept. 1933, 4. And also in a story about a debate between Gareth Jones and Hamilton Fyfe. "World's Window," *Syracuse Herald*, 23 Oct. 1933, 8.

18 "Sees Review of Red Army Troops, Moscow," *Lethbridge Herald*, 20 Feb. 1935, 3.
19 "Do zakhidno-ukraïns'kykh robitnykiv i selian," *Ukraïns'ki robitnychi visty*, 21 Sept. 1933, 3.
20 "No Chance Early War," *Edmonton Journal*, 27 Feb. 1934, 6.
21 "Vidchyty pro Rosiiu," *Ukraïns'kyi holos*, 27 Dec. 1933, 2.
22 "Famine Lecture Presents Findings of Holodomor Demography Research Team," *Canadian Association of Slavists Newsletter* 53, no. 108 (2010–2011): 23. In that lecture, presented at the University of Toronto, demographer Oleh Wolowyna noted that direct losses from the famine in Ukraine were 100,700 in 1932; 3,597,500 in 1933; and 204,500 in 1934. In 1933, Wolowyna noted, "Ukraine's famine mortality rate was 118/1,000 compared to 22/1,000 for Russia overall and 45/1,000 for Southern Russia, the agricultural region of the Russian SFSR (which included the heavily Ukrainian Kuban) that experienced the Russian republic's most significant famine losses. (Excepting Kazakhstan, where the famine had its own particular dynamic)." Ibid., 23–24.
23 Rudnytskyi et al., "Man-Made Human Catastrophe," 62, 65.
24 "Stalin Unmasked," *Winnipeg Free Press*, 30 Nov. 1939, 3, 19.
25 "Ukraïna rynel," *Ukraïns'ki visty*, 21 June 1933, 2. From the *Salt Lake Tribune* in June 1933: "The grain that Moscow has been secretly purchasing abroad in the last fortnight will not be used to feed the starving Ukrainian peasantry. Famine relief is being secretly organized and includes only the 28 larger Ukrainian cities, whose total population is less than four million.... The G.P.U. (soviet espionage system) has been ordered to complete the issuance of passports to inhabitants listed in Ukrainian cities and to expel the declassed element" ("Millions in Russ District Face Famine," 4 June 1933, B1). In March 1933, the *Montreal Star* (citing the Associated Press) mentioned a report in a Soviet regional newspaper of a relief action that was taking place. The North Caucasus Regional Communist Party Committee, it reported, had threatened "stoppage of 'food assistance' as one of the measures taken against collective farms and villages failing in proper preparations for planting." An entire village and three collective farms were put on the "dreaded 'black board' as a warning, accompanied by the withdrawal of the Government's food doles and loans for seed and fodder." Food where needed, according to the edict that was issued, "will be allowed only those showing diligent work" ("Starving Farmers are Fed by Soviet Government," 10 Mar. 1933, 1).
26 Oleh Wolowyna, "Demographic Complexity of the Holodomor: Beyond the Controversy on the Number of Losses" (lecture, CIUS Seminar Series, University of Alberta, Edmonton, 24 Nov. 2014). Wolowyna was responding to a question at his lecture.

27 Andrew Cairns (Empire Marketing Board) to John E. Brownlee, 8 Dec. 1932, in the Andrew Cairns Papers, Marshall Library of Economics, Cambridge University. Andrew Cairns died in a plane crash in India in 1958. "Ex-City Man Killed in India Crash," *Winnipeg Free Press*, 16 May 1958, 1.
28 Instructive in this regard is the thesis of Harvard University economist Amartya Kumar Sen: "There has never been a famine in any country that's been a democracy with a relatively free press." Sen provides the example of India, which had no episodes of mass starvation since independence in 1947 despite experiencing occasional years of food shortages. He then contends, "My point really is that if famine is about to develop, democracy can guarantee that it won't. When newspapers are controlled, it's amazing how ignorant and immune from pressure the government can be." "The Politics of Famine: It's Never Fair to Blame Just the Weather," *Edmonton Journal*, 24 Jan. 1993; reprinted from the *New York Times*.
29 "A Girl Drops In on Moscow," *Vancouver Sun*, 8 Aug. 1933, 5.
30 Viktor Suvorov, *Icebreaker: Who Started the Second World War?* (London: Hamish Hamilton, 1990), 107.
31 "Children 'Scourge' to Reds," *Montreal Star*, 7 June 1933, 10.
32 "Record-Breaking Talkie Coming to Elite Theatre," *Star* (Wainwright), 8 Aug. 1934, 5. For a study of homeless children in the USSR, including during the period of the famine, see Margaret K. Stolee, "Children in the USSR, 1917–1957," *Soviet Studies* 40, no. 1 (1988): 64–83.

BIBLIOGRAPHY

Archives

Cairns, Andrew. Papers. Marshall Library of Economics. Cambridge University, UK.
Elektronnyi arkhiv ukraïns'koho vyzvol'noho rukhu. http://avr.org.ua.
Foreign Office Papers. Public Record Office (now the National Archives), London.
Kyforuk/Nay Fonds. Bohdan Medwidsky Ukrainian Folklore Archives. University of Alberta, Edmonton.
Library and Archives Canada, Ottawa.
Provincial Archives of Alberta, Edmonton.
Roosevelt, Franklin D., Papers as President: The President's Secretary's File (PSF), 1933–1945. FDR Presidential Library and Museum, New York. http://www.fdrlibrary.marist.edu/archives/collections/franklin/.
Saskatchewan Archives Board, Regina.
Skoropadska, Ielysaveta. Papers. Committee to Aid Victims of the Famine in Ukraine, 1933–44. V. Lypynsky East European Research Institute Archives, Philadelphia.
St. Vladimir's Ukrainian Orthodox Congregation Library and Archives, Calgary.
Ukrainian Canadian Archives and Museum of Alberta, Edmonton.
Ukrainian Catholic Archeparchy of Winnipeg Archives.
Ukrainian Cultural and Educational Centre (Oseredok), Winnipeg.

Newspapers and Magazines

ABC (Madrid), 1933
Aberdeen Press and Journal, 1932
Almonte Gazette (Almonte, ON), 1933
American Mercury (New York), 1935
Barrier Miner (Broken Hill, Australia), 1933
Blairmore Enterprise (Blairmore, AB), 1933, 1934
Border Cities Star (Windsor, ON), 1933, 1934

Calgary Herald, 1933, 1934
Canadian Baptist (Toronto), 1934
Canadian Dimension (Winnipeg), 2004
Canadian Jewish Chronicle (Montreal), 1932, 1933
Charlottetown Guardian, 1933, 1934, 1943
Chicago Tribune, 1933
Chilliwack Progress (Chilliwack, BC), 1933
Conversation (Cambridge, MA), 2015
Courier and Advertiser (Dundee), 1934
Daily Colonist (Victoria, BC), 1933
Daily Mail (London), 1933
Day (Kyiv), 2006
Der Bote (Rosthern, SK), 1933, 1934
Deseret News (Salt Lake City), 1932
Le Devoir (Montreal), 1933, 1934
Devon and Exeter Gazette (UK), 1934
Drummondville Spokesman (Drummondville, QC), 1933
Edmonton Bulletin, 1933, 1935
Edmonton Journal, 1932, 1933, 1934, 1941, 1993
Evening Record (Ellensburg, WA), 1932
Evening Telegraph and Post (Dundee), 1933
Globe (Toronto), 1932, 1933
Irma Times (Irma, AB), 1932
Jewish Telegraphic Agency (New York), 1933
Jewish Western Bulletin (Vancouver), 1933
Journal de Genève, 1933
Kanadskii gudok (Winnipeg), 1933
Kanadyis'kyi farmer (Winnipeg), 1933, 1934
Kingsville Reporter (Kingsville, ON), 1933, 1934
Leader-Post (Regina), 1933
Lethbridge Herald, 1932, 1933, 1934
La Liberté (Winnipeg), 1933
Life, 1953
Literary Digest (New York), 1932
Maclean's, 1933
Manchester Guardian, 1933, 1934
Manitoban (Winnipeg), 1934
Le Matin (Paris), 1933
Mercury (Hobart, Australia), 1935
Montreal Gazette, 1933
Montreal Star, 1933, 1934
New Outlook (Toronto), 1934
New York Times, 1932, 1933, 1934, 1946

Nottingham Evening Post, 1933
Novyi shliakh (Edmonton/Saskatoon), 1933, 1934, [*New Pathway*] 2010
Ottawa Citizen, 1933, 1934, 1936
Ottawa Journal, 1932, 1933, 1934, 1950
Oyen News (Oyen, AB), 1933
Perthshire Advertiser (Scotland), 2010
Pravda (Moscow), 1933
La Presse (Montreal), 1933, 1934
Prince George Citizen (Prince George, BC), 1932, 1934
Radisson Comet (Radisson, SK), 1933
Rassvet (Chicago), 1933
Redcliff Review (Redcliff, AB), 1932
Santa Cruz Evening News, 1933
Saturday Night (Toronto), 1933, 1934
Sil's'ki visti (Kyiv), 2013
Soviet Russia Today (Toronto), 1933, 1934
Star (Wainwright, AB), 1933, 1934
Star-Phoenix (Saskatoon), 1933
Stony Plain Sun (Stony Plain, AB), 1933
Stouffville Sun Tribune (Stouffville, ON), 1933
La Survivance (Edmonton), 1932, 1933
Svoboda (Jersey City), 1916, 1932, 1933, 1934, 1935, 1958
Sydney Morning Herald, 1933, 1934, 1953
Syracuse Herald, 1933
Times (London), 1933, 1934, 1935, 1936
Times of India, 1933
Times-Union (Albany, NY), 1933
Toronto Star, 1932, 1933, 1934, 2014
Toronto Telegram, 1932, 1933
Ukrainian Bureau Bulletin (London), 1932, 1933, 1934
Ukrainian Weekly (Jersey City, NJ), 1934, 1935, 1976, 1983, 1988, 2012
Ukraïns'ki visty (Edmonton), 1932, 1933, 1934, 1941
Ukraïns'ki robitnychi visty (Winnipeg), 1932, 1933, 1934
Ukraïns'kyi holos (Winnipeg), 1933, 1934
Vancouver Province, 1932, 1933
Vancouver Sun, 1933
Vegreville Observer (Vegreville, AB), 1933
Vozrozhdenie (Paris), 1934
Wall Street Journal, 1933
Western Catholic (Edmonton), 1933, 1934
Western Globe (Lacombe, AB), 1933
Windsor Daily Star, 1936
Winnipeg Free Press, 1932, 1933, 1934
Winnipeg Tribune, 1932, 1933, 1934, 1936

Government Publications

Canada Year Book 1933. Ottawa: King's Printer, 1933.
Dominion of Canada. Parliament. *Official Report of Debates [Hansard].* 1933 and 1934.
Parliamentary Debates [UK]. House of Commons. 5th series. 1932–34.
Parliamentary Debates [UK]. House of Lords. 5th series. 1934.
Report of the Canadian Delegates to the Fifteenth Assembly of the League of Nations, Geneva, 10–27 September 1934. Ottawa: Department of Foreign Affairs, 1935.
"The Depression Years, Part II, 1935 [Weekly Summary Report on Revolutionary Organizations and Agitators in Canada]." *R.C.M.P. Security Bulletins.* https://journals.lib.unb.ca/index.php/RCMP/index.

Encyclopedias and Virtual Resources

The Canadian Encyclopedia. www.thecanadianencyclopedia.ca/.
Encyclopedia of Canada's Peoples. Edited by Paul Robert Magocsi. Toronto: University of Toronto Press for the Multicultural History Society of Ontario, 1999.
Encyclopedia of Saskatchewan. Regina: Canadian Plains Research Center, 2006–. http://esask.uregina.ca/.
Encyclopedia of Ukraine. Vol. 2. Edited by Volodymyr Kubijovyč. Toronto: University of Toronto Press, 1988.
Global Anabaptist Mennonite Encyclopedia Online. http://gameo.org/.
Harvard Encyclopedia of American Ethnic Groups. Edited by Stephan Thernstrom. Cambridge, MA: Belknap Press of Harvard University, 1980.
Internet Encyclopedia of Ukraine. Edmonton and Toronto: Canadian Institute of Ukrainian Studies. http://www.encyclopediaofukraine.com.
Ukrainians in the United Kingdom Online Encyclopaedia. http://www.ukrainiansintheuk.info.
Virtual Museum of Canada. Ottawa: Canadian Museum of History, 2014–. http://www.virtualmuseum.ca/.

Scholarly and Other Sources

50ème anniversaire de la famine-génocide en Ukraine, 1933–1983. Paris: Club de Amis de l'Ukraine, 1983.
Ammende, Ewald. *Human Life in Russia.* London: G. Allen & Unwin, [1936].
Andriewsky, Olga. "Towards a Decentred History: The Study of the Holodomor and Ukrainian Historiography." *East/West: Journal of Ukrainian Studies* 2, no. 1 (2015): 18–52.
Angus, Ian. *Canadian Bolsheviks: The Early Years of the Communist Party of Canada.* Victoria, BC: Trafford, 2004.
Anholenko, V. "Z poshty 1932–1933 za todishnyi holod." *Ukraïns'kyi filatelistychnyi visnyk* 2 (2002): 26–27.

Balan, Jars. "Rhea Clyman: A Forgotten Eyewitness to the Hunger of 1932." *Ukraina Moderna*, 21 November 2014, http://uamoderna.com/.

Balan, Jars. "The Gathering Storm: The Mainstream Canadian Press Coverage of the Soviet Union in the Lead-Up to Ukraine's Great Famine-Holodomor." *Canadian Ethnic Studies* 42, nos. 2–3 (2010): 205–43.

Basciani, Alberto. "From Collectivization to the Great Famine: Eyewitness Statements on the Holodomor by Refugees from the Ukrainian SSR, 1930–1933." *Holodomor Studies* 3, nos. 1–2 (2011): 1–27.

Bednarek, Jerzy, ed. *Poland and Ukraine in the 1930s–1940s: Unknown Documents from the Archives of the Secret Services*. Vol. 7, *Holodomor: The Great Famine in Ukraine 1932–1933*. Warsaw: Institute of National Remembrance, Commission of the Prosecution of Crimes against the Polish Nation, 2009.

Black, J. L. *Canada in the Soviet Mirror: Ideology and Perception in Soviet Foreign Affairs, 1917–1991*. Ottawa: Carleton University Press, 1998.

Bohachevsky-Chomiak, Martha. *Feminists despite Themselves: Women in Ukrainian Community Life, 1884–1939*. Edmonton: CIUS Press, 1988.

Boriak, Hennadii. "Sources and Resources on the Famine in Ukraine's State Archival System." *Harvard Ukrainian Studies* 27, nos. 1–4 (2004–2005): 117–47.

Bridenthal, Renate. "Germans from Russia: The Political Network of a Double Diaspora." In *The Heimat Abroad: The Boundaries of Germanness*, edited by K. Molly O'Donnell, Renate Bridenthal, and Nancy Reagin, 187–218. Ann Arbor: University of Michigan Press, 2005.

Bruski, Jan Jacek, comp. *Hołodomor 1932–1933. Wielki Głód na Ukrainie w dokumentach polskiej dyplomacji i wywiadu*. Warsaw: Wyd. Polski Instytut Spraw Międzynarodowych, 2008.

Burian, L. M., and I. E. Rikun, comps. *Holodomor v Ukraïni 1932–1933 rr.: Bibliohrafichnyi pokazhchyk*. Odesa: Vyd-vo M.P. Kots, 2001.

Burness, Catriona. "Count up to Twenty-One: Scottish Women in Formal Politics, 1918–1990." In *Women and Citizenship in Ireland in the Twentieth Century: What Difference Did the Vote Make?*, edited by Esther Breitenbach and Pat Thane, 45–62. London: Continuum, 2010.

Cairns, Andrew. *The Soviet Famine 1932–33: An Eye-Witness Account of Conditions in the Spring and Summer of 1932*, edited by Tony Kuz. Edmonton: CIUS Press, 1989.

Carynnyk, Marco. "Chairman's Remarks." In *Multiculturalism and Ukrainian Canadians: Identity, Homeland Ties, and the Community's Future*, edited by Stella M. Hryniuk and Lubomyr Y. Luciuk, 42–43. Toronto: Multicultural History Society of Ontario, 1993.

———. "Swallowing Stalinism: Pro-Communist Ukrainian Canadians and Soviet Ukraine in the 1930s." In *Canada's Ukrainians: Negotiating an Identity*, edited by Lubomyr Luciuk and Stella Hryniuk, 187–205. Toronto: University of Toronto Press, 1991.

———, Lubomyr Y. Luciuk, and Bohdan S. Kordan, eds. *The Foreign Office and the Famine: British Documents on Ukraine and the Great Famine of 1932–1933*. Kingston: Limestone, 1988.

Cherfas, Teresa. "Reporting Stalin's Famine: Jones and Muggeridge: A Case of Forgetting and Rediscovery." *Kritika: Explorations in Russian and Eurasian History* 14, no. 4 (2013): 775–804.

Dalrymple, Dana G. Review of *Herbert Hoover and Famine Relief to Soviet Russia, 1921–1923*, by Benjamin M. Weissman. *Soviet Studies* 27, no. 3 (1975): 504–8.

Davies, Alan, and Marilyn F. Nefsky. *How Silent Were the Churches? Canadian Protestantism and the Jewish Plight during the Nazi Era*. Waterloo, ON: Wilfrid Laurier University Press, 1998.

Davies, R. W., and Stephen G. Wheatcroft. *The Years of Hunger: Soviet Agriculture, 1931–1933*. New York: Palgrave Macmillan, 2004.

Duranty, Walter. *I Write as I Please*. New York: Simon & Schuster, 1935.

Endicott, Stephen Lyon. *Bienfait: The Saskatchewan Miners' Struggle of '31*. Toronto: University of Toronto, 2002.

Epp, Frank H. *Mennonite Exodus: The Rescue and Resettlement of the Russian Mennonites since the Communist Revolution*. Altona, MB: D. W. Friesen, 1967.

Epp, Marlene. "The Semiotics of Zwieback: Feast and Famine in Narratives of Mennonite Refugee Women." In *Sisters or Strangers? Immigrant, Ethnic, and Racialized Women in Canadian History*, edited by Marlene Epp and Franca Iacovetta, 314–40. Toronto: University of Toronto Press, 2004.

"Famine Lecture Presents Findings of Holodomor Demography Research Team." *Canadian Association of Slavists Newsletter* 53, no. 108 (2010–11): 23–24.

Fleming, Keith Robson. *The World Is Our Parish: John King Gordon, 1900–1989: An Intellectual Biography*. Toronto: University of Toronto Press, 2015.

Foran, Max. "Hooves for Gallons: The Canada-Russia Barter Deal of 1932–33." *Alberta History* 49, no. 2 (2001): 12–19.

Fortier, J. W. Guy. "Growing Up in Lower Town." *Heritage Ottawa Newsletter* 30, no. 2 (2003): 6–8.

Frolick, Stanley. *Between Two Worlds: The Memoirs of Stanley Frolick*, edited by Lubomyr Y. Luciuk and Marco Carynnyk. Toronto: Multicultural History Society of Ontario, 1990.

Gelb, Michael. Review of *After the Holodomor: The Enduring Impact of the Great Famine on Ukraine*, edited by Andrea Graziosi, Lubomyr A. Hajda, and Halyna Hryn. *Agricultural History* 89, no. 3 (2015): 446–48.

Glazov, Jamie. *Canadian Policy toward Khrushchev's Soviet Union*. Montreal and Kingston: McGill-Queen's University Press, 2002.

Goldman, Emma. *Living My Life: Two Volumes in One*. New York: Cosimo Classics, 2011.

Goldsborough, Gordon, and Christian Cassidy. "Memorable Manitobans: Jacob Penner (1880–1965)." *Manitoba Historical Society*. Last revised 5 November 2016. http://www.mhs.mb.ca/docs/people/penner_j.shtml.

Graziosi, Andrea. "The Impact of Holodomor Studies on the Understanding of the USSR." *East/West: Journal of Ukrainian Studies* 2, no. 1 (2015): 53–80.

———, Lubomyr A. Hajda, and Halyna Hryn, eds. *After the Holodomor: The Enduring Impact of the Great Famine on Ukraine*. Cambridge, MA: Harvard University Press, 2013.

———, Lubomyr A. Hajda, and Halyna Hryn. Introduction to Graziosi, Lubomyr, and Hryn, *After the Holodomor*, xv–xxvii.

Griffin, Frederick. *Soviet Scene: A Newspaperman's Close-Ups of New Russia*. Toronto: Macmillan, 1932.

Halton, David. *Dispatches from the Front: Matthew Halton, Canada's Voice at War*. Toronto: McClelland & Stewart, 2014.

Harder, Helmut. *David Toews Was Here, 1870–1947*. Winnipeg: CMBC, 2002.

Harwood, Philip J. "Axis Radio Personalities." In *The Guide to United States Popular Culture*, edited by Ray Broadus Browne and Pat Browne, 53. Bowling Green, Ohio: Bowling Green State University Popular Press, 2001.

Heinzen, James W. *Inventing a Soviet Countryside: State Power and the Transformation of Rural Russia, 1917–1929*. Pittsburgh: University of Pittsburgh Press, 2004.

Himka, John-Paul. "Encumbered Memory: The Ukrainian Famine of 1932–33." *Kritika: Explorations in Russian and Eurasian History* 14, no. 2 (2013): 413–38.

———. "The Holodomor in the Ukrainian-Jewish Encounter Initiative." Paper presented at the meeting of the Ukrainian Jewish Encounter Initiative, Ditchley Park, England, 14–16 December 2009. http://www.academia.edu/499209/The_Holodomor_in_the_Ukrainian-Jewish_Encounter_Initiative.

Hinther, Rhonda L. "'Sincerest Revolutionary Greetings': Progressive Ukrainians in Twentieth Century Canada." PhD dissertation, McMaster University, 2005.

Horn, Michiel. *The Great Depression of the 1930s in Canada*. Historical Booklet No. 39. Ottawa: Canadian Historical Association, 1984.

Housden, Martyn. *On Their Own Behalf: Ewald Ammende, Europe's National Minorities and the Campaign for Cultural Autonomy, 1920–1936*. Amsterdam: Rodopi, 2014.

Howard-Hassmann, Rhoda E. *State Food Crimes*. Cambridge: Cambridge University Press, 2016.

Hrynevych, Liudmyla. *Khronika kolektyvizatsiï ta holodomoru v Ukraïni, 1927–1933*. Kyiv: Krytyka, 2008.

Ignatieff, Michael. *The Russian Album*. Toronto: Penguin Canada, 2009.

Ignatieff, Nicholas. *The Russian Emerges: A Native Assessment of the Soviet Experiment*. Toronto: Macmillan, 1932.

Isajiw, Wsevolod W. "The Impact of the Man-Made Famine on the Structure of Ukrainian Society." In *Famine in Ukraine 1932–1933*, edited by Roman Serbyn and Bohdan Krawchenko, 139–46. Edmonton: CIUS Press, 1986.

Johnston, Robert H. *"New Mecca, New Babylon": Paris and the Russian Exiles, 1920–1945*. Montreal and Kingston: McGill-Queen's University Press, 1988.

Ketchum, Carleton J. "The Russia of Today." 30 November 1933. Transcript. *The Empire Club of Canada Addresses*. http://speeches.empireclub.org/60735/data.

Khlevniuk, Oleg. "Comments on the Short-Term Consequences of the Holodomor." In Graziosi, Lubomyr, and Hryn, *After the Holodomor*, 149–61.

King, Charles. *The Moldovans: Romania, Russia, and the Politics of Culture*. Stanford: Hoover Institution Press, 2000.

Klid, Bohdan, and Alexander J. Motyl, comps. and eds. *The Holodomor Reader: A Sourcebook on the Famine of 1932–1933 in Ukraine*. Edmonton: CIUS Press, 2012.

Kolasky, John, ed. and trans. *Prophets and Proletarians: Documents on the History of the Rise and Decline of Ukrainian Communism in Canada.* Edmonton: CIUS Press, 1990.

———. *The Shattered Illusion: The History of Ukrainian Pro-Communist Organizations in Canada.* Toronto: PMA, 1979.

Kondrashin, V. V. "Fenomen stalinizma v kontekste mirovoi i otechestvennoi istoricheskoi praktiki resheniia krest'ianskogo voprosa." In *Stalinizm i krest'ianstvo: Sbornik nauchnykh statei i materialov kruglykh stolov i zasedanii teoreticheskogo seminara "Krest'ianskii vopros v otechestvennoi i mirovoi istorii,"* 97–105. Moscow: Izdatel'stvo Ispolitova, 2014.

———. "Hunger in 1932–1933: A Tragedy of the Peoples of the USSR." *Holodomor Studies* 1, no. 2 (2009): 16–21.

Koshiw, Jaroslaw V. "The 1932–33 Famine in the British Government Archives." In *Famine-Genocide in Ukraine 1932–1933: Western Archives, Testimonies and New Research*, edited by Wsevolod W. Isajiw, 51–65. Toronto: Ukrainian Canadian Research and Documentation Centre, 2003.

———. *British Foreign Office Files on Ukraine and Ukrainians, 1917–1948.* Research Report No. 60. Edmonton: CIUS Press, 1997.

———. Review of *Human Life in Russia* [reprint ed.], by Ewald Ammende. *Journal of Ukrainian Studies* 10, no. 2 (1985): 101–7.

Koval'chuk, Olena, and Tamara Marusyk. *Holodomor 1932–1933rr. v USRR i ukraïns'ka diaspora Pivnichnoï Ameryky.* Chernivtsi: Nashi knyhy, 2010.

Kramar, O. S. "Tovarystva tekhnichnoï dopomohy ta reemihratsiia zarubizhnoï ukraïns'koi hromads'kosti u polityci komunistychnoho rezhymu (1921–1925 rr.)." *Hileia: Naukovyi visnyk* 20 (2009): 70–79.

Krawchenko, Bohdan. *Social Change and National Consciousness in Twentieth-Century Ukraine.* Basingstoke, Hampshire: Macmillan, 1985.

Krawchuk, Andrii. "Protesting against the Famine: The Statement of the Ukrainian Catholic Bishops in 1933." *Journal of Ukrainian Studies* 8, no. 2 (1983): 59–62.

Kukushkin, Vadim. "Back in the USSR." *Beaver* 86, no. 4 (2006): 33–36.

Kulchytsky, George P. "Western Relief Efforts during the 'Stalin Famine.'" *Ukrainian Quarterly* 49, no. 2 (1993): 152–64.

Kul'chyts'kyi, Stanislav. "The Holodomor of 1932–33: How and Why?" *East/West: Journal of Ukrainian Studies* 2, no. 1 (2015): 93–116.

Kuromiya, Hiroaki. "The Soviet Famine of 1932–1933 Reconsidered." *Europe-Asia Studies* 60, no. 4 (2008): 663–75.

———. *The Voices of the Dead: Stalin's Great Terror in the 1930s.* New Haven: Yale University Press, 2007.

Kushnezh [Kuśnierz], R. "L'vivs'ka ukraïns'ka presa pro Holodomor v USRR." *Ukraïns'kyi istorychnyi zhurnal* 3 (2006): 199–209.

Lang, Harry. "A Trip to the Jewish Kolkhozy of Ukraine and White Russia." *Jewish Daily Forward* (New York), 30 December 1933. Reprinted in *Holodomor Studies* 2, no. 2 (2010): 229–40.

Laqueur, Walter. *Russia and Germany: A Century of Conflict.* London: Weidenfeld & Nicolson, 1965.

Lawton, Lancelot. "Russian Economic Realities." *Fortnightly Review* 135 (August 1934): 171–79.
Lazebnyk, Stanislav. "Ukraïntsi za kordonom: ekskurs v istoriiu." *Personal Plius* 20, no. 282 (2008). http://www.personal-plus.net/272/3274.html.
Lebid-Wynnyckyj, Iroida. "Ukrainian Canadian Drama from the Beginnings of Immigration to 1942." MA thesis, University of Waterloo, 1976.
Leshchenko, O. L. "Z istoriï sil'kohospodars'kykh komun kanads'kykh ukraïntsiv na Ukraïni." *Ukraïns'kyi istorychnyi zhurnal* 10 (1991): 58–69.
Letkemann, Peter. "The Fate of Mennonites in the Volga-Ural Region, 1929–1941." *Journal of Mennonite Studies* 26 (2008): 181–200.
Luchkovich, Michael. "An Open Letter to Mr. Dean Rusk." *Ukrainian Review* 9, nos. 1–2 (1962): 104–6.
Lyons, Eugene. *Assignment in Utopia*. London: George G. Harrap, 1938.
Makuch, Andrij. "Fighting for the Soul of the Ukrainian Progressive Movement in Canada: The Lobayites and the Ukrainian Labour-Farmer Temple Association." In *Re-Imagining Ukrainian-Canadians: History, Politics, and Identity*, edited by Rhonda L. Hinther and Jim Mochoruk, 376–400. Toronto: University of Toronto Press, 2011.
———. "The Petliura Legacy in Interwar Canada." Paper presented at the annual convention of the Canadian Association of Slavists, University of Victoria, 27 May 2012.
———. "Ukrainian Patriots, Communist Sympathizers, and the Holodomor Issue in 1933 Canada." Paper presented at the annual convention of the Canadian Association of Slavists, University of New Brunswick / St. Thomas University, Fredericton, 28 May 2011.
Marples, David. "Ethnic Issues in the Famine of 1932–1933 in Ukraine." *Europe-Asia Studies* 61, no. 3 (2009): 505–18.
———. Eduard Baidaus, and Mariya Melentyeva. "Causes of the 1932 Famine in Soviet Ukraine: Debates at the Third All-Ukrainian Party Conference." *Canadian Slavonic Papers* 56, nos. 3–4 (2014): 291–312.
Martin, Terry. *Affirmative Action Empire: Nations and Nationalism in the Soviet Union, 1923–1939*. Ithaca: Cornell University Press, 2001.
———. "Collectivization, Famine, and Terror, 1926–1934." *Conrad Grebel Review* 20, no. 1 (2002): 23–39.
Martynowych, Orest T. "Sympathy for the Devil: The Attitude of Ukrainian War Veterans in Canada to Nazi Germany and the Jews, 1933–1939." In *Re-Imagining Ukrainian-Canadians: History, Politics, and Identity*, edited by Rhonda L. Hinther and Jim Mochoruk, 173–220. Toronto: University of Toronto Press, 2011.
———. "A Ukrainian Canadian in London: Vladimir J. (Kaye) Kysilewsky and the Ukrainian Bureau, 1931–40." *Canadian Ethnic Studies* 42, nos. 2–3 (2010): 263–88.
———. *Ukrainians in Canada: The Formative Years, 1891–1924*. Edmonton: CIUS Press, 1991.
———. *Ukrainians in Canada: The Interwar Years*. Bk. 1, *Social Structure, Religious Institutions, and Mass Organizations*. Edmonton: CIUS Press, 2016.

Marunchak, Mykhailo H. *Natsiia v borot'bi za svoie isnuvannia: 1932 i 1933 v Ukraïni i diiaspori*. Winnipeg: UVAN, 1985.

Mazepa, I. "Ukrainia under Bolshevist Rule." *Slavonic and East European Review* 12, no. 35 (January 1934): 334–46.

McVay, Athanasius D. *God's Martyr, History's Witness: Blessed Nykyta Budka, the First Ukrainian Catholic Bishop in Canada*. Edmonton: Ukrainian Catholic Eparchy of Edmonton and the Metropolitan Andrey Sheptytsky Institute of Eastern Christian Studies, 2014.

——— and Lubomyr Y. Luciuk, eds. *The Holy See and the Holodomor: Documents from the Vatican Secret Archives on the Great Famine of 1932–1933 in Soviet Ukraine*. Kingston: Kashtan, 2011.

Mironov, Alexandru-Murad. "And Quiet Flows the Dnister: Life and Death on the Romanian-Soviet Border, 1918–1940." *Arhivele Totalitarismului* 19, nos. 3–4 (2011): 32–58.

Momryk, Myron. "A Western Communist Eyewitness to the Famine." *Holodomor Studies* 3, nos. 1–2 (2011): 123–31.

Monkhouse, Allan. *Moscow, 1911–1933: Being the Memoirs of Allan Monkhouse*. London: V. Gollancz, 1933.

———. "Present Position of the U.S.S.R." 8 November 1934. Transcript. *The Empire Club of Canada Addresses*. http://speeches.empireclub.org/60031/data.

Morris, M. Wayne. *Stalin's Famine and Roosevelt's Recognition of Russia*. Lanham, MD: University Press of America, 1994.

Naimark, Norman M. "How the Holodomor Can Be Integrated into Our Understanding of Genocide." *East/West: Journal of Ukrainian Studies* 2, no. 1 (2015): 117–31.

Naulko, Vsevolod, Ihor Vynnychenko, and Rostyslav Sossa. *Ukrainians of the Eastern Diaspora: An Atlas*, translated by Serge Cipko and Myroslav Yurkevich. Kyiv: Mapa / Toronto: CIUS Press, 1993.

Neufeldt, Colin P. "The Fate of Mennonites in Ukraine and the Crimea during Soviet Collectivization and the Famine (1930–1933)." PhD dissertation, University of Alberta, 1999.

———. "Fifth Column? New Light on the Soviet Germans and Their Relationship to the Third Reich." *Journal of Ukrainian Studies* 24 (1988): 65–81.

———. "The Public and Private Lives of Mennonite Kolkhoz Chairmen in the Khortytsia and Molochansk German National Raiony in Ukraine (1928–1934)." *Carl Beck Papers in Russian and East European Studies*, no. 2305 (January 2015): 1–87.

———. "The 'Zborni' of Khortytsia, Ukraine: The Last Stop for Some Kulaks En Route to Stalin's Special Settlements." *Journal of Ukrainian Studies* 35–36 (2010–2011): 207–23.

Niergarth, Kirk. "Gender and the Great Experiment." Unpublished paper, 2015.

——— and J. L. Black. "Revisiting the Canadian–Soviet Barter Proposal of 1932–1933: The Soviet Perspective." *International Journal* 71, no. 3 (2016): 409–32.

North, Don. *Inappropriate Conduct: Mystery of a Disgraced War Correspondent*. Bloomington, IN: iUniverse, 2013.

Osokina, Elena A. *Zoloto dlia industrializatsii: Torgsin*. Moscow: ROSSPEN, 2009.

Paassen, Pierre van. *Visions Rise and Change*. New York: Dial Press, 1955.

Papuha, Iaroslav. "Pozytsiia Varshavy shchodo Holodomoru 1932–1933 rr." *Mandrivets*, no. 4 (2010): 38–42.

———. *Zakhidna Ukraïna i holodomor 1932–1933 rokiv: moral'no-politychna i material'na dopomoha postrazhdalym*. Lviv: Astroliabniia, 2008.

Petracchi, Giorgio. "Il fascismo, la diplomazia italiana e la 'questione Ucraina': La politica orientale dell'Italia e il problema dell'Ucraina (1933–1941)." In *La morte della terra: La grande "carestía" in Ucraina nel 1932–33*, edited by Gabriele De Rosa and Francesca Lomastro, 263–310. Rome: Viella, 2004.

Petryshyn, J. "R.B. Bennett and the Communists: 1930–1935." *Journal of Canadian Studies* 9, no. 4 (1974): 43–55.

Pidhainy, S. O. "Portraits of Solowky Exiles." In *Black Deeds of the Kremlin: A White Book*, edited by S. O. Pidhainy, 1:326–67. Toronto: Ukrainian Association of Victims of Russian Communist Terror, 1953.

Pitner, Yana. "Mass Murder or Massive Incompetence?" Review of *Hunger by Design: The Great Ukrainian Famine and Its Soviet Context*, edited by Halyna Hryn. *H-Russia / H-Net Reviews* (October 2010). http://www.h-net.org/reviews/showrev.php?id=30622.

Polonsky, Antony. *The Jews in Poland and Russia*. Vol. 3, *1914 to 2008*. Oxford: Littman Library of Jewish Civilization, 2012.

Pomakoy, Keith. *Helping Humanity: American Policy and Genocide Rescue*. Lanham, MD: Lexington Books, 2011.

Prokip, N. Z. "Reaktsiia Zakhidnoï Ukraïny ta mizhnarodnoï spil'nota na Holodomor 1932–1933 rr. v Ukraïni." *Visnyk Natsional'noho universytetu L'vivs'ka politekhnika*, no. 993 (2011): 181–87.

Prokopenko, Havrylo Nykyforovych. "Ukrainian Famine Memoirs: Eyewitness Testimony of Havrylo Nykyforovych Prokopenko." Translated by Marta D. Olynyk. Montreal Institute for Genocide and Human Rights Studies, Concordia University. Accessed 23 February 2017. https://www.concordia.ca/research/migs/resources/ukrainian-famine-memoirs.html.

Prymak, Thomas M. *Gathering a Heritage: Ukrainian, Slavonic, and Ethnic Canada and the USA*. Toronto: University of Toronto Press, 2015.

Pylypenko, P. *Smert' komisara Skrypnyka, abo Holod na Ukraini*. Winnipeg: Nakladom Ukraïns'koï knyharni, n.d.

Rippley, LaVern J. "F. W. Sallet and the *Dakota Freie Presse*." *North Dakota History* (1992): 2–20.

Romanyshyn, Oleh, Orest Steciw, and Andrew Gregorovich, comps. *Holodomor: The Ukrainian Genocide 1932–1933*. Toronto: League of Ukrainian Canadians and Ucrainica Research Institute, 2014.

Rudnytskyi, Omelian, Nataliia Levchuk, Oleh Wolowyna, Pavlo Shevchuk, and Alla Kovbasiuk (Savchuk). "Demography of a Man-Made Human Catastrophe: The Case of Massive Famine in Ukraine 1932–1933." *Canadian Studies in Population* 42, nos. 1–2 (2015): 53–80.

Schmidt, Alyssa Erin. "After History: Famine Plays of an Gorta Mór and the Holodomor." PhD dissertation, Tufts University, 2012.

Schmitz, Gerald. *The Famine in the Ukraine, 1932–33: A Canadian Retrospective after Fifty Years.* Ottawa: Library of Parliament, 1982.

Serbyn, Roman. "The First Man-Made Famine in Soviet Ukraine 1921–1923," *Ukrainian Weekly,* 6 Nov. 1988, 5–12.

———. "The Great Famine of 1933 and the Ukrainian Lobby at the League of Nations and the International Red-Cross." *Holodomor Studies* 1, no. 1 (2009): 91–133.

———. comp. and ed. *Holod 1921–1923 i ukraïns'ka presa v Kanadi.* Toronto: Ukraïns'ko-kanads'kyi doslidcho-dokumentatsiinyi tsentr, 1992.

———. "Lemkin on Genocide of Nations." *Journal of International Criminal Justice* 7 (2009): 123–30.

———. "Public Pressure on the International Committee of the Red-Cross as It Waited for the Soviet Reply on the Ukrainian Famine." *Holodomor Studies* 1, no. 2 (2009): 101–41.

Shkandrij, Myroslav. *Jews in Ukrainian Literature: Representation and Identity.* New Haven: Yale University Press, 2009.

———. "Ukrainianization, Terror and Famine: Coverage in Lviv's Dilo and the Nationalist Press of the 1930s." *Nationalities Papers* 40, no. 3 (2012): 431–51.

———. *Ukrainian Nationalism: Politics, Ideology, and Literature, 1929–1956.* New Haven: Yale University Press, 2015.

Shkandrij, Myroslav, and Olga Bertelsen. "The Secret Police and the Campaign against Galicians in Soviet Ukraine, 1929–34." *Nationalities Papers* 42, no. 1 (2014): 37–62.

———. "The Soviet Regime's National Operations in Ukraine, 1929–1934." *Canadian Slavonic Papers* 55, nos. 3–4 (2013): 417–47.

Shlepakov, A. M., and N. M. Kravchenko. *Ukraïns'ki kanadtsi v istorychnykh zv'iazkakh iz zemleiu bat'kiv.* Kyiv: Dnipro, 1990.

Shulgin, Alexander. "Ukraine and Its Political Aspirations." *Slavonic and East European Review* 13, no. 38 (1935): 350–62.

Simpson, Sir John Hope. *The Refugee Problem: Report of a Survey.* London: Oxford University Press, 1939.

Snyder, Timothy. *Bloodlands: Europe between Hitler and Stalin.* New York: Basic Books, 2010.

———. "Covert Polish Missions across the Soviet Ukrainian Border, 1928–1933." In *Confini: Costruzioni, attraversamenti, rappresentazioni,* edited by Silvia Salvatici, 55–78. Soveria Mannelli: Rubbettino, 2005.

St. Andrew's-Wesley Church: Reflections, 1933–1993. Vancouver: St. Andrew's-Wesley Church, 1993.

Stewart-Murray, Katharine Marjory (Duchess of Atholl). *Working Partnership: Being the Lives of John George, 8th Duke of Atholl, and of his Wife, Katharine Marjory Ramsay.* London: Arthur Baker, 1958.

Stolee, Margaret K. "Children in the USSR, 1917–1957." *Soviet Studies* 40, no. 1 (1988): 64–83.

Subtelny, Orest. *Ukraine: A History.* Toronto: University of Toronto Press with the Canadian Institute of Ukrainian Studies, 1988.

Suvorov, Viktor. *Icebreaker: Who Started the Second World War?* London: Hamish Hamilton, 1990.

Sysyn, Frank. "Thirty Years of Research on the Holodomor: A Balance Sheet." *East/West: Journal of Ukrainian Studies* 2, no. 1 (2015): 3–16.

———. "The Ukrainian Famine of 1932–3: The Role of the Ukrainian Diaspora in Research and Public Discussion." In *Studies in Comparative Genocide*, edited by Levron Chorbajian and George Shirinian, 182–215. New York: St. Martin's Press, 1999.

Tauger, Mark B. Review of *After the Holodomor: The Enduring Impact of the Great Famine on Ukraine*, edited by Andrea Graziosi, Lubomyr A. Hajda, and Halyna Hryn. *Nationalities Papers* 43, no. 3 (2015): 514–18.

Taylor, S. J. *Stalin's Apologist: Walter Duranty: The New York Times's Man in Moscow.* Oxford: Oxford University Press, 1990.

Thom, Françoise. "Reflections on Stalin and the Holodomor." *East/West: Journal of Ukrainian Studies* 2, no. 1 (2015): 81–92.

Timoshenko, Vladimir P. "Agriculture in the Soviet Spotlight." *Foreign Affairs* 32, no. 2 (1954): 244–58.

"Ukrajinské a cizí pomocné výbory." *Hlad na Ukrajině*, nos. 1–2 (November 1933): 24.

Veidlinger, Jeffrey. *In the Shadow of the Shtetl: Small-Town Jewish Life in Soviet Ukraine.* Bloomington: Indiana University Press, 2013.

Waite, P. B. *In Search of R.B. Bennett.* Montreal and Kingston: McGill-Queen's University Press, 2012.

Weiss-Wendt, Anton. "Hostage of Politics: Raphael Lemkin on 'Soviet Genocide.'" *Journal of Genocide Research* 7, no. 4 (2005): 551–59.

Werth, Nicholas. "Keynote Address for the Holodomor Conference, Harvard Ukrainian Research Institute, 17–18 November 2008." In Graziosi, Lubomyr, and Hryn, *After the Holodomor*, xxix–xxviii.

Woycenko, Ol'ha. "Community Organizations." In *A Heritage in Transition: Essays in the History of Ukrainians in Canada*, edited by Manoly R. Lupul, 173–94. Toronto: McClelland & Stewart, 1982.

Wright, Patrick. *Iron Curtain: From Stage to Cold War.* Oxford: Oxford University Press, 2007.

Wysocki, Roman. "Reactions to the Famine in Poland." In Graziosi, Lubomyr, and Hryn, *After the Holodomor*, 49–67.

PERMISSIONS ACKNOWLEDGEMENTS

Map of Ukraine, 1933 (Figure 2, page xviii) is used by permission of the Canadian Institute of Ukrainian Studies Press.

"Food Shortage During Wheat Glut," *Saskatoon Star-Phoenix*, August 28, 1933, p. 7 (Figure 3, page 71) and "Victims of Famine," *Saskatoon Star-Phoenix*, August 3, 1933, p. 4 (Figure 6, page 177) are republished with the express permission of Saskatoon Star Phoenix, a division of Postmedia Network Inc.

The handbill announcing the performance of *The Death of Commissar Skrypnyk, or Famine in Ukraine* (Figure 4, page 97) and the postcard of the Elizabeth Skoropadsky Committee to Aid Victims of the Famine in Ukraine (Figure 5, page 171) are from the Demetrius Elcheshen fonds, Ukrainian Cultural and Educational Centre. Used with permission.

INDEX

Page references in *italics* indicate illustrations.

Agricultural Russia and the Wheat Problem (Timoshenko), 127
Alliluyeva, Nadezhda, 14, 241n55, 241n58
All-Russian Evangelical Christian Union: famine relief work, 260–1n41
American Committee of Aid to the Starving in Ukraine, 195–6
Ameryka (newspaper), 144
Ammende, Ewald: Canadian tour, 194–5; correspondence of, 193, 199–201; credentials, 190; death of, 312n26; on European affairs, 200; on famine in Ukraine, 190–2, 193, 199, 311n22; *Human Life in Russia,* 196, 312n26; meeting with Bennett, 194; memorandum of, 143; on Soviet reply to International Red Cross, 264n68; Ukrainian Canadian press about, 105; on USSR's entry to the League of Nations, 200; visit to North America, 190–2, 193–5, 216
Anderson, James T. M., 35, 106
Andriewsky, Olga, xv
anti-famine protests in North America, 101–3, 107–10, 216
Asatkin, Alexander, 89, 112, 218, 221
Ashby, Corbett, 82
Atholl, Katharine Marjory Stewart-Murray, Duchess of: *The Conscription of a People,* 314n44; correspondence, 201, 203–4; lobbyist for the famine victims, xvi, xvii, 202–3, 221; on USSR's entrance to the League of Nations, 204

Bachynsky, Nicolas Volodymir, 106
Basciani, Alberto, 8
Batytsky, V., 173
Beaudry, Laurent, 198
Beck, Józef, 208
Beneš, Edvard, 200
Benn, Walter, 318n17
Bennett, Richard Bedford: anti-Communist policies, 131; awareness of famine in Ukraine, 22–3; call for resignation, 132–3; Canada-Soviet trade relations and, 27, 135, 194, 287n25, 287n29; correspondence, 133–4, 186–7, 188, 199–200, 204, 311n17; donations, 284n2; hunger marches and, 21; meeting with Ammende, 194; non-interference policy, 45; opinion of Duchess of Atholl, 314n44; petition from religious representatives to, 196, 197–8; relation with Skelton, 208; threatening letters to, 133, 286n18; on USSR's admission to the League of Nations, 195, 204, 208, 314–15n46; visit to Geneva, 194–5
Bentley, Roy D., 113–4

338 Index

Berlin Committee *See* Committee to Aid Victims of the Famine in Ukraine
Bertelsen, Olga, 247n35
Biggar, J. L., 83, 84
Bilec, Leon, 246n31
Birchall, Frederick T., 262n56
Birmingham Bureau of Research on Russian Economic Conditions, 20–1
Black, J. L., 134, 245n16
Black, W. J., 147
Blumenfeld, Hans, 297n123
Boberskyj, Ivan, 245n19
Bohachevsky-Chomiak, Martha, 216
Boivin, P. H., 72
Border Cities Star: comments on Luchkovich's statements, 181; image of the USSR, 41, 49, 66–7, 111–12; report on Clark's address on life in Soviet Union, 31; resolution of Windsor's meeting of BCWEC, 76–7; on situation in Ukraine, 75; on Soviet import of grain, 112, 113
Border Cities Workers' Educational Circle (BCWEC), 74–7
Boriak, Hennadii, 242n60
Bouchette, Bob, 122, 215
Boychuk, John, 130
Bracken, John, 128
Brandon Sun, 41
Braun, Isaac, 92
Brewing, Willard, 279n97
Brookhart, Smith Wildman, 276n73
Brown, Harrison, 239n38
Brown, John, 30, 148, 246n31
Brownlee, John E., 3, 4
Brüder in Not (Brethren in Need) relief organization, 46, 47, 83, 89, 305–6n43, 312n27, 317n13
Bryant, James F., 35
Budka, Nykyta, 272n46
Bullitt, William C., 269–70n23

Cairns, Andrew: correspondence, 2–5; occupation, 235n16; on situation in the Soviet countryside, 2, 3–4; on Soviet standard of living, 4–5; trips to the USSR, 2, 3, 234–5n9; on validity of reports about Soviet Union, 213, 222; on Western journalists in Moscow, 222; witness of famine, 2–3, 5
Calder, J. K., 73–4, 148, 259–60n33
Calgary Herald, 54–5, 69, 102, 103, 183, 308n68
Canada: anti-Semitism, 138–9; Communist propaganda in, 277n83, 285–6n14, 295n90; deportations from, 131, 132, 266n94; emigration from, 9; ethnic groups, xx, xxi; famine relief efforts, 167, 168–9; foreign policy, 20, 131, 133–4, 187, 207–8, 215, 216; grain export question, 216; Great Depression, 214, 219; perception of situation in Ukraine, 213, 216, 218, 219–21; Soviet sympathizers in, 137, 288–9n50, 288n48; surplus of wheat, 243n10; territory and population, xx
Canada-Soviet trade relations, 27–8, 33, 135, 246n25, 283n124, 287n25, 287n29
Canadian communards in Ukraine, 299n142
Canadian Jewish Chronicle, 174, 221
Canadian Labour Defence League, 132
Canadian press: on Alliluyeva's suicide, 14; anti-Semitic, 290–1n67; on Five-Year Plan, 9–10; foreign-language newspapers, xx, 233n22, 234n25; reports on famine in Ukraine, xix–xx, 1, 2, 259n27; on travel restrictions in the USSR, 78–9; on Ukrainian refugees in Romania, 7
Canadian Red Cross, 11, 83, 264n70
cannibalism in Ukraine: Canadian press on, 15, 26–7, 245–6n24, 252n10; European press on, 101, 312n27; scale and investigations of, 242n60; Slusarenko's account of, 162

Carynnyk, Marco, 202, 290n60
Catholic Church: concern of famine in Ukraine, 79–81, 90
Cecil-Smith, E., 281–2n108
Cerezke, Louisa, 176
Cerezke, Robert, 176
Chamberlin, William Henry, xvi, 89, 114, 186, 222
Charlottetown Guardian, 7, 13–14, 246n25
Chicago Tribune, 269n15
China: famine in, xiii–xiv, 178; resale of American wheat to the USSR, 248n48
Choulguine, Alexandre, 188, 189, 302n17, 310n9–10
Churchill, Winston S., 58
CILACC ("Centre international de lutte active contre le communisme"), 263n58
Clark, Herbert Spencer, 31
Clyman, Rhea, 13–14, 214, 241n58
Cohen, Sam, 91
collective farms, 299n143
collectivization, 160, 244n11; *See also* kulaks (individual farmers)
Committee to Aid Victims of the Famine in Ukraine: branches of, 170; Canadian connections, 172; criticism of, 172; foundation of, 166–7, 173; fundraising efforts, 168, 169, 170, 303–4n25; letters to state leaders, 168, 302–3n18; postcard campaign, 169, *171*, 305n38; representatives of, 303n20; shipment of aid to Soviet Ukraine, 170
Communist Party of Canada, 130, 135
Congress of European Nationalities, 200
Connelly, Marc, 117
Co-operative Commonwealth Federation (CCF), 179–80
Cossacks, deportations of, 244n13
Courier and Advertiser, 218
Cowan, Jack, 138, 289n51

Cromie, Robert J., 67, 68–70, 71, 214, 258–9n24, 282n108
Cummings, A. C., 20
Cummins, O. F., 134

Daily Colonist, 70, 258n20
Datskiv, Teodor, 182, 195
Day, Donald, 59, 60, 68, 255n29
Death of Commissar Skrypnyk, or Famine in Ukraine, The (play), 96–7, 217
Denbigh, Rudolph William Basil Fielding, Earl of, 205–6
Denikin, Anton, 233n18
Derry, George Herman, 31
Derus, Maria, 175
Derus, Peter, 175
Detroit Free Press, 101
Dilo (newspaper), 173
Dnipropetrovsk: workers' protest in, 242n59
Dniprostroi Dam, 2, 12, 148
Dnister River, 6–7, 8
Dojacek, Frank, xxii, 234n25
Doumer, Paul: assassination of, 5–6, 72, 259n25
Dovzhenko, Oleksandr, 234n4
Drach, Ivan, xv
Dragan, George, 273n48
Duggan, S. P., 191
Durant, Will, 314n46
Duranty, Walter, xvi, 12, 49, 89, 117, 222
Dyk, Joseph, 134

Echlin, Erland, 250n81
Eddy, Sherwood, 247n33
Edmonton Bulletin: on anti-famine protests, 109; editorial on famine in the USSR, 87, 275n66; on family of Rabbi Isaac Haft, 110; on invitation of the USSR to the League of Nations, 313n36; letter criticizing Cromie, 69; on Romanchych's decline of Soviet visa, 117; on situation in Ukraine, 219

340 *Index*

Edmonton Journal: on anti-famine protests, 109; editorial about Cromie's address, 258–9n24; editorial on famine in Ukraine, 81–2; editorial "What to Believe about Russia?," 215; on emigration from Canada, 9; on execution of Soviet officials, 19–20; on harvesting in Ukraine, 11; Lazarowich's article on famine, 98–9; letters to the editor, 159; on protest rally in Edmonton, 53–4; on situation in the USSR, 1, 23, 67, 93
Elcheshen, Demetrius, 182, 308–9n74
Ellis, Walter E., 31
Ens, Gerard, 32
Enukidze, Abel, 85
Epp, Frank H., 44, 45, 141

famine and democracy, 320n28
famine in the Soviet Union: areas affected by, xv–xvi; comparison to horsemen of the Apocalypse, xiii–xiv, xvi; consequence of, xv; foreign press on, xiv, xvi–xvii; government concealment of, xiv, xvi, 37; in historiography, xv–xvi
famine in Ukraine: American press on, 191–2; attempts to escape, 61; beginning of, 164; blame of kulaks for, 248n37; Canadian press on, 67–8, 217, 218–21, 250n73, 263n57, 290n60, 292n74; Catholic church and, 79–81; causes of, 77, 160–1, 163, 165; chronology, xix; comparison to 1921-23 famine, 202, 213; contradictory information about, 305–6n43, 311n22, 312n27; death rate, xix, 48, 90, 99, 164–5, 220–1, 230–1n9, 278n94, 291n69, 311n22, 319n22; debates in the House of Lords about, 205; debates in the League of Nations about, 82–5; economic blockade, 231n9; European press on, 72–3, 317n7; eyewitness accounts, 62–3, 221–2, 229n2, 247–8n36, 247n34; as genocide against Ukrainian nation, 230n8; Hitler's comments on, 46–7; horrors of, 161–2; in Kyiv region, 161, 164–5; lack of effective actions against, 79; Polish reaction to, 273n50; protest meetings in Canada, 110, 274n60; roots of, 57, 98; scale of, 60, 164; scavenging and cannibalism, 10, 161–2, 165; skepticism about, 122; sources of information about, 282n108; Soviet officials' attitude to, 220, 255n29; stories of victims of, 175–6, 177, 178; suppression of anti-famine riots, 63; Western Ukrainian press on, 273n50; *See also* Holodomor
famine of 1921-23: causes, 82; comparison to 1932-33 famine, 202, 213; death rate, 59, 60; images from, 71; opposition to foreign aid during, 246n29; relief actions, 33, 173, 296n112; scale, vii, 99
famine relief: in 1921-23, 296n112; donations from individuals and groups, 273n59; European organizations, 89, 196; Ewald Ammende's plan on, 105–6; famine relief committee in Paris, 272n45; fundraising campaigns, 173, 262n56; international relief committee, 99; for Mennonite families, 47; money sent to relatives in Ukraine, 88; organized by Soviet government, 319n25; Red Cross activities, 11–12; of Ukrainian Canadians, 99, 216; of Ukrainian immigrants in Belgium, 304n34
Farley, Samuel, 37, 38, 248n49
Fedorovich, Ivan, 169
Fedyk, T., 152
Finlayson, R. K., 118, 189
First Five-Year Plan, 2, 22, 148, 163–4

Fish, Hamilton, 205
Florinsky, M., 255n29
Forsey, Eugene, 278–9n95
four horsemen of the Apocalypse, xiii
Fox, J. F., 32, 149
Frank, Solomon, 198
French-language press: on famine in Ukraine, 82
Friends of the Soviet Union, 133, 135–6
Frolick, Stanley, 273n50

Gardiner, James G., 36, 42, 106, 225–8, 248n49
Gelb, Michael, 230n9
Germans in Canada, 233n23
Germans in Ukraine, 307n60
Germany *See* Nazi Germany
Gilchrist, J. M., 127
Glazov, Jamie, 44, 187
Globe, 41–2, 66, 260–1n41, 278n88, 305n36
Gold, Henry S., 69
Goldman, Emma, 260n39
Gordeenko, Dmitri, 111
Gordon, John King, 278–9n95
Gordon, Wesley Ashton, 147, 148
Gorguloff, Paul (Pavel Gorgulov), 5–6, 72, 235n20, 236n21
Great Britain: embargo on trade with the USSR, 56; non-interference principle in diplomacy, 44; popular opinion of the Soviet Union, 186; reaction on trial of British engineers, 313n40
Great Depression, 129–30
Griffin, Frederick, 14, 22, 148, 241n57
Gryzhak, Dmytro, 152

Haft, Isaac, 110
Halton, Matthew H., 179
Harasymchuk, D., 151
Harasymchuk-Artamenko, O., 151
Harris, Morris J., xiv
Hearst press: anti-Communist campaign, 280n103

Henry, Howard R. L., 125
Herriot, Édouard: criticism of, 116; political career, 259n25; visit to the USSR, 71, 72–3, 318n17
Hetman, M., 169
Hilliard, Edward, 313–14n40
Himka, John-Paul, 293n78
Hitler, Adolf: chancellor of Germany, 138; on famine in Ukraine, 46–7; view of, 141–2
Hogarth, D. M., 243n8
Holland, G. R., 40
Holmes, Dan (Danylo Homitsky), 92
Holodomor, xv, 230–1n9
Hood, Stanley, 1–2, 246n31
Hoover, Herbert, 19, 100, 270n24
Hrushevsky, Mykhailo, 317n12
Hryhorczuk, Nicholas Apoluner, 106
Human Life in Russia (Ammende), 196
"Hunger Bennett," 132; *See also* Bennett, Richard Bedford
hunger marches during Great Depression, 21
Hurtig, Thomas, 198

Ignatieff, Nicholas, 56, 57, 254n20, 278n94
Independent Canadian Doukhobors, 151
Innitzer, Theodor, Cardinal, 79, 110, 180, 196, 262n52, 272n46
Interconfessional and International Relief Committee for the Starving Districts of the Soviet Union, 79–80, 190
International Red Cross, 264n68
Intourist, 316n3
Investigator, 62
Irchan, Myroslav, 131, 151, 156, 300n148
Ireton, Robert E., 101–2
Isajiw, Wsevolod W., 301n6
Ivan (film), 234n4
Ivasenko, Viktor, 15
Izvestia (newspaper), 237–8n31

Japanese-Soviet relations, 275–6n72, 276n73
Jewish Western Bulletin, 292n73
Jews: blame for famine, 290n59; in Canada, xx; mortality during famine, 294n80; in North America, *Ukraïns'kyi holos* editorial on, 141; in Soviet state apparatus, 289n56, 293n78; in the Soviet Union, persecution of, 138, 139; in Ukraine, starvation of, 143, 144, 294n80
Jones, Gareth, 48–9, 54, 202, 214, 252–3n12, 318n16–17
Judeo-Bolshevism: myth of, 139–40, 144

Kalyniuk, T. P., 151
Kanadyis'kyi farmer (Canadian farmer): on child labour in the Soviet Union, 111; circulation of, 234n25; coverage of Luchkovich's speech, 181; on entry of the USSR to the League of Nations, 209; on formation of the Berlin Committee, 168; on fundraising for famine relief, 312–13n31; letter of gratitude to Mowinckel, 85; ownership of, 234n25; report on Ketchum's speech in Winnipeg, 122–3; on Russian refugees in Poland, 238n32; subscribers, xxii; testimony of Marie Zuk, 93–5; Torgsin advertisement, 174, 221
Kaye, Vladimir, 25, 317n12
Kelly, Robert, 102
Kerensky, Alexander, 70, 98, 233n18, 235n20
Kerr, A. E., 118, 279n97
Ketchum, Carleton J.: address in Mount Royal Hotel in Montreal, 124–5; claim against Canadian government, 283n125; correspondence with Canadian politicians, 124, 125; criticism of, 123, 124; Duranty and, 120; on famine in Ukraine, 118–19, 120, 220; political aspirations, 123–4; public lectures, 118–27, 218, 281n107; on repression of kulaks, 119–20; speech at Ukrainian Institute Prosvita, 122–4; travel to the USSR, 119; visit to collective farm, 280n102
Khrystos Nasha Syla, 88
Khvylovy, Mykola, 66, 293n79
King, William Lyon Mackenzie, 32, 37, 125
Kingsville Reporter, 138
Kitching, Oscar, 76
Klassen, C. F., 198
Klimchuk, F., 153
Knickerbocker, H. R., 49
Kolasky, John, 156
Kondrashin, Viktor, 231n9
Konosevych, F., 77
Konovalets, Ievhen, 233n18
Kopachuk, Mykola, 102
Korab, Henry de, 84
Kordan, Bohdan S., 202
Korostovets, Volodymyr, 167–8
Koski, J., 246n31
Kostiuk, Mykhailo, 268n14
Kovaliv, Omeliian, 298n131
Kritzevosky, Rose, 52
Krotkoff, L., 76
Kuban: political repression in, 23–4; revolt in Tikhoretsky district, 24; Ukrainian population, xvii
Kufliuk, Semen, 247n34
kulaks (individual farmers): blame for famine, 248n37; border crossing, 237–8n31; liquidation of, 279n97, 280–1n104, 280n103; opposition to collectivization, 283n127; origin of term, 6; property confiscation, 305n36; registration requirements, 305n36
Kul'chyts'kyi, Stanislav, xv
Kunitz, Joshua, 276n78
Kurdydyk, George I., 208, 311n17
Kuromiya, Hiroaki, 231n9, 298n125

Kysilewsky, Vladimir, 194–5, 245n19, 247n34, 252–3n12, 271–2n41, 306n43

Ladyka, Basil (Vasylii), 89, 91, 147, 198
La Liberté (weekly newspaper), 79
Lang, Cosmo Gordon (Archbishop of Canterbury): Ammende's committee and, 191, 192; speech on famine in the House of Lords, 187, 199, 203–4, 205, 279n97, 314n45
Lang, Harry, 143, 294n80
La Presse, 82, 181
Laval, Pierre, 259n25
Lawson, Clarke, 118
Lawton, Lancelot, xiv, 230n4
Lazarowich, Peter J., 81, 98–9
Leader-Post, 219
League of Nations: debates on admission of the USSR in, 187–9, 194–5, 196–7, 203, 206–8, 313n36, 315n50, 315n54; expulsion of the USSR from, 316n62; famine in Ukraine and, 82–5, 167, 198; Ukrainian delegations at, 82; vote on USSR's entry to, 199, 206–7, 209
Lebrun, Francois, 259n25
Le Devoir, 79, 80, 181
Legislative Assembly of Saskatchewan: debates on famine relief, 28, 34–42; resolution on barter trade with Russia, 36; response in the Ukrainian community, 42–3; Ukrainian representative in, 273n48
Le Matin, 84
Lemkin, Raphael, 230n8
Lemyk, Mykola, 103, 104, 271n39
Lenin, Vladimir, 213, 282n112
Leningrad: outbreak of typhus in, 4–5
Leschishin, Dmytro D., 85
Leshchenko, O. L., 299n142
Lethbridge Herald, 49, 114
letters from the USSR: censorship of, 46, 49; on collective farm system, 126–7; description of famine, 10, 219; on difficulty to buy bread, 88–9; on food sales for hard currency, 55; from former residents of Canada, 151–2; positive image of the Soviet Union in, 151–3; quantity of, 45; stories of famine victims, 175–6, 178; on theft of food, 35–6, 54–5; on Torgsin stores, 175
Liaison Committee of Women's International Organizations, 189–90
Literary Digest, 317n8
Litvinov, Maxim, 72, 101, 142, 208
Lloyd George, David, 106, 251n91
Luchkovich, Michael: correspondence with Ammende, 193; correspondence with Lord Phillimore, 185–6; on deportation from Canada, 266n94; letter to Rusk, 308n66; opposition to CCF, 180; political career, 106; press on, 308n68; at rally about famine, 107; speech in the House of Commons, 178–83; telegram from Ukrainian representatives to, 192–3; visit to Winnipeg, 311n16
Luciuk, Lubomyr Y., 202
Luhovy, Rev., 197
Lutsky, Ostap, 195
Lyons, Eugene, 221

MacDonald, Finlay, 135
MacDonald, Ramsay, 96, 189, 227
Mackay, Rev. John, 193, 197, 198–9
Mackie, Herbert, 20, 29
Maclean's, 74
MacNicol, John R., 179
MacPherson, Murdoch A., 35, 127
Maier-Mykhalsky, Denys, 8
Mailov, Aleksandr: assassination of, 103–4
Makhno, Nestor, 233n18
Makins, Paul, 172
Makohin, Jacob, 25

Makovsky, I., 152
Makuch, Andrij, 268n10
Manchester Guardian: article about the famine, 48–9; Bernard Shaw's letter, 251–2n93; on Ukrainian refugees, 237n31; on USSR's entrance to the League of Nations, 206–7
Mandryka, Mykyta, 95, 268n10
March, Cyril, 32
Margolis, Jacob, 77
Martin, Terry, 307n60
Martynowych, Orest, 139, 140, 290n67, 293n79
Marunchak, Mykhailo, xvi
Maryglad, Tomas, 238n34
Masiutin, Vasily, 169, *171*
May Day celebration in Winnipeg, 137
Mazurkevych, Il., 168–9
McIntyre, Marvin H., 100
Mennonites: famine relief efforts, 44–8, 209–10; immigrants from the USSR, 233n23; population statistics, xx
Mennonites in the Soviet Union: letters about famine, 28–9, 34–5; mortality during famine, 48; role in carrying out Soviet policies, 301n8; settlements in Ukraine, 251n88; starvation of, 221
Merriam, Arthur, 69, 124
Mertzka, Alice, 13
Michailoff, I., 76
Mikkelson, P., 219, 318n15
Miller, Jack, 75
Mironov, Alexandru-Murad, 7
Miskew, Peter, 106, 107
Mitchell, Humphrey: accounts of Soviet life, 179, 186; delegate to the British Trades Union, 256–7n6; on Lenin, 282n111; public appearances, 260n36; on situation in Europe, 186; visit to the USSR, 66–7
Moir, Elsie F., 11

Moldavian Autonomous Soviet Socialist Republic, 6
Molotov, Viacheslav, 244n11
Monkhouse, Allan, 58, 135–26, 254n22
Montreal Gazette: on famine in Ukraine, 20
Montreal Star: on Ammende's visit to Canada, 194; on famine in Ukraine, 312n27, 319n25; on mobilization for harvest work, 111; on Soviet homeless children, 223–4
Morning Post: on food riots in Yekaterinburg, 12
Morrison, Hugh Whitney, 87
Moscow, 1911–1933 (Monkhouse), 126
Mosion, Max, 142
Motherwell, William Richard, 22, 243n10
Motta, M. Giuseppe, 206, 315n50
Mountford, T. E., 219
Mowinckel, Johan Ludwig, 82, 84, 85, 167, 209, 264n68
Muggeridge, Malcolm, xvi, 48, 58–9, 202
Mussolini, Benito, 96, 302n18
Mykytiak, Arkadii, 315n50
Mykytiuk, Dmytro, 94
Myroniuk, Mariika, 152

Nakoff, Jack, 137
National Office of the Friends of the Soviet Union, 246n31
National Ukrainian Government in Exile, 188
Nazi Germany: anti-Semitism, 138, 290n59; refugees from USSR in, 237n31; trade relations with the USSR, 250n81
Nesbitt, Russell, 135
Neufeld, John, 92
Neufeldt, Colin P., 45, 251n88
New Economic Policy, 143, 160
New York Times: Calder's obituary, 259–60n33; coverage of Ammende's visit, 190–1; on food shortage

in Ukraine, 78; on foreign aid rejection by Soviet government, 172–3; on Lemyk's sentence, 271n39; on Ukrainian refugees in Romania, 237n30; on USSR's entrance to the League of Nations, 206, 207
Ney, F. J., 121
Nicholson, G. B., 135
Niergarth, Kirk, 134
Nippold, Otto, 290n59
Nova Zoria (newspaper), 105
Novyi shliakh (New Pathway): appeal of Ukrainian National Federation, 109; on donations for famine relief, 273n59; on famine in Ukraine, 143–4, 284n131; owner of, xxii; publication of Slusarenko's speech, 159, 163

Odoevzev, A. S., 76, 77
OGPU, 162, 247n35
Olenchuk, Mykola, 115, 116–17
Omelchenko, Anastasia, 111
Organization for Jewish Colonization in Russia (ICOR), 142
Oshawa Daily Times, 115–16
Ostry, Ethel, 277n79
Ottawa Citizen: on Ammende's visit to Canada, 311n22; doubts of scale of famine, 101; on U.S. recognition of the USSR, 101
Ottawa Journal: on famine in Ukraine, 142–3, 292n74
Ovey, Esmond, 3

Paassen, Pierre van: on agrarian policy in Ukraine, 13; article on Morocco, 318n17; on czarist pogrom of Jews, 291n69; on Dniprostroi, 12; education and career, 86; on famine in Ukraine, 86, 219, 265n77, 291n69; on Herriot's visit to the USSR, 318–19n17; on Pavlo Skoropadsky, 291n69; professional reputation, 10, 87–8, 148, 239n38; reports about Soviet Union, 9–10, 86–8, 148, 214–15, 318–19n17; on situation in Spain, xvi; termination of employment, 239n38; *Visions Rise and Change,* 265n77
Paliiv, Dmytro, 317n12
Palmer, George, 113–14, 149, 218–19, 277n83
Pankiv, Andrii, 288n48
Patmont, Louis R., 277n84
Patterson, Sam, 30, 138, 148, 246n31
Peebles, John, 66
Pelekhovych, Neonilia, 196
Pelensky, Zenon, 83
Penner, Jacob, 137, 183
Perazic, M. N., 146
Perley, Ernest Edward, 44
Perry, Anne Anderson, 14
Petliura, Symon, 141, 291n69
Phillimore, Godfrey Walter, 185–7
Pickering, Edward, 125
Piłsudski, Józef, 112, 291n69
Pius XI, Pope, 80, 90, 91
Plawiuk, W. S., 42
Poland: relations with Soviet Union, 103–4, 143; Ukrainian refugees in, 238n32
Polonsky, Antony, 293n78
Popoff, M., 194
Popowich, Matthew, 130
Porayko, Alexander, 153
Postyshev, Pavel, 65, 96
Pravda (newspaper): article about Cromie, 214; on crop expectations, 199
Prince George Citizen: on collective farm system, 126–7; comparison of Monkhouse and Ketchum reports, 125–6; on famine in Ukraine, 283n127; on Gorguloff's execution, 236n21
Prokopenko, Havrylo Nykyforovych, 229n2

Prosvita Hall in Windsor: meeting of Ukrainian Canadians in, 145–6
Prymak, Thomas M., 234n25
Purkis, Thorton, 12, 240n46

Raby, William, 219
Radisson Comet: on Soviet agricultural development, 215–16
Rassvet (newspaper), 260n38
Rayner, Ralph, 314n44
Red Cross *See* Canadian Red Cross; International Red Cross; Russian Red Cross
Regina Leader-Post: on Communist system, 39–40; editorial about conditions in the USSR, 40–1; on famine in Russia, 34; Gardiner's speech, 38; on Russian agricultural production, 39–40; "Soviet State Impresses Two Western Men," 30
Richert, Charles, 23
Riddell, Walter A., 208
Riga: anti-Soviet activities in, 298n125
Ripley, Robert L., 278n94
Road to Life (film), 224, 295n99
Robins, Raymond, 269n17
Romanchych, Hanka, 117
Romania: demonstration against Soviet policies in Ukraine, 271–2n41; refugee and attempted crossings from USSR into, 7, 8, 236n28, 237n29–31, 237n30
Roosevelt, Franklin Delano, 19, 94, 100
Roosevelt, Theodor, 270n24, 302n17, 302n18
Ross, J. J., 198
Rubin, H., 280–1n104
Rudnycka, Milena, 83, 201, 237n30, 302n14
Rusk, Dean, 308n66
Russian-Canadian Workers' Federation, 77
Russian Coordinating Committee of The House of Lords, 185

Russian Missionary Group: "four-page folder" on famine issued by, 258n20
Russian Red Cross, 260–1n41
Russian Workers' and Farmers' Clubs (RWFC), 132, 153

Sabline, E., 258n20
Sachynsky, Feodor, 175, 307n55
Sallet, Richard, 68, 257n12
Salt Lake Tribune: on famine relief efforts, 319n25
Sanders, A. B., 258n20
Sanderson, J. E., 38
Sandler, Rickard Johannes, 189–90
Sarchuk, W. J., 43
Saskatchewan legislature *See* Legislative Assembly of Saskatchewan
Satanove, H., 93
Saturday Night: on roots of famine in Ukraine, 56–7
Saucier, J. J., 201
Save the Children Fund, 41, 314n41
Sawchuk, S., 192, 198
Schiller, Otto, 4
Schmitz, Gerald, 180, 181, 213
Schoor, L., 144
Schwartzbard, Sholom, 141
Sembay, John (Ivan), 91–2, 131, 137, 156
Sembay, Julius, 300n148
Sembay, Olga, 300n148
Semenov, Gregory, 72
Sen, Amartya Kumar, 320n28
Seraphim, Russian Orthodox Bishop, 262n52
Serkau, G. G., 134
Sharman, William, 247–8n36
Shaw, George Bernard, 49, 251–2n93, 285–6n14
Sheinon, Sophia, 92
Sheptytsky, Andrei, 79
Shevchenko, Taras, 162
Shields, E. E., 26, 245–6n24
Shiels, R. L., 286n23
Shinbane, A. N., 139

Shirer, William, 237n31
Shkandrij, Myroslav, 247n35, 272n42, 293n78, 294n80
Sigvaldson, B. I., 144
Sikevich, V., 115, 116
Simon, John, 203
Simons, I. Iu., 48
Sinnott, Alfred, 198
Skelton, Oscar, 207–9, 210, 315n54
Skoblak, Stephen, 267n6
Skoropadsky, Elizabeth, 167, 301n11, 304n36
Skoropadsky, Pavlo, xix, 168, 172, 291n69
Skrypnyk, Mykola: famine in Ukraine and, 269n15, 293n79; suicide of, 65–6, 217, 300n149; Western media on, 217–18, 256n4, 317n8
Skvirsky, Boris, 215, 276n75
Slusarenko, Sophie: on abandoned children, 161; background, 62–3; eyewitness account of famine, 160, 161, 163; on grain-procurement quotas, 160; on press censorship, 162; on scavenging and cannibalism, 161–2; on Soviet international pacts, 163
Smith, Ella, 252n93
Snyder, Timothy, 231n9
Solovetsky Islands: forced labour in, 251–2n93
Soviet Ukraine *See* Ukraine
Soviet Union *See* USSR
Soviet Union Today, 248n37, 259n26, 281–2n108
Speechly, J. M., 42
Stalin, Joseph: agricultural policy of, 269–70n23; distrust of foreign journalists, 240–1n52; on the First Five-Year Plan, 22, 280n103; interviews, 269n17; on the League of Nations, 189; on progress in the Soviet Union, 214; rejection of foreign aid, 213, 246n29; support of Soviet parachute program, 223; on victory of collectivization, 244n11

stamp with four horsemen, xiii, *xiv*
Standret, L. A., 115
Star-Phoenix: accounts of famine, 71, 175; on activities of Ukrainian Baptists, 312–13n31; comment on barter resolution, 38; on meeting in Hague, 40; on protest rally in Saskatoon, 53; Sachynsky family story, 175, *177*, 307n55
Stechishin, J. W., 53
Stevens, H. H., 69, 287n29
Stewart, H. A., 134
Strang, William, 21
St. Raphael Ukrainian Immigrants' Welfare Association, 309n7
Stringer, Isaac O., 198
Strong, Anna Louise, 248n37
Stronsky, Mykola, 104–5, 272n42
Suomi Local (Canadian Finnish organization): ban of, 136
Suvorov, Viktor, 223
Svoboda, 195–6, 288n48
Sydney Morning Herald, 217–18, 280n103
Sysyn, Frank, 280n103
Sysyn, Lesio, 264n70

Talan, K., 76
Taschereau, Louis-Alexandre, 295n90
Tchernavin, V., 251–2n93
Teodorovych, Ioann, 140
Times, The: letters to the editor, 166–7, 187, 199; report on Skrypnyk's suicide, 66
Times of India: on Skrypnyk's suicide, 217
Timoshenko, Vladimir P., 127–8, 284n131
TODOVYRNAZU (Association for Aid to the Liberation Movement in Western Ukraine), 136, 137, 149
Toews, David, 28, 29, 32, 33, 44–5, 209–11
Tokarzewski-Karaszewicz, Jan, 73
Tolstoy, Alexandra L., 23, 24–5, 244–5n14
Torgsin stores: advertisements in Canadian press, 174, 221, 306n51–2; aid distribution through, 89, 170,

174, 175, 178, 306n52; as currency resource for Soviet regime, 178; goods and prices, 306n51; growing number of, 174; meaning of Torgsin abbreviation, 250n78

Toronto Star: coverage of Ammende's visit in Canada, 194; on famine in China, 178; on the First Five-Year Plan, 22; on situation in the USSR, 12–13; Torgsin advertisement, 174, 221, 306n52; on White Sea–Baltic canal, 276n78

Toronto Telegram: on anti-Communist rallies in Canada, 54; on cannibalism in the USSR, 252n10; on demonstrations in New York, 103; on exchange of silver for food, 16; on exit visa from the USSR, 52; on famine relief in North Caucasus, 28; publication of Clyman's articles, 13; on Soviet passport system, 253n15; story of Wolchok family, 243n8; on suicide of Nadezhda Alliluyeva, 241n58

Trofymovych, A. H., 152

Trotsky, Leon, 57, 233n18, 254n19

Troyanovsky, Alexander, 191, 283n124

Tryzub (newspaper), 7, 84

Turnbull, Franklin W., 24, 47–8

Uhrich, John M., 34, 35, 44, 248n45

Ukraine: aftermath of Skrypnyk's suicide, 317n12; antireligious campaign, 165–6, 304n36; class struggle, 87; collectivization, 160, 254n20; delays in harvesting, 11; deportations, 26; food shortage, 11, 155–6, 165; former residents of Canada in, 151, 156; grain requisition policy, 154–5, 166; Jews in, 294n80; map, *xviii*; peasant resistance to regime, 12; plan for famine relief, 11; population, xvii, 232–3n17; repressions of peasants, 164; school system, 165; settlement of families from Russia, 301n6; shipment of wheat out of, 98; territories, xvii; Torgsin stores, 46; travel restrictions, 95; urban protests, 242n59; *See also* famine in Ukraine

Ukrainian Bureau in London: publications of, 25–6; visit of Ukrainians from Canada, 245n19

Ukrainian Catholic Church, xxi, 79, 107–8

Ukrainian Civic Committee for the Salvation of Ukraine, 79, 89, 170, 173, 216, 304n33

Ukrainian Conservative Club, 309n74

Ukrainian diaspora: in Belgium, famine relief efforts of, 304n34; as political force, xvii, xix; in the United States, 233n19; *See also* Ukrainians in Canada

Ukrainian Famine Relief Committee, 181–3, 309n75

Ukrainian Greek Orthodox Church of Canada, 108

Ukrainian Labour-Farmer Temple Association (ULFTA): annual convention, 136, 137; arrest of leaders, 156–7; challenges, 131; confrontation with Ukrainian National Council, 136–7; famine relief efforts in 1921-22, 130–1; formation of, 130; police raid of headquarters, 131, 136; response to Skrypnyk's suicide, 218; Soviet propaganda and, 300n148; support of Ukrainian SSR, xxi

Ukrainian National Council (UNC): confrontation with ULFTA, 136–7; formation of, 95–6; letters to Franklin D. Roosevelt, 94, 100; members of, 267n6; objectives of, 182; press coverage, 268n10

Ukrainian National Federation, xxi, 107–10, 159–60

Ukrainian Orthodox Church, xxi
Ukrainian press in Canada: coverage of events in Ukraine, xxii–xxiii, 105–6; newspapers, xxii; *See also* individual periodicals
Ukrainian Red Cross (Belgium), 109
Ukrainian refugees, 237n30–1, 238n32, 238n34, 261n47
Ukrainian Self-Reliance League of Canada, 11, 109, 173, 182, 188, 216
Ukrainians in Canada: activities of Ukrainian Baptists, 312–13n31; anti-Communist campaigns, 146–7, 278n88; Arborg tax riot, 144–5; attitude to Jews, 139–40; in Canadian politics, 106–7; churches, xxi; Communism and, 144–8; famine relief efforts, xxii, 42–3, 302n14, 302n17; immigrants from the USSR, 163; letter of gratitude to Lord Denbigh, 205–6; organizations and associations, xxi; population statistics, xix, xx–xxi; public meetings, 51, 53–4, 62, 85, 101, 102, 115–16, 145–6; support of the Ukrainian National Republic, xxi; Western policy toward Soviet Union and, 141–2; Western Ukrainian view of, 233n20
Ukrainian Sporting Sitch Association of Canada (USSAC), xxi, xxii, 62, 145, 168–70, 303n22
Ukrainian SSR *See* Ukraine
Ukraïns'ki robitnychi visty (Ukrainian Labour News): on achievement of Soviet system, 148; advertisement of tourist trip to the USSR, 288n49; on American–Soviet relations, 149–50; on Ammende's visit to Canada, 195; on Chinese refugees in the USSR, 149; criticism of anti-Soviet policy, 153; on hunger in western Ukrainian territories, 150; on Ketchum's lectures in Winnipeg, 123; letters from the Soviet Union, 150–7, 220; owner of, xxii, 130; print run, 130; on situation in Soviet Ukraine, 149, 154–5; Torgsin advertisement, 174, 221

Ukraïns'ki visty (Ukrainian News): on Ammende's visit to North America, 193, 194, 312n26; on assassination of Mailov, 104; on congress called by Cardinal Innitzer, 272n46; coverage of Luchkovich's speech, 181; on deportations in the Soviet Union, 51, 60; on deportees from Canada, 91–2; on disturbances in urban centers, 52; on duty of Ukrainian diaspora, 62; on elimination of religious life in Ukraine, 62; on famine relief efforts, 89, 91, 221; on labour law in the USSR, 15–16; publishing and distribution of, xxii, 233n22; on refusal of Soviet regime to accept foreign aid, 172–3; report on Volga region, 51; on resistance to Soviet government policies, 14–15; on situation in Ukraine, 54, 55, 59–62, 88–91, 217; stories about cannibalism, 15, 17, 59, 60; on suppression of scholarship in Soviet Ukraine, 89; Torgsin advertisement, 221, 306n51; on Ukrainian refugees in Romania, 236n28; on voice of Catholic Church about tragedy of Ukraine, 90

Ukraïns'kyi holos (Ukrainian Voice): on arrest of ULFTA leaders, 156; coverage of Luchkovich's speech, 181; on famine in Ukraine, 140–1, 166, 220; on immigrants from Soviet Ukraine, 163–5; on Jews in Soviet government, 140; on Ketchum's lectures in Winnipeg, 123; on protest meetings, 108; on Russian settlers in Ukraine, 301n6; story

of Galician immigrant, 238n34; on Stronsky's suicide, 104–5; Torgsin advertisement, 174, 221
United Hetman Classocrats, 205–6
United States: rallies of Ukrainian organizations, 102–3; recognition of the USSR, 19, 100–1, 187, 214; trade with the USSR, 276n75, 287n29
United Ukrainian Organizations of the United States, 100
Unruh, Benjamin H., 47
USSAC *See* Ukrainian Sporting Sitch Association of Canada
USSR (Union of Soviet Socialist Republics): agricultural development, 110, 192, 194, 215–16, 247n33, 264n67, 298n131, 316n4; aid to Communist organizations abroad, 135; Alliance of Red Cross and Red Crescent Societies, 85; amnesty to prisoners, 113; British recognition of, 27; Canadians in, 21–2; censorship, 46; child labour, 111; class struggle, 220; collectivization, 126–7, 160, 164, 244n11; concentration camps in, 251–2n93; convict labour, 276n78; decline of rural population, 231n9; denial of famine, 191, 214, 264n70, 314n41; deportation of Cossacks, 244n13; emigration to and from, 9, 163, 243n8, 288n48, 297n116, 298n127; exit visa cost, 52, 163; food riots, 12; foreign credits, 121; foreign policy, 6, 15, 103–4, 112, 143, 186, 255n29; foreign specialists in, 73, 288–9n50; foundation of, xxi; grain export and import, 61, 90, 112, 243–4n10, 255n29; homeless children, 223–4, 295n99; human losses due to famine, 231n9; industrial development, 121, 214, 220; League of Nations and, 204, 206–8, 209, 316n62; military preparations, 226–7; money transfer restrictions, 88; negative image of, 31–2, 49, 261n42; neglect of people's lives, 120–1; organized tourism, 118; parachute program, 223; passport system, 26, 56, 60, 146, 221, 253n15; population, 68; positive image of, 31, 32, 40, 49, 76, 278–9n95, 289n51; prisons in, 162, 277n79; propaganda, xvi; punishment for theft of state property, 113; rejection of foreign aid, 172–3, 175, 190, 216, 264n68; reports of famine in Siberia, 251n91; repressions of peasants, 164; sale of silver articles in exchange for food, 16, 242n64; sources of information about, 21; state planning, 289n51; trade relations with Canada and U.S., 33, 276n75, 283n124, 287n25, 287n29; travel restrictions, 78, 89, 117–18, 146, 163, 221, 261n42, 278n94; treatment of minorities, 187; trial of British engineers, 55–6, 58, 313n40; typhus outbreak in Moscow, 253n15; Ukrainianization policy, xxii; U.S. recognition of, 19, 100–1, 187, 214; Western press on situation in, 214–15, 217–18, 219–20; Western travellers in, 30

Vancouver Province, 60, 70, 238n32
Vancouver Sun, 49, 222–3
Vegreville Observer, 107, 181
Veidlinger, Jeffrey, 294n80
Verchomin, I., 54
Verigin, Peter, 19, 91
Villard, Oswald Garrison, 280n103
Villeneuve, Jean-Marie-Rodrigue, 195
Volodin, Eugene, 75, 76
Vorozhbet, Stepan, 92
Vozrozhdenie (newspaper), 72, 73, 89
Vyshinsky, Andrey, 223

Waagen, Mary E., 11
Wallace, Len, 297n116

Webb, Ralph H., 28, 147, 148, 181–2, 243–4n10
Wells, Carveth, 282n108
Wensel, Luisa, 176, 178
Werth, Nicholas, xv
Western Catholic: articles about famine, 80, 312–13n31
Western Jewish Bulletin: on Jews in the Soviet Union, 142
White, William Allen, 111
White Sea-Baltic canal, 276n78
Wiebe, Cornelius, 61–2, 106
Wienerberger, Alexander, 317n13
Williams, George H., 40, 44
Williams, Whiting, 180
Willis, John A., 247–8n36
Wilson, Grace, 153
Winnipeg Free Press: coverage of Ammende's visit to Canada, 191–2; on demonstrations in Chicago, 103; editorial about famine, 78–9; on food scarcity in the Soviet Union, 16–17; Hitler's quote in, 47; publications of anonymous letters, 290n57; reports on famine in Ukraine, 40, 58–9, 63; "Soviets War on the Peasants," 59; on White Sea-Baltic canal, 276n78
Winnipeg Tribune: on case of Rose Kritzevosky, 52; coverage of Ammende's visit to Canada, 192; on grain production in Russia, 316n4; letter about conditions in the USSR, 34; on Luchkovich's speech, 181; on Manitoba's ethnic communities, 148; on play about famine in Ukraine, 96; report of Canadian deal with the USSR, 246n25; on tax riots in Manitoba, 144–5; on Ukrainian Famine Relief Committee, 182
Wolowyna, Oleh, 319n22
Women's Auxiliary of the Chinese Church of Christ, 178
Woodsworth, James Shaver, 24, 66, 131, 132, 245n16
Workers' Benevolent Association (WBA), 131, 136, 137
Worobeck, Stefan, 136
Wysocki, Roman, 238n32, 273n50

Yakimischak, D., 188, 198
Yelle, Emile, 198

Zakharchenko, Marta, 15
Zilberstein, Oscar, 139
Zuk, Marie, 93–5
Zynchuk, Nick, 132

SERGE CIPKO is assistant director of research at the Canadian Institute of Ukrainian Studies at the University of Alberta. He is the author of *Ukrainians in Argentina, 1897–1950: The Making of a Community* and co-author, with Glenna Roberts, of *One-Way Ticket: The Soviet Return-to-the-Homeland Campaign, 1955–1960*.

www.ingramcontent.com/pod-product-compliance
Lightning Source LLC
Chambersburg PA
CBHW020055020526
44112CB00031B/150